The
Mother to Mother
Baby Care Book

"*In every child who is born, under no matter what circumstances and of no matter what parents, the potentiality of the human race is born again.*"

—James Agee

The
Mother to Mother
Baby Care Book

BARBARA SILLS and JEANNE HENRY

AVON
PUBLISHERS OF BARD, CAMELOT, DISCUS AND FLARE BOOKS

AVON BOOKS
A division of
The Hearst Corporation
959 Eighth Avenue
New York, New York 10019

Copyright © 1980 Camaro Publishing Company
Published by arrangement with Camaro Publishing Company
Library of Congress Catalog Card Number: 79-15708
ISBN: 0-380-53074-0

Cover photograph Copyright © 1981 by Nancy Brown
Illustrations by Barry Brenner
Back cover photographs by Garth Bishop

First Avon Printing, March, 1981

The Camaro Publishing Company edition contains the following
Library of Congress Cataloging in Publication Data:

Sills, Barbara Wilcox
  Mother to mother baby care book.

  Bibliography: p.
  Includes index.
  1. Children—Management. 2. Infants—Care and
hygiene. 3. Children—Care and hygiene. 4. Mother and
child. 5. Mother and child—Bibliography. I. Henry,
Jeanne Heffernan, joint author. II. Title.

For our mothers

Emma G. Heffernan
and
Marion L. Wilcox

Introduction

No pediatrician or other expert tells us how to get gum
out of hair.

In this era of working women, smaller families, and dis-
tant relatives, firsthand mothering advice is hard to come by.
A brand new mother may have plenty of "work" colleagues
but no mothering ones at all to help with on-the-job training
when she starts raising her own child. But it is other mothers,
nevertheless, who are the best help. It is from them, fellows
on the front lines, that one finds advice the easiest to take.
It is also with them that one sifts through the overwhelming
glut of secondhand advice to figure out what really works,
what really can be accomplished.

It is before you develop your own mother network (and
a good one may take years) that this book will be most useful.

The book began as we talked in one of our kitchens on a
summer day four years ago. Jeanne Henry, a journalist, had
just finished investigating so many local nursery schools for
her daughter that she was determined to share the information
she had put together. The only person who seemed to know
more about the array of schools was the old friend across
the table, Barbara Sills, a preschool and parent education
teacher. We resolved to write a guide to preschools in our
area of Los Angeles. But because of editor Garth Bishop's
encouragement, we began to think bigger. Why not compile
and share the whole range of child care know-how so pain-
fully built up by ourselves and other mothers? While books
by psychologists and doctors abound, books by mothers do
not. The encyclopedic reference book for the crucial first
three years, one that shared practical mothering advice, certainly did not exist. We decided to try to fill the gap.

Eventually we were to involve over 200 other parents
in the book. Some were members of Barbara's Child Growth

and Development class at the South Bay Adult School in Manhattan Beach, California. Others were friends and neighbors. A few were fathers who do full time parenting. Many others contributed their experience by answering a long questionnaire distributed in other parts of the country by our friends, relatives, and colleagues. Most of the mothers had children under 5, but more than a few had grown children.

From our own experience, we knew the questions mothers ask even if not all the answers. Between us we have four children: Anne and Nicholas Henry and David and Jonas Sills. We were learning about the basic concerns of parents and about ways to ask questions when we first met—as students working for Master's degrees in Childhood Education and Journalism, respectively, at Columbia University.

We asked the mothers to share what they knew they had done right. We asked what they would change if they had the first years to do over again. Many relished the chance to pass on information about everything from buying equipment to discipline to finding a babysitter—hints that had taken months or years to learn the hard way. We tried to cover all the basic concerns of new mothers and then to share the lore in a way that recognizes the uniqueness of each child, each parent, each home.

To protect the privacy of children and of the mothers who shared both proud and trying moments with us, names and locations in the text have been changed. But the names of actual contributors and those of their children are listed in the Acknowledgments section.

We are more grateful than we can say to all of the contributors for opening their hearts and minds to us over the telephone, at the park, in the classroom and on paper.

Besides offering the practical, compassionate advice of other mothers, we made this book a one-stop source for information that might otherwise require many trips to the library or involve misspent dollars in the marketplace. For example, how do you make your own baby food? What do you need to know about car restraints? What's a good chair and table height for a preschool child? What are the best books for a 2-year-old? Where can you write for catalogs of school suppliers and manufacturers of outdoor play equipment?

Every child desperately needs a chief caregiver who thinks that *that child* is wonderful and unique. But before we can get outside ourselves to marvel at a child, it helps to feel we are pretty unique and worth caring for ourselves. Therefore, the last chapter, "Taking Care of You." It is far from the least important.

Why the emphasis on mothers? Although we applaud the move toward shared child care, we wear no rose-colored glasses. Recognizing economic and social realities, we know that in most homes where there are young children, Mom is *still* either the chief caregiver or the person who finds and oversees a chief caregiver. So while our book is meant for anyone who cares for a new person for hours at a time— mother, father, day-care worker, grandparent, babysitter— the title reflects the current real world. Mothers are still the ones to ask for advice if you have trouble getting a baby to *take* the medicine a doctor prescribes. Mothers are still the ones most often seeking the advice.

A book like this is never complete. Times change, medicine advances, equipment manufacturers come out with new things, and new mothers create new and better ways to take care of their children. We therefore appeal to you to share with us any insights, ideas or hints that we may have overlooked. Please write to us in care of the publisher. We hope that future editions will add even more information and will be ever more useful for busy new parents.

If we have discovered anything as mothers, it is that we must keep learning. No matter what the age, a child is always changing. As soon as we figure out one stage, the child is well into another.

We have done our best learning from other mothers. They have helped us to grow through this most stupendous of adventures, raising a child. We wish you, the reader, as much joy and satisfaction as we have found in the work of these years and we hope our book will stimulate and encourage you to find the same fulfillment.

Jeanne Henry

Barbara Sills

Los Angeles, California

Contents

Chapter Table of Contents

MOTHER AND CHILD

1

Pregnancy, Childbirth, and You

You've missed your period. Your breasts are sensitive. You fall asleep during your favorite TV show. You take the test and your suspicions are confirmed. You're pregnant!

It's time to plan and make some decisions. How do you choose a doctor? What methods of childbirth and delivery will be best for you? When should you stop working? What should you eat and drink? Since each woman is different, each of you will find answers to these questions in your own way.

The information in this chapter will help you start finding the way. We share current advice from experts on issues such as working, smoking, eating, and drinking. We discuss books, magazines, and organizations, both here and in the Mother's Resource List in the back of this book. And we give a variety of hints and suggestions from women who shared their *unique* experiences with us to help you take charge of your own *unique* pregnancy and childbirth.

"Pregnancy is looking in the mirror and smiling because I am almost a mother. It is looking in the mirror and crying because I look so ugly. It is feeling physically wonderful, able to do everything and anything. It is feeling physically exhausted and depressed. It is being afraid of what's to come because of that real live baby inside me."

Mother-to-be / Lubbock, Tex.

"I'd been gunning for something my whole life. Get into college. Finish college. Get a good job. Do a good job. Get married. Keep working. Save money. Get furniture. Travel. After six years of marriage, I was pregnant. For really the first time I slowed down. I felt like I wanted to know what life was about outside the walls of our apartment, outside my office. I felt like I was planting a garden in the sunshine and the earth felt good."   *Mother of one / Troy, N.Y.*

"Wonder and sorrow are two great words describing pregnancy. You can't help but marvel at the way nature provides us with this magnificent event. To feel movement inside of you and know that you're creating a person is grand. And once it's over you have such a feeling of accomplishment. Now for the sorrow part. After looking at your large, swollen body you wonder if you'll ever be the same again. And you won't, not quite. You'll never completely regain your previous figure. And you'll be 'three' instead of 'two,' with all the wonder and sorrow of *that* experience."

Mother of three / Grand Rapids, Mich.

CHOOSING THE DOCTOR

Give a lot of thought to how you want to experience childbirth before you choose a doctor. Most doctors follow the same general procedures in caring for pregnant women, but they have different approaches to labor and delivery: some are vehemently in favor of unmedicated childbirth; some are lukewarm; and some are opposed. If you want an unmedicated childbirth, you will naturally want a doctor who will support you. If you've decided on an anesthetized birth, then you will want a doctor who is well versed in anesthetics.

"The right doctor makes all the difference," commented one woman. "I wanted natural childbirth with my first pregnancy. I read all the books and practiced the exercises on my own. I had no choice of doctors, however, since there was only one in town. He was a delightful, traditional, family-style physician who convinced me to let him take charge. Everything was beautiful—until labor, which was one of the most terrifying experiences of my life. The medication and anesthetics the doctor used did almost nothing to alleviate my pain and fear.

"We had moved to San Francisco when I became pregnant the second time," she added. "I called several obstetricians to find out who advocated natural childbirth. On my third call, I found the right one. Although the second labor was longer than the first, it was a thrilling experience to give birth on my own—to be informed and in control myself without being all doped up with drugs."

"I had my first child at 35. I'm a total coward about pain, so I researched anesthetics and decided that a caudal would relieve most of the pain of labor. I then hunted for a doctor who used caudal blocks. I had both of my daughters this way and it was just fine." *Mother of two / Washington, D.C.*

"I called fifty physicians to find one who would deliver my baby at home. I couldn't find exactly what I wanted but my research paid off. We found the Birth Center. It was typical of most doctors' offices, with a waiting room, examining room, and so forth. Untypical was the birthroom, which was tucked away in the back of the suite of offices. It looked like a bedroom, complete with patchwork wallpaper, private bath, patio, and a door that locked from the inside. It seemed a private, cheery place to have a baby."
Mother of one / Hermosa Beach, Calif.

Are you considering unmedicated birth? Do you want your husband with you during labor? Does he want to be in the delivery room? Are you thinking of having your baby at home or in a doctor's office? Do you want "family-centered childbirth" in a birth center, with your relatives and friends encouraged to visit? You don't have to make a final decision at the beginning of your pregnancy, but you should keep your general attitudes in mind when you choose a doctor.

You might find an excellent obstetrician through recommendations of friends, instructors of childbirth classes, nurses in the obstetrics sections of hospitals, the local county chapter of the American Medical Association, your family physician, or even the yellow pages of your phone book.

"I questioned my family doctor, and then I called the medical board and asked the same questions. The obstetrician recommended was the one I chose, but the decision was not made until after I met him, questioned him, and felt entirely comfortable." *Mother of two / Dallas, Tex.*

"When I was taken to the emergency room after I miscarried very early in my first pregnancy, I asked an obstetrical nurse for the name of a doctor for the next time. She gave me my present obstetrician's name. He is very highly respected by the nurses he works with. Asking a nurse can be the best way since they see the doctors in action and should know the good from the bad." *Mother of three / Salt Lake City, Utah*

Here are some points to consider before making a final decision in choosing a doctor.

• What is the doctor's preferred method of delivery? Does this coincide with your desires?

• Does he practice alone or with a group? If it is a group practice, how is it set up? Will he alone care for you and deliver your baby or is responsibility divided among group members? If responsibility is divided, do all the doctors have the same philosophy about childbirth?

• What does he charge? How does he prefer payment? Show your doctor your insurance policy. Some doctors require you to pay only the difference between insurance coverage and total charges. Others require the full amount in advance and then you collect from your insurance company later.

• Does he have a procedure for answering routine questions over the phone? (What's best is a call-back procedure, where he returns your call, or a call-in hour when he isn't seeing patients.) Is he available on weekends or late at night for emergencies?

• Will he handle medical problems not related to pregnancy?

• How frequently does he want you to see him? (Once a month for the first seven months, two visits in the eighth month, and once a week in the ninth month is common.)

• What hospital does he use?

- Does he encourage full participation of the father? Will there be an opportunity for the father to talk with the doctor during the pregnancy? Does he welcome fathers during labor and delivery?

- And last, but not least, do you like your doctor? Do you trust him? Are you comfortable asking him questions and do you agree with most of his methods and advice? If you occasionally disagree with him, are you comfortable expressing and working out your differences? In her book *Pregnancy and Childbirth* Tracy Hotchner says, "Trust has to go both ways, so that while it is important for you to find out as much as possible about the doctor's ideology, it is equally important for him to believe that you respect and trust him." We agree, and feel that if you like and trust your doctor, you can then work together for the best possible pregnancy and childbirth experience.

"I wish I'd listened to my doctor. He told me to stay off my feet and take it very easy when I started spotting in the third month. I quit work but I just didn't feel bad enough to stay in bed all day. Our baby was born at *seven* months and we now have a host of problems connected with his prematurity to contend with. I often wonder what things would be like if I'd stayed in bed and if I'd carried him even a few weeks longer." *Mother of one / Cherry Hill, N.J.*

While you're choosing an obstetrician for yourself, consider finding a pediatrician for your baby. Read the section on choosing a pediatrician in Chapter 9 for some pointers.

CHOOSING THE HOSPITAL

Hospitals also differ in the policies about childbirth, and some may not allow the innovations your own doctor might approve. Therefore, if there are several hospitals in your area, you might want to settle on one *before* you pick a doctor. One mother said, "You'll spend a lot more time with the labor room nurses than you will with your doctor. And you're choosing not just care for yourself, but for your baby, so be as choosy about the hospital as you are about your doctor."

Since many hospitals have tours of their maternity wings, and others should at least let you visit, arrange to see the facilities and talk with the staff. When you find a hospital where you feel comfortable, ask for a list of obstetricians who practice there. If a doctor is on the staff, he's a particularly good bet.

"We were new in town, and I didn't know anyone or anything about the hospitals or doctors. One day I bought a bunch of daffodils and went to a local hospital during visiting hours. I walked around on the maternity floor until I found a woman without any visitors. I gave her the flowers, explaining that I was pregnant and was looking for a hospital to have my baby. She seemed to enjoy answering my questions. I did this with another hospital, and that time I found my hospital, my doctor, and also a good friend, since I later became close to one of the women with whom I talked." *Mother of two / Chicago, Ill.*

These are some of the things you should consider when looking for a hospital.

• What is the policy on childbirth? Are anesthetics routinely given, or is unmedicated childbirth encouraged? Does the hospital allow Leboyer births (dimmed lights, quiet atmosphere, warm bath, and gentle handling of babies)?

• Will your baby's father be encouraged to help during labor and delivery? Will he be allowed to be present for a Caesarean birth using regional anesthesia? Is the father encouraged to get to know his baby after birth? Can he stay during the day and is he permitted to hold and care for the baby? Early contact is helpful for the "bonding process"—the father needs to see and hold his child in the minutes, hours, and days after birth just as the mother does.

• Does the hospital offer "rooming-in," an arrangement where mother and baby share a room? If it does, will the nurses take over when a mother wants to rest? If it doesn't, how soon, how frequently, and for how long are infants brought to their mothers? The more time with mother the better.

• Is the nursing staff supportive of mothers who want to breast feed their babies? Are babies encouraged to nurse on demand, eating whenever they are hungry? Will aides bring the baby for the two a.m. feeding? Is there a breast-feeding expert on the staff, someone who has breast fed her own babies and can assist a new mother?

• Have there been any staph infections during the last five years at the hospital, particularly in the nursery?

• What are visiting hours and procedures? Can older children visit? Are relatives and friends allowed to visit? (Some new mothers prefer a "no visitor" rule, excluding everyone except the immediate family, because they appreciate the chance to rest.)

• Can the length of your hospital stay be flexible if necessary? Will you be allowed to leave early if you feel ready or extend your stay a little if you don't feel up to going home at the appointed time?

• Does the hospital have those "little extras" to make a mother comfortable, such as shampoo and hair-care facilities and sitz baths for those troubled by hemorrhoids?

• Is there an alternative to a normal labor and delivery room set-up? You might want to consider a family-centered plan, where birth occurs in homelike surroundings, husbands and other family members are encouraged to participate, a midwife performs delivery, and the hospital stay is very brief.

• Is there a parent-education program? Some hospitals hold baby-bath demonstrations, give breast- and bottle-feeding instructions, and offer other information many new parents find helpful.

• Does the hospital have a perinatal center (a facility equipped to give the best possible care to premature or high-risk babies)? If there is no perinatal center, does the hospital have an arrangement with another hospital for babies in need of special care?

You probably won't find the perfect doctor or the perfect hospital, but the more you know ahead of time, the more likely you are to get close to it. "With my first baby,

I was too trusting," one woman told us. "I'm pregnant again, but this time I'm armed. I know the childbirth section in *Our Bodies Ourselves* cold and my husband does too. I know there are dangers and discomforts to fetal-monitoring devices during labor, to forceps deliveries, to practically all kinds of anesthesia. I feel like I'm fighting for the healthiest possible baby and learning all this stuff is part of the fight. When the time comes my doctor is going to make the decisions *with* us, not on his own."

"We had our second child, Josh, with the Leboyer method—what a lovely experience! The lights of the delivery room were dimmed, the room was calm and quiet, and a tub of warm water was awaiting the birth of our child. Upon delivery the doctor handed our son to my husband so that he could put Josh in the warm water. It was a most beautiful sight. Josh seemed to feel so comforted and relaxed in the water, and Mike beamed as he held his son for the first time. It was a special moment in our lives, and it was only possible because I chose a doctor and hospital that encouraged Leboyer births." *Mother of two / Boston, Mass.*

"Sarah was born in my doctor's office. She was placed, whimpering and squirming, on my hollow belly. We were so taken with this newborn that it was a few minutes before either of us thought to check her sex. She was lying on her tummy and we were stroking her back and just loving her. We continued to get acquainted while the doctor busied himself with the umbilical cord and my stitches. When he was finished I nursed her for a few minutes—then it was into the shower for me, while Daddy took the baby and bathed her." *Mother of one / Hermosa Beach, Calif.*

LABOR AND DELIVERY: WHICH METHOD FOR YOU?

The most common methods of childbirth are: natural (or "prepared"), without anesthetics; natural, with anesthetics; anesthetics of some kind used throughout labor and delivery; and Caesarean section.

It is very difficult to find unbiased reports about methods of childbirth, since the issues are often clouded by their authors' viewpoints. In some books and articles written by physicians, the adverse effects of medications on mother and baby are minimized, giving the impression that drugs will provide a perfect, painless childbirth. In some books and articles by natural-childbirth advocates, on the other hand, a glowing picture is painted of painless childbirth as a result of proper exercises and breathing.

There is no easy solution. Our recommendation is to take the natural-childbirth courses, read the books, and prepare yourself for unmedicated childbirth; it's the safest way for both mother and child. However, be prepared to accept the possibility of medication if there should be complications or you have prolonged labor.

"My first pregnancy was in 1969. At that time, natural child-birth was not so popular so I chose a saddleblock anesthe-sia. I was pretty scared during labor, not knowing how bad it was going to be having a baby. The labor was painful but short, and when I got back to my room after my daugh-ter's birth I was very sick. The second time, three years later, I decided to have the baby naturally. The labor was almost easy and the delivery was a thrill. I think, from my own experience, natural childbirth is the only way to go."
Mother of two / St. Louis, Mo.

"I could write a short book on natural childbirth. I think it should be a prerequisite for having a baby. My husband and I took the Lamaze classes for both of our children, and the unity we shared when we experienced their births was invaluable for years afterward. I felt so sorry for my room-mates and their husbands, waiting in the halls, while Don and I progressed together through the birth of our babies."
Mother of two / Manhattan Beach, Calif.

In general, the mothers who used prepared-childbirth techniques, without medication, said that birth was a mar-velous experience. "I felt strong, in control, as if I was a general fighting a hard battle. And I won!" said one mother.

"A nurse practically insisted that I have some Demerol," said another woman. "Since we had learned in class that I could refuse it, I asked her to save it for later. But there wasn't any later. I was thrilled and overwhelmed with the miracle of it all."

"I had no medication during my daughter's birth," said a third mother. "I had an eight-hour labor, and an easy birth. If my labor had gone on for a long time, I might have chosen to have medication."

Some women whose labor was prolonged did choose to have medication. One woman who is actively involved in women's health care said, "I thought I would surely have a natural childbirth. My husband and I were convinced that it was the best way. We took a Lamaze class, read numerous books, and had the techniques down pat. But after twenty hours of labor, the breathing techniques and other processes were totally ineffective. I gladly accepted my doctor's offer of a paracervical block. Our daughter was born an hour later, perfectly healthy, perfectly normal, perfectly beautiful."

"During the labor of my second pregnancy, my contractions were coming so fast and strong that I insisted on medication for relief. I had already experienced the Lamaze childbirth with my first child, but with my second I was terribly frightened by the intensity and frequency of the contractions. I was given a caudal, which was a tremendous relief— so much so that I actually enjoyed the rest of my labor. I'm convinced that the medication didn't harm my child in any noticeable way. He was alert at birth and certainly had a healthy set of lungs."

Mother of two / Washington, D.C.

So that you will be aware of the different kinds of anesthetics, their uses and effects, here is a brief description of the drugs most commonly used during childbirth.

Analgesics (Narcotics and Tranquilizers)

Narcotics (like Demerol, Dolophine, or Nisenti) reduce or diminish pain. They are frequently used with tranquilizers (like Valium) that reduce tension and anxiety.

Benefits. Take the edge off the pain during the early part of labor and help the woman to relax.

Drawbacks. May slow down labor. Can have a serious depressant effect on fetal respiration. A newborn's responses may be sluggish because of these drugs.

Mothers' Comments. "After I was in labor a few hours, they gave me Demerol. It was really a help. I even slept a little between contractions," one mother said. "I didn't like the dopey, drunk feeling I got with Demerol. I would drift off to sleep, then suddenly wake up with a nightmare of a contraction," said another mother.

General Anesthetics

General anesthetics—cyclopropane, halothane, and pentothal—cause total unconsciousness.

Benefits. General anesthetics are used only in an emergency, for difficult breech births, Caesareans, multiple births, or when the risks of delivery outweigh the risks of using the anesthetic.

Drawbacks. May adversely affect the cardiovascular and respiratory systems of both mother and baby.

Regional Anesthetics

Regional anesthetics numb specific areas of the body.

PUDENDAL BLOCK

Anesthetizes the vulva, the outer portion of a woman's genitalia.

Benefits. It is usually used at the end of labor before the episiotomy (the incision to enlarge the opening through which the baby will pass)—if an episiotomy is necessary—or to numb the area for a forceps delivery.

Drawbacks. There is a slight effect on the fetus (it reaches the baby in fifteen minutes), although it is minimal and wears off a half hour after birth.

PARACERVICAL BLOCK

Stops pain in pelvis from uterus and cervix. Lasts for about an hour, but can be reinjected.

Benefits. Stops the pain of labor without stopping the contractions. Can be used fairly early in labor, and is helpful when there is minimal dilation.

Drawbacks. Some anesthesiologists are now questioning the safety of this anesthetic for both mother and baby. It must be very skillfully administered so that it does not penetrate the presenting end of the fetus. Since the injection site is close to the main artery to the uterus, the anesthetic crosses the placenta in three to four minutes, and there is a greater chance of absorption by the placenta and depression of the fetus. It has also been known to cause severe hypotension (a drop in blood pressure, with shocklike symptoms, altered heart rate, nausea) and convulsions during labor.

Mothers' Comments. One close friend who had a paracervical said, "Yes, even though I know the risks, I would do it over again if I had to. I had a twenty-four-hour labor, with almost no dilation. My doctor suggested a paracervical, saying that if it didn't relax me he would do a Caesarean. I can still vividly recall my feelings of relief when the pain ended. In an hour I had reached transition stage. I was then able to cope, without any more drugs, and had a 'natural childbirth' with my husband at my side."

SPINAL BLOCK

Spinal blocks anesthetize the complete birth area, from the waist to the knees (the popular *saddle block* is a variation of the spinal). It is usually given near the end of labor, often after the baby's head has appeared, because earlier use can stop contractions.

Benefits. Stops all sensations of labor and delivery.

Drawbacks. Since the pushing urge is obliterated by the anesthetic, sometimes forceps must be used for delivery. For the mother, there is a possibility of hypotension. Also, some women report severe headaches for days or even weeks after a spinal. A minor drawback is that a woman must lie flat on her back for several hours after having a spinal. The effects on the baby are minimal, since it is given close to birth. However, it does cause a slowed heart rate and a decreased flow of blood and oxygen.

Mothers' Comments. This was the most frequently used anesthetic among the women we questioned. One said, "I had a saddle block with my son. I really needed it for the first." Another commented, "I went through almost until the end, using techniques from my Lamaze class. But the pushing hurt like hell, so I readily agreed to a saddle block. I did it that way with both of my children." "The next time I'll forget a spinal," said a third mother. "My son was born within minutes after the doctor injected the anesthetic. I would gladly have endured a few more minutes of pain to have avoided an additional six hours of discomfort lying flat on my back with a full bladder, which I just couldn't seem to empty in that position."

Continuous Regional Anesthetics

Caudal blocks or lumbar epidural blocks are given during the first stage of labor and then continued through to delivery.

CAUDAL BLOCK

A catheter is put into the lower back and the anesthetic is injected into the catheter. More is used as needed.

Benefits. Can be used during the last part (transition) of the first stage of labor, which is the hardest part for most women. Stops the sensations of labor without stopping the contractions.

Drawbacks. Since more anesthetic is used than in spinal or epidural blocks, there is a greater chance of hypotension for the mother and loss of oxygen to the baby, since it transfers quickly to the fetus.

Mothers' Comments. "I had two births, two caudals, and both were great!" said one mother. "It was hard on my own body and very hard on my baby," said another. "Both my husband and I regretted not pursuing natural childbirth more adamantly. We felt I could have been more help, and that the baby would have been in better shape had I had less medication. My son had problems off and on for the first year of his life. Some of these just might have been caused by medication."

EPIDURAL BLOCK

Like the caudal, the epidural block stops pain without stopping contractions, and can be administered early in labor (at around five centimeters' dilation). Less anesthetic is used than with the caudal block, and it is slower to reach the fetus.

Drawbacks. Possible hypotension in mother. Requires an expert anesthesiologist since serious complications can occur as a result of incorrect placement of the catheter. Also, several other hospital routines may have to be performed, such as fetal monitoring, frequent blood pressure checks, artificial rupture of membranes, and sometimes additional drugs to speed up labor.

Comments. The authors of *Our Bodies Ourselves* assert: "When we choose epidural anesthesia, we are choosing to have a doctor/hospital-controlled labor and delivery. We are accepting the risks and possible side effects of many procedures and drugs; and we are casually taking for granted the skill of doctors and attendants."

This statement from *Our Bodies Ourselves* could easily apply to the whole range of anesthetics. For some women, however, the risks are worth it. If a woman's labor is prolonged, if there are complications, or if she has an extremely low pain threshold, she should not have to apologize for taking the risk of using anesthetics. John Miller, M.D., said, in *Childbirth*, "There is no justification in withholding the safety and comfort of anesthesia in situations where it is necessary. There is even less justification in the routine administration of anesthesia to every woman in labor."

What women have won in the long struggle about childbirth is the right to make up their own minds about what is going to happen to their bodies and their babies.

"I feel very strongly that mothers should read about and take natural-childbirth classes. They have nothing to lose and so much to gain. Why not help make it as easy as possible? But I do not feel they should carry this to unreasonable lengths—if things do not go well, take medication. And do not feel as if you have failed."

Mother of two / Lawton, Okla.

Caesarean Section

Doctors perform Caesareans for about one in every ten births, and the rate appears to be increasing. They are performed when the mother's pelvis is too small to allow passage. Other indications for a Caesarean include: placenta previa (the placenta precedes the baby), placenta abruptio (the placenta is either completely or partially detached from the uterine wall before birth), or a prolapsed cord (the umbilical cord slips in front of the baby). Caesareans are sometimes performed when there is an RH problem, when the baby is in a breech (buttocks first) or transverse (sideways) position, when there is fetal distress, when the baby is at least two weeks past due date, or when there is maternal disease such as diabetes or toxemia.

If you know ahead of time that you will have a Caesarean, check our Resource List for names of organizations that will give you information about Caesarean groups in your area. If there are no groups, ask your doctor if he knows of any women who would be willing to share their experiences with you. Discuss anesthetics with your doctor. Several of the women we questioned had had Caesareans, and all had used regional, rather than general, anesthetics.

If you and your husband want to be together in the delivery room, *emphatically* express your wishes. Comparatively recent policy changes in some hospitals allow fathers to attend Caesarean births provided that the mother does not need a general anesthetic.

In an article in *The American Baby*, Crystal Sada, director of Caesarean Way, says, "We feel, as a group, that education is the best tool for relaxation. Although it is a shock to learn you need to have surgery, the more information you find out on the subject, the less scary it becomes."

Although no woman is overjoyed at the thought of having major surgery, many might find Caesareans more acceptable if they realized that, in the long run, both baby and mother are benefited by this type of birth if the conditions exist that make a Caesarean the wisest choice of delivery. Medical experts say that a Caesarean lessens the chance of harm to the fetus and to the mother when difficulties are expected.

One friend, however, a nurse in an obstetrician's office, told us that once or twice a month new patients come in and request a Caesarean because they are afraid of labor or want to have their babies on a particular day. Although the operation is safer today, it is nevertheless major surgery and therefore there are risks of complications. *No woman should have a Caesarean unless it is absolutely necessary.*

Another friend told us about her experiences with her three Caesarean births. "My first was an unexpected Caesarean when I was 17," she said. "An unwed mother, I went to birth classes at the YWCA, preparing myself for natural childbirth. After twenty hours of labor and minimal dilation, I was given a saddle block and taken into emergency delivery. A five-and-a-half-pound girl was born and adopted privately through a lawyer. I had a long convalescence, but I believe the emotions of giving up a child prolonged my recovery. It is important to get up the day after surgery, to alleviate the feeling that you're going to pop back open, and also to keep your stomach from filling with gas. I just didn't feel like moving much, and spent ten days lying around in the hospital.

"When I became pregnant the second time, five years later, married, and very ready to have and keep my own child, I searched far and wide for a doctor who would agree to let me have another chance with a normal delivery. I finally found one, and went to Lamaze classes with my husband, with the understanding that chances for a normal delivery were fifty/fifty.

"Again I had a long labor, and when the doctor made a decision for a Caesarean I was disappointed, but also relieved to end the labor. I was given a spinal. They made the incision on top of my old scar. The only physical sensation I felt was the pulling of my rib cage and upper body as they pressed and squeezed trying to pop the baby out. My daughter was brought to my side immediately after the cord was cut and was examined and cleaned right next to me, and then taken to see her dad, where he was allowed to watch the nurses perform their duties on her.

"My greatest concern after my third Caesarean was for my husband. I felt badly that he was being cheated as a father in not being able to witness the birth of his own children. For days the feeling haunted me, until I broke into tears with apologies. Loving person that he is, he shared his feeling that this was no real concern, and he eventually helped to eradicate the guilt I felt. Very few hospitals allow the father to be present during a Caesarean birth, but if we keep asking for it, they may eventually give in."

PREPARATION AND TRAINING FOR CHILDBIRTH

"The Lamaze class was a tremendous preparation for child-birth. Before I took the course I had a lot of apprehension about labor and delivery. Upon completing the course I felt fully educated, confident, and very well prepared to bring my child into the world."

Mother of two / New Haven, Conn.

"My prepared-childbirth class was marvelous. I learned what would happen to me, to my body, and to my baby during childbirth. My fears were eliminated. I learned breathing techniques and positions to make the pain more bearable. My husband worked with me daily and attended classes, so it was a mutual experience. Most important, I was so psychologically ready I felt I could conquer the world. I looked forward even to the pain as a challenge and desirable experience." *Mother of two / Lancaster, Pa.*

If you have never skied before, you may be able to put on a pair of skis and somehow make it down a hill. But you'll avoid a lot of pain and anxiety if you prepare yourself be-forehand by learning how to move and hold the poles. The same holds true for childbirth.

More than 70 percent of all expectant mothers in this country now receive some kind of education for labor and delivery. The women we questioned reflected this trend. When asked to name the most important thing they did to get ready for a baby, many said it was taking a childbirth-preparation class. "I used the Lamaze method of child-birth and felt as if I could handle most situations," said one.

If you decide to take a prepared-childbirth class, you

will learn to relax and control the muscles used in childbirth. You will be taught techniques of breathing that ease
and facilitate labor. You will learn methods to help in di-
verting and controlling pain. You will discuss the anatomy
and physiology of pregnancy and the three stages of labor.
You will receive up-to-date information about medication,
as well as about forceps and Caesarean deliveries. And most
important, you will discover that you have the right, the
knowledge, and the ability to have some say during your
labor and delivery.

Classes are offered by hospitals, Y's, and organizations
such as American Society for Psychoprophylaxis in Obstetrics (Lamaze method). To find a class, check our Resource
List.

There are several points you might consider before choosing a class.

• Try to find a small class. Most have at least ten couples,
but the smaller the better, to give you a chance to ask questions.

• The instructor should be qualified by either personal or
professional experience in prepared childbirth. She should
herself have had a baby using the techniques she is teaching
and/or have participated as a coach in several such births.

• The class should present a balance of materials on both
pregnancy and birth, and should give you enough time to
learn and practice the relaxing and breathing techniques.

• Classes usually meet once a week, for two hours, for six
to ten weeks during the last two months of pregnancy. A
refresher session should be available if your labor is delayed.

• If the class is offered by a hospital, make certain that it
is not just a propaganda program to teach you to go along
with hospital routines.

• Some classes will prepare you for parenthood as well as
childbirth, discussing such topics as breast feeding and
child care.

• Classes can be found to fit all pocketbooks. Prices range
from a few dollars to fifty or sixty dollars.

Childbirth has traditionally been the subject of many frightening half truths and myths, which will be explored and debunked during prepared-childbirth classes. But as a result of the interest in natural childbirth itself, some new myths have blossomed.

Myth 1: If you take a prepared-childbirth class you can't request medication during labor. There is absolutely no truth to this. No doctor, no childbirth instructor—not even one who is totally dedicated to unmedicated childbirth— would insist that there is no place for medication in childbirth.

Myth 2: Prepared childbirth will prevent all pain. In his book, *Childbirth*, Dr. John Miller says: "One cannot avoid all pain in life except by continuous anesthesia (as the alcoholic attempts), and some pain is an absolute prerequisite to accomplishing almost any worthwhile goal. So painless childbirth is a contradiction in terms. The only way to avoid the pain of childbirth is not to bear children."

Because they want to alleviate fear, some prepared-childbirth instructors de-emphasize the pain. Most mothers, however, admit that the contractions of advanced labor are painful. One said, "My only criticism of my Lamaze course was that nobody told me that labor would *hurt!* My mind was prepared to conquer all pain but my body didn't believe what my mind was telling it."

Myth 3: There's no point in taking a class if your husband won't agree to participate actively. You'll get something out of it even if you go alone. If your husband is totally opposed, a friend might be willing and eager to come with you. And your husband may eventually change his mind. One woman said, "Although my husband dragged his feet at the start, he eventually became so actively involved that he felt capable of delivering his own baby."

FATHERS IN THE LABOR AND DELIVERY ROOM

At the start of your pregnancy, your partner may not be as involved as you are. "I was too busy worrying about how I was going to support the kid to think about seeing him born," commented one father. "However, I did see him born and it was one of life's great experiences—the only way to have a baby."

Every couple we talked with who were together for their child's birth were lyrically happy about starting their family as a threesome.

"I'm sure I love my daughter a little more because I saw her born," one father said. "I felt so proud of my wife, of myself, of my daughter."

"It was a snap!" beamed another father. "The thrill of a lifetime."

"I thought it was terrific. I couldn't have just sat in the waiting room—I would have come unglued. I wouldn't have wanted it any other way," said another father.

"I must admit I wasn't too wild about the idea at the beginning," admitted another. "I was afraid I would pass out, or just not hack it. But I was too busy helping my wife to even think about myself, and hearing my son's first cry— boy, that was something!"

The mothers' reports were just as glowing.

"After my son was born, we genuinely felt as though we had had the baby," said one.

"My husband was a godsend. I would have gone stark, raving mad without him there. I hardly let him leave the room, even to use the bathroom. If it had come to a choice between him and the doctor, I would have chosen to go it alone with my husband," commented another.

One father who did not see his son born still regretted it eight years later: "I wish I had been there. I feel like I missed out on something important."

"I wish he had been there, too," added his wife. "I cried tears of happiness when our son was born. They were also tears of loneliness since I wanted to share the birth of our son with my man."

"My husband was so enthusiastic about being in the delivery room that he's the one who talks about it whenever the subject of birth comes up—at home, at a party, even in his office. He attended all the classes with me and coached me through the roughest part of labor with his positive attitude and encouragement. I'm expecting our third child and he's so excited about repeating this experience. He thinks it's terrific that I carry the child for nine months and then he gets the glory of seeing the baby first, not me. I think he'd make a great mother."

Mother of two / Atlanta, Ga.

"Nothing could convince my husband to be with me during labor and delivery, and since he was so uptight about the whole idea I didn't try to force him—I didn't need to worry about *two* babies. As an alternative, I asked my sister to be my coach. She had two children herself, and was both delighted and fascinated at having this opportunity. Afterward we were so close and discussed the experience so often that my husband changed his mind and now wants to be with me during my second labor and delivery."

Mother of one / Bayshore, N.Y.

TAKING CARE OF YOURSELF

Pregnancy will motivate you toward self-care. Not only what you eat but cigarettes, alcohol, medications, and drugs—all these affect and may harm your baby. Many women change habits acquired over a lifetime in order to give their babies the healthiest possible start in life.

Diet

Over the years there have been many changes in opinion about how much a pregnant woman should eat. Our mothers were encouraged to stuff themselves because they were "eating for two." Then the trend changed and women were advised to gain as little as possible, or even to reduce if they were overweight. Lately physicians seems to be reversing themselves again. Many now feel that while excessive weight gain is dangerous for both mother and baby, a restricted diet may also be harmful.

"I gained forty pounds while I was pregnant," said one mother, "but since I ate mainly protein, fruits, and vegetables I had no problems losing the weight after I gave birth." Most other women gained between twenty-five and thirty pounds, and those who lost their extra weight most easily were the ones who had eaten nutritious food during pregnancy. The ones who gorged on "junk food" had more difficulty with weight loss.

Ask your doctor about foods to avoid. One may be liver. Dr. Frank Rauscher, director of the National Cancer Institute, has advised pregnant women not to eat it because DES, a synthetic estrogen fed to animals to encourage weight gain, tends to collect in the animal's liver and kidneys. DES has been linked to vaginal cancer in daughters of women who took it in the form of hormones to prevent miscarriages.

You may also have to cut down on coffee and tea. One doctor has said that the caffeine in both coffee and tea has a pronounced effect on the fetus, and advises pregnant women to switch to decaffeinated coffee. If this is impossible, at least keep regular coffee or tea consumption to an absolute minimum.

If you need to overhaul your eating habits read *Nourishing Your Unborn Child: Nutrition and Natural Foods in Pregnancy* by Phyllis Williams, who is a nurse and a mother. If you have problems with overeating, another excellent book is *A Woman Doctor's Diet for Women* by Barbara Edelstein, M.D. Dr. Edelstein thoroughly understands the psyche of the overweight woman and offers numerous suggestions to help women watch what they eat. She also offers a special diet for overweight pregnant women.

Smoking

Women who smoke during pregnancy are nearly twice as likely to lose their babies through miscarriage as women who are nonsmokers, according to a Columbia University study. Other studies have shown that smoking results in smaller babies, that it increases the likelihood of premature births, and that it increases the risk of birth defects. And to make the picture even bleaker, a recent study suggests a possible link between smoking and crib death (Sudden Infant Death Syndrome), the leading cause of death of infants between the ages of 1 month and a year.

One group of British scientists, looking at the long-term influences of prenatal exposure to smoking, found that children of smokers at age 7, and later at 11, were not only shorter but also were slower in math and reading than children of nonsmoking mothers.

If you smoke, make every effort to quit when you become pregnant. "I quit smoking during the first trimester of my first pregnancy," said one friend. "Cold turkey was the method. It wasn't easy, but my motivation was strong. Five years later, I'm still a nonsmoker. I can say that it's certainly one thing in my life that I have absolutely no regrets about." Another woman quit after taking a course sponsored by the American Cancer Society, and still another paid $500 for a stop-smoking program and swore it was worth every penny.

A fourth friend who didn't quit reported that one day while she was watching a TV program showing the effect of cigarettes on the fetus her 10-year-old son said, "Gee, Mom, maybe if you hadn't smoked I wouldn't be so short."

If you can't quit, at least cut down. Experts say the effect on the fetus is related to the number of cigarettes smoked, and that smoking more than ten cigarettes a day is a *proven* risk factor. Also, since 60 percent of the tars and nicotine are in the last half of a cigarette, try to smoke only the first half. Change to a brand lower in tars and nicotine. Choose a brand you don't like; you may smoke less. Take a walk, knit a blanket, or suck on a lollipop whenever you have the urge to smoke.

"I took ten or fifteen showers a day when I quit smoking," said one mother. "Ever try to smoke in the shower?"

Cats, Raw Meat, and Insecticides

Cats often carry an infectious organism called toxoplasma, which can cause birth defects if transmitted to a fetus. Over 3,000 babies are born with it each year in the United States. The best way to guard against it: don't empty your cat's litter box while pregnant, and wash your hands thoroughly after you handle the cat and its favorite things. Raw or rare meat can also carry the organism; make certain that the meat you eat is well done.

It's also wise to avoid strong cleaning solvents and paints while you are pregnant, because of possible risk to the fetus. Avoid cleaning, painting, or refinishing anything with strong sprays or materials. Also avoid spraying your garden and house plants with strong insecticides.

Drugs and Medications

Remember the thalidomide tragedy? Women who took what they thought was a perfectly harmless drug later gave birth to deformed babies. Since almost everything ingested by the mother is passed along to the fetus within a few minutes when you're pregnant, it's important to avoid *all* drugs not prescribed or approved by your doctor, including such over-the-counter remedies as aspirin and antihistamines. Valium is as prevalent in many people's medicine cabinet as aspirin. It should not be used during pregnancy.

No one knows yet what effect marijuana has on an unborn child, but why take the chance?

Alcohol

The National Institute on Alcohol Abuse and Alcoholism warned recently that women who take more than two drinks a day during pregnancy run the risk of giving birth to mentally retarded and physically deformed babies. The Food and Drug Administration warns that this is not only a problem for women who are alcoholics, but also for any pregnant woman who might drink two or more ounces of liquor on any given day. Another study showed that women who drink two to four ounces a day ran a 10 percent risk of giving birth to retarded babies, and women who drink four or more ounces had a 19 percent risk. Increasing evidence shows that a pregnant woman should severely limit, or even stop, drinking alcohol.

In her book, Tracy Hotchner says, "*Alcohol* is a poison. In large amounts it may damage the nerve cells of the brain. Some of the alcohol you drink reaches the baby, and during the critical developmental period you don't want its brain cells exposed." It's best for your baby if you *stop drinking* while you are pregnant. If you do have an occasional drink, don't have more than one ounce of hard liquor, two glasses of wine, or two glasses of beer on any one day.

Exercise

If you are an extremely active person, you can probably continue to be very active during your pregnancy until your body—or your doctor—tells you it's time to stop. One mother went surfing until her eighth month, and some women have participated in the Olympics while pregnant. A friend continued with yoga, adapting her methods to routines given in Jeannine Medvin's book *Prenatal Yoga and Natural Birth.*

ONE MOTHER WENT SURFING UNTIL HER 8TH MONTH.

"I'm a runner, but with my first child I had a cyst the doctor was afraid would rupture, so I sat around for nine months—and gained sixty pounds. My second pregnancy was fine, but I only ran the first four months. I did play tennis up until the end, but I still gained forty pounds. During my third pregnancy, I ran the entire time and only gained twenty-five pounds. For me that's good.

"Running is my mental, as well as my physical, conditioning. Every day during those nine months I got out and jogged three to six miles, and I didn't notice the discomfort of the baby. My goal during that pregnancy was to run the Manhattan Beach ten-kilometer run, and I did it! It was fantastic during the race to hear the astounded comments of other runners as I slowly plodded my way to, and *across,* the finish line."

Mother of three / Manhattan Beach, Calif.

On the other hand, if you are an inactive person, don't begin a strenuous exercise program once you are pregnant. Instead, find ways to include a little mild exercise in your daily routine. "I was in better shape after pregnancy than before," said one mother. "My husband and I walked every day. Sometimes we would stroll for hours. The hospital was two miles from home, so we even walked to the entrance when my labor started."

WORKING

"I felt wonderful while I was pregnant. I had so much energy, and my appetite was terrific. I worked until a few days before I delivered, which was greatly beneficial—physically, mentally, and financially. I felt capable of anything."

Mother of one / Flagstaff, Ariz.

If you feel up to it, and your doctor approves, by all means continue working for as long as you like. At any given time in the United States some 3.5 million women are pregnant, and most of those who are expecting a first child work, according to Dr. Ervin E. Nichols, coordinator of "Guidelines on Pregnancy and Work," a pamphlet issued by the American College of Obstetrics and Gynecology.

Dr. Nichols estimates that 85 percent of these jobs hold no danger to the pregnant worker. But he and other experts suggest that pregnant women tell their doctor immediately about the type of work they do, including:

• Physical stress (heat, noise, vibration, long periods spent sitting or standing in one place).

• Chemical or radiation exposure.

• Exposure to animals or to raw meat.

• Conditions affecting oxygen and carbon monoxide levels in the blood (airline personnel, toll-booth operators, and other outdoor workers may have abnormal levels, especially if they smoke).

Your job is probably one of those that pose no danger; however, it certainly pays to be safe. If you have doubts, read *Women's Work, Women's Health* by Jeanne Mager Stellman.

Some of the women we questioned worked until a week or so before giving birth. One said, "I taught until a week before my due date. It was the best possible way for me, since I kept physically and mentally active throughout my whole pregnancy and earned money at the same time."

Others quit their jobs two or three months beforehand. "I quit work three months before my first child was born," one mother told us. "It was ten years and three children ago, but I still look back on those three months as the best possible baby gift. I read, fixed up a nursery, visited art galleries, and went to the movies. And I spent blissful minutes and hours just sitting by myself and dreaming. There are times now in my life of children, husband, home, and work when I would give it all up just to have ten minutes alone to sit and dream."

Congress has enacted a slate of rights for pregnant women. These rights include:

• Women who return to work after maternity leave are not to be treated as new employees and do not have to start over with pension and other benefits. Also, they are not to lose status in regard to seniority, pay, or promotions.

• Pregnant women may work as long as they are able and willing to do so.

• A company cannot refuse to hire pregnant women merely because they are pregnant and cannot fire employees because they become pregnant.

• A company is required to pay full benefits for pregnancy and childbirth if its pregnant employees are covered by the company's group health insurance.

• Pregnant women may collect sick-leave pay and disability benefits both for problems connected with pregnancy and for maternity leaves.

Check with your employer about your benefits, and make sure you receive everything that is rightfully due to you.

When and If to Return to Work

You may have no choice about whether or not to return to work after the birth of your baby. If working is a financial necessity, your decision is easy: you will return to work. The advice most often offered by working mothers was expressed by one young woman who said, "Spend as much time looking and as much money as you can afford for the best in child care. Working has been a positive experience for my daughter and me. I spent months looking for my sitter. After interviewing many, many women I found the perfect sitter—an older woman who became our substitute grandmother. In some ways she is as close to our family as my daughter's real grandmother." If you must return to work, be sure to read Chapter 16 for more information on finding the "best in child care."

"These early years have been wonderful, more rewarding than I ever imagined. I had planned to return to work when Cindy was 3 months old, but took the full year, returning to work mornings only when she was a year old. If at all possible, I feel the mother or father should be the major caregiver until the child is 3." *Mother of one / Belmont, Mass.*

"My part-time job was perfect. I worked five hours a day, which gave me time to be with other adults in a stimulating environment, and yet I still had plenty of time to meet the needs of a small infant. Full-time work would have been too demanding, but working part time gave me the best of both worlds." *Mother of two / Durham, N.C.*

If you must return to work, don't rush immediately back to the job. Spend as much time at home with your baby as you possibly can. During the first few months a mother and child establish lasting bonds. It is important to your future relationship that your baby spend time in your arms so that he knows, physically, that you are his mother and you know, physically, that he is your child.

If you have a choice, reserve final judgment about working until after the baby is born. A Houston lab technician who went back to work immediately after her daughter's birth told us, "Until I had a child I thought surely I'd continue working. Then I had her. Instead of enjoying her, it was 'Hurry up!' all day long. I'd mutter to her, 'I've got to get to work . . . I've got to get you to the sitter's . . . I've got to get a load of wash in!' " This woman quit her full-time job and is now happily working part time.

"The three years of full-time mothering I was able to give my eldest son were a joy. It was a privilege to be with him, to share his growth. I had to go back to work when my second son was 2 months old, and although we both made a good adjustment, I still have lingering regrets seven years later. When my sons ask me to tell them what they were like as babies, I can clearly recall numerous stories about the eldest. But I can't remember much about the youngest, since I just wasn't there." *Mother of two / Detroit, Mich.*

Ten years ago most child-development experts were in firm agreement that a baby needed full-time mothering. When more and more women began to go to work, however, the experts began to modify their opinions, saying that it wasn't too bad for the baby as long as the mother was happy with her decision. We heard the phrase "It's the quality —not the quantity—of time you spend with your children that really counts" so often it became a cliché.

Now some authorities are strongly dissenting. In her book *Every Child's Birthright: In Defense of Mothering*, Selma Fraiberg voices concern about social pressures and policies that send increasing numbers of mothers to work at a time when good substitute-mother services are extremely hard to find. She suggests that laws, customs, and even values must change if children's genuine needs are to be met.

In the book *The Challenge of Day Care*, child-development experts Sally Provence, Audrey Naylor, and June Patterson describe a day-care center they developed under the auspices of the Yale Child Study Center. They attempted to create the very best, but even with the best, they noted, "Ideas about the subjective experience of very young children away from their mothers for the whole day are conjecture, but one can see that their feelings range from a sense of bewilderment to acute longing for mother and home and that their adaptive capacities are increasingly overtaxed as the hours lengthen."

Perhaps "quantity" *is* just as important as "quality" in mothering. If you are wavering in your decision about returning to work, you might wish to read these books; they may help you to make up your mind. And even if you do return to work, you might read them because they may help you in choosing care for your baby.

YOUR SEX LIFE

Some women report that pregnancy enhances their sexual desire and responsiveness. "The best thing about pregnancy was the special closeness between me and my husband—and that feeling of being special enhanced our whole sex experience," commented one mother. Other women candidly admitted that they did not enjoy sex during pregnancy. "I felt that my body belonged to the baby," one mother told us, "and this feeling lasted right through breast feeding."

Whatever your feelings, talk them over with your husband, as he may also be feeling doubts and concern. "I was afraid I'd hurt the baby," said one man. "But then my wife and I visited the obstetrician together and the three of us discussed the question of sex during pregnancy. The doctor helped me get rid of my fears."

Some couples find that their favorite positions become uncomfortable or impossible during the last weeks of pregnancy. If this gets to be a problem a bit of experimentation may be in order. "We tried all kinds of different positions when I was pregnant," confided one friend. "We also learned to enjoy mutual masturbation during the last month, when intercourse became so uncomfortable for me that I couldn't possibly enjoy it." Although many doctors used to advise abstinence from intercourse during the last two months of pregnancy, many are now revising this stand. Check with your doctor if you have concerns about limiting intercourse. However, you shouldn't engage in intercourse or masturbation if you have vaginal or abdominal pain, uterine bleeding, or ruptured membranes, or if you have reason to fear miscarriage.

Opinions vary on when to resume intercourse after a baby is born, so be sure to check with your doctor *beforehand* about when he thinks it's safe for you. Six weeks is the traditional length of time that many of us have heard from our mothers, our friends, and our doctors. However, some women don't wait that long. One who did said later, "I could have screamed when I checked with my doctor and he said, 'Who told you six weeks? I didn't.'"

Some new mothers, however, found intercourse uncomfortable for a least eight to ten weeks after giving birth. "It was extremely painful for me—and I felt more like a mother than a lover," one woman said. "I began to feel more and more more guilty as my husband became more and more frustrated. Then one night I burst into tears in the middle of intercourse. We quit, and talked for at least an hour. My husband agreed to let me take the lead and let him know when I felt like sex. Gradually, I began to enjoy it again."

Remember, you can get pregnant again almost immediately, and *breast feeding is not an adequate form of birth control.* So also check on birth-control methods with your doctor before resuming sexual relations.

HOW YOU'LL FEEL DURING PREGNANCY

"My two pregnancies were as different as my two sons. The first pregnancy was delightful. I felt physically strong and healthy, worked up until the last month, controlled my weight, and was unusually happy and alive. It was such a beautiful feeling knowing that a little person was growing inside me. I never had morning sickness or any other irritating ailments. I just assumed that I was one of those lucky women who blossomed while pregnant. Well, I was wrong. During my second pregnancy I was a complete physical and emotional wreck. The veins in my legs became so painful that for eight months I had to wear stockings that had to be specially made. I continually felt sorry for myself. That pregnancy was a real burden, but how glad I was, finally, to give birth to a healthy and dearly loved son." *Mother of two / Elgin, Ill.*

Some women felt marvelous throughout their pregnancies and enjoyed every minute of the experience. "I loved it," said one. "I felt as though my life had opened up incredibly. I felt vulnerable at moments, strong at others. It was a time of fine closeness for my husband and me. I felt like a queen receiving homage and respect. It was always positive, and it felt good."

Other women were less enthusiastic. "I disliked being pregnant," commented one friend bluntly. "I was gawky and couldn't do things right; it kind of slowed me down. I'm just not one of those who thinks being pregnant is great. I did it twice, and would do it again if I wanted a third child. But the end, that's the good part—a new and exciting baby."

"It was just about like not being pregnant. There were some good days, some not so good, and some bad," said a third mother. Most women would agree. Their most common complaints were of annoyances rather than disabling problems. Here are the ones they reported and the things they did to help.

Early Months

The following ailments and complaints are common during the first months of pregnancy. Since each woman is different, however, you may experience only some—or none—of these problems during any part of your pregnancy.

Fatigue. During the first few months you will probably tire easily and need more sleep than usual because your body is rapidly changing to accommodate your baby. When you are tired, rest. In a few months your system will adjust and you'll stop feeling so tired. One mother suggested, "Along with the extra vitamins one takes during pregnancy, I found that a hearty protein drink really helped me through the tired, sagging feelings. I still have this drink every morning and will do so as long as I continue to nurse."

Morning sickness. Although many theories have been advanced to explain the cause of nausea during pregnancy, no one really knows why about half of all pregnant women in our country experience it. During the first three months you may experience nausea, and it can occur at any time of the day, not just the morning. When we asked what worked for nausea, many women stated emphatically, "Absolutely nothing!"

One mother went into it in more detail. "I found that nothing worked. I knew I was going to throw up so I thought I might as well get it over with. I would drink a glass of milk every morning, go into the bathroom, throw it up, and be fine for the rest of the day," she said. Other women found relief in different ways, and here are some of their suggestions:

• Before going to bed prepare a snack of dry toast or saltines and a thermos of tea. Set your alarm a few minutes early and remain in bed a little longer than usual. Have your snack before getting out of bed. Sip your tea, munch your crackers, listen to music, look around the room. Then get up slowly and start your day relaxed.

● Eat lightly and frequently throughout the day. "I was very sick and found nothing helped at first," recalled one mother. "After losing nine pounds I forced myself to eat out of fear for my unborn infant. Soda crackers, V-8 juice, apricot juice, and hunks of cheese were the only things I could stomach at first. I nibbled all day, and slowly went back on a normal diet."

● Keeping very busy was a solution for one mother; resting a lot was a solution for another.

● Several mothers recommended adding vitamin B-6 to the diet.

Your emotions. One mother described pregnancy this way: "It is as close to being psychotic as most women will ever get. I have a close friend who is now pregnant. She's up one minute, down the next. She moans that she can't eat a thing and then five minutes later devours everything in the refrigerator. One day she regrets that she even considered bringing a child into this overpopulated world, and the next she's thrilled with the wonder of being pregnant and anticipating the joys of motherhood. I can put up with her swings in mood because I vividly recall being exactly the same way myself when I was pregnant."

"Do I remember the ups and downs! I would be happily sewing, dreaming of the baby, and suddenly find myself in tears, terrified that he wouldn't be normal. The more I tried to get a handle on what was bothering me, to try and figure out what caused my feelings, the more bothered I would get. I finally realized that I just couldn't track down any reason for my swings in mood and that negative feelings just had to pass."
Mother of three / Sacramento, Calif.

What do you do when you're feeling blue?

Do something nice for you. Take a bubble bath; go window shopping; buy some sexy perfume; read a good book; talk to a close friend.

Go ahead and give in to the mood. Cry a little or a lot. Stomp your feet, pound a pillow, express your feelings. "It was marvelous!" said one woman. "It usually take something catastrophic to release my tears, but when I was pregnant I could cry and cry, and let all the bad feelings wash away. It was like being a very little girl again, only better, because nobody told me that pregnant ladies shouldn't cry."

"Keep busy," suggested a father. "Whenever my wife was bored, she got the blues. Rather than let her feel sorry for herself, I encouraged her to get involved with her pottery, or go visit a friend, or jump in the sack with me. Usually one of these did the trick."

"I wouldn't let myself feel blue," said another mother. "I believed the old wives' tale that a 'happy pregnancy means a happy baby.'"

One of the universal preoccupations during pregnancy is wondering about the sex of the baby. One mother told us: "Throughout the months of my first and second pregnancies I mulled over the question 'Is it a boy or a girl?' I was 42 when I became pregnant a third time. On my first visit the doctor suggested amniocentesis, a test that would determine whether or not my baby had Downs Syndrome, which is more prevalent with older women. The test also reveals the sex of a baby. The day came to find out the results. My baby was normal, and my doctor asked if I wanted to know its sex. I suddenly felt like a child being forced to celebrate Christmas six months early. I told him 'no,' and spent the rest of my pregnancy happily mulling over the question, 'Is it a boy or a girl?'"

Middle Months

The middle part of pregnancy is often characterized by a feeling of extreme well-being, both physical and mental. The nausea and fatigue of early pregnancy will usually lessen or disappear, and emotions become calmer. Many women report feeling absolutely fantastic during these months.

Last Months

"The bloom has worn off, the reality is here," moaned a mother-to-be in her eighth month. "I'm gigantic, I'm ugly, I'm uncomfortable. My back hurts and my legs ache. Everyone tells me I'm blooming. Actually, I'm wilting. I wish I could go to sleep and wake up and find it's all over. But the trouble is, I can't sleep and I'm not ready, even if it were all over."

Minor pains of mind and body often accompany the last months of pregnancy. Since you can't use aspirin or other drugs to gain temporary relief, try some of these suggestions.

Backache. A firm mattress is a must. If you don't have one, use a board to firm a sagging mattress. Try sleeping with a pillow under the small of your back. One woman said, "During my first pregnancy I had severe backache, but during my second I had absolutely none because I slept in a heated water bed."

A Hydrocollator, which is a moist-heat steam pack manufactured by the Chattanooga Pharmacal Company, has provided temporary relief to many who suffer from chronic lower-back problems. It's made of a fabric that absorbs moisture when placed in boiling water and emits moist heat when applied to your back. It's available in most pharmacies in a variety of sizes—small enough to use on your neck or large enough to apply to your whole spine. It costs under ten dollars, lasts for years, and can be used in place of a heating pad.

Leg cramps. Keep off your feet, elevate your legs at night, and gently massage the cramped area. A Hydrocollator may also help.

"Whenever I had minor aches and pains, I practiced techniques from my Lamaze class. The progressive relaxation technique was particularly effective. I tensed, then completely relaxed, the muscles in my body and very often my backache or leg aches would disappear," one mother told us.

Rib aches. About the only thing that helps with these is to change your position. Stand up if you are sitting down, sit if standing, change from side to side when lying down. One mother said, "I just reached down and shoved my baby into another position when she made me hurt."

Insomnia. It's ironic. Just at the point when you need to rest, to store up energy for the birth of your baby, you may find it impossible to sleep at night. If night sleep is a problem, try napping during the day. Then get up at night and read, sew, watch TV, or do something soothing. One mother felt that in a way her insomnia had been a blessing because it prepared her for waking at night with her new daughter.

Sleeping. Getting comfortable at night can be a problem. Experiment with different positions, and try using extra pillows under the small of your back, under or between your legs, and under your arms or breasts. "I was only comfortable lying on my side in a fetal position with pillows under my legs and upper arm in the last month," one mother said.

Mild swelling of hands or feet. Be sure to report swelling to your doctor, since it can be a danger signal. He may advise you to cut down on salt and on diet soda, which has a high sodium count.

Constipation. Follow a moderate exercise program; eat leafy green vegetables and whole-grain cereals and breads; have some fruit before going to bed. A glass of prune juice a day will work wonders, and some women swear by raisins. Don't strain or push during bowel movements, since this may cause another problem, hemorrhoids.

Hemorrhoids. "If I had it to do over, I'd try to avoid the hemorrhoids that made my first days at home after the baby came very difficult," said a mother. "I'd be very conscious of roughage in the diet. I'd also learn to push right during birth giving it everything I've got."

Flatulence (more commonly known as gas). I was full of gas when I was pregnant," one mother told us. "It sounds gross, but I found that getting down on all fours with my knees under my stomache, resting some weight on my elbows, and my bottom up in the air enabled the gas to rise and pass unobstructed."

PREPARING FOR BABY CARE

If you are inexperienced in handling babies, by all means take a Red Cross course in caring for newborns. If your husband wants to go with you, all the better. One study showed that women who attended prenatal classes for instruction in child care had significantly less emotional upset when they began caring for their babies than women who did not attend such classes. And those whose husbands attended classes with them

DANGER SIGNALS
Symptoms That Warrant an Immediate Call to Your Doctor

● Vaginal bleeding at any time during pregnancy.

● Sudden swelling or puffiness of face, eyes, or fingers.

● Severe headache, especially during the second half of pregnancy.

● Leakage of clear fluid from the vagina.

● Blurring of vision, particularly during the second half of pregnancy.

● Severe abdominal pain at any time during pregnancy and any place in your abdomen.

● Any significant illness characterized by high fever, severe nausea, or diarrhea.

● Burning or painful urination, or decreased urine output.

● Fainting, dizzy spells, or convulsions.

● A weight gain of more than two pounds in one week.

● Any long period of inactivity on the part of your baby after it has started to move around a lot.

● Any other problem that has you drastically worried. Your doctor may laugh and tell you everything is fine, but it's better to call and risk being laughed at than to neglect a symptom that may mean something is seriously wrong.

experienced even fewer emotional disturbances, after birth, than did the women who went by themselves.

"I read all the current books on raising *psychologically* healthy babies, but Spock was not fashionable then, and I didn't even give a minute's thought to the *physical* care of a baby. I came home from the hospital with a list. 'Protect the circumcision with Vaseline . . . Sponge bathe the baby until the umbilical cord heals . . . Burp the baby after each feeding.' But the list didn't tell how to 'protect,' 'sponge,' or 'burp.' Somehow, we survived. I sent my husband to the drugstore for a copy of

Spock, and gave my son his first tub bath with the book at my side. Now I know I should have included practical child-care books on my pre-baby reading list, should have taken a course in baby care, should have asked for rooming-in, and definitely should have picked the brains of the nurses in the hospital." *Mother of two / New York, N.Y.*

"I was *not* prepared for motherhood and I increasingly resent my poor preparation. I am an only child who was never permitted to babysit. I learned how to raise children by reading and by trial and error. I wish I had gained practical knowledge of children to experience the give and take, the disappointments, and the joys so that I would have had a better perspective on child raising." *Mother of two / Baton Rouge, La.*

To gain practical experience with a baby, spend some time with an infant. If you have a friend with a newborn, ask her to let you watch as she feeds, bathes, and changes her baby. Volunteer to babysit so that you can do some of these tasks yourself. One mother said, "The best help I got was from a friend. She let me use her baby as a laboratory. At first I was scared to death, but eventually I relaxed. My husband and I took care of the baby for a weekend. We both felt like pros by the time our baby was born."

Another friend joined a babysitting co-op when she was six months pregnant. "Both my husband and I babysat. We learned to care for children of all ages, and we stored up many advance hours of babysitting time. It was fantastic when I brought my own daughter home and needed to get out."

One of the best ways to learn to care for your baby is to ask for "rooming-in" in the hospital. You will feed your baby on demand. You and your husband will establish a family bond shortly after birth, since you can both hold, rock, and cuddle the baby. And you will learn to bathe, change, feed, and care for your baby with the help of experienced nurses.

"Rooming-in was fantastic! My daughter was in my room five hours after her birth. I held her, cuddled her, fed her, changed her, and bathed her myself. My husband also spent time with us, and got to know his daughter. Whenever I wanted to take a nap, I alerted the nurses and they took over."
Mother of two / Hyattsville, Md.

Some mothers found rooming in to be tiring, and a little more than they were up to so soon after giving birth. In a hospital with a staff sympathetic to rooming in this wouldn't be so much of a problem because the nurses would be on hand when you needed them. But if the staff *isn't* supportive you may find yourself being "punished" by nurses who insist that caring for the newborn is entirely up to you. For this reason, you should be especially careful of your choice of hospitals if you decide you want rooming in; if the hospital is grudging about it, perhaps you should either abandon the idea or find a more accepting hospital—or gird yourself for a battle of wills with the nursing staff.

BREAST OR BOTTLE FEEDING?

Feeding can be a volatile issue for a pregnant woman. Should you feed by breast or by bottle? Only you and your husband should make this decision. To help you decide, we will briefly list the plus factors for both breast and bottle feeding. More detailed information about feeding is given in Chapters 2 and 3.

Breast Feeding

● Breast milk is easy for a baby to digest. It contains antibodies not contained in formula that help to protect a baby from some diseases. It is cheaper than formula and requires no preparation. It is readily available wherever a mother and baby may go together.

● Breast feeding is a fulfilling and sensual experience for many mothers. One said, "I missed that special part-of-me closeness that I had with my son while I was pregnant. Nursing brought us together again."

● Breast feeding requires a natural sucking motion. Some dentists say this prevents later tooth-alignment problems that can develop from sucking on a bottle the wrong way.

● Breast feeding is physically good for a mother, since it causes the uterus to contract and return more quickly to its normal size.

● Breast feeding requires a mother to sit down, relax, and hold her baby close and secure, and that's good not only for mothers but for babies.

Bottle Feeding

• A few mothers feel very uncomfortable about the idea of breast feeding and for them bottles are better. One said, "Breast feeding just wasn't my thing. I held my daughter while feeding her a bottle and felt as close to her as I would have if she was sucking at my breast."

• Using a bottle, a new mother knows exactly how much milk her baby is getting.

• Both mother and father can feed their baby and thereby establish the bond that naturally comes with giving nourishment.

• A mother can more easily go back to work or go places for longer periods of time without her baby.

Most of the women we talked with breast fed their infants, and very few of them had regrets. Some women who didn't give it a chance, however, *did* express regrets. "I was afraid to give nursing a chance," one mother said. "I was nervous about my figure. I was also a nervous mother, and I was afraid I'd pass along my feelings to my children. Now I'm sorry I didn't try breast feeding. After all, if it doesn't work out, you can always stop. But once you decide to use bottles, it's almost impossible to give them up and breast feed."

If you are considering breast feeding, you may want to prepare your nipples while you are pregnant. To do so, use only water to wash your nipples during the last two months, as soap dries them out. During the last month, massage your nipples with a coarse towel, ten times on each side.

One husband helped his wife by sucking on her nipples for a minute or two each night and she swears that this was the reason she had no soreness in nursing her baby. Another woman exposed her breasts to the sun for a few minutes each day; she's convinced that this toughened her nipples so that she had no trouble nursing.

Colostrum, a yellowish substance that precedes your milk, begins to build up in your breasts, especially during the last months. To help open your milk ducts, press out (express) some of this colostrum during the last month. In the back of the nipple of each breast, under the areola (the brown area), are ducts through which the milk flows. Gently massage the areola, pressing in and around your nipples.

"I nursed both of my boys. During the month before my first son's birth, I toughened my breasts by massaging my nipples and expressing colostrum. Nursing presented absolutely no problems, and my breasts and nipples were fine. My second son was born a month prematurely and I had had no time to prepare my breasts. I suffered with cracked and sore nipples for most of the first month of nursing."
Mother of two / Manchester, N.H.

Besides preparing your nipples, we suggest you read Karen Pryor's *Nursing Your Baby*, which can prevent all sorts of problems in the hospital. You'll know what to ask for and what to insist on. For example, the author warns that hospital help who have never nursed may, in the interest of "schedules," abruptly take the baby from you just as the milk "lets down." Or they may not want to bring the baby to you for a two a.m. feeding. Also, if your baby consistently isn't hungry when the nurse brings her to you for feeding, check to see whether she isn't being given bottles in the nursery. Make sure that she's brought to you as soon as she is hungry, even if this doesn't coincide with the feeding schedules.

"I found it difficult to get information and help about nursing," one mother said. "Responsibility seemed to fall in the crack between my obstetrician's area of concern and my pediatrician's. Neither one seemed to be up on it." One source of help may be a nurse who has breast fed her own babies. If you find such a nurse, ask her for help. Also, particularly after you go home, you can get both moral support and practical advice from nursing mothers' groups such as the La Leche League.

Don't give up if nursing in the hospital isn't totally successful. Relaxation is the key to a good nursing experience, and very few women are really relaxed in a hospital. Once you get home and can relax and do things in your own way, you may find that breast-feeding problems immediately resolve themselves.

ADDITIONAL HELP

We have not intended this chapter to be used as a substitute
for your doctor's advice. It merely reflects the opinions and
experiences of mothers and of the many books on pregnancy
and childbirth we've read. We hope it has given you an overview of pregnancy and of the choices and decisions that you,
as a mother-to-be, have the right to make before your child
is born.

In addition to the information found here, you may wish
to read a more specialized book such as *Pregnancy and Childbirth* by Tracy Hotchner, an excellent guide detailing virtually
everything you'll want to know about the subject. Alan Guttmacher, M.D., in his book *Pregnancy, Birth, and Family Planning*, is very good at giving clear explanations of the mechanics
of pregnancy and birth. If you've decided on natural childbirth,
you might also like to read Lester Hazell's helpful book,
Commonsense Childbirth.

If you're reading this book while you're still pregnant,
give particular attention to the following: Chapter 2 provides
information on what to do during the first days with your
baby and will guide you in finding help at home for those
days—something you will have to make arrangements for
before you go to the hospital. Chapter 5 will give you up-to-
date specifics on everything you'll need to buy for your
baby's first years. Chapters 15 and 16 will help you begin
the search for babysitters and/or day care while you're still
pregnant. The Resource List will direct you to other books
and services on pregnancy and child rearing.

See the Naming Your Baby section at the end of the
book for guidelines in making this exciting decision.

2

Bringing Baby Home: First-Day Care

"I just don't know what to expect. I've prepared a nursery, I've read books, and I've cared for a friend's 6-month-old, but all the information is a jumble. What I need is a primer, with just enough help to get me through the first few days."
                    Mother-to-be / Torrance, Calif.

Your main job during the first days will be to feed and change your baby and to see that he gets rest and sleep. You will bathe him and care for his navel. If you have a boy who has been circumcised, you will care for the circumcision until it heals. And you should have certain items of clothing, equipment, and supplies on hand.

In the first half of this chapter we give you a "First-Days Primer" with basic information about the physical care your baby needs during the first days. Although the actual tasks are minimal, it may all seem horrendous. You may have to feed your baby ten or twelve times a day; you may have to change her fifteen or twenty times; and, as you will be "on call" twenty-four hours a day, you'll probably be exhausted. Here you'll find mothers' advice about feeding, diapering, sleeping, and bathing as well as a list of the minimum of necessary clothing and supplies to get you through the first few days.

In the second half of this chapter—titled "Coping with a Newborn"—we give information and share mothers' experiences to help you deal with some of the often overpowering aspects of your first days at home. We discuss a newborn's innate abilities and emotional needs as well as a new mother's instincts and emotional needs. We give medical pointers, including specific information from a pediatrician on when to call a doctor. And we share feelings, both positive and negative, from mothers and fathers about their first days as parents.

First-Days Primer

FEEDING

Many babies aren't very hungry the first few days, and then become ravenous the third or fourth day. Eventually they settle down to their own natural schedule, eating every three or four hours. On the first few days most mothers and experts agree—let your baby eat whenever he seems hungry. He may want to eat every two hours. He may not want to eat much at all. Whatever his pattern, there's nothing you can do to change it at the beginning.

Have a soothing drink yourself while feeding the baby. Take the phone off the hook, hang a Do Not Disturb sign on the door, relax, and enjoy.

Starting Breast Feeding

Nature provides beautifully for most breast-feeding mothers and babies. Colostrum, a thick yellowish fluid that is present in the breasts before birth and for a few days thereafter, is said to play a role in protecting your baby against disease, giving him antibodies. Although it has no nutritional value, colostrum is adequate for a newborn baby who isn't very hungry. Milk usually comes in on the third or fourth day, just when a baby starts getting hungry.

Your supply of breast milk may be erratic at the start. One day you may be engorged, brimming over with milk, and the next you may not have enough. One day your baby may be ravenous and the next show little interest. Don't despair—eventually your baby's demands and your milk supply will adjust to each other.

One word of warning comes from Dr. Spock in *Baby and Child Care*. He cautions nursing mothers to realize that breast-fed babies may show a dramatic increase in appetite between the third and sixth days, wanting to eat every two hours— ten to twelve times a day. "The baby is now settling down to the serious business of eating and growing," Spock says, and "is providing the breasts with the stimulation they must have if they are to meet his increasing needs."

"At the very first I was terrified the baby wasn't getting enough milk, but a La Leche League mother reassured me. If an infant's managing to wet eight to ten diapers a day, she told me, that means he's probably getting as much milk as he needs."   *Mother of one / Page, Ariz.*

"You're so dithered the first few days home it's easy for a new nursing mom to forget a simple thing: drinking enough liquids. A sure sign you're not drinking enough is that your own urine is darker than usual. The nursing bras from Penney's open easiest. And get some washable cloth nursing pads. They're cheaper than the disposable kind, plus they look better under clothes."   *Mother of three / Memphis, Tenn.*

Starting Bottle Feeding

Not every mother is able to breast feed, and not every mother *wants* to breast feed. In spite of what may seem to be an overwhelming preponderance of opinion in favor of breast feeding these days, if it isn't for you don't agonize over it or feel inadequate if you bottle feed your baby. To make it as easy as possible for yourself, use liquid formula and a presterilized nursing kit for the first few days. (A nursing kit has a cylindrical form that holds a sterile plastic bag. Formula is poured into the bag and the bag is thrown away after using.) Specific pointers on breast and bottle feeding will be found in Chapter 3; information on bottles and other feeding implements is in Chapter 5.

"I wanted no work bottles. I got a Playtex nurser kit and extra boxes of disposable bottles. All I have to do is scrub

the nipples (they turn inside out easily)—
then boil them, and that's it! I store them
in a glass peanut butter jar, also boiled."
Mother of two / Council Bluffs, Iowa

"As a going-home present, my hospital
gave me a six-pack of premeasured,
premixed prepared bottles with disposable nipples. What a relief! I didn't have
to measure or wash anything, not even
the nipples, since I threw each one away
after using it."
Mother of three / Boston, Mass.

"A common mistake new mothers make
is not watching while eager relatives,
friends, and babysitters give the baby
a bottle. Make sure that milk is filling
the nipple and the top part of the bottle
all the time the baby is drinking so that
she doesn't suck in air along with the
milk, which may give her gas pains.
The bottle should always be tilted up-
wards."
Mother of four / Olympia, Wash.

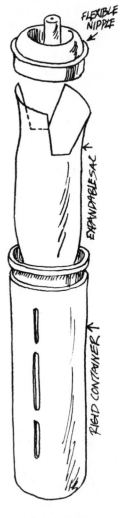

SLEEP—WHAT TO EXPECT

"The first thing I recall when I think of
the first day home is sleep: trying to
soothe my fussy baby, to get him to
sleep so I could get the sleep that I so
desperately needed."
Mother of three / Atlanta, Ga.

Most newborn babies sleep a great deal
of the time. Your baby may sleep 80
percent of the day and night, taking
one long rest of three to four hours and
then eight or nine shorter naps. A few newborn babies,
however, are alert and wakeful from birth. If your baby is
naturally wakeful and doesn't require much sleep, there's

not much you can do, without a doctor's advice, to change
this normal sleep pattern. At the start, the number and
length of naps is up to the baby.

Your baby was undoubtedly the best baby in the hospital.
She slept around the clock, waking only to nurse from breast
or bottle. You couldn't wait to take her home. But on the
first night home she won't stop howling. Now what, coach?

Don't panic. A few nights of crying are perfectly normal.
Your baby may be having trouble getting used to the quiet
of your home. Eventually she'll calm down and adjust to her
new surroundings.

Encourage your baby to sleep on her stomach, because
if she vomits she is not likely to choke, and if she's colicky
the pressure on her stomach may help to relieve her. Tuck
her securely into her crib or cradle to give her the feeling
that she is swaddled and secure, just as she was in the womb.
Keep her snugly wrapped, even on warm days.

"In the hospital I put on a little of my favorite perfume
just before the nurses brought Kerry in for feedings. Then
at home I used it often and also put a few drops on Kerry's
sheets. I'm sure this familiar smell helped Kerry sleep."
Mother of three / Milwaukee, Wisc.

"Both a womb and a newborn nursery in a hospital are relatively noisy places, and I think one reason a baby has sleep
problems when he's brought home from the hospital is simply that things are too quiet. An ace in the hole for us those
first few days home was a record called 'Lullaby from the
Womb' (Capitol)—an actual recording of a heartbeat and
other womb noises. I played it in the middle of the first
night when my son was restless, and it seemed to soothe
him." *Mother of two / Des Moines, Iowa*

"It was August, and hot, when my first son was born, so I
dressed him lightly and put him to bed with a receiving blanket flung over him. For the first two days he had enormous
trouble sleeping. He thrashed and jerked and woke up screaming. A friend suggested that I tuck the blanket around him,

and it was like magic. He immediately began to sleep for three and four hours at a stretch."

Mother of two / Landover, Md.

Barbara Sills reports that both David and Jonas slept in her room for the first month: "We felt more secure knowing they were there. Bernie often got up with me. Also, all we had to do when the baby woke for his early-morning feeding was reach over, take him out of the car bed, change him on the changing table in our room, feed him, and slip him back into bed. If a diaper was messy, we just left it in a small trash can till morning."

Other mothers report that from the start their babies slept in another room, yet close enough to be easily heard. In either case, don't be alarmed by the many normal noises a sleeping infant makes.

DIAPERING BASICS

First bowel movements are greenish-brown or black. Two or three days after birth, breast-fed babies have yellowish curdy-liquid stools, while bottle-fed babies have more solid yellowish-brown stools. The time and frequency of bowel movements may vary. Some babies have one or more after each feeding; others have only one a day or even less.

"I was terrified when my first daughter had three enormous liquid bowel movements within an hour on the first day home. I called the doctor, who assured me that this was perfectly normal."   *Mother of two / Rochester, N.Y.*

Change your baby on a waist-high surface, either a changing table, a sink, or some other suitable place. Wash your baby with soap and water after each bowel movement, but only with water after urination.

When should you change your baby? This is often a dilemma for both new and experienced mothers, especially at the two a.m. feeding, when babies invariably wake up wet or soiled or both. If you decide to wait until *after* feeding your baby to change him, the problem is that he may fall asleep while being fed—and then you'll have to wake him again to change him, and he may object vociferously. Faced with this situation, a mother may prefer to change her baby *before* feeding him; there's a pretty good chance that he won't wet or soil himself while being fed, and then if he falls asleep while eating he can be put back to bed clean and dry.

One mother, however, handled the problem differently. "Even if she was wet or soiled, I nursed my daughter from one breast and *then* changed her," this mother told us. "This actually served two purposes. Not only did it get her back to bed clean, but if she had fallen asleep during the first half of her meal—as she often did—changing her would wake her up enough to eat a little more." This method would of course work for bottle-fed babies, too. We suggest you try both these methods and see which one works best for you.

"I used Huggies disposables a lot at first. A newborn's stools are *very* liquid and the elasticized thighs on Huggies helps contain the mess. They save the need for rubber pants which I hate to use." *Mother of two / Dallas, Tex.*

"One friend's baby gift to me was to do my washing for a month. She took it every day and brought it back the next, all neatly folded. It was by far the best gift I received." *Mother of two / Arlington, Va.*

BATHING

Hold off on tub bathing for the first few days. You may be nervous, trying to hold on to a slippery, wiggly baby, and your baby may be miserable, since he can't be held securely in a tub. Most mothers, and many doctors, recommend sponge bathing.

"I gave my son a tub bath on the first day home. What a disaster! It was one of the scariest of my firsts. My husband and I read all the directions from the pediatrician, laid out the equipment, and did several run-throughs without the baby. When the Big Moment arrived, my husband was standing by with his camera to record our son's joy and delight with his first bath. Ha! Our son was enraged. He cried so hard that his arms turned purple up to his shoulders. After that, I stuck to sponge baths, and it was a month before I got up the nerve to try a regular bath again. Then he gurgled, kicked, and really enjoyed it."

Mother of one / Bloomington, Ind.

Don't be disappointed or worry if your baby dislikes even his first sponge baths. Many new babies don't like being unswaddled. They will jerk and twist and eventually begin to cry in an instinctive effort to increase circulation and warm themselves up. If you're planning to photograph this important first, be prepared to record tears.

Sponge-Bathing Tips

1. Feed your baby before you bathe her. If she's hungry, neither of you will enjoy bathtime.

2. Gather all needed materials beforehand—soap, washcloth, towels, bowl of water, complete change of clothing.

3. Cover your changing table or sink area with an absorbent pad or towel.

4. Undress your baby. Cradle her with your arm, holding her arm with your hand. Don't let go of her, and take her with you if you must interrupt the bath for any reason.

5. Wash her face and hair with a washcloth and warm water. Rub a little soap on your hand and gently soap her, taking care to reach the crevices of her neck, arms, and legs. Rinse her thoroughly with the washcloth and pat her dry.

Lotion, baby oil, and powder are not needed for good skin care. In fact, some doctors are completely opposed to their use. Many mothers, however, associate the smell of baby powder with the smell of a clean baby. If you do use powder, don't shake it directly on the baby as she might inhale it, which could cause serious long-term problems because of the talc in the powder. Rather, shake a little on your hand and then smooth it sparingly on the baby. Or try Cornstarch. It's not only cheaper than powder, but is a natural skin soother without any perfumes or other additives.

Don't use cotton swabs to clean your baby's ears or nose. Rather than pull out dirt, you may push it in. The word is: if you can't see it and easily reach it, don't clean it.

THE NAVEL, THE FONTANEL, AND CIRCUMCISION

The Navel

The stump of umbilical cord left on your baby will wither away and drop off, usually during the first week. When it falls off it may leave a raw spot that may take a few weeks to scab over and completely heal.

Keep the navel dry. Some doctors recommend dabbing a drop of rubbing alcohol on the navel with cotton; others recommend merely drying the navel with cotton once or twice a day. Keep your baby's diaper pinned below the unhealed navel to prevent irritation.

The Fontanel

The fontanel is the soft spot on the top of your baby's head where the skull bones have not yet completely fused. There is a tough membrane covering the fontanel, so there is little chance of harming your baby by touching this soft spot. It will take a year for it to fuse completely.

Circumcision

If you have a boy and he was circumcised, protect the unhealed circumcision with a liberal amount of petroleum jelly. One mother's suggestion: "I squeezed out a ribbon of Vaseline from the tube, swirling it around the circumcised tip of the penis, like decorating a cake with frosting."

PIN DIAPER BELOW UNHEALED NAVEL

A First-Day Starter Set:
Clothing, Equipment, and Supplies

Some women like to shop ahead of time, and spend many happy hours setting up a nursery and preparing everything. Others prefer to wait until after the baby is born. If you plan to shop ahead, see Chapter 5 for a complete shopping list. If you're the last-minute type, the following list contains only essentials needed for survival the first few days.

Clothing
diapers - 1 dozen
newborn size disposable diapers - 2 boxes
diaper safety pins - 4
cotton shirts - 3
gowns, sacque sets, or stretch suits - 3
receiving blankets - 3
sweater set - 1
waterproof pants - 3

Bathing and Bedding
toiletries - soap, diaper ointment, cotton balls, petroleum jelly, rubbing alcohol, moist towelettes
fitted crib or cradle sheets - 3
crib-size rubber sheet - 1
quilted crib pad - 1
lap-size flannelized rubber pads - 3
crib blankets - 2 or more, depending on weather

Nursery Equipment
baby bed (bassinette, cradle, car bed, portacrib, or regular crib)
firm mattress that fits tightly in the bed

Feeding Needs
If breast feeding:
    bottles - 2 or 3, and nipples to fit
    1 six-pack of liquid formula
If bottle feeding:
    nurser (bottle) kit
    2 six-packs of liquid formula
    1 can of powdered formula

Miscellaneous
auto safety seat
birth announcements
camera and film
nursing bra and nursing pads
pacifier
rectal thermometer
Dr. Spock's *Baby and Child Care*
Mother to Mother Baby-Care Book

Coping with a Newborn

YOUR BABY'S INBORN ABILITIES

Even at birth, your baby has some innate abilities and capacities to take care of himself. "Try to keep in mind that this little bundle is much more durable and forgiving than he looks," advised one mother. Your baby is born with many reflexes, which help him survive. He can lift and turn his head, if placed on his belly. He can twist his head, pucker his lips, and even bat his arms to dislodge a light object placed over his mouth and nose. He will "root"—search for the nipple with his mouth, move his tongue, and turn his head if his cheek or palm is stroked—which helps him find his food. He has a strong sucking urge, a gag reflex to aid in spitting up mucus, and a blink reflex to protect his eyes. He will pull in his limbs, shiver, and eventually start to cry if exposed to a sudden drop in temperature. He will try to avoid pain by jerking and pulling away.

More and more research studies are proving what mothers have known for years. A newborn baby is an intelligent, perceiving individual. Your baby is sensitive to the world, soaking up impressions through the pores of his skin. He reacts to sounds and smells and can see objects held nearby. "The newborn's most impressive powers are sensory," says Frank Caplan in *The First Twelve Months of Life*. "Skin contact and warmth from mother's body are probably the most potent stimulation for infants in the first few months of life."

BABY'S AND MOTHER'S FIRST NEEDS

"Getting to Know You," the well-known song from *The King and I*, could be the theme song for both you and your baby when you first begin to care for him.

"It may sound absurd, but I even enjoyed changing my baby's diaper. The first day he howled with rage every time I changed him. I thought, that's good, at least he has a temper. In the next few days he began to trust me more, and after the first week we used diaper-changing time to chat with each other." *Mother of one / Chicago, Ill.*

Your baby's needs and your needs are remarkably similar for the first few days. You both need rest and nutritious foods. You also need to bond yourself to each other, to get to know and love each other. Most of this bonding takes place by means of sensory impressions. Your baby will hear the sound of your voice, see your face, and feel the warmth of your body as you feed her, change her, bathe her. You'll spend hours looking at and examining every part of her body and get to recognize her smell, the sound of her cries of anger and slurps of contentment. You'll sense her moods in the "feel" of her body as you feed her, change her, and bathe her.

Your new baby needs assurance that you are her mother and the world is safe. You will automatically give this feeling to her as you care for her. However, you also need assurance and you may not get it as easily as you give it. Your baby may be disoriented the first few days at home. She may not eat well, sleep well, or respond with total bliss to your cuddling, feeding, bathing, and soothing. She may not make you feel that she loves you, or even likes you. Visiting relatives may rave about the baby but totally forget to pay any attention to you. Friends with children may want to share your experience, but often they may laugh off your concerns, launch into their own present concerns, and talk about *their* babies.

Even your husband, who was so marvelous during your pregnancy and a tower of strength during delivery, may not be able to give you the help and assurance you desperately crave. In fact, he may be looking to *you* for assurance that he will be an adequate and caring father and that he is still part of this suddenly expanded family.

The best help for a new mother is another new mother. It pays to cultivate a friendship with someone who also has a new baby. If you are still pregnant, get to know someone in your childbirth class; or, later, make friends with another new mother in the hospital. Join the La Leche League before or after giving birth, not only to get help with and information about nursing but to get to know other mothers. You may not be kindred spirits or form an everlasting relationship, but the bond of having a new baby is strong; the help and mutual support you can derive from a friendship of this sort is invaluable.

Barbara and Bernie Sills became very close to a couple giving birth the same day that David was born. Sherrie and Barbara had adjoining labor rooms, and kept pace with each other throughout labor and delivery. Bernie and Bill met in the hospital corridor while their wives were in labor. "We were put in the same hospital room," Barbara says. "The first day we talked for hours about labor and birth. The second and third days we chattered endlessly about breast feeding, changing diapers, and bathing. We shared our hopes and our previously hidden fears. When we went home, we called each other two, three, and sometimes four or five times a day. We're still close friends, and recently David and Carrie celebrated their ninth birthday, together."

HELP IN THE HOUSE

"I had mixed feelings about going home from the hospital after my daughter's birth. The primary feeling was one of joy—our first baby, in our own home. The second feeling was fear—a huge responsibility for a brand-new life at a time when I still needed someone to take care of *me.*"

Mother of two / Tucumcari, N.M.

Most new mothers want to care for their babies as much as possible, but most can use a little pampering and some help around the house. A few mothers chose to be alone with their babies, but most told us that help was essential. If at all possible, try to get someone to help for at least an hour or so during the first few days.

If both of you feel comfortable about the idea, your husband may be your best source of help. The plus factor is that the two of you together can learn how to care for your new baby—sharing the first bath, feeding, changing, loving. One mother told us, "The most important thing is to make a family. I believe it happens in the first few days. That's why my husband stayed home. We shut out the world, forgetting everything except making our previous warm twosome into a warm threesome."

"I was very fortunate because my husband Don very much wanted to be the one to care for me and Lynn after she was delivered by Caesarean section. We worked out a great system. I stayed in bed as much as I needed, since I tired easily, and Don took over Lynn's care: he changed her diapers and gowns, and brought her to me whenever it was time for her to nurse. He also got up during the night to bring her to me. And he was the one who cleaned her up and returned her to bed. I'm sure that Don's great care during that first week at home helped me in my recovery. I'm also sure it helped cement an extremely close love between father and daughter."

Mother of two / Newport, R.I.

The minus factor of husband staying home is that both of you are likely to be emotionally keyed up about all the new responsibilities of parenting. As one new mother put it, "After three days of constant togetherness my husband and I were snapping and snarling at each other. We were both relieved when he decided to go back to work a little early."

One friend made arrangements for a cleaning service. "I asked around and found two women who came in a few times during my pregnancy," she said. "They cleaned the oven, the windows, everything. They came again when I was in the hospital, and once again after I had been home for a few weeks."

Another woman hired a 16-year-old girl to help her. "I worked with her for two months before my baby was born, and she was able to do most of the housework when I came home from the hospital. She then became our babysitter. Now she's almost like one of the family."

If you are willing and a close relative is able, count yourself blessed. "Have your mother come and stay with you, if you get along," advised one mother. "My mom was so much help, but most of all it was comforting just to know she was there."

In *The Mother Knot*, author Jane Lazarre said that when she first came home with her baby all she wanted to do was lie in a very clean room and feed her child. Many new mothers will immediately identify with that feeling. If you are going to have help to provide that "very clean room," plan ahead and decide exactly what you want your help to do. Then be sure and share your plans with this person, be it he or she, hired or family. One mother said, "I hired a lady on the recommendation of a friend to help during my first week home. We talked briefly and liked each other. She arrived the day I came home and took over my baby. It took me two days to get up enough nerve to let her know that I wanted to take care of the baby myself. 'But dear,' she said. 'I'm not a cleaning lady. I'm a baby nurse!'"

"If you have someone helping you, make a written list telling them what you would like done. A list is especially helpful for a relative, since it's easier to ask a relative to do something like scrub out the toilet if it's on a list. My mother-in-law came to help me, and she was the one who suggested that I just jot down the things I'd like her to do."

Mother of three / Billings, Mont.

"I'd read everything there was on care of newborns and we'd both taken the Red Cross baby-care course, so I felt fairly confident. My husband picked us up at the hospital, brought us home, and then went right back to work. He was the kind who thought that because I was a woman I'd know what to do about everything. So there I was, alone in the apartment with that tiny thing. I felt weak and suddenly terrified. I called an old friend of ours who has four children and she came over right away. She showed me how to take a baby's temperature rectally, which somehow made me feel better, don't ask me why. We talked a while. Then she got up and called Pete at work. She literally ordered him to come home. He did and then he stayed home from work for two more days. When our second child was born, he took two weeks of vacation time and everything was fine!"

Mother of two / Collingswood, N.J.

Possibly you may decide, as one woman did, to be alone with your new baby. She said, "My mother would love to have come to help, but this was one time I was selfish and I'm glad I was. She would have had to fly across the country and stay in our small apartment. She sleeps fitfully anyway and wouldn't have held up very well under the two a.m. squalls. But mostly I didn't want to have to run interference between Mom and my husband in our first days as a family.

"We made out fine," she added. "I'm not a meticulous housekeeper and Joe knows his way around a kitchen and washing machine. He came home for lunch. Everything in our small apartment was only steps away. Friends were considerate about visiting when we wanted them to. The only problem was my hemorrhoids, and Mom couldn't have helped that!"

"The first nights after I got home from the hospital I'd wake up shaking and perspiring. I think it was just the aftershocks of giving birth. What a big thing for your body to go through! Until those 'shakes' stopped I knew I'd better take it easy and not overdo, for everone's sake."

Mother of one / Wheeling, W. Va.

In her book *Commonsense Childbirth*, Lester Hazell says, "Here is a rule of thumb with regard to what housekeeping should be done: nothing that does not come easily at the discretion of the wife for a full six weeks. That means that she cares for the emotional needs of the family, but not necessarily for such items as dirty dishes."

Keeping this in mind, make a mental or written "must list," including only those things that you absolutely must do in order to survive. Remember that for the first few weeks after birth your energy level will be very low. As one mother put it, "After giving birth, when energy is gone, it's gone! It's unlike any other experience—a totally blotto feeling."

We asked a friend who was pregnant with her second child to think of her musts. She said later, "I realized that there are very few musts. I must take care of the baby, feed her, change her, bathe her, snuggle her. I must give some special time to my 2-year-old son. I must find some way or someone to help with the laundry and cooking, and I must spend some time alone with my husband. The whole thing should be very easy if I can make myself stick only to the musts."

"My friends got together and gave me the best of all possible baby gifts when I had my first child—a different friend brought over a meal each night for a week. And they didn't stop to chat!" *Mother of two / Los Angeles, Calif.*

HANDLING VISITORS AT HOME

As mentioned earlier, both you and your baby will need extra rest when you first come home from the hospital. And both of you need protection against illness. Keep these two factors in mind when you establish a visitors' policy. Some mothers thrive on excitement and it doesn't interfere with their rest. "I loved showing off my baby," said one mother. "Every day was a party. Fortunately, I can sleep through anything, so frequently I'd announce, 'I'm tired, so I'm going to bed,' and would leave my friends to enjoy each other and watch the baby while I took a nap."

Other women need to be alone, and for them visitors can be a strain. "The first few days, friends and relatives dropped in all day long. I was exhausted, so I finally posted a 'Do Not Disturb—Mother and Baby Napping' sign on my front door and told people who called that I was under strict doctor's orders to limit visitors. I then gained badly needed privacy to relax and get to know my son."

RELY ON YOUR INSTINCTS

"I sincerely believe that mother knows best, even a new mother, and I insisted on following my 'mother instincts' just five hours after my son was born. The hospital had a rooming-in policy, but wouldn't bring a baby to a mother until it had had three ounces of formula in the nursery. My son refused to eat, and the hospital staff refused to bring him to me. I got more and more frantic, and when a friend called I started bawling. 'Of course he won't eat,' my friend said, 'because he needs *you*—you're his mother.' So I hung up and then I raised such a fuss that the staff allowed me to feed my baby in the nursery. Right away he seemed to know me, and drank the three ounces of formula. That experience convinced me that I knew what I was doing and that I could care for my baby better than anyone else."

Mother of one / Kansas City, Mo.

The phrase "mother's instinct" has been out of vogue for the past few years, but it's gradually creeping back in as a valid and real influence in child rearing. Your baby is unique, and he is yours. If you're in doubt, listen carefully to your inner voice and rely on it.

For example, your milk is in and your baby has nursed for fifteen minutes. He falls asleep, but then wakes up, howling, a half hour later. You try to comfort him, but he still cries. Your instincts tell you that he's hungry even though he's just eaten. Go ahead and feed him again if that's what your instincts tell you.

Or, when you check your sleeping baby you sense that something is wrong. She's breathing strangely, her color has changed. You don't want to call the doctor needlessly, but you get more and more concerned. Give in to your instincts —call the doctor. Your feelings may be wrong, but they may also be right, and why take the chance?

"Both Ryan and I made a good adjustment to nursing in the hospital, and his first three feedings at home went smoothly. I put him down at eight p.m. for a long evening's nap and then went to sleep myself. An hour later, he woke howling. My mother suggested that I give him water. My husband said to let him cry. All my books warned against giving him a bottle, but my milk was gone and I felt he was hungry. I gave him water and held and rocked him. After an hour I prepared a bottle of formula. He drank three ounces and immediately went back to sleep. He woke four hours later, eager and anxious to nurse. I nursed Ryan for a year after that first nervous night when I was afraid my breast would dry up and wither away to nothing if I offered him a bottle."

Mother of one / Hyattsville, Md.

NEWBORN MEDICAL CARE: SOME POINTERS

Your own instincts can help guide the way in some situations, but it also helps to have some basic information about keeping newborn babies safe. Having a few key telephone numbers handy, knowing some of the most common reasons for a call to the doctor, and knowing how to take a baby's temperature will go a long way toward dispelling some of the trepidation you may feel during those first days at home.

Make a list that includes your pediatrician's phone number, the number of the nearest hospital emergency room, and a number for the paramedics or other rescue units in your area and post it near your phone. Also make sure you know how to get to a nearby hospital emergency room and know where to park when you get there. Both parents should carry insurance identification to facilitate emergency treatment.

"If you ever have to give medicine to a newborn or a very young baby and it keeps dribbling back out of her mouth, try this. Put it in a nipple and let her suck from that."
Mother of three / Boise, Ida.

When to Call the Doctor

A pediatrician we know gives the following list to parents when they leave the hospital with their baby and asks them to call if the baby has any of the symptoms on the list during the first few days. We suggest that you look over this list and also ask your own pediatrician for any additional suggestions. Then memorize the list or keep it posted by your phone along with your emergency numbers.

Call the doctor if there is:

1. Fever of 101 degrees or higher, by a rectal reading.

2. Vomiting. This means throwing up a significant amount, not "spitting up" or the sort of drooling of excess milk that is common with most newborns.

3. Refusal of food several times in a row.

4. Excessive crying.

5. Listlessness.

6. Loose, runny bowels accompanied by mucus and foul odor.

7. An unusual rash.

8. Anything else that has you seriously worried.

Taking the Baby's Temperature

"I was awfully squeamish about taking my infant's temperature rectally the first time. But, truly, it's not that hard. It takes just a minute, and it helps so much to know whether or not she has a real fever."
Mother of two / Palos Verdes, Calif.

Here's how to take your baby's temperature rectally.

1. Shake down a rectal thermometer (one with a rounded bulb on the end) over a bed or other soft surface so that it won't break if you drop it. It should read lower than 97 degrees.

2. Lubricate the bulb with petroleum jelly.

3. Sit down and place your baby over your knees so that he's resting on his stomach.

4. Gently guide the thermometer into his rectum. Don't push; let it glide in by itself.

5. Rest your hand against your baby's bottom and cradle the thermometer between two fingers.

6. The temperature will register in just about a minute. If your baby is squirmy, take a twenty-second reading; the mercury will rise to within one degree of the actual temperature.

7. A normal rectal temperature can range from 98.6 to 100.6 degrees; 101 or higher is considered a fever, and your pediatrician should be notified.

FEELINGS

Your first few days at home with your baby will probably be filled with new emotions. You may feel happy one minute and miserable the next. You will probably have strong feelings of love for your baby, but you might also feel detached and uninterested. You may feel competent and strong like one of those women who are "made for motherhood," or you may feel incompetent and afraid, and fear that you're someone who just wasn't meant to have children. You may feel exhilarated or you may feel depressed.

Some of these feelings are caused by a hormone imbalance. After giving birth there will be a drop in the amount of estrogen and progesterone in your system, causing an imbalance of these hormones. If you're subject to premenstrual moods, you may be particularly sensitive to hormonal imbalance and thus experience especially strong swings in moods after your baby is born. If a depression develops or continues after the first few weeks at home, you should see your doctor.

If you have strong feelings, either positive or negative, during the first few days, however, realize that your feelings are perfectly normal. Some women used the word "joy" to describe their feelings on the first day home; others used the word "terror." Here we share some mothers' feelings about their first days with their babies.

"The first day in our home with Craig was so joyous and fulfilling that I found napping and even sleeping that night impossible. I was hyper with an incredible awe. I just couldn't believe that I had created such a perfectly unique human being. I became bubbly, talkative, and wanted to invite in the whole world to see what I had wrought."

Mother of two / Little Rock, Ark.

"While I was still in the hospital I was thrilled as I had never been before. I was 29 and had eagerly anticipated becoming a mother. But when I brought Eddie home I was more terrified than I had ever been in my life. What a responsibility! I thought I'd turned out to be one of those rare mothers who just couldn't hack it, who would have to give up my baby for adoption to someone more competent. Becoming a mother was the most drastic change in my life, before or since. If my son and I survived—and we did—then anyone can, believe me." *Mother of three / Duluth, Minn.*

"I felt like I was a child playing house at first. It all seemed so unreal. I was nervous and defensive and took suggestions as criticism. I wanted to be left alone. My advice to another nervous new mother is: *relax*. Trust your own instincts, but also be willing to accept help from others." *Mother of two / Miami, Fla.*

"I never realized the amount of love I would feel for my newborn child. It was overwhelming. I loved every minute of my time with her, even the wee hours of the morning since they were so peaceful—just the two of us with no interruptions." *Mother of two / Akron, Ohio*

"I didn't truly love my baby from the start. I held her, fondled her, talked to her, but often I couldn't wait to get rid of her so I could simply dream about her. At first the dream was better than the reality. It wasn't until the second week—when my husband went back to work and my mother went home and I had my daughter all to myself—that I felt I knew and loved her." *Mother of one / Louisville, Ky.*

How will my partner react to the baby? What will he do to help? Each new mother will ask herself these questions. Since each new father is an individual with his own emotions, each will react in his own way. Some new fathers will be thrilled with the baby and eager to participate in all aspects of baby care, while others may be lukewarm and frightened of holding and caring for the baby. And some may feel negative about fatherhood and even about the baby.

We asked some mothers and fathers to write about their feelings toward their new babies and the very early days of parenthood. Here are a few of their responses.

"I was in rapture over my son's birth. I assisted with his birth and felt awed at the process. I felt a closeness to my son and wife that was unbelievable. At first I was timid

about handling newborns, but became more relaxed, especially as he grew a little."—*Father* / "Don's biggest help was
in allowing me to satisfy my need to mother to the fullest
by taking on my 'housewife' role. He cooked or brought
meals home, did the laundry, and tried to be neat (a very
difficult job for him!)."—*Mother*

"I was laid off from my job in the aerospace industry a
month before my son's birth and was so depressed and concerned about myself that I didn't want to go near him. To
be honest, I felt strong resentment—if it hadn't been for him,
at least my wife would have been working and bringing in
some money."—*Father* / "All my husband did was sit around
reading the want ads all morning and guzzle beer all afternoon
and evening. He's made up for it since by being a marvelous
father. But that time was really the pits!"—*Mother*

"My initial feelings about my newborn child were of won-
derment, happiness, and closeness to both my child and my
wife."—*Father* / "My husband changed diapers, gave bottles,
helped with the first bath. He was a *great* floorwalker that
first night. And when the kids were fussy, he would sing or
rock them to sleep."—*Mother*

"The boy we'd been expecting for nine months turned out to
be a girl. No football player there. I didn't say so to anyone,
and certainly not to my wife, but I was very disappointed. I
remember envying the men who watched blue blankets in
the nursery. Then I remember things like feeling a little disgusted when my wife, in desperation to stop the baby's crying,
started nursing her right at the dinner table the second night
home. I can admit this now and smile, but I had no idea then
how that little girl would grow on me. Now I even feel sorry
for guys who will never have a daughter. As far as I'm concerned, there's so much going on those first few days you
just have to plow forward and have faith that things will work
out. It's like the first days of school or the first days in the
Marines or the first days of anything else momentous."—
Father / "The first few days are a blur. I remember feeling
that if the relatives would only go home maybe my husband
would get a chance to do something for the baby. Then, too,

she always seemed to be asleep when he was home. It was at about three weeks that I remember finally feeling like a family. The three of us were on the couch after dinner, it was snowing outside, and my husband actually got the baby to smile her first smile."—*Mother*

"My first-born son was the only baby in the world, and I had to protect him. The day I drove my wife and son home from the hospital, every car on the road was a potential threat—enemies stay away."—*Father* / "My husband shopped, cooked, and took care of the house. He made a steak dinner my first night home. He held the baby nervously and was afraid to change diapers—in fact, he didn't do this job for almost two months. However, he did compose a song for our son. And in the long run, that's much more important than changing diapers."—*Mother*

"The thing I remember about the baby's first day home is all those trips to the store—once for diaper pins, once for Vaseline, and once again for a roll of film so that we could always remember those first moments together with our son."—*Father* / "I remember my first day home with the baby as a wonderful time—unwinding in my own bed, feeding the baby, savoring every precious moment."—*Mother*

"I'm now a grandfather. When I had my children I was brainwashed into believing that holding and cuddling a baby and changing diapers were things only a henpecked husband would do. I had to stifle my desires to truly participate. I envy my son and his new baby. They're really involved."—*Father* / "My husband was a marvelous provider, but he was so frightened of our children. He's a different person with his grandson—gentle, loving, and caring."—*Mother*

* * *

A Typical First Day Home

(Some new and some not so new mothers receive a great
deal of pleasure and satisfaction from keeping a "baby
diary." Here we share with you excerpts from a friend's
diary about her first day at home with her new daughter.)

All the relatives have gone home except Grandma. She's
taking a nap and your dad has gone out for a walk. You, my
darling Emily, are sleeping in your cradle. I now have a few
minutes to write to let you know about your first day at home.

I'm filled with awe that I gave birth to someone as perfect
as you. I still can't believe you're real. But I'm also filled with
fear. Can I do it? Can I be a good mother? It all seemed so
easy while I was pregnant, and even while I was "rooming-
in" at the hospital. I hardly needed any help feeding you,
changing you, and taking care of you. But now we're home,
and I'm responsible for keeping you alive. It all seems overpowering, especially after your first few hours under my care.

All went smoothly for the first five miles of the ride
home. You slept in your car seat and I sat next to you, just
soaking in every detail about you. Then the unbelievable
happened—the car began to swerve. Your dad brought it
under control, but I was shaking all over as he got out to see
what was wrong. Sure enough, the rear tire was flat.

So you and I drove up to our front door with a friendly
neighbor, leaving your dad to change the tire. Your grandma,
Aunt Judi, Aunt Mary, and Uncle Paul were waiting to welcome us home. Their oohs and ahs woke you, and both of
us, mother and child, started bawling—you from hunger, me
from fatigue.

Your grandma took you from my arms and led us into
the bedroom. She put you into your cradle, helped me into
a nightgown, pulled back the covers, and settled me in bed.
She handed you to me, went out of the room, and closed
the door.

Ahhh, my very own bed. How good it felt. I snuggled
you and guided a nipple into your mouth. And, wonder of
wonders, you greedily nursed. You slurped and sucked for
fifteen minutes. How marvelous to be alone with you—no

nurses, no roommate, no relatives—and, may he forgive me, no Daddy.

I wanted to continue the peace, so I got up to change your diaper alone, even though every movement was painful because of my stitches and hemorrhoids. I took off your sopping disposable diaper and expertly cleaned you. Then I took a snowy diaper-service diaper, folded it under you, and searched for diaper pins. Disaster! No pins! And no disposable diapers with handy tabs, either.

Your aunts and uncles began a frantic search for any kind of pin, but not one could be found, so I put you to bed with a flapping diaper, and then I collapsed in another shower of tears. How easily the tears flow. Oh, Lord, how can I be a mature, responsible mother when all I seem to do is cry like a baby myself?

Your grandma brought me a glass of wine and handed me two books. One was this book, filled with empty pages. The other was an old diary, filled with the events of my own babyhood and with my own mother's fears and apprehensions. And, as I read the words of my own first days and started writing about yours, I feel comforted.

I'm very tired. I think I can sleep now. Someday, perhaps when you have your own first-born, I'll give you this book. And perhaps you too will be comforted by your beginnings. For you, my darling daughter, are so precious and dear to me. I can only find clichés to express my love.

I'm crying again, but these tears are just fine. Sleep well, my love, and welcome home.

3

Baby Care:
The First Months

"No matter how much reading and talking you do ahead of time, there is simply no way to realistically anticipate the major life adjustment you'll be making with your new baby. After I had struggled with the frequent feedings and erratic sleep habits of my baby for a few weeks a friend said, 'Quit fighting it. You chose to have this child, and if you aren't willing to keep him fed, warm, and dry—which are really his only needs right now—you shouldn't have had him!' That hurt, but I realized she was right. I revised my priorities and devoted more time to just getting to know my son. Somehow this made the whole family's adjustment easier."
                                    Mother of one / St. Louis, Mo.

The words of this young mother just about say it all. In this chapter you'll find hints from other mothers which we hope will help you keep your new son or daughter "fed, warm, and dry" during the first months. You can then relax, and in the process get to know each other.

SLEEPING

After the first few weeks your baby will begin to sleep for longer periods. He may take three or four daytime naps and begin to sleep for as long as five or six hours at nighttime. Babies seem to have inborn sleep habits and patterns. Some babies require a set sleep schedule; they sleep and wake up at about the same time every day, and are miserable and act impossible if their sleep is interrupted or their pattern is changed. Other babies thrive on irregularity. One night they fall asleep at eight and wake at ten, the next they sleep from six until twelve. If a baby with an irregular sleep pattern is wakened before the end of his naptime he can easily catch up on his sleep at some other time. To some extent, these sleep patterns will continue into childhood and possibly even adulthood.

Observe your baby for the first few weeks, and then figure out a sleep schedule based on *his* pattern rather than imposing a schedule on him. You may also have to consider your baby's sleep patterns when planning for visitors, outside excursions, and trips to the doctor. Play it by ear if someone drops over to see your baby when he's sleeping. Consider the importance of the visitor as well as the baby's sleep habits; for example, if the visitor is Great-Aunt Zelda, who's in town only for the afternoon, go ahead and wake the baby. Some things are more important than sleep.

Let your baby get used to sleeping in a variety of places and in noisy, as well as quiet, surroundings. Occasionally move his portacrib or car bed from room to room. Take him with you when you go visiting and let him sleep in someone else's house. Don't go around shushing everyone every time the baby is sleeping. Some babies seem to prefer quiet, while others don't mind noise at all. However, if you expose your baby to both quiet and noisy sleeping environments he'll eventually get used to sleeping under both kinds of conditions.

"It was always quiet at bedtime when I was growing up, and when I went away to college I was miserable. I just couldn't get to sleep until everyone else on my dormitory floor was quiet. My husband can sleep through anything, since he comes from a very lively family. We've purposely exposed our kids to noise, almost from birth, and they're such sound sleepers that all three—our two sons and my husband—slept through a good-sized California earthquake."
Mother of two / Lawndale, Calif.

"My son started waking up at night as soon as we went to

bed. He wasn't hungry, wet, or sick, but it seemed he could sense the exact moment I fell asleep and would wake up howling. Since he slept through noise and confusion during the day, I finally realized that he had gotten used to noise but couldn't sleep when it was quiet. So before we went to bed, I turned on a radio in his room and sure enough he stayed asleep. Gradually, I got him accustomed to sleeping through quiet as well as through noise."

Mother of four / Chicago, Ill.

"My oldest daughter was a restless sleeper, and I found a variety of ways to help soothe her so she could go to sleep. I felt she needed the warmth of my body to help her calm down when she was colicky, so I carried her in a front pack for the first months; that way I could comfort her and still have the use of both hands. Sound, rather than quiet, was also effective, so I left the radio on while she slept. I also danced her to sleep, resting her head on my shoulder and swaying and swooping to the music. Usually she'd only last about five minutes before sawing logs. And when all else failed, there was my last-resort stand-by, the midnight ride of the old VW—around and around the block until, finally, she fell asleep." *Mother of two / Madison, Wisc.*

FEEDING

"The first three months were hard. My son was awake most of the day, and cried continuously. I tried to stick to the four-hour schedule my doctor recommended. For the last hour I walked him, fed him bottles of water, did everything possible to stretch the time to keep to that schedule. But by then he'd be so exhausted that he couldn't eat well and would fall into a deep sleep. If I had it to do over again, I'd forget the schedule and feed him whenever he seemed hungry."

Mother of two / Raleigh, N.C.

That mother realized too late that it's better to feed your baby on demand, at least at the beginning. Assume that he knows best how often to eat, and eventually he'll establish a schedule that both of you can live with.

But if your baby is still on an erratic feeding schedule

after the first month, you might gradually begin to lengthen the time between his feedings to nudge him toward a four-hour daytime schedule and even longer periods at night. One mother tried several techniques to regulate her baby's eating patterns. She let him wake on his own in the morning, fed him, noted the time, and tried to help him to go for four more hours until the next feeding. If he woke early for a feeding, she rocked him and gave him a pacifier and sometimes a bottle of sugar water. If he was still howling with hunger, she went ahead and fed him. If he slept through a feeding, she woke him to get him used to eating on a regular four-hour schedule. "It took about two weeks to get him to adjust to a four-hour schedule," this mother said, " and then—he was just 6 weeks old—he began sleeping through the night."

"I had to wake my baby for her ten p.m. feeding," said another woman. "I made sure she was well fed, and then she began to sleep through until three, then four, and finally through the night."

"Since day and night seem to blend together in those early days and it's hard to keep track of when you did what—even when you last fed the baby—I took to carrying a pad with me to keep track of the last feeding, bath, and so on. From this I later worked up a schedule that fit my baby's natural pattern." *Mother of two / Great Falls, Mont.*

"The other day a woman with a 17-day-old baby stopped by to drop off an application form for our babysitting co-op. She had dark circles halfway down her face. We got talking and she confided that her pediatrician had told her to feed her son at midnight and at six a.m. Her son was waking up at four every morning and she said she hated listening to him scream until she could feed him again at six. I was horrified. I told her to look at the size of her baby's tummy. It didn't look like it could *hold* six hours' worth of milk yet! You've got to use your own mind sometimes." *Mother of four / Santa Fe, N.M.*

Breast Feeding

"The best thing about breast feeding my 1-month-old is in

the middle of the night when he snuggles up to me in bed.
His mommy is so very important to him. And we're all alone.
No 2-year-old brother, no 4-year-old brother, no phone calls,
no house to clean, just the two of us, so warm and needy.
It's hard to explain how it makes me feel in words, except
it's *love*. I am that little warm, cuddly baby's whole world,
and he is mine, for those few precious moments."

Mother of three / Cincinnati, Ohio

In the words of one mother's doctor, "Don't listen to anyone who says you won't be able to nurse your baby. Eventually he'll get hungry enough to adapt himself to you, no
matter what the size and shape of your breasts and nipples."
Here is some information that may help you with breast
feeding.

Milk is formed in glands throughout the breast and is
stored in "sinuses" located behind the areola (the dark area
surrounding the nipple). A duct leads from the sinuses to
the nipple. Make sure your baby has most of the areola in
his mouth; as he sucks on the areola he will squeeze the sinuses and push milk out of them, through the nipple, and
into his mouth. If he's slow getting started, gently but firmly grasp the areola and squeeze out a little milk. Once he
gets a little taste, he may be more motivated to suck.

Most mothers nurse for five to ten minutes the first two
or three days; ten to fifteen minutes the next few days; and,
finally, about twenty minutes. Nursing for longer periods
may hurt your nipples—and may not be so good for your
baby, either. One mother says that she made the mistake
of letting her daughter nurse for as long as an hour. "I
thought she'd stop when she'd had enough, but one day
she projectile-vomited clear across the room. I called the
doctor, and when I told him how long she'd been nursing,
he was appalled."

Once your milk is fully established, let your baby empty
one breast at each feeding, since a breast needs to be emptied
in order to produce new milk. After ten or fifteen minutes
the breast is virtually empty. Let her nurse for a few more
minutes at the other breast if she's still hungry. Alternate
breasts at each feeding. (If you can't tell by looking, by the
way, tie a ribbon or clip a pin to your bra strap to remind

you which breast the baby last emptied.)

Leave your bra flap open for several minutes after nursing to let your nipples dry thoroughly, if they tend to become sore. Unless you have toughened your nipples before the baby was born, they are bound to be a little tender. Cut down on nursing time if you start to experience discomfort. Massé Cream is a special ointment designed to protect and heal sore breasts. Buy some from a pharmacy and rub it into your nipples. Nipple shields (a bottle-like nipple with a plastic cuff that encircles your own nipple) can also help. Squeeze a little milk into the nipple and nurse your baby with the shield on. Then try nursing with it off, since your baby may not have to suck so hard once the milk is flowing. And be sure to put your finger into your baby's mouth to break the suction when she's finished nursing. Otherwise she'll pull on your nipple when you pull her away, and that hurts! Call your doctor if you're having significant pain.

"I received a lovely small white pillow with an eyelet cover for a shower present. How pretty but how impractical, I thought. However, it turned out that I used it every day. The pillowcase was drip-dry, and the pillow was just the right size to prop up the baby in my lap so that I was comfortable nursing. It's also behind the baby propping her up in a Windsor chair in the first picture I ever took of her."
Mother of one / Fontana, Calif.

Use the most cozy and relaxing chair in the house in which to nurse. Although any comfortable chair will do, a rocking chair is especially soothing and relaxing for both mother and baby. Rest your baby partly in your lap to avoid tiring your arm. Use pillows to make yourself more comfortable—behind your back, under your arm, or even in your lap under the baby.

However, if you're more relaxed in bed, nurse there. Rest on your side with one arm over your head and put your baby on her side, facing you. Guide the nipple into her mouth with your free hand, and raise or lower the nipple by rolling your body.

"From a supportive nurse, I picked up two helpful tips on

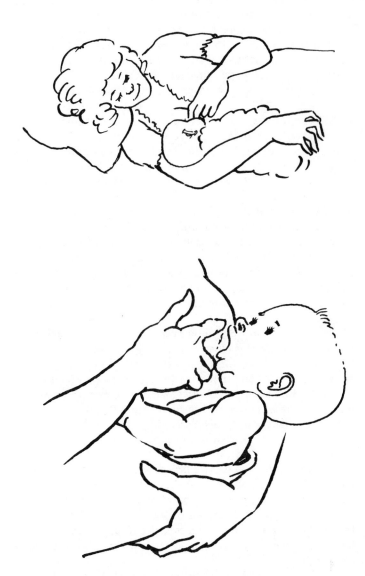

breast feeding while I was in the hospital. To help your baby find the nipple of your breast, touch it to his cheek. He will instinctively turn toward the touch. Don't touch the other side of his head, or he'll turn that way. If he falls asleep at your breast and you still want to nurse, tickle his feet or even snap them with your thumb and forefinger. This may wake him up enough to nurse a little longer."

Mother of one / Atlanta, Ga.

After the first few days of nursing, give your baby an occasional bottle of formula. If you don't, she may become so hooked on the breast that she'll refuse to take a bottle. Some babies associate Mom with breast, and won't take a bottle from her. You might want to let your husband give the baby her first bottles.

If you encounter problems with nursing but don't want to stop, call the nearest chapter of the La Leche League. Not only can this organization help you with breast feeding, but it will put you in touch with other mothers of young babies. *You Can Breastfeed Your Baby . . . Even in Special Situations* by Dorothy Brewster is also an excellent resource for mothers having problems with nursing.

"I was able to nurse my baby even though I went back to work. I chose a sitter close to my office and went there at lunchtime to nurse him. I also expressed one feeding into a sterile bottle and left that with the sitter for one feeding. And I fed him again at the sitter's before going home at night. Yes, it was an added hassle for me. But it was worth it, and my baby and I both thrived."

Mother of one / Baltimore, Md.

Although it takes a little practice, once you've learned to hand-express milk, you'll find the technique useful throughout the time you nurse your baby, either simply to relieve pressure from too-full breasts or to save the milk for use in bottles later. You could use a breast pump, but some doctors feel that complications can arise from its use and thus advise against it.

To hand-express or "milk" your breast, first put both hands around the breast at the base and gently stroke toward the nipple to bring the milk up to the nipple. Next encircle the areola with your thumb at the top, your forefinger at the bottom. Squeeze your thumb and forefinger together, keeping them on the areola, not the nipple. Squeeze eight or ten times, and then move your finger and thumb to another position and "milk" again. If you're hand-expressing your milk to use later, catch it in a cup; if you're doing it to relieve pressure, do it while you're showering, or squirt it into a sink.

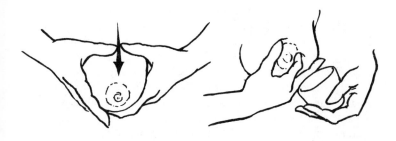

Bottle Feeding

"I was one of those rare mothers who had the RH factor, which created a problem with breast feeding. Both of my children were born with jaundice, and breast feeding my oldest girl was unsuccessful because of the antibodies built into my milk. I feel that not enough warning is given to RH mothers about the possibility of not being able to breast feed successfully."   *Mother of two / Salem, Ore.*

"When my son was born, my life was so chaotic that I found it difficult to keep nursing time quiet and relaxed. There were so many needs to be met—I was exhausted beyond belief. I was nursing several times during the night and dragging through the day. My son didn't respond favorably, either. He would suck for a few minutes, and then stop. I then felt rejected, and as I became more tense, *he* became more tense. After a month of struggle, I quickly weaned him to the bottle. What a relief! He loved lying in my arms and drinking his bottle. I loved the feeling of freedom it gave me. We're both flourishing, in spite of bottles."

Mother of two / Denver, Colo.

Present-day formulas take most of the fuss out of preparing a bottle for your baby. As mentioned in Chapter 2, to make it as easy as possible during the first few days, you might want to use a liquid formula and a nursing kit. Then switch to a powdered formula for everyday feeding, since it's inexpensive and relatively simple to prepare. (You may want to keep a six-pack of liquid formula on hand for emergency situations.)

Many doctors now say it isn't necessary to sterilize bottles or water, so you can prepare each bottle just before feeding. Read the directions on the can, put in the required amount of powder, pour in the water, shake, and you're ready to feed. One mother said, "It took me a long time to figure out that all I had to do before a trip was put a little powdered formula in the bottom of a clean, dry bottle; when my daughter was ready to be fed, all I had to do was fill the bottle with water in a restroom or at a drinking fountain."

If your baby is crying with hunger, feed him as soon as possible, because if he cries for a long time his stomach will fill with air, making feeding difficult. Hold him in a fairly upright position so that any air he swallows will easily rise. Hold the bottle at such an angle that the nipple is always filled with formula, not with air. Burp your baby before, in the middle, and after bottle feeding.

If formula comes out of the bottle too slowly, loosen the cap slightly. If it's still too slow, enlarge the nipple hole by sterilizing a needle in a hot flame and jabbing it quickly into the hole. Or put a toothpick through the hole and then boil the nipple *and* the toothpick for five minutes. If formula comes out too fast, tighten the cap. Store nipples, caps, and rings in a plastic berry box; store bottles in a soft-drink carrying carton.

Your baby may drink between three and four ounces at each feeding every two, three, or four hours during the day at the beginning. She will gradually increase the amount of milk she drinks. However, the amounts and times will vary with each baby, so it may take some time to figure out your baby's needs and preferences. Throw out any unused formula and start over with a fresh bottle for the next feeding.

Your husband might like to give the baby at least one bottle each day, and he may volunteer to get up once or twice during the night for those early-morning feedings, to give you a chance to catch up on your rest. Discourage relatives and visitors from feeding your baby, however, at least for the first few weeks. You and the new one need to get to know each other and develop close ties through feeding.

One of the biggest criticisms that many mothers and doctors have in regard to bottle feeding is that it's insidiously easy to start the habit of propping your baby's bottle. And once you start, it's hard to stop. The *quality* of the time you spend feeding the baby is most important. Find the most comfortable chair in the house, cuddle the baby in your arms, hold her close, and give her the same feeling of love and security you would if you were nursing her.

"Even though I didn't breast feed my baby, I was determined to give him the feeling of closeness that naturally comes with breast feeding. Switch arms when you bottle feed, just as a breast-feeding mother would. A nurse in the hospital told me this helps a baby's eye coordination which, to me, seems to make a kind of 'natural' sense."

Mother of two / Davenport, Iowa

Feeding your baby in your arms may also avoid future teeth problems. Stephen J. Moss, a dentist and author of *Your Child's Teeth*, says that many children who wear braces were bottle fed as infants. It's not the bottle itself, but the way it's held that causes the problem according to Moss. He feels that, used incorrectly, a bottle can interfere with the natural alignment of the tooth buds that are forming in a baby's mouth.

He suggests that mothers who bottle feed their infants should hold the bottle in such a way that the nipple will be presented in the same alignment as a mother's nipple is in breast feeding. "The thing I want mothers to get away from is sticking the bottle in the baby's mouth while the baby is on his back. The tonguing is abnormal in such a position," he says.

Dentists say that a bottle in bed encourages tooth decay, since the baby sucks in his sleep and milk remains on his teeth. Pediatricians say that letting a baby take a bottle to bed will prolong the bottle habit and may contribute to ear infections. It's a good idea to avoid this habit by not starting it at all. If possible, feed your baby his nighttime bottle in your arms. If this isn't possible, let him hold it himself before going to bed. Beware, from many who have taken the first step, that giving a baby one bottle in bed is like giving just one drink to an alcoholic. Once it's started neither you nor your baby will find it easy to stop.

One friend was at her wits' end with her very active baby, who from birth wiggled and moved around so much that holding her still for a feeding was almost impossible. "I finally learned to wrap her tightly in a terry-cloth towel," she said. "The texture of the towel made it easy to hold on to the baby."

Burping

If a stubborn bubble just won't come up, try putting your baby across your knees and gently rocking him back and forth as you pat his back. Be sure to put a diaper over your

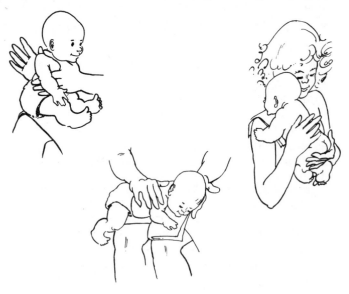

knees to catch any spit-up milk. If that doesn't work, sit him up in your lap, support his chest and neck with one hand, and pat or rub his back with the other hand. And at the same time you may gently rock him back and forth.

For some reason, we found that the two a.m. burp always seemed to take the longest. After a month of nursing David for fifteen minutes and burping him for another fifteen minutes, Barbara finally asked the doctor what to do. "Put him back to bed without burping," he said. "If he's uncomfortable, he'll wake up crying and you can try again."

Sleeping Through the Night

By three months, your baby should have given up the two a.m. feeding. If he hasn't, be firm. Pick a night when you are well rested and can get along without much sleep. When baby wakes for his early-morning snack, let him cry. Be forewarned that you will be tempted to give in and feed him, especially if he cries for more than fifteen minutes. Try to keep your wits about you. Realize that he may not really be hungry; he's just in the habit of having a snack then.

Jonas, Barbara's son, was born with a possible heart defect. She was anxious about him, especially at night, and afraid to let him cry. When she told her pediatrician that Jonas was still waking for an early-morning feeding at 3½ months, he insisted that she let the baby cry it out. She says she tried three times, unsuccessfully, before she could withstand his anguished howls. "When I finally took a stand and let him cry it out, it took only two nights to get him over the habit of eating at two a.m.," she reports.

"My son was very small at birth, so I nursed him every three hours around the clock. He rapidly caught up on his weight, but I was a basket case from not getting enough sleep. At my pediatrician's suggestion, I began spacing out his night feedings until he was waking up only once each night. After three months, my husband, my pediatrician, and I decided that Charles should go through the night without eating. When my son started crying, my husband woke up with me and held my hand. We held hands for an hour while Charles clamored for attention. That night was one of the most difficult experiences in rearing our child."

Mother of one / New York, N.Y.

DIAPERING

Changing Diapers

"My 2-month-old used to cry the whole time I changed his diaper on the dressing table. One day, to my utter amazement, he didn't cry. Instead, he was entranced by the baby on the Pampers box, which I had inadvertently set on the dressing table near his head. Now whenever I change his diapers, I put the box close to him and he coos and giggles and smiles all over the place while he talks to his little friend."

Mother of three / Tulsa, Okla.

You'll probably spend more time changing your baby in the first months than doing any other care chore except feeding. To make this job more enjoyable, use changing time to talk and play with your baby. "My daughter first smiled, and also laughed out loud for the first time, while she was being changed. I'd go through ridiculous antics while changing her —blowing bubbles, kissing her belly, clicking my tongue, letting my hair fall down on her face."

"My 3-year-old son loves music," said another mother. "and we'd always use changing time to sing. At first I did the singing, but soon he began to join me, making funny little chirping sounds. And now that he's 3 he does all the singing—in the tub, while putting on his shoes, any time he's getting dressed or undressed."

Body games are great fun when you're changing the baby. Even when he's an infant, touch or kiss his eyes, nose, and mouth, and make a game of naming these and other body

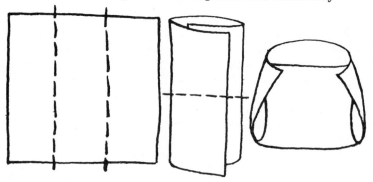

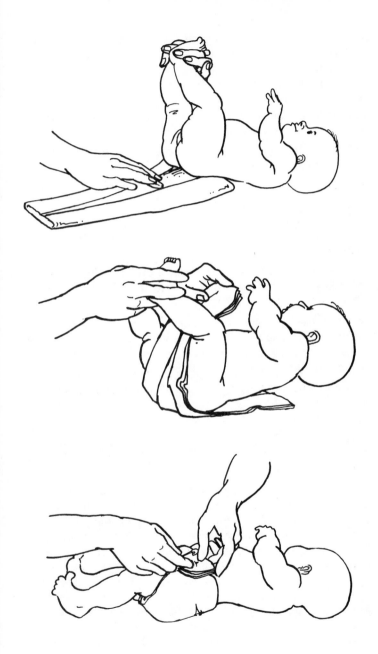

parts. You can also hang a mirror or mobile over the changing area and decorate the wall with pictures. You can even use changing time for exercising your baby by giving him a gentle massage, concentrating on different parts of his body at each change.

To make the work of changing as easy as possible, try some of the following hints:

• Keep your thumb inside the diaper to protect the baby in case you push the pin too far.

• Wash the baby's bottom with plain water or a disposable wipe, even if he has only urinated.

• Be sure to use a rubber lap pad to cover a boy baby's penis to avoid being sprayed; pull the pad away just before you pin the diapers.

• Fold cloth diapers with the double thickness in front for both boys and girls, and use diaper liners for the first month or so to cut down on the mess.

• If you use disposable diapers, keep a roll of masking tape handy so you can replace the tabs when they lose their stickiness or for those times, such as bathtime, when you've taken off a clean diaper and want to use it again.

• If you store diaper pins in a bar of soap that's still in its box the pins will easily slip through the diapers. Or run the tine of the pin through your hair.

• Keep a spray bottle filled with water on the changing table and a roll of toilet paper attached to the end of the table to be ready for emergencies.

Some mothers are hesitant to use waterproof pants on infants for fear of contributing to diaper rash. While waterproof pants do indeed keep moisture next to baby's skin, a more likely cause of diaper rash is the tendency to change the baby's diaper less frequently when he's wearing these pants. So go ahead and use them from the start; just remember to change the baby often, and leave the pants off for a day or so if he develops a rash. You probably won't need waterproof pants if you use disposable diapers unless your baby has diarrhea. To soften stiff waterproof pants, by the way, put them in your dryer with a load of towels.

Washing Diapers

Even if you use disposables, you should slosh most of the
feces out before you throw them out; it's important, for
sanitary and ecological reasons, to follow the instructions
for disposal on the box. Many mothers tear a hole in the
outer layer of the diaper and let the soggy filling in the middle go down the toilet, unless plumbing is old or goes into
a septic tank. Slosh wet and soiled cloth diapers in the toilet
to remove urine and the worst of the stools. Then fill a bucket about half full of water, stir in a couple of capfuls of disinfectant, and put the rinsed-out diapers in. When you're
down to five or ten clean diapers, pour the bucketful of soaking diapers, water and all, into your automatic washer. Set
the dial to the spin cycle and spin out all the excess water.
Then, using very hot water and a mild detergent, run the
diapers through a complete wash-and-rinse cycle. Reset the
machine and rinse again. Even if you have a passion for snowy-
white diapers, go easy on bleach. It's not only hard on diapers, it's hard on baby's skin.

One mother boasts, "I never folded a single diaper. I just
pulled the diapers out of the dryer into a pretty basket, then
folded them right on my baby."

Barbara bought a heavy plastic laundry hamper to use
as a diaper pail after the flimsy bucket she first used sprang
a leak.

"I tried a suggestion from the "Heloise" column in our local
paper—making diaper liners out of tulle—and it's really helped
save diaper-washing time. Here's the hint. Buy half a yard of
tulle, a netlike fabric often used to make bridal veils. (Be sure
and get tulle, which is soft, rather than nylon net, which is
rough.) Cut the tulle into sizes to fit diapers, and use one
piece to line a diaper each time you change your baby. Most
of the soil will be caught by the tulle, and is easily sloshed
out. The diapers hardly get dirty at all. These liners can be
washed along with diapers and used over and over again."

Mother of two / Portland, Me.

If your baby gets diaper rash and you want to make sure
his diapers are perfectly clean, try this remedy from a grandmother who raised six children, washing all their diapers by

hand, without seeing even one serious case of diaper rash. Rinse the diapers and put them in a large metal bucket. Fill the bucket with water, put it on the stove, and bring it to a boil. Let the diapers stew for at least a half hour. Allow them to cool, pour them into your washing machine, and wash them as usual. (For more information on diaper rash, see Chapter 9.)

BATHING

Bathe your baby whenever and wherever it's convenient for you. Some mothers use the kitchen sink; some use a plastic dishpan or tub on the kitchen table; others start right out by putting baby in the family bathtub, even though it's hard on the washer's back. There is no "right" time for bathing babies. If you work best on a schedule, set aside a certain time of the day to give the baby her bath. If you're not a scheduled person, bathe her at ten a.m. one day and ten p.m. the next. It won't matter to her. And it won't bother her, either, if she doesn't have a bath every single day.

"I kept forgetting things like soap or a towel, so I finally decided to keep everything I needed for the bath in a plastic dishpan," said one mother. The essentials: two washcloths, soap, one or two towels, shampoo, a fresh change of clothing.

If you have no idea how to bathe a baby, here is one method:

1. Gather together all of your materials. Spread a towel or a piece of foam rubber on the sink drainboard or table.

2. Fill the tub with warm water. Bring the baby to the table *next* to the tub and quickly undress her. Thoroughly wash her bottom and, using a different washcloth, wash her face and ears. Wet your hand and soap her down. Two or three times a week, wet her hair and rub in a little shampoo.

3. Finally, test the water temperature and, if it's all right slip her into the tub. (If you have the baby sit on a wash-cloth, it will "anchor" her.) Hold her across your arm, firmly supporting her head and encircling her arm with your hand. Make sure you have a secure (though comfortable) grip on her before you lower her into the water. Rinse her with your free hand and then take her from the tub and

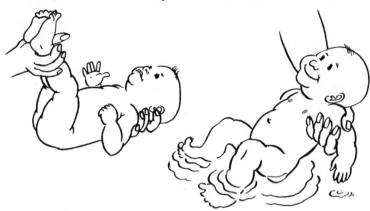

thoroughly dry her.

One mother suggests sharing bathtime with Daddy. Four hands make the job much easier, and it usually ends up being enjoyable for everybody. Another mother said, "I feed my baby from one breast, bathe him, and then nurse him from the other breast. He falls asleep clean and full."

"My daughter and I both enjoyed getting in the tub together. I would lie down with her on top of me, and she'd have a lot of fun kicking and splashing and get a bath at the same time. Another fun thing to do is soap the baby and then hold her to you—what a funny, fishy sensation."

Mother of two / Birmingham, Ala.

MISCELLANEOUS TIPS

Several mothers found that a small, inexpensive suitcase is more convenient than a conventional diaper bag for taking trips with a baby. Keep the bag stocked with disposable diapers, throwaway wipes, small and large lap pads, a clean bottle, a can of premixed formula, and a change of clothes. Restock the bag immediately after each trip so that you'll be ready to go at a moment's notice.

One friend keeps in her car a bottle, a few cans of formula, disposable diapers, and a bottle warmer that plugs into the car's cigarette lighter. "That way, we're prepared for any emergency."

Pacifiers—to use or not to use, that is the question. If you hate the sight of a baby sucking on a pacifier, don't use one. If your baby keeps spitting it out and shows no interest in it, forget it. But if you or your baby have no strong feelings one way or the other, go ahead and give pacifiers a try. If your baby needs extra sucking, he may find his thumb, and the pacifier habit is much easier to get rid of than the thumbsucking habit.

"The hospital where my son was born used a bottle nipple stuffed with a piece of cotton as a pacifier. This impromptu device turned out to be a lifesaver the day I managed to misplace all three of my 1-month-old's pacifiers."

Mother of two / Charleston, W. Va.

To wipe up vomit, use a damp rag sprinkled with baking soda, which both cleans up the mess and absorbs the odor.

Practice carrying your baby in a "football hold." In days gone by, before backpacks and baby carriers, many a mother did her housework with baby's head cradled in her free hand and his feet tucked securely under her arm.

Slip a large rubber sheet in your diaper bag and spread it on the floor to make a safe bed for the baby when you're visiting friends. This sheet will also provide you with a changing place wherever you might be, as it will protect the baby from a floor or rug—and protect the floor or rug from *her*— while you change her.

Never leave babies unattended on a bed or couch, even surrounded by pillows. Babies can move around more than you might expect—and they can move fast. Tiny babies have been known to be suffocated by pillows, to have fallen off beds, and even to have gotten themselves caught between mattresses and headboards.

A Typical Day in the Life of a 2-Month-Old

I wake suddenly. It's five o'clock! I leap from bed and rush to Brian's room. He's still breathing, and still sleeping. He's slept through the night! I feel marvelous. For the first time in months, I've had a full six hours' sleep. I've been a zombie these last two months, drooping and yearning only for sleep.

When Brian wakes at five-thirty I nurse him in my rocking chair. Another miracle. My hemorrhoids are all gone. I can sit without any pain.

I take Brian to the kitchen, and from his infant seat he watches me and waves his hands and makes chirpy noises while I fix breakfast. Dave and I have breakfast together; Brian, in his infant seat in the middle of the table, makes the most gorgeous centerpiece imaginable.

After Dave leaves for work I put Brian back to bed and do some housework. At ten o'clock the phone rings and Brian wakes up, howling. It's Pam on the phone. She's home alone with her newborn daughter, Jenny, and desperately needs some things from the store. I agree to get them for her and say Brian and I will be there as soon as possible.

I nurse Brian and dress him, and we go to the store and then to Pam's. What a difference two months make. Brian looks and acts like a mature person compared to Jenny, who still has that other-world newborn look, as if she's not all the way here yet. Brian is now real. He kicks, he bats with his hands, he smiles, he eats with gusto. In fact, he cries all the way home, and it's a harried half-hour ride through noon-hour traffic. As soon as we get home I nurse him, and then both of us take a nap.

A half-hour later I am rudely awakened by a piercing cry. I'm beginning to understand Brian's cries, but this one is new and extremely frightening. I check his diaper pins and his diapers, but there's nothing wrong there. I try to burp him. I rock him, walk him, and try to feed him, but he pushes away from my breast, stiffening and screaming.

Frantic, I call the doctor. His nurse asks me to describe Brian's symptoms, but all I can say is that he's crying as though he's in pain.

"Have you taken his temperature?" she asks me and I

confess that I don't know how to use a rectal thermometer. I almost expect her to chide me for my ignorance, but she just calmly tells me how to do it and asks me to let her know the results. Such a lovely lady—so understanding of nervous new mothers. I follow her instructions, but as soon as I insert the thermometer Brian has a huge bowel movement, all over me, himself, the chair. He stops crying! So *that* was what was bothering him. It's a terrible mess, but I'm so relieved! I call the doctor's nurse to tell her the emergency is over and then flop down on the living-room couch, too tired to sleep, to read, to do anything but watch the soaps.

Dave calls around four. We talk briefly, mainly about Brian, the subject of most of our conversations these days. He tells me he'll bring home some fried chicken for dinner, which is grand, because I've totally forgotten about cooking, and everything edible is still in the freezer.

Dave gets home at six, and we decide to eat before I feed Brian. Wrong decision. Brian has the most sensitive ears, or nose, or something. I chomp down on my chicken and immediately he begins to cry. Dave changes him and brings him to me. I nurse him at the table while I eat my chicken. Then we put him in his infant seat, in his usual place in the center of the table, and after dinner Dave sits in the rocking chair and talks with his son while I take a long bubble bath. I put on my "let's do it" nightgown and slither back into the living room. Dave whistles, and for the first time all day I feel like something other than a mother.

* * *

A Typical Day in the Life of an 8-Month-Old

I get up at six-fifteen, even though it's Saturday, have a cup of coffee, and glance through the paper. It's just so nice to have some time alone without having to rush, rush, rush to get John and myself ready so I can get him to the sitter and make it to work on time.

John wakes at seven. I change him, dress him, feed him. He creeps after me as I give the house a once-over-lightly cleaning. I change the beds and change him. A friend is coming for lunch. I pick up the pots and pans John has strewn all over the house. I let out the dog and pick up bits of Pampers he's strewn all over the bathroom.

My friend comes, with *her* 8-month-old. We compare notes. I come out ahead, or even, on everything except teeth. Her daughter has two; my son has none. I'm furious, and shaken by the ridiculousness of my fury.

She leaves and I put John to bed. I get out the vacuum cleaner and try to finish just one of the hundreds of things I can't do during the week after work or any time John is awake. (ITEM—Whatever happened to my plan to have nap hours to enjoy myself?)

I get John up and look at all the other undone tasks. I decide to chuck them all, and off we go to the beach. I plunk John down on the sand and stretch out. John grabs a handful of sand and comes to show it to me to admire—and is astonished that the sand is gone. He sits down by my head, and over and over again grabs fistfuls of sand and watches them dribble through his fingers. He then begins to crawl on my head. We roll and tumble together, giggling and laughing.

He loses interest in me and goes off to explore. He joins a family group, a man with two children. "Ah ha," I think. "Perhaps a divorced father out for the day?" But no, a woman joins the group.

We spend two glorious hours at the beach, and then go home. I give John the pots and pans while I fix his dinner. Then I feed him and the dog.

Bob, a man I've been seeing, drops over unexpectedly, eager to talk and share his day. As we're having a drink he gives a "look" at the pots and pans and other litter on the living-room floor. I angrily slam the pots and pans into the cupboard in the kitchen. Bob and I talk as I try to keep John from playing with the stereo set, pulling on an electric cord, yanking the dog's tail. I relent and let him play with the pots and pans again. (ITEM—In what moment of insanity did I decide against a playpen?)

Bob leaves and I put John to bed and eat a TV dinner.

I go in to cover John. He's curled up in a fetal position, holding on to his yellow blanket, breathing softly, gently. So sweet, so loving, so beautiful. Ahh, life's not so bad after all, with my marvelous 8-month-old son. In fact, life's pretty good when he's sleeping!

4

Child Care:
The First Years

During the first years your "baby" is rapidly growing into your "child." He will give up his two a.m. feeding, his bottle, his morning nap. He will begin to eat solids, to feed himself, to dress himself. He will want to touch, taste, and explore everything in his immediate world.

Taking care of your baby after the first few months may become a little easier for you. Your baby is not so fragile and you will have developed experience and confidence in your own ability. But it may also become more of a challenge. You will continually have to stay one step ahead of him to keep him safe and encourage him in his quest for growth and independence.

In this chapter we discuss the common concerns about baby and child care during the first years. We offer suggestions for feeding, weaning, sleeping, bathing, grooming, and dressing—and for teaching your child how to learn to do these things for himself. Just as important, we discuss keeping your baby safe so that he will survive to be a child.

"In some ways it's much easier to take care of my 1-year-old. I'm not so afraid I'll drop her or drown her or starve her. But it's also getting harder, since I'm afraid she'll fall, or drown herself, or starve herself."

Mother of one / Eugene, Ore.

"One minute my 18-month-old wants to be my baby. He snuggles in my arms; he wants me to hold his bottle; he walks around saying 'up, up'; he demands all my time. The next minute he wants to be a teenager. 'No, Yonny do it!' he shrieks as I try to put on his shoes."

Mother of four / Chicago, Ill.

"It's a matter of living life while your children are here. It's like taking time to see the sun rise or a rainbow. In fact, kids are like rainbows—if you don't stop while they're here, they're gone." *Mother of six / Hartford, Conn.*

FEEDING

Weaning from the Breast

There is no agreement about the best time to wean a baby from the breast. Our recommendation is to go ahead and nurse as long as both you and the baby still enjoy it. It may be one week, one month, or one year.

When you decide to wean, try to do it gradually. Cut out one feeding; several days later, cut out a second feeding. After a few more days, cut out the last feeding. Your milk supply will gradually decrease. If you are uncomfortable, manually express a small amount—just enough to relieve the pressure.

A few mothers report that the gradual method didn't work for them and that they had to switch their babies from breast to bottle all at once. If gradual weaning doesn't work for you, either, switch to bottles if your baby is under a year old or, if the baby is older, straight to drinking from cups, if you prefer. In either case, consult with your doctor if you decide to quit cold turkey. He may want to give you medication to help dry up your milk.

"I could not gradually wean any of my three children. When they were old enough to wean (at about 9 months) they wouldn't give up one meal at a time. They whined and cried, wanting me. So I prepared for weaning by giving them a cup of milk at each meal and then nursing them. And then all at once I completely stopped, and it worked."

Mother of three / Seattle, Wash.

Weaning from the Bottle

Unless she violently rejects a bottle, you shouldn't wean
your baby to a cup before she is a year old. She needs to
suck, and if she gives up her bottle too early she may turn
to her thumb to satisfy her sucking urges.

Gradual weaning works well with some babies. First
eliminate the bottle your child desires the least, then gradually get rid of the others. Once she's kicked the habit, throw
all the bottles away. If, in a moment of stress, you slip her
a bottle to get her to sleep "just this once," be warned that
you'll start the habit all over again.

"When I weaned my oldest from the bottle, I first took away
the bottle I gave him at naptime and substituted looking at
a book while holding and rocking him. This was relaxing for
him, and when I put him down he was ready to go to sleep."
Mother of two / Atlanta, Ga.

"When weaning from the bottle, don't be overly concerned
about how much milk your child drinks. At first, my children drastically cut their milk drinking, but in three or four
weeks they were drinking plenty from the cup. As long as
they had a well-balanced diet, I didn't worry about the
milk." *Mother of two / Cleveland, Ohio*

"My best advice came from my children's pediatrician: to
have a 'bottle-tossing party.' I talked about this special event
to come, we planned a dinner of my son's favorite foods,
and I wrapped up a new cup for him to open as a present.
The night of our party, my son, my husband, and I went
through the house looking for all the bottles, which I had
previously hidden in a few obvious places; we took them outside and tossed them, one by one, into the trash can. Then
we went in and had our celebration. When my son asked for
his bottle that night, I reminded him that they were all gone.
I suggested that he look through the house to see if we forgot one. He looked, but not one bottle turned up. That settled the issue once and for all."
Mother of two / Oakland, Calif.

Solids

Listen to your pediatrician's advice about starting solid food. There is a wide difference of opinion about when to do this, and no two books, pediatricians, or mothers seem to agree.

"I gave both my children some cereal for their ten o'clock feeding when they were a month old. Although many friends told me this was a terrible idea, I felt it was worth a try since I had to get up in the morning and work, and I couldn't function on the job without a good night's rest. By the end of six weeks both kids were sleeping through the night, and I'm convinced the cereal helped."
Mother of two / Burlington, Vt.

"How much easier it is, now, the second time around. I was so vulnerable the first time. People made me feel like a crud. But now that I'm experienced, I don't feel threatened by people. For example, I don't give my 4-month-old solids, although two friends think that's the height of neglect. Breast feeding is enough for her and easy for me. She's getting along just fine." *Mother of two / Phoenix, Ariz.*

Your baby will require a few weeks to adjust to eating solids. For a while he'll eat just enough to get used to the idea, and he'll still be filling most of his nutritional needs from milk rather than solids. While he's learning to eat from a spoon, feed him some milk first—half a bottle or from one breast—because if he's howling with hunger he won't enjoy eating food from a spoon.

Traditionally, babies are started on cereal and then progress to fruits, vegetables, and finally meat. Barbara, however, started Jonas on fruit. He loved it and quickly learned to swallow. A few weeks later, when she introduced cereal, he greedily lapped it up. If you do start with cereal, make it single-grain, mixing about one tablespoon of cereal with one tablespoon of formula. And if your baby is prone to food allergies, it might be best to use rice, corn, oat, or barley rather than wheat cereal, as he may be allergic to wheat.

Put your baby in his infant seat on the kitchen or dining-room table and, using a small-bowled long-handled spoon, feed him a minuscule amount of cereal. He'll probably spit it out; if so, scrape it off his chin, talk to him cheerfully, and spoon it back in. Eventually a little will get into his mouth and into his stomach. Warning: Baby cereal dries to the consistency of plaster. Wipe up spills immediately.

Introduce new foods gradually, waiting at least a week before starting each new food to make sure he does not have an allergy. He may express a violent dislike for some new addition to his menu. If he does, hold off on that food for a few weeks before trying it again.

Give your baby a few sips of juice or milk from a cup at around six months. Finish off each meal with a few sips from the cup. He won't drink much, but he'll get used to drinking from a cup.

If you use a high chair, don't put the dish on the tray when you are feeding the baby because he may throw it at you or on the floor. Give him a spoon or rattle to shake or bang while you spoon in the food. When he can sit up without support, let him start on a few simple finger foods.

In theory, feeding a baby is easy: if you prepare nutritious food, he will be eager to eat it all. In reality, it's not so easy. There probably isn't a mother alive who hasn't, at some time during the first year or so, worried about her child's eating habits. Is he eating too much? Is he eating too little? He hates meat. He eats only meat. He won't drink enough milk. He drinks too much milk. The list could go on endlessly.

During his second year your baby's growth rate will slow dramatically, and his appetite may slow down too. Also, he may have strong food preferences. At times he won't eat much; at other times he'll be ravenous. If your baby is gaining weight at a normal rate and is generally healthy, assume that he knows best about how much and what to eat. The menu is up to you; eating or not eating is up to him.

"My first child was a very picky eater," said a New York mother with four grown children, "probably because I hovered over him and worried that he wasn't eating enough; he's still choosy. The other three weren't hard to please because I had a more relaxed attitude toward eating."

"From the first time they could understand the words 'silly' and 'growing,' we made this distinction in relation to foods: the 'silly' foods versus the 'growing' foods. During the day, and at each meal, their bodies required that they eat more of the growing foods. Silly foods (chips, crackers, cookies) were okay, within limits, after a meal. Now that my kids are 4 and 7, we call them nutritious foods and junk foods."

Mother of two / Houston, Tex.

Gradually switch from baby food to regular table food. One mother said, "From one year on, the children ate what we ate. If they didn't like it, they didn't eat. Occasionally I would make a meal of their favorite hot dogs or hamburgers, and then my husband and I ate what *they* liked. Now they eat almost everything." That mother probably has the right idea. If you hover over your child and make a big fuss about what, and how much, he eats, you may be on the way to producing a picky eater. Try to maintain a relaxed attitude about eating from the very beginning. (See Chapters 6 and 7 for more information on feeding your children and making your own baby food.)

SLEEPING

"My first child was not a sleeper. She would stay up indefinitely if it were left to her. I tried everything. I finally closed her in her room—a *mistake*, because it caused a fear of the dark, and then she wouldn't sleep in her room. She'd leave her room and we'd find her in the morning curled up at the foot of our bed or even on the floor in the hall. I was much more relaxed with my second and third children than I was with my first—I put the younger children to bed when they seemed tired and more or less left a sleeping schedule up to them. But my oldest daughter still has sleeping problems at age 9." *Mother of three / Springfield, Mo.*

"We decided when our children should go to bed and stood firmly to our ground. They knew we meant it and we've had no problems." *Mother of two / Columbia, S.C.*

Wouldn't it be marvelous if mothers and fathers woke at six every morning as full of energy as their 2-year-olds? One mother set aside a box of special toys to be played with only when Mommy was sleeping. "I put dry cereal or a peanut butter sandwich and fruit in a brown paper bag and leave it at the bottom of my daughter's crib," said another mother. "She wakes up, finds her sack breakfast, and sometimes lets me sleep an extra hour."

As she gets older, your baby will sleep less and less. By 6 months she'll probably be down to two naps, morning and afternoon. During the first year, your baby will know best how much sleep she needs. After that, you may have to take charge. Most babies are down to an afternoon nap at one year. Some take a late-morning nap and wake at one or two; others take an early-afternoon nap. If your child fusses halfheartedly before falling asleep, her nap schedule and bedtime hour are probably right for her. However, if she cries violently for more than fifteen or twenty minutes, you may have to adjust her schedule to let her stay up a little longer.

"Naptime was important to me since it was *my* rest time, too. With my first child, at about a year we would read a story and then I'd snuggle with her until she went to sleep. Sometimes we both slept, snuggled close together. I continued this with my second child, and even now, when they are 8 and 6, we have a read and rest when they first come home from school."   *Mother of two / Worcester, Mass.*

"I always found it helpful to take my baby for a short ride in the stroller just before naptime. The fresh air seemed to make her sleepy."   *Mother of two / Denver, Colo.*

When a baby gives up her morning nap, the transition is fairly easy: all you have to do is move up lunchtime and gradually adjust her naptime—from ten-thirty to eleven and then to noon or later.

Maybe you'll be lucky enough to have a child who requires an afternoon nap until she is 3, 4, or even 5. However, you may discover that your child doesn't really need an afternoon nap. Some children give up napping at 2, or even before. If she cries and complains for an hour when you put her down for her nap at one p.m., finally falls asleep, and doesn't wake till four, she probably can do without her nap.

If you continue to insist on an afternoon nap, she'll probably fuss and stay awake for a long time when you put her to bed at night.

Transition periods for some children are hard on everyone's nerves. To help make life a little easier, try one or both of these suggestions. (1) Insist that your child remain quiet in her room after lunch for two hours. If she falls asleep, be sure to wake her after two hours so she won't stay awake at night. (2) Skip naptime altogether. If you choose this option, however, be aware that every few days your child may conk out at four or five o'clock and wake at nine raring to go. If this happens, wake her after a half hour and then pop her into the tub to alleviate her natural distress at being awakened. Barbara says that Jonas was in a transition period for more than a year. Sometimes he took a morning nap; sometimes he took an afternoon nap; sometimes he fell asleep at five and slept through the night; and sometimes he fell asleep at four and woke at seven. Whatever his self-imposed schedule, Barbara reports, she put him to bed at his regular bedtime and told him that he didn't have to go to sleep, but he did have to read or play quietly.

By the way, after the first few months, blankets are useless; most babies older than 3 months kick them off. If the weather is cool, zip the baby into a blanket sleeper. In any case, it pays to buy good-quality sleepers; good ones will outlast cheap ones three times over.

"My baby stopped napping at 15 months. Yes, it was hard in the afternoon. But the good news is that he went to sleep for the night at six p.m., which gave my husband and me long evenings together." *Mother of one / Annapolis, Md.*

"My 2½-year-old son began to resist going to sleep at night when I was seven months into my second pregnancy. For a month I tried everything: rocking him, singing to him, reading to him. I finally resorted to letting him sleep in our bed just to get some rest myself.

"Then I discovered a technique that worked like magic. I came home from my Lamaze class one night, and there was Kevin, wide awake. 'Come on, Kevin,' I announced. 'We're going to play a game.' I put him to bed, and sooth-

ingly improvised on the progressive relaxation techniques
I had learned that night in class. 'Go to sleep, feet, re—lax,'
I crooned. I went over his whole body, touching, patting,
and crooning, and by the time I got to 'Close your eyes, relax, go to sleep,' he was sound asleep."

Mother of two / Gainesville, Fla.

BATHING AND GROOMING

Diapering

Some very active babies have a hard time holding still long
enough to have their diapers changed. If every change is a
struggle and singing songs doesn't do the trick, be firm. Tell
your child, "Changing time is not messing-around time. You
must lie still while I change your diaper." Hold him down
and do the job as quickly as possible. Once he understands
that you won't tolerate too much moving around, you can
go back to fun and games while changing diapers.

Tub Baths

Your baby will enjoy bathtime more and more as he gets
older. If he's sitting up and his thrashing and splashing un-
nerve you, put him in the tub in a large laundry basket.
The water will surround him in his own "boat," and he can
move without slipping and crawling all over the tub.

Give an older baby his own washcloth and let him scrub
himself. About once a week, scrub him down yourself from
head to toe. The rest of the time, give special attention to
his face and bottom. He'll get the rest clean just by playing
in the tub.

"I put all the little bits and pieces of left-over soap into a
white sock, knotted the end of the sock, and gave it to my
2½-year-old daughter to replace both soap and washcloth
when she took a bath. She enjoyed using her own sock soap
and quickly learned to hang it on the faucet when she was
finished. It also conserved soap, since we used every bit, and
there were no longer any bars of soap slowly dissolving in
the bottom of the tub."

Mother of one / Madison, Wisc.

A mother told us that she frequently took her daughters into the shower with her, starting at two or three months. They thoroughly enjoyed the water falling on their heads and never developed a fear of water. Both daughters, now 5 and 8, are excellent swimmers.

Never leave a child alone in the tub before he is 3 years old. Even after that, be extremely cautious. Make frequent tub checks. We still remember a news story several years ago about a 5-year-old who drowned in the tub while his mother was on the phone.

Rigidly enforce the following tub rules: no standing, no jumping, no lying down. Punish infractions by immediately removing your child from the tub.

Some children are afraid that when the water flows out of the tub they'll go down the drain too, so it's a good idea to wait to pull the plug until your child is out of the bathroom.

Face and Hands

Almost all children hate to have their faces washed, and many aren't exactly overjoyed by having their hands scrubbed. Give your baby a washcloth and let him do as much of the washing as possible by himself.

When you have to get off all the dirt for a visit to Great-Aunt Zelda or the yearly Christmas photographs, move slowly and work gently. Use a small washcloth and go after the dirt one section at a time. To many of us, face and hand washing tends to be an afterthought. "Oh, oh," we say. "Quick, let's wash your hands—dinner is getting cold" or "Oh dear, you can't go to nursery school with that filthy face." If we could take some of the rush and panic out of washing away dirt, maybe it wouldn't be such an ordeal for our children.

A hint from one mother: "Let your child spread shaving cream on his face, then 'shave' it away with a washcloth."

"When my baby is about 2, I'm going to put one of those long-handled gadgets they sell in baby stores on the bathroom light switch so he can turn it on himself. I'll put a mirror on the bathroom wall at his eye level and I'll put a towel rack down where he can reach it. We've already replaced the cold-

water faucet handle with one a child can turn more easily.
No wonder my oldest was so difficult when it came to cleaning up. It was physically hard for her in that adult bathroom."

Mother of two / Spokane, Wash.

Hair

Hair washing may turn into a struggle at some time before
baby's first birthday. To make this task easier and more fun,
try one of the following ideas.

Jeanne Henry let Anne lie on a towel on the bathroom
counter top. She wet the baby's hair thoroughly, rubbed in
a little shampoo, then rinsed it out over the sink with a spray
attachment. During the second soaping they made "rabbit
ears" and after the final rinse they wrapped a towel around
Anne's head and tried to decide if she still looked like a girl.

Barbara got in the tub with David and Jonas, held them
in her lap, and played "Row, row, row your boat" with
them. At the end of each verse she soaped them, and on
each "row" she dipped their heads into the water. Both
boys enjoyed this hair-washing game for a long time.

Brush your child's hair in front of a mirror and tell him
how good it looks. Use a wide-toothed "natural" comb to
get out snarls.

Getting gum out of a child's hair is only amusing if it's
someone else's child. If it's your own, it's not so funny, and
it's an all-too-common problem.

If your child has short, curly hair and it's a big wad, scissors may be the only solution. However, if the hair is fairly
straight and there's not too much gum, try the following:

1. Apply a good amount of cold cream to the gum and surrounding hair.

2. Work the cold cream in for about five minutes, until you
feel that it has gotten underneath, between the hair and the
gum, reducing the adhesion.

3. Holding the gum firmly, gently pull the hair away from it
a couple of strands at a time. The gum may come away in
little pieces, something like pencil-eraser leavings. Repeat
this procedure if necessary.

4. Once most of the gum is out, the problem becomes one
of removing the cold cream. Washing with a mild baby

shampoo won't do it. Carefully use your own shampoo— or a little liquid detergent—to get it out.

Barbara once tried to get a hunk of bubble gum out of Jonas' very curly, short hair. She tried peanut butter, cold cream, and ice, but nothing worked. She finally had to cut the gum out.

"I'll never forget the day our 170-pound mastiff somehow managed to cover himself from one end to the other with gum. My husband went crazy trying to get it out. He used turpentine, and both he and the dog were in agony.

"I vaguely remembered hearing that peanut butter worked well for removing gum. So I got our jar of chunky peanut butter and massaged it into the dog's hair by the handfuls. I waited about ten minutes, then used soap and water. And immediately our dog was back to normal. I've since used it on my son's hair, and it works just as well on humans."   *Mother of two / Manhattan Beach, Calif.*

DRESSING

At some time during her second year, your child will declare her dressing independence and shriek, "No, me do it!" She'll want to put on her own shoes, but she won't get them on the right feet; she'll want to take off her shirt, but it will get stuck on her head. To handle some of the conflicts that crop up during a "me do it" stage, try some of the following suggestions.

When you're in an enormous rush and want to get your child dressed quickly, tell her, "I know you want to do it yourself, but we're late. Now see if you can help Mommy do the job fast."

Give her a shirt to hold while you change her diaper. Give her her shoes to hold while you put on her socks.

Even if she is almost 3, when you're in a hurry and need to do the job yourself, dress her on her changing table. If you're persistent, it will dawn on her that she has to be still when she's on the changing table.

When she's in a rush, one mother tells her 2-year-old, "If you won't let me get you dressed you'll have to stay home." So far, she says, the threat has worked. But she doesn't know what she'll do if her daughter calls her bluff.

"I found it helpful, when my son started to dress himself, to keep only clothes that were suitable to the season in the drawers he could reach. That narrowed his choices and also eliminated some arguments about whether what he'd decide to wear was okay for the weather."

Mother of one / Sheridan, Wyo.

Another mother told us, "Nothing worked with my daughter until I insisted she be dressed every day before 'Mister Rogers' came on TV at seven-thirty."

It's much better, however, if you can plan ahead and allow enough time so that you don't have to rush. Having to do things in a hurry can make both mother and baby cranky.

A friend says, "I know that my 2-year-old wants to do everything for herself, so I stand back and let her do it. I always try to leave her enough time to dress and feed herself. Any time you have to hurry through something, you're probably not going to enjoy the experience—and certainly your child won't enjoy it."

Once your child has learned to dress and undress herself, she may practice this new skill endlessly. Many children go through their entire wardrobes in one day, dressing and undressing. To avoid letting a child litter the house with clothes, insist that all dressing and undressing be done in her room. If you enforce that rule, you can easily scoop discarded clothes back into the drawer for another day.

"You must keep them away from babies, but plastic vegetable bags are handy for one thing for older children. The only way I know to get boots on over sneakers is to put one of those bags over each shoe—then the foot slides into the boot easily. Another tip about boots: I put colored tape on the backs of my kids' boots so they know which ones are theirs in nursery school." *Mother of four / Minneapolis, Minn.*

"I teach my children which shoe goes on which foot by putting a dab of red nail polish on the inside lining of every *right* shoe, slipper, sneaker, and boot they own. I also point out that the big toe must go in the longer part of the shoe."

Mother of three / Springfield, Ill.

To teach your child to put on his own coat or sweater, try this method, used in many nursery schools and day-care centers. The instructions will take only a few minutes, and your child should have instant success. (1) Spread the coat wrong side out on the floor. (2) Stand your child in front of the coat collar, facing the coat. (3) Tell him to stoop and push his arms into the coat sleeves. (4) Help him raise his arms and flip the coat over his head. Voila! It's on.

SAFEKEEPING

You can go bananas thinking about all the things that could kill or injure your child. Some mothers become so paranoid about safety that they never let their children out of their sight. Other mothers seem so careless that one wonders how their children make it past three months.

We feel mild paranoia is better than carelessness. After all, you've put a lot of time, effort, and money into your baby; you don't want to have to start over with a new model.

Dangers at Home

"My son was fascinated by electrical outlets. He quickly figured out how to remove the plug-in coverings, much to our dismay. We replaced the whole outlet plate with a kind in which the openings are in the opposite direction from the openings of the outlet. This proved to be so difficult to remove that he lost interest in them."

Mother of one / New York, N.Y.

"I've heard that coffee tables are the number-one cause of maiming accidents in the home, and after our experience I believe it. We had very carefully childproofed our home for our 2-year-old, removing everything breakable or dangerous from his reach or sight—everything but the coffee table. One evening shortly before my husband was to return home from work, my son did a flying jump off the couch and landed face down on the coffee table. When he stood up, his face was covered with blood and he was holding his tooth—root and all. We removed the damn table, and haven't replaced it to this day." *Mother of one / Detroit, Mich.*

Before your baby is mobile enough to get into things, go through a baby store or your local hardware store, thinking of everything you want to keep away from the baby. Buy as many latches, locks, and gates as it will take to do the job. Install them the very next day.

Plug up unused electrical outlets with blank plugs. Tape lamp cords and wiring to the backs of furniture or to the wall, or wrap them around table legs and then tape them down. One day in Barbara's classroom a 5-year-old who was old enough to know better absent-mindedly picked up a record-player cord lying near him on the rug and started to chew it. Fortunately, the player wasn't plugged in.

Vacuum daily in all the rooms to which a crawling child has free access. Doing so often takes less time than checking the floors for little scraps and bits that a baby might attempt to eat.

Throw out plastic dry-cleaning bags—in the outside trash. A doctor once warned Barbara against carrying diapers in a

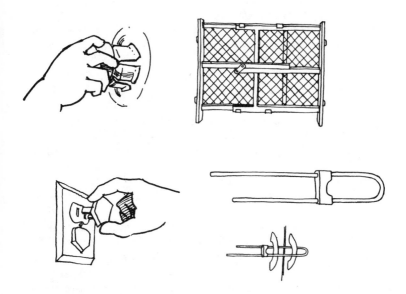

plastic vegetable bag from the supermarket. He told her that he had once treated a child who had almost suffocated after putting one of these bags over his head.

"My 2-month-old suddenly developed a red swollen toe and cried in pain. I drove her to the emergency room, where a nurse immediately guessed what was wrong. A colorless plastic thread from the baby's stretch suit had gotten wound around her toe so tightly that the flesh had swelled up around it. All the nurse had to do was snip the thread. After that, I washed the baby's clothes inside out and always checked for loose threads." *Mother of one / Cincinnati, Ohio*

A playpen can help a busy mother keep an active baby safe. If you have space for a playpen, you may want to consider one. As one mother said, "Sure, he may learn more without a playpen, but I want him alive as well as bright."

If you decide on a playpen, start early and put your baby in it long before she begins to move. If she gets used to her playpen when she's 2 or 3 months old, before she's really moving around very much, she'll feel more comfortable in it when she begins to crawl.

If you have a small house or can scrupulously babyproof your house, you may not want or need a playpen. One mother told us, "The only thing we used our playpen for was the Christmas tree. When our son was 9 months old, we put the tree in the playpen so he couldn't get to it. The rest of the year the pen stayed folded up in the garage, because it just took up too much room in our already overcrowded house."

If you decide against a playpen, begin to childproof well before your baby begins to crawl. Also invest in a gate, since there are bound to be rooms which you'll want to block off and turn into sort of a giant playpen.

Accidental poisoning is the number-one emergency that has to be dealt with in pediatric medicine, especially with children between 1 and 3. So keep anything that is not meant to be eaten by a child well out of her reach. The list is endless. Your child could get very sick if she drank enough of your best bourbon. She could die if she swallowed oven cleaner, toilet-bowl cleaner, aspirin, or even your iron pills. Store poisonous substances as close to the ceiling as possible. However, anticipate the fact that your 5-month-old will someday be an accomplished climber.

Actually, you can explain a lot to children once they've learned to talk, so be sure to make them understand how important it is not to eat or drink *anything* that isn't meant to be eaten or drunk. Give them examples and then show them all the different kinds of things they should not experiment with, both inside the home and outdoors.

Most mothers do fairly well at storing things out of reach. Actually, sheer carelessness is the cause of most poisonings. The phone rings while you're cleaning the toilet. In your hurry to answer it, you leave the can of cleanser on the floor. Late for a dinner party, you spray on some last-minute perfume and leave the bottle on the coffee table. If you are normally careless about putting things back in their places, don't buy poisonous cleansers. Instead, borrow from your next-door neighbor and periodically replace her supply. (See Chapter 9 for what to do in case of poisoning.)

If you have any sliding glass doors in the house, be sure to stick a decal or colored tape on the glass at your child's eye level. Otherwise a racing 2-year-old can easily forget the door is closed.

"My daughter had a bad accident when she was 3, and what's worse was that it happened at home; I heard it but couldn't stop it in time. Two older children were over to play with her brother for the afternoon, and they decided to get flashlights and play in the closet. My daughter's fingers got caught in the hinge part of the door. She ended up with two badly broken fingers that will never look quite the same."   *Mother of two / Santa Monica, Calif.*

Falls

Falls kill more children than any other kind of mishap except traffic accidents, according to safety experts. Falls from open windows, for example, cause far more deaths in the toddler age group than do accidents from poisoning, fire, or drowning, says Dr. Vincent J. Fontana, author of *A Parents' Guide to Child Safety.* Toddlers can lean against screens in open windows and fall through them or even work loose the hooks attaching screens to window frames, push out the screens, and then fall out the window. If you live in a two-story house or above the first floor in an apartment house, you must be especially watchful, but even in a one-story house or first-floor apartment children can be hurt in a fall from a window to a hard surface below.

To prevent a child from falling out of a window:

• Be certain that all screens are in good condition and attached securely to window frames but don't rely on screens alone to prevent falls.

• Don't put a child's crib, bed, or any type of furniture near a window.

• If you need to open windows where a young child plays or sleeps, open them from the top or, if from the bottom, not more than five inches. Safety devices are available at hardware stores that can prevent the windows from being opened further.

• If you live in a hot climate and must keep windows open more than several inches, fasten a metal protective screen over the opening.

• There is no substitute for keeping an eye on any child near an open window.

To avoid other types of falls, make sure all stairwells have handrails that children can reach; make sure the stairwells are well lighted, carpeted (or at least not waxed), and kept clear of tripping hazards; make it a house rule to keep traffic areas clear of stray toys; anchor throw rugs; avoid highly waxed floors; never allow young children to climb ladders; and invest in two gates, one for the top and one for the bottom of stairs, until children can go up and down safely.

"When my daughter began climbing up and down stairs, I put a gate across the stairs about four steps up from the bottom. She could then climb safely up and down as much as she liked, and I stopped worrying about broken limbs and brain concussions." *Mother of two / Ridgefield, N.J.*

Jeanne still gets shaky when she recalls a day when Anne, 3, awoke from her nap early and yelled to be taken out. Jeanne stalled, trying to finish a telephone call. She heard a thump from the bedroom but didn't think much of it and completed the call. Then she went upstairs to find that Anne, apparently frustrated at not being able to open her bedroom door, had climbed on top of her dresser, which was underneath a window. Wood paddle-toy in her fist, she had smashed a hole through the closed window. Only the jagged edges of broken glass had stopped her from going further. Some lessons were learned by her mother: the dresser was moved, the doorknob oiled, the paddle thrown out, and all thumps and noises were given priority over telephone calls.

The Perilous Outdoors

"When my first daughter started to crawl, and at the same time developed a passion for the taste of anything small, like cigarette butts or small pieces of glass, I began to de-litter parks, playgrounds, and beaches wherever we went. I took along a large bag and spent five or ten minutes picking up anything she might discover to cram into her mouth.

Frequently other mothers and older children would help, and we would clean up a park in just a few minutes."
Mother of two / Des Moines, Iowa

Don't let your child eat any leaf or plant that he picks up outside. If you allow him to pull up a carrot and eat it, the next day he may decide to eat something less nutritious. Until he's old enough to know the difference, make testing plants an absolute no-no. (And why don't nurseries indicate whether plants are poisonous on those little sticks that tell you their names in Latin?)

Provide an enclosed play yard for very young children. The memory of a child under 3 just isn't reliable enough to keep her from running into the street.

Even if he protests, insist that your child hold your hand when walking in a parking lot or crossing the street. If your arms are full of packages and he pulls away, put down the packages and, if necessary, carry him to the car. Your purchases are a lot easier to replace than your child.

Safety in the Car

Buy and use car restraints, even for short trips, and don't start the car's engine until everyone is securely buckled up. If your children distract you by crying or fighting while you're driving, pull over to the side of the road to settle the problem. (See Chapter 5 for detailed information on car restraints.)

"From the very start I insisted that my son—as a baby and as a toddler—be buckled into the car, first in an infant car seat, then in a toddler seat, and now with an adult seat belt. It's a hard-and-fast rule. And he sits *still* when he's in the car. For long trips, I keep a basket filled with books, crayons, dolls, and playdough. Since he's used to doing nothing when taking short drives, he's thrilled with this activity basket on long trips."   *Mother of two / Lynchburg, Va.*

If you have a four-door car and a 2- or 3-year-old, you may want to buy a pair of locking devices for the rear doors. Many dealers sell a relatively inexpensive "child-guard door lock" that fits under the regular locking knob. This means *you* control exit and entry from the car, and car doors are potential finger-choppers in a child's world. However, safety experts' warn that such devices may hamper quick removal of victims of an auto accident. This is a case when you have to judge the relative risks. One mother of a rambunctious 3-year-old boy and an 8-month-old girl says these locks have made her car outings easier. "Since I unlock his door, Peter gets out when I'm ready for him to, and I can grab his hand so he won't dart away," she says.

Emergencies

It can't be said too often: if your safety precautions don't work and an accident happens, call for help immediately. Keep a list of emergency numbers permanently attached to your phone or a nearby wall. Include on it the numbers of the rescue squad, the fire department, your doctor, the poison-control center, the emergency room of your local hospital, your own phone number, and your husband's number at work. Also, be sure you know the shortest route to the closest emergency room.

Every mother—every teenager and adult, for that matter—should know what to do in acute crisis when help may not arrive in time. If you don't know how to attempt to resuscitate a person who has stopped breathing, stanch the flow of blood from a severed vein or artery, relieve an obstruction that is causing a person to choke, or treat a person in deep shock, sign up for a first-aid course. The life you save may be your child's.

"I've had both a suspected poisoning and a definite choking, and if I hadn't been prepared and known what to do I would almost certainly have had a severely injured or dead child."
Mother of two / Palos Verdes, Calif.

* * *

A Typical Day in the Life of a 2-Year-Old

It's five-fifteen in the morning. "Mommy, Mommy!" Oh no, I mutter. Not yet, Josh, please.

Josh plops down on top of me. "Mommy, I'm wet . . . I want to get dressed . . . I want to wear my Superman shirt with my blue shorts and my white socks with the green stripes . . . I don't want zips, I want sandals . . . I want juice and Cheerios in the yellow bowl . . . I want to watch 'Mister Rogers' on TV with my nigh nigh (blanket) . . . "

I get up, dress Josh, and turn on the TV to show him the test pattern to prove there is no "Mister Rogers" yet.

By seven the rest of the family is up. Josh is fascinated watching his daddy shave. He discovers the button on the shaving cream and squirts it—on the mirror, the counter, his clothes—and massages some into his hair. Off with the clothes, into the tub, and on with another argument about what to wear.

We sit down for breakfast. "I don't want apple juice, I want grape juice . . . I want my Superman cup . . . I want raisin bread." He throws himself to the floor, kicking and screaming and spilling his grape juice in one of his frequent tantrums, this time because we're out of raisin bread. The rest of us—my husband, my older son David, and I—have learned to ignore him. We finish breakfast, he finishes his tantrum. I send him out to the back yard to play with David.

Ahh, how marvelous, I think, two little brothers being good friends out in the back yard. I go upstairs to dress in some cool white pants and a T-shirt. It's time to take David to nursery school, so I call the boys.

Surprise, surprise. Josh has discovered the mud hole that David and his friend dug yesterday. He is covered with mud. Into the tub for yet another bath.

Well, we make it to school with David by nine. "We're going to do some errands, now," I tell Josh. "Ooh! I want to do errands!" We go to the bank. "I want to do errands," he whines. I explain about errands. We go to the cleaner's, the gas station, the grocery store. "I want to do errands," he insists before and after each stop. He can't understand my explanation, and I can't figure out what it is that he thinks "errands" might be. At noon we pick up David at school. All the way through lunch, Josh repeats his refrain, and finally, at naptime, cries himself to sleep murmuring, "Mommy, I want to do errands!"

By this time I am exhausted, irritable, and in no mood to clean the house and get ready for the dinner guests coming this evening. When Josh wakes up David is still sleeping, so we spend a peaceful twenty minutes reading. Miraculously, Josh and David play beautifully the rest of the afternoon, so I'm able to make dinner and get dressed. I give the boys a forty-five-minute bubble bath and leave them in their room playing with their new cassette player.

A half hour later, I hear a shriek and rush to their room, where I find Josh tangled in a pile of spaghetti-like tape from a cassette. "Put it back! Put it all back!" he screams. He throws himself down and hits the dresser. "I hurt my hair! I hurt my hair!" He grabs several cassettes and wildly throws them around the room.

Just then Daddy comes home with two important business associates. He manages to calm Josh and plays with him and David while I entertain the guests. Finally it's time for the boys to go to bed, and once again the demands begin. "I want a story . . . It's too dark in here . . . I want milk . . . My pants are wet . . . I want my Superman pajamas . . . " Finally, in a rage, I grab Josh and practically throw him in bed. Coldly, I say goodnight and close the door.

"Mommy!" he howls.

I open the door, absolutely furious, and snarl, "What is it now, Josh?"

"Mommy, I wuv you."

Tears fill my eyes. "I love you too Josh," I say, hugging and kissing him. "Oh well, tomorrow's another day," I mutter.

"Nother day, nother day," I hear him say, as I walk away. "Nother day, do errands."

* * *

A Typical Day in the Life of a 3-Year-Old

At six-thirty the alarm goes off and I pounce on it. Then I roll over and fall halfway back to sleep. I hear Shannon as she peeps in at our door, uses the bathroom, and pads downstairs to join her 5-year-old brother, Craig. They prepare breakfast for themselves—juice and cereal.

By seven I'm awake again, ready to begin my morning routine. I put away cereal and milk and prepare breakfast for my husband, Doug. Shannon pulls the tall stool over to the counter and acts as a stage director, questioning and discussing everything in the kitchen, every move I make. "Why are you using that knife? . . . Why is the sponge squishy? . . . Can I have a cookie? . . . Why is the faucet dripping? . . . Put Daddy's eggs on the table . . . Daddy likes milk in his coffee . . . " I'm still too groggy to do anything more than nod my head, but that's okay. She chatters away throughout the day, and usually requires no response. Her dolls, her animals, the television, even a blank wall are things to talk to.

But sometimes her fantasy stories require an audience. At eight o'clock she calls me excitedly. "Mommy, Mommy! The trash man just came!" Her voice quivers and she waves her arms, jumping up and down with an enthusiasm that's impossible to resist. I stoop down to really listen. "He did? That's fantastic," I say.

"Yes, he did!" Shannon says seriously. "The truck ate all the trashes! He ate all the trashes!" She rushes to the window, points to the empty barrel, and rushes back to me. "He ate all the trees. The truck ate all the cars! He ate all the houses."

"Really, Shannon?"

"Oh yeah! He ate Michael's house. He ate the street!" She is still chattering as she goes to the other room to tell her story to her favorite bear.

I finish the breakfast dishes and send Shannon to her room to dress. Her clothes are laid out and she puts everything on herself, with some help with her shoes. She brushes her teeth, I brush her hair, and it's off to nursery school.

After school she has a quick lunch, and then straight to

a long nap. With her in bed are *four* security "blankies," one of her bears, and several dolls. She tells them all a story and sings to them for an hour before finally falling asleep.

She wakes from her nap crying and comes whining down the stairs. "Don't look at me. Don't, don't, don't!" she screams at Craig.

Craig teases back, "Shannon is a baby, nanny nanny billy goat." And so goes the afternoon. From three to six is always the worst time for both my kids.

I turn on the TV cartoons, which distract them both for a while, but soon they're sniping at each other again. This delightful afternoon drags on. Finally it's five-thirty and time for Daddy to come home. Both kids are watching for him at the window, all the fight magically gone. Dad and kids frolic, racing around the back yard, and then take the dog for a walk.

After dinner, Doug helps them with their baths and pajamas while I do the dishes. Then they pick out some books and come downstairs. The four of us read together, snuggled on the living-room couch, and all the day's tension disappears. We take them upstairs for tooth brushing, water, bedside songs, hugs and kisses. I turn off the light, turn on the night light, and we go downstairs.

Eight o'clock. How *quiet* the house is! An evening left to get in touch with my husband. It's hard not to utter a long, long sigh.

* * *

BUYING, FEEDING, DOCTORING

5

Clothing, Equipment, Toys and Books: What to Get Year by Year

Shopping for baby paraphernalia was often fun for us. It would have been even more fun if we had known then what we know now.

This chapter is designed to help you make wise buying decisions—ones you won't regret later. The section headed What You Do Need: The Basic Facts contains an alphabetical category-by-category listing of those things many mothers have found to be the most helpful to have, along with advice and opinions about the usefulness and the safety of these products. There is enough detail here to let you walk into a store and act like a seasoned parent.

Following the basic-facts section are direct quotes from mothers on how they would parcel out their child-related dollars differently if they could do the first three years over again. The one observation that was made most frequently? "We spent too much on toys and clothes, and not enough on babysitting."

At the end of this chapter is a year-by-year No-Frills Shopping List that represents the collective wisdom of many mothers regarding a sane minimum of equipment, clothes, toys, and books for the first three years. These items are what we would buy if we had it to do over again. We kept

138 / Mother to Mother

the list lean. If you follow it fairly closely, the clutter level caused by the new resident will be bearably low.

But first, some general advice on setting up your child-raising shop.

DON'T BUY IF YOU CAN BEG OR BORROW

Postpone buying stretch suits, sweater sets, stuffed toys, and blankets. Babies receive many as gifts. If you are overloaded with gifts in one category, some baby stores will exchange unneeded brand-name items for other things you do need.

Friends whose children have outgrown still-serviceable clothes and equipment will be eager to give or lend them to you. Take them. "If we were planning more children, I'd set up a swap-and-shop secondhand store," a forthright mother of one told us. "Now I constantly keep my baby supplies in circulation by lending them to trusted friends. Eventually I'll have a vasectomy sale and use the money for clothes, shoes, and toys suitable for my son now." There are many parents like her around, and all are a good source of free or inexpensive baby things.

However, another mother cautions, "I love to have friends give my kids hand-me-down clothes, but I make sure it's understood they won't be returned. I'm just not as meticulous about stains and buttons as lots of them are. If I had to worry about returning the stuff in the same condition it would drive me nuts."

Garage sales and thrift shops are the answer for many of us. Ask friends who frequent them to alert you when they stumble on a load of children's things.

Buy ahead. While the weather is still warm, check the thrift shops for jackets before you head for children's clothing stores.

Consider buying from catalogs. Even after postage and handling charges are added, catalog shopping is sometimes less expensive and certainly less brain-scrambling than touring the stores with an ornery baby or a 2-year-old. More important, you may never come across the best books, toys, or records in your local discount or department store. A walk through the pages of a school-supply catalog (see Resource List for addresses) can be more instructive than a day in a shopping center.

WHAT YOU DON'T NEED

What you don't need is guilt about not being able to buy everything on our No-Frills Shopping List or on any other list. No single item mentioned in this chapter will make or break your child's first three years. Love, energy, and ingenuity can cope with anything. Do without a cradle (use a pretty basket or a padded bureau drawer), a playpen (childproof the house), disposable diapers (wash prefolded ones), a crib (use a portable model).

But there *are* lots of handy things out there that can make your job easier. It is the informed setting of priorities that is important. This mother of one sounds like she knows herself, her house, and her baby: "Nobody needs a scale, and it's possible to borrow a swing and a walker. We did have a crib upstairs and a portacrib in the downstairs den so I didn't have to run the baby up and down for short naps. Everyone should have a rocking chair, though, and a bathroom near the baby's room. My umbrella stroller set me free and I feel a car seat that meets current safety standards is a must."

We agree. What we call the "mobility" items like the car restraint and umbrella stroller should be at or near the top of everyone's list. As for the many baby-oriented things not on our shopping list—the scale, walker, warming dish, bathinette, hobby horse, toy chest, and on and on—they fall into the "ignore it" or "if for free, take!" category.

Remember, too, that what is "essential" in one home may not be in another. We did not put a wind-up baby swing on the No-Frills Shopping List, for example, because of its expense in relation to the amount of use it will get in most households. However, the mother quoted below would take issue with this assessment:

"The three most worthwhile things we bought when the children were babies were an infant seat, a wind-up swing, and a changing table. There's nothing worse than a whining child, and from the time my kids were a month old whenever they started to whine I'd plop them in the swing with a pillow behind them—and it would rock them to sleep. The changing table was worth it (even though my husband thought we should use a dresser top) because I could hold the baby with one hand and reach everything I needed with the other."

Mother of two / Oklahoma City, Okla.

It seems clear that a swing could turn out to be either a regretted "clutter item" if you have a calm baby who dislikes jiggling or an essential godsend if you have a colicky infant who seems to need a lot of steady, soothing diversion. Just because something isn't on the No-Frills List doesn't mean it might not be of use to you. The list is what it says it is—there are no frills. If you're careful and take your time, you should be able to decide which of the many not-so-essential items may be worth buying for your baby.

Certainly one splurge on a real luxury—a ruffled bassinet, say, if you've always dreamed of having one—can be worth it. One mother, an antiques lover, stopped traffic in her New Jersey neighborhood for months as she wheeled her son about in a handsome sixty-year-old white wicker carriage lined with yellow gingham.

WHAT YOU DO NEED: THE BASIC FACTS

Following is a categorized list of everything you'll really need along with the necessary information to help you buy wisely. The categories included are: clothes and shoes, diapers, feeding implements, furniture, mobility equipment (including car restraints and strollers), toys, books and records.

Clothes

According to several experienced sales clerks in children's departments, mothers buy less than half the clothes children wear from birth to 3. The rest come as gifts or hand-me-downs. Mom buys the basics.

When buying clothes, stick to one color scheme. Red-white-blue is good, for example, because that combination is appropriate for children of both sexes and because those colors manage to look crisper than pastels do after a morning's hard wear. A white sweater in a washable material will go with everything. It also shows up at dusk in a supermarket parking lot or in the street. Light- or bright-colored jackets or sweaters are safer for children of all ages.

"As far as clothes go, I would have been even more firm about discouraging friends and relatives from buying all those fancy little outfits when I really needed more stretch sleep-and-play suits, T-shirts, plastic pants, and so on. Joe rarely wore 'real' clothes until he was 6 months old, and he never complained. I believe he was more comfortable and easy-going because we didn't fuss with fancy clothes."

Mother of one / Milwaukee, Wisc.

Don't buy anything that isn't machine washable and reasonably well made. When buying or making overalls or jumpers, choose buckle fasteners instead of buttons so that you won't need to move buttons every few months as the child grows.

A young child's job is to learn to use her body. Clothing that does not interfere with this work is essential. Most of the time you can dress your child in sturdy, practical clothing. This often means long pants for little girls, too. In hot weather, an infant may be happiest dressed only in a diaper and a cotton T-shirt.

A pediatrician we know warns against dressing children in synthetics in hot weather: "Cotton and wool 'breathe,' but synthetics don't. It's like sealing them up to put them in synthetics on a really hot day." She also warns against bundling children in too many clothes in cool weather. One California teacher says, "I can tell the kids are going to be perspiring by ten a.m. on a rainy day. Some mothers here think it's snowing when we get a little rain."

"The most expensive are not always the best, especially in play clothes. When a lot of money is invested in clothes, you feel you should hand them down no matter how bad they look on the second child."

Mother of three / Portland, Me.

What about pajamas? Do you buy ones chemically treated for fire retardancy, and then breathe easy with the knowledge that they won't ignite fast from a dropped match? Or do you buy untreated fabric, make your own, and stay free from the fear of possible cancer-causing chemicals while you worry about fire?

Tris, the fire-retardant substance suspected of causing cancer in animals, was banned by the Consumer Product Safety Commission in 1977. It was once used in over half of all children's sleepwear made in the United States. You may want to avoid hand-me-down pajamas if they contain *acetate, triacetate, polyester,* or *polyester-cotton* combinations, in all of which Tris or its questionable substitute Fyrol has been used. (Three washings remove the surface Tris, but there is disagreement over whether this takes care of the danger.)

A CPSC spokesman advises parents to ask retailers whether a garment has been chemically treated. If you don't get a satisfactory answer, don't buy. There are, after all, several fabrics that are inherently flame retardant (modacrylic, vinyon, matrix, wool), and others can be made so without the use of chemicals.

Recognizing the possible danger of the chemicals, the CPSC is now suggesting that all flammability standards be dropped for *infant* sleepwear on the ground that small babies are not mobile and therefore are less exposed to fire sources than older children.

If you would like additional information in this area, call the CPSC toll-free consumer hotline for advice: 800-638-8326.

Shoes

Children of 5 or younger account for almost one-fourth of the sales of the U.S. shoe industry. You can count on buying a new pair of shoes about every four to six months after a child starts walking. Unless the doctor recommends otherwise, a child is as well off with a pair of sturdy sneakers as anything else. They provide good traction for climbing ladders and for confident running.

If your child toes in or out, your doctor may advise buying high-top orthopedic shoes. These are not so expensive in the long run as they seem at first because they wear well and take the place of both sneakers and dress shoes. And the cost may be tax deductible as a medical expense.

"My boys never wore shoes until they walked and then they wore tennies outside and bare feet inside. Children's feet *do* develop just fine without white leather combat boots in size 3 at $18 or more a pair!"

Mother of two / Birmingham, Ala.

Although sandals are easier to fasten than sneakers or orthopedic shoes, and although they look fine without socks, if you have ever watched a child trying to run in sandals, curling his toes in an attempt to get traction, you may reconsider. One orthopedic specialist warns, "Two hours in a pair of sandals undoes the good of wearing orthopedic shoes for a month."

"Kids learn to buckle long before they can tie knots. From 2 on, I buy my girls oxfords that buckle, and that's one more thing they can do for themselves."

Mother of three / Pikeville, Ky.

Socks that are too tight are as bad as shoes that are too small. Good socks, made largely of cotton, are worth the extra money. Many brands come with color marks knit into the toes to help in sorting if you wash clothes for more than one child.

Diapers

Cloth or disposable? A good case can be made for either kind. You will use roughly eighty diapers a week during the first year, fifty a week the second year, thirty-five a week the third year. Here are some considerations.

Money. Disposables, in the long run, will cost about four times as much as cloth diapers washed at home in a machine, if you consider the labor of the diaper washer to be free. The cost of diaper service is somewhere in the middle.

Time. A diaper washer will spend many hours a week at the job during the first year. Using cloth diapers requires presoaking, occasional bleaching, washing, rinsing, drying, folding, and putting away.

Convenience. Using disposables is easier for many families. The rubber-pants step is usually nonexistent. Fathers, baby-sitters, and grandparents seem less fearful of changing a wiggling baby if they don't have to worry about puncturing her. When no pins are involved, a squirming, impatient child can be tackled more easily—from front or rear, standing or sitting. You can throw away disposables in a plastic bag when you are traveling or visiting instead of accumulating a soggy pile to take home.

Ecology. Many ecologically concerned parents reject disposable diapers as being wasteful; they feel that the extra effort required to maintain cloth diapers is a small price to pay for the cause of conservation of natural resources. They tend, however, to overlook the energy needed to run washers, dryers, and hot-water heaters as well as the fact that few detergents are ecologically harmless. As for throwaways, the American Paper Institute claims that they add no new or dangerous materials to the environment. These claims notwithstanding, conservationists in Oregon are attempting to ban the sale of disposables because, they say, these diapers clog land fills and take too long to biodegrade.

Sanitation authorities advise parents who use throwaway diapers to follow manufacturers' directions for disposal in order to avoid causing sewage problems. If your house has a septic tank or cesspool, most plumbers advise you *not* to flush away the absorbent material that serves as the middle part of the disposable diaper "sandwich." When you're away from home, save your friends from potential plumbing problems; put disposables into a plastic bag and toss that into the household garbage.

"When it came to diapers, I tried everything. The costs of disposables and diaper service were so high that I changed to cloth ones and laundered them myself. I did, however, use disposable diapers at night because they seemed more absorbent."   *Mother of one / Creve Coeur, Mo.*

"I bought my disposable diapers by the case from a wholesale grocer who was willing to deal with the public. It saved us a little money and even more time."
                              Mother of two / Palos Verdes, Calif.

Anne Henry wore only disposables for two and a half years. Jonas and David Sills wore cloth diapers washed at home. Both of us believe that we would do it the same way again.

After analyzing the costs of disposables, diaper service and washing diapers at home, Lee Edwards Benning recommends all three in her book *How to Bring Up a Child Without Spending a Fortune:* diaper service for the first six months (free pail, free deodorant cakes, less chance of not noticing the need for a change and hence less diaper rash), do-it-yourself cheap the second year (without extra rinses needed to prevent diaper rash in the young infant), disposables the third year (pressure taken out of toilet training).

Whatever you decide, remember that disposables are handy for travel and that cloth diapers are handy when you run out of disposables. And, by the way, soft, used cloth diapers make the world's best cleaning rags.

Feeding Implements

Few of us use glass bottles anymore. The plastic kind is lighter to hold, of course, and has the nice bonus that it doesn't break when tossed away by a toddler. Nursers are another form of bottle—cylindrical plastic forms that hold flexible plastic bags which in turn hold the milk, formula, water, juice, or whatever. These are thrown away after use; replacement bags cost only pennies each.

The bags on nursers collapse as the baby drinks, so less air is taken in with the liquid, which makes the burping procedure less bothersome. Older babies, however, can rip off the bags and make a sodden mess of things, and nursers can leak when put into a diaper bag. Still, it's nice not to have to scrub out bottles every day. Actually, neither plastic bottles nor nursers are particularly expensive items (as baby paraphernalia goes), so you may want to buy a set of each to see which you prefer. One nurser manufacturer sells a "trial kit" for a dollar or two.

"Buy feeding spoons with very small bowls. Resist the temptation to buy the kind with rubberized bowls, which are sold in many supermarkets. For one thing, they taste awful, and for another they're too big."

Mother of two / Las Vegas, Nev.

Nipples are important. Whatever kind comes with your bottles, make sure the liquid doesn't come out too easily and that the nipple doesn't go too far into the baby's mouth— it should only reach the roof of the mouth.

Furniture

No single piece of furniture is essential. We know a mother who even did without a crib by borrowing a portable model and using it until her child was a year old. Thereafter, the child slept on a normal-size mattress on the floor until she was 3, when the parents put a bed frame under the mattress. What equipment you get depends on how much room you have—and, of course, on your budget.

Portable crib. This is useful in many ways. If you plan to do exchange sitting or to invite a friend with a baby over for the day, it's handy to have another crib for the second child. Most portable models fold up to fit into the trunk of a car. A wooden model, with the mattress in the highest position, can serve as a changing table; with the mattress in the lowest position, it can be used as a small playpen. Mesh and aluminum versions, although less sturdy than wood, are lighter to carry.

"My portable crib has been so useful. It was a shower gift accompanied by a long yellow skirt my sister made. It has served as a bassinet, playpen, crib on vacation, and now as a bed for small visitors."   *Mother of three / Scranton, Pa.*

"A handy thing we came up with was to take the floor and front wheels off our old wooden portacrib, making it super light so that it could be carried across the beach or through a bowling alley. We punched holes in the corner of a waterproof pad that had been cut to replace the floor and tied it into the crib. The result was a baby who could go anywhere comfortably contained in an area small enough not to be in the way."   *Mother of one / St. Petersburg, Fla.*

Standard crib. This is one of the most important purchases you will make in terms of the length of time a child will use it. In 1973 the federal government set standards for crib safety after a study showed that crib accidents resulted in 150 to 200 deaths and 50,000 injuries each year. Infants could get their heads stuck in between the slats or in the gaps between the crib sides and mattress. The maximum space now allowed between slats is just under two and a half inches. Inside dimensions are fixed so that a standard-size crib mattress fits snugly.

Babies used to be able to roll out of some cribs if the drop side was down. Older toddlers could climb out over a raised side. To prevent the former accident, standards now require that the top of the lowered side be at least nine inches above the mattress support at its highest position. To make it tough on climbing toddlers, the top of the raised side must now be at least twenty-six inches above the mattress support at its lowest position. (Mothers of climbers at some point give in to reality and keep the drop side down all the time and the mattress in the lowest position. They also place a soft rug, with a pad under it, on the floor at the side of the crib.)

"I think a sturdy, good-quality crib is a good investment if you plan to have more than one child, but I wouldn't keep a child in a crib much past the age of 2. Both my children could climb out before then. My son, who will be 3 next month, is getting a bed as a birthday present; he's now sleeping in a sleeping bag on the floor because he insists that cribs are for babies."   *Mother of two / Dallas, Tex.*

If you are given a hand-me-down crib or if you buy a secondhand crib or one made in another country, check it for all of the above safety standards. Since all *new* cribs sold now are reasonably safe, the only consideration, other than price and style, is whether to have a single or double drop side. We see no advantage in spending the extra money for double drop sides, since most cribs are put against a wall on one side anyway.

Don't worry if the crib seems a little wobbly. Most are not rigid, but that doesn't mean they aren't stable. A metal stabilizer bar helps a little, but a crib without a bar will hold up just as well. The drop-side mechanisms on most cribs are foot-operated, but you also have to lift the top rail as you press the foot lever. This means that an accidental bump against the foot lever by an older child will not release the crib side.

Most cribs (and playpens) come with plastic teething rails. If you have an older crib, you can buy new teething rails at well-stocked baby-equipment stores.

Mattresses are sold separately. A sturdy inner-spring mattress is worth the investment, particularly if you expect to have more than one child. Be sure to buy a plastic-zippered mattress protector for it. The same mattress can be used on some youth beds for children long past crib age. Also sold separately are bumper pads that go around the top of the mattress to cushion the baby's head and prevent arms and legs from getting wedged between bars. (Often an infant placed in the middle of a crib will work her way into a position in which her head is against the pad, where, perhaps, she feels more secure.) Get a set of pads that tie or snap around the crib bars in six places. Clip off any parts of strips hanging loose so that the baby can't chew on them, and remove the pads entirely when the baby starts pulling herself up; otherwise, the pads may collapse under her and her head may be pushed into the bars.

"Crib mattresses are handy long after your child's in a regular bed. We put ours on the floor at the side of our son's big bed while he got used to sleeping in it. Later we built a platform and put the mattress on top to use as the base of a couch for his room. One of my friends removed one of the sliding doors from her daughter's wall-length closet and put the crib mattress on the closet floor, where it served as her bed until she was 5. That way the whole room was a giant playroom, and she decorated the sleeping part so it looked like a cozy hideaway."   *Mother of two / Des Moines, Iowa*

High chair. Do not get an antique. An old wood one may look wonderful next to an oak table, but it can swing and sway dangerously with the weight of an antsy child. Today's models, with legs set far apart, are much safer. A rambunctious child will be in it for hours every day, from the time she sits up until she can sit on a telephone book at the table with adults.

Each year high chairs are involved in some 7,000 injuries serious enough to require treatment in hospital emergency rooms. A safety belt or harness for the very young child is a must. A good one is easy to put on and fasten and holds a child so tightly that standing up is impossible. A crotch strap running from the front of the seat to a waist strap will keep the child from slipping under the tray and then down to the floor. Perhaps even better than a strap for a very young baby is an inexpensive fabric "safe chair" we've seen in well-stocked baby shops. It can be used on high chairs in restaurants, which often do not have straps; for an older baby, it can be used to convert a regular chair into a high chair at Grandma's.

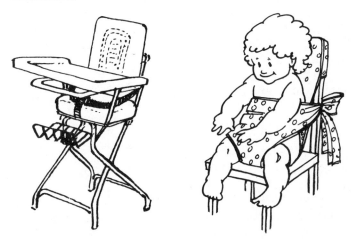

After safety, ease of cleaning should be the next consideration. Food gets caught everywhere. A folding model is easier to store if you want to hide it during a dinner party or put it in the trunk of the car, but it may not be as sturdy as other models.

The tray should be the large, wraparound kind that gives support to the child's elbows, and the tray edges should be raised so as to catch the worst of the spills. The tray should be removable so it can be washed at the sink after a meal, and it should lock firmly but easily into place. Plastic makes a quiet surface for the beginning drummer. The foot rest should be adjustable. Also, consider how the chair would fit without the tray at the adult eating table, since a 2-year-old may enjoy eating with the family.

A last word on high chairs: Do *not* do as Anne's mother did—push the high chair up to the sink and let a child play at "watering" plants and "cooking." Anne slipped one day, fell to the floor, and jarred a front tooth loose.

Feeding table. Instead of a high chair, you may want to use a close-to-the-ground feeding table. The advantage here is that there is much less distance to fall and less chance of it because the child is propped in the middle of a square table. (In some convertible models the seat back flips down to make a play table when the child is older.) One disadvantage is that sometimes it's nice to have the whole family, including the baby, up there at adult-table level for dinner. Also, the shape of these tables is usually square and larger than a conventional high chair, which can make it awkward to have in a small kitchen (but they can be stored under the regular dining table when not in use). Other points to consider: it can be hard on a mother's back to feed a child who is in a feeding table instead of in a high chair, and it's harder to put a baby in and get her out than it is with a high chair.

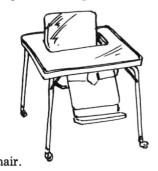

Child's table and chair. The sooner the high chair goes, the better. Even the best have a degree of risk. A 2-year-old wants to explore and to feel that he can control his own movements. A high chair is soon a prison to him—or, worse, a ladder to get to alluring heights. We believe that a table and a chair at which a child can spread out his things and work or play or eat is the most important piece of furniture to buy, after the crib.

The larger the table, the better. Jeanne found a sturdy Parsons table in an unfinished-furniture store and covered it with oilcloth. From the same store, she got two attractive, sturdy spindle-back children's chairs. Childcraft and other school suppliers have wonderfully sturdy tables, some with adjustable legs, and chairs to match.

For the longest possible use of a growing child, get a comfortable chair with a seat roughly thirteen inches from the floor. The table should be at least twenty by thirty inches on top and twenty-two to twenty-four inches high. The space between table top and chair seat should be eight to ten inches, to allow for knee room. You will find such a table and chair more useful than any dozen toys.

One school supplier includes the chart below in its catalog.

Age	Chair Height	Table Height
1½ - 2	9"	16"
3 - 5	10"	18"
4 - 5	12"	20"
5 - 7	14"	22"
Adult	17"	26"

"My son is 5 and for over three years he's spent a large part of every day 'working' at his table in the kitchen. Even when he's watching TV, he's usually back and forth visiting some project he's got going on the table."

Mother of one / New York, N.Y.

Playpen. When you shop for a playpen, remember that a mesh-sided model is lighter if you expect to move it around much, although a wood version might be more pleasant to look at in the living room.

Safety hazards to be aware of: buttons or fingers can get caught in mesh, and some children learn to climb out by putting their toes through the holes. In wood models, the spacing between slats should be the same as that for cribs.

Changing table. Instead of the conventional type, which you will probably get rid of when the child nears 2, consider using a low chest of drawers covered with a foam pad. (But don't use the drawers for the baby's everyday things—holding a baby with one hand and rummaging in a drawer with the other is dangerous.) A portable crib raised to its highest position might also do. All these alternatives require a table or shelf nearby for diapers and equipment. The basic necessities are a sturdy surface at a comfortable height for Mom; shelf space for diapers, clothes, and a container of water; a roll of toilet paper attached to the wall out of baby's reach; and a wastebasket.

Jeanne's diaper center for Anne's first few months was a portable crib. After that she used the large counter area adjacent to the bathroom sink. Anne's clothes were kept in the cupboard underneath. Jonas and David had a conventional changing table, and Barbara thought it well worth the expense.

Mobility Equipment

We've observed that new parents who seem to come through the first three years most happily get out of the house often. Today's umbrella stroller, backpacks, and car seats make the baby carriages of our childhood seem like dinosaurs. No wonder it's so much easier now to take the baby everywhere than it was for our parents.

This "new" equipment is not really new. For centuries Navajo mothers have used a cradle board that resembles a cross between an infant seat and a backpack. Infants in Bali are rarely laid down, even when asleep. Their mothers carry them around in net bags slung around their necks and supported on their hips. One traveler who recently visited Bali saw 8-year-old girls playing tag with babies in nets on their backs.

We recommend that new parents get these items before anything else:

Infant carrier. We've used this term to mean any fabric or leather sling or wrap in which an infant who does not yet sit up can be held against the parent's chest or back or supported on one hip. Some mothers prefer a sling or "pleat seat" that cradles the infant between arm and hip. Other mothers prefer a sturdy carrier that can be worn in front or in back, leaving both hands free for cooking, raking leaves, walking, or bicycling.

"When I was nursing and we took family outings—hikes, visits to museums, antiquing, or birdwatching—so I could get out but still be able to nurse also, we used the frontwrap carrier. Now that the baby's older, we go out after his nap and put him in the backpack. We go places you could never go with a carriage or even a stroller."

Mother of one / Omaha, Neb.

Infant seat. This is a lightweight plastic inclined seat with a waist and crotch strap that can be used with infants up to the age of 5 or 6 months. The seat is helpful for feeding, for trips to the grocery store (some fit nicely in the front section of grocery carts), and for any time one wants to gently confine a child but allow her to see what's going on. In hot weather, for example, an infant seat may be more comfortable for her than Mom's arms. Get as sturdy-looking a version as you can find; it should have a base that is larger than the seat so that it won't tip over and seat adjustments that hold securely in each position. Some 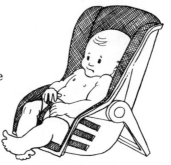 models have rockers as a base; we don't think this is at all necessary. Be sure, always, to use the strap, and be sure the seat is on the floor, not a countertop, if you leave the room for even a moment. *Never* use infant seats as car seats. They aren't strong enough to provide protection in an accident.

Backpack. After a child can sit up by himself and support his own back and head fairly well, he probably weighs enough so that an aluminum-frame-and-canvas pack is more comfortable for the parent than an infant carrier. Moreover, the child now wants a clear view of everything—not just his parent's shirt. One model has padded straps adjustable to fit either parent, a padded chin rest for the baby, an adjustable inner seat so the baby sits lower as he gets bigger, a "seat belt" to keep the baby from slipping out or crawling up your neck, and a folding stand that lets you prop both pack

and child on the ground during a rest stop. Many of these carriers can be used for children weighing up to twenty-five pounds. Try out different models for comfort (using your own or borrowed baby) before you buy one.

"I never thought I was the type to walk around with a baby in a pack on my back, but I do. It's the only way to cook dinner when the baby's crotchety and it's the only way to shop with both hands free."

Mother of two / New Haven, Conn.

Car restraints. Infants are so fragile that they can be badly injured by even a minor accident. For children 1 through 4, auto accidents are the leading cause of death.

Clearly, restraining a child in a moving auto makes sense. A 3-year-old who has always ridden in a car restraint does not object to being confined in this way, and he can't roll down the windows, throw things out of the car, open the door, or otherwise distract the driver. At least one study has shown that children who ride in car restraints behave better in the car than those who do not.

Why not use the adult seat belt to restrain a child and prevent serious injury in case of an accident? Most safety experts say a lap belt buckled over a child's hips is better than no restraint at all, but in a severe crash a lap belt used alone for a baby or child could possibly cause internal injuries. A young child needs devices designed to distribute the force of impact over a large area of her body. Also, you should never ride with a child on your lap and the seat belt around you both; in a crash, your own weight—greatly increased by collision—would force the belt to cut deeply into your child, which could cause serious or even fatal injuries. A car safety "seat" or a harness held in place by an adult lap belt is essential for children under 4 who weigh less than forty pounds.

"We had our accident a block from home—I did $1,000
worth of damage to the front end of our car late one afternoon when I was blinded by the sun coming over the top of
the hill and plowed right into a parked car. Thank God it
was one of the times my daughter was strapped into her car
seat. Even now it's hard for me to make myself buckle her
in, but I do it. And I make my husband and my friends in
the car pool do it too."

Mother of one / San Francisco, Calif.

What kind of car restraint should you buy?

The best single thing a busy parent can do to find out is
to get the latest edition of "Don't Risk Your Child's Life,"
a pamphlet published by Physicians for Automotive Safety.
To order, send 35 cents and a long, stamped, self-addressed
envelope to: PAS, P.O. Box 208, Rye, New York 10580.
This organization keeps up with changes in car-restraint
technology, and in its frequently revised pamphlet gives a
list of safe crash-tested devices, complete with brand names
and model numbers plus other very useful information. If
you study this pamphlet you will know a lot more about
the restraints than do most of the salesmen in places where
they are sold.

Beyond studying the pamphlet, a parent about to buy a
car restraint should keep in mind these practical considerations brought up by mothers:

1. *Will the model fit in your car?* Try the model you're considering *in your car* before you decide to buy it. Some bucket seats, for example, are not large enough to hold some
models; or the back seat of your car may not be deep enough
to hold some convertible models; or your seat belts may not
be long enough to stretch across rear-facing infant seats.

2. *Will a toddler or older child be able to see out?* A baby
may not care, but an older child *wants* to be able to see the
world go by. What's more, parents enjoy pointing out the
passing parade and talking about it with their child. This is
probably the biggest reason why many parents buy two car
restraints: for an infant, a rear-facing bucket-type seat that
can be used as a carrier-feeder-sleeper when you reach your
destination; for an older baby or young child, an elevated

model that faces forward. Many safe models are available that fit both stages, but they don't always allow the older child to see out.

"Here's something you wouldn't think of unless you already have a child. It makes it easier for you to get them in the seat if they know that when they get in it they can see out. And I think it helps keep them from getting car sick when they can see." *Mother of two / Minneapolis, Minn.*

3. *Does the model you want have to be tethered?* Safety experts have called the top-tethered seats preferable to any other kind—*if* you do the tethering. This is very important. If the seat is in front you must anchor a strap attached to the top of the restraint onto a rear seat belt; if the seat is in the back, you must anchor the strap onto a permanent latch installed by drilling a hole through the steel support of the rear package shelf. There is talk of making the anchor fixture mandatory in all new cars, but until that time parents must go to the inconvenience and expense of installing the anchor fixture themselves in every family vehicle. (Extra anchor hardware is available at well-stocked baby stores.) Safety experts are appalled by studies of cars in supermarket parking lots which show that 80 percent of the tether straps are not in use or are installed improperly. This could mean that in an accident the car seat itself could slam forward and back, taking the child with it. *Unless you plan to follow through on tethering, safety experts warn that your child will be far safer riding in a device designed to give crash protection without the need for top anchoring.*

4. *Is a harness or a shield used to keep the child in the car seat?* The regular seat belt keeps the car *restraint* in place in a crash. A harness or shield keeps the *child* in place in the *restraint* in a way that distributes the force of impact all over his body. Although safety experts praise the shield, an especially active child can wriggle out of it while you're driving, and in warm weather the shield may trap heat. But a harness is no picnic to attach either.

5. *Is the restraint sturdy?* Most models are built to last a while but some are sturdier than others. Some mothers told

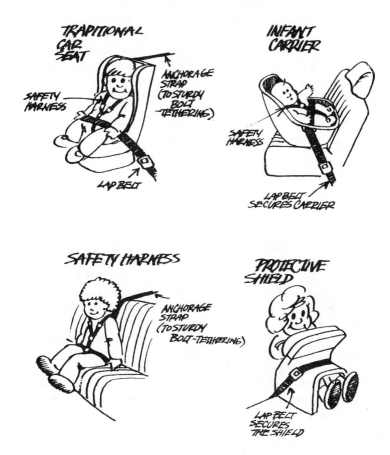

us their heavy molded-plastic restraints survived being tossed unboxed into baggage compartments of planes for trips to grandma's. Others mentioned they were disappointed that padding and foam rubber on other models was chewed up and grubby-looking after use by just one child.

6. *What can you afford?* If cost is a big factor, consider the following. In more than twenty states and Canada, Jaycee **auxiliary groups** sponsor a "Buckle Up Babes" program **through which** you can *rent* an infant car restraint for nine **months at a** reasonable price. Also, since many infant-size

bucket-seat restraints are used only until the baby sits up well by herself, they are often available at the garage sales. Or, since they are virtually indestructible, many mothers are happy to lend infant seats to others. For an older baby or young child the least expensive safe car restraint is probably a safety harness that is secured with a lap belt and a top tether strap. The child can sit on a cushion for elevation.

"My son is 3 and doesn't take naps anymore, but he does take cat naps when we're riding in the car. I'm so glad we got one of the restraints with side panels that he can lean his head against. He looks quite comfortable during these naps, and his head doesn't flop around while he sleeps."
Mother of one / Charleston, W. Va.

At this time the government still does not require simulated-crash testing of child safety seats and harnesses (although it is expected to do so soon.) Many manufacturers have gone ahead and done this on their own. Private consumer groups like Consumers Union also do testing and organizations like Physicians for Automotive Safety keep track of which devices are crash-tested and have been proven safe. So be sure that whatever restraint you get has been *approved by consumer organizations*.

Proper use is as important as choosing a safe style. Be sure you understand how to use all the gadgets and straps the manufacturer includes, and then make yourself use them —not an easy task, we know from personal experience. A small pillow facilitates sleeping in most restraints designed for the older baby and young child. On long trips try to stop at least every hour so children can run about. Babies should be taken from the infant car restraints and allowed to lie on their stomachs and kick for a few minutes.

Remember that it is best if your child rides in the back seat unless, for some reason, you must supervise her closely. The center of the rear seat is the safest spot of all.

Car beds. As of this writing, we know of no kind of infant car bed that provides the safety of a car restraint, and federal safety regulations do not yet cover car beds. They're dangerous because they just don't restrain a child sufficiently. Rather than a car bed, use a car restraint. Medical experts agree that sleeping in a semi-upright position in a car restraint does not harm an infant or young child. You should, however, put a rolled-up receiving blanket around a newborn's head and shoulders to provide additional support.

"A car bed was one of my musts, although I never used it in the car. Instead, I used it in the house, moving my baby's resting place from room to room. I also took it with me when we visited friends so I could stow the baby in a back room in his own bed."   *Mother of two / Santa Fe, N.M.*

Strollers. An umbrella stroller is invaluable. Lightweight and collapsible, it can be carried on one of your arms via its "umbrella" type handles. You can carry it onto planes and use it the minute you get off. You can go up escalators, into elevators, onto buses, over sand, up steps, and into the houses of friends, where it serves as a seat and snoozing spot. Umbrella strollers weigh as little as five pounds and can be used from the time an infant can hold his head up until, as a 2-year-old, he gets tired at the zoo. Since they are light and have aluminum frames, they are not as sturdy as conventional strollers; a baby or child should never be left unattended so that he might tip it over. Don't bother with the sun-screen attachment, but you may want the optional snap-on carrying pouch for shopping.

   If you live in a neighborhood where you will do a lot of walking on sidewalks, a sturdy collapsible stroller may be your choice. It is a far more useful purchase than a carriage,

FOLDING UMBRELLA STROLLER

STURDIER STROLLER

which is needed for only six months or so. A conventional stroller can hold more packages than an umbrella stroller, and even a boisterous 2-year-old would have a hard time tipping it over. Some have reclining seats for napping and room for an older child to ride standing up. A model that folds up for compact storage in a hall closet or car trunk is useful.

Toys

Most of the mothers we questioned said they would spend less on toys during the years from birth to 3 if they had it to do over. It is all too easy to buy the wrong toys for the wrong reasons. One of the most sensible shoppers we know admitted: "Whenever I was depressed when Jeff was a toddler, I'd go out and buy him a toy." According to one psychologist the average 18-month-old plays with the average toy designed for that age for an average of ninety seconds.

Long before a child is 3 he senses his parents' values through their attitudes toward toys, books, and television. He also observes how much time we allot to such active pursuits as walks and visits with other children. Our values are revealed by the relative importance we attach to each of these activities.

What about "educational" toys? The American Academy of Pediatrics' Committee on the Infant and Preschool Child has stated that parents may be wasting money if they buy "developmental" toys in the hope of increasing a child's IQ. And psychologist James Kavanagh, director of the National Institute of Child Health and Human Development, believes that the least boring and most educational toys for preschool children are homemade.

Always consider the real version of something before you buy a toy. A real plastic lunchbox and plastic-lined vacuum bottle are prized by a 2-year-old. The same goes for a real hammer and nails used under supervision, a real used typewriter instead of a plastic toy model, and a real record player (when she nears 4)—perhaps one from a school-supply house. It will outlast a toy phonograph by ten years. Here are some other everyday household items that can double as "educational" toys.

For the child under 1 year. Telephone with button taped down, measuring spoons, coasters, transistor radio, cylindrical oatmeal box decorated with colored tape, box or drawer filled with safe kitchen utensils, masking tape, paper bags, nesting plastic or metal bowls.

From 1 to 2. Wooden bowl filled with walnuts in their shells, bowl of water and sponge, a new plumber's helper of his own, paper plates and cups, flour sifter, colander plus a shoestring knotted at one end to thread in and out, and inexpensive scrapbooks or albums filled with cut-out magazine pictures of animals, shapes, numbers, or colors.

From 2 to 3. Brown wrapping paper taped to a wall for large-scale artworks, padlock and key, real magnet and real bolts, card table covered by a sheet to make a cave, a small tray holding tongs and several small objects, flashlight, a box full of hats and shoes from a thrift shop, alphabet letters cut from sheets of sandpaper, basket of poker chips.

For the few conventional toys that we and many other mothers consider classics and absolutely worth buying both for fun and development, see the No-Frills Shopping List at the end of this chapter. Above all, as one mother of four told us, "Try not to get into the habit of buying a small cheap toy for your children every time you go out. Let them carry one around the store, if necessary, because usually a small child will lose interest by the time you get to the checkout."

Consider safety. More than 900 manufacturers of toys, games, and craft kits fight it out in this fiercely competitive industry. Understandably, perhaps, some of them are more concerned about financial survival than safety. The Child Protection and Safety Act gives the FDA the power to outlaw toys that do not meet its safety standards. The body that checks up on toys is the Consumer Product Safety Commission. Since it was formed, it has banned 1,500 toys— that is, *after* children were hurt. Toys are *not* tested by the commission before they go on the market. Unlike cribs, toys for sale may be unsafe. (If you want to obtain or report information about hazardous toys, write to the Toy Safety Review Committee, Bureau of Product Safety, U.S. Food and Drug Administration, 5401 W. Bard Ave., Bethesda, Maryland 20016.)

When buying toys for infants, avoid those that have

cords longer than twelve inches, that are small enough to swallow, and that have parts (such as button eyes) that can fall off or be picked off and swallowed.

Know your toddler's personality. If he's a fledgling major-league pitcher, make sure his toys are soft and pliable. Check all toys frequently for loose parts or sharp edges. Also, make sure that a toy is appropriate to your child's age. Many toy manufacturers print a recommended age on toy packages, which protects them in case of accidents if younger children use the toys.

Before you buy a toy, consider whether it demands active involvement by the child. Will it help him work off energy? Will it encourage him to use his imagination? Such toys as balls, tricycles, blocks, and finger puppets are, we feel, well worth the money. Mechanical or battery-operated toys usually are not. One mother changed her toy-buying habits, she told us, when her 20-month-old child showed her a beautifully carved wooden duck and asked, "How does it work, Mommy?"

"Our all-time best toys: a combination blackboard-pegboard desk set (for 18 months and older), tyke bike, hot-wheels tricycle, Mattel's shopping cart, puzzles, cash register, assortment of hats, and 'Sesame Street' and story records."
Mother of two / Nashville, Tenn.

We recommend that you maintain a stack of toy catalogs (see Resource List) and buy through them instead of shopping with children in tow, at least during the first three years. Or, better yet, "shop" by exchanging toys with friends or using a toy loan library, if any civic group operates one in your area.

A mother of an energetic 3-year-old boy said the best thing she'd bought during the past year was a punching bag from a school-supply house. And many other mothers mentioned that instead of buying many small toys they wish they had invested in a dome climber or other outdoor exercise toy (see the Resource List for names of school suppliers who are good sources for these toys). We hope an entrepreneur will one day open a *rental* operation for this kind of expensive equipment, which becomes more attractive the farther you live from trees and empty lots or hillsides where children can move freely and expend energy.

"Beware of toys with many small pieces, although some get lots of use, such as the Fisher Price Village, Gas Station, etc. Nothing can clutter a house more easily than a toddler and a toy with thirty-two pieces!"
Mother of two / Detroit, Mich.

"I buy a lot of toys cheaply at garage and yard sales, and I have an unstructured toy exchange with two friends. I also buy new toys on sale after Christmas and save them for rainy days and to give as birthday presents for the children's friends." *Mother of four / Seattle, Wash.*

A parent is capable of appreciating a twenty-dollar doll. A 2-year-old is not. If you have spent a lot of money on a toy, the temptation to pressure your child to play with it spoils some of the fun.

In the end, the best toys are the ones we can share with our children. David Sills' father, a commercial artist, spread a "Sesame Street" mural over two walls of his son's bedroom and later built with him a book of drawings about David's daily life. The book is in shreds from almost daily reading over six years. Anne Henry and her father, an engineer, have some of their best times together with a large set of wood blocks, building steep roads, tunnels, and castles on the living-room coffee table.

Books

Of the 40,000 children's books in print in the United States today, which ones are worth buying? There's the rub. Many of us, in the course of hurried visits to the library, bookstore, or market, snatch up a colorful-looking book only to be disappointed when it fails to interest our toddler and bores us on the first reading.

The books on our No-Frills Shopping List are described in detail below. These are the ones we consider worth buying or reserving at the library. They are the ones we wish we had bought ahead of time, the ones not to be missed in the rush of life. All have been recommended by many parents and librarians, and all delighted our own children. Many can be appreciated on two levels—while the child enjoys the story, the adult can genuinely savor the art or wit.

There are hundreds of other good books. Many of the best are decades old. In the mysterious ways that allow the fittest to survive, those books have lasted because they have been loved.

The first mention of specific children's books to buy is on the part of our No-Frills Shopping List for 1- and 2-year-olds, but you may want to buy two of these books even sooner. These are the "toy" books, such as Dorothy Kunhardt's *Pat the Bunny* (one page has a felt bunny to touch, another has a mirror) and H. A. Rey's *Anybody at Home?* (lift the flaps and see what lives in a garage, a snail shell, a house, a bird's nest).

We like the Dr. Seuss *Cat in the Hat Dictionary* enough to put on the list for a 1-year-old and up because the illustrations are simple and some are humorous. A picture dictionary helps a toddler increase her vocabulary and thus make more sense of her world.

Mother Goose collections, elegant or simple, are fun, particularly for the sounds and the exercises in fantasy they offer. *The Rooster Crows*, a book of American rhymes and jingles first published in 1945, has finger games a child will like at 18 months, illustrations of "Lazy Mary" and "Engine Engine Number Nine" that a parent will savor, and even a few prize rope-skipping rhymes.

At some time during the second year a child will be ready for a simple story told in few words. In *Goodnight Moon* by Margaret Wise Brown, which has less than 130 words, after a bunny is tucked into bed, he whispers goodnight to the familiar things in his comfortable room. After dozens of readings, your child may notice the tiny mouse that appears in a different spot in each picture of the bunny nursery, where a fire is lit and a nanny rabbit rocks away. The phrases rhyme; the room grows darker; the moon appears outside the window. It's no surprise to us that this is the best-selling children's book at a big Los Angeles bookstore noted for its collection of children's books.

"My children's favorite 'books' since the age of 1½ have been real photo albums. I put the best pictures we take of each child doing various things into albums that become each child's property. At 5, Melissa is on her fifth album, and Burt, nearly 3, is close to the end of his second. They get *immense* pleasure from looking at themselves as infants and in remembering things like playing in the snow, what their birthday cake looked like, and their first swimming lesson."

Mother of two / Lawndale, Calif.

The Golden Song Book makes a nice change from reading stories. There are attractive illustrations and simple arrangements for piano of fifty-six classic songs and singing games. This book, first published by Golden Press in 1945, had its twenty-sixth printing in 1974.

A book can subtly teach a child about paradox while offering a practical message. In *Play with Me* a child learns that she can try *too* hard, as she grabs at a grasshopper, frog, and other wildlife during a morning visit to a meadow. When she gives up and sits quietly on a rock watching a bug, all the insects and animals she had wanted to play with slowly come back.

Also delightful to children from 1 to 3 are: (1) absurd stories like *Are You My Mother?* (your child will roar "No!" each time a newly hatched bird asks "Are you my mother?" of a kitten, a hen, a cow, and a bullfrog); (2) fantastic stories like *Harold and the Purple Crayon* (Harold draws a one-color world of monsters and trees until finally, after drawing his own bed, he gets into it, drops the crayon on the floor, and efficiently goes to sleep); and (3) realistic stories about busy people like *Who Knows the Little Man?* (the little man catches a fish that nibbled at his toe, then goes home to set a table so sparsely elegant that a parent drools) and *The Carrot Seed* (a small boy, despite the doubts of his parents and big brother, plants a seed and patiently waters and weeds until, finally, carrot greenery sprouts up).

Very satisfying to both children and parents are books like *Look at Me Now!* In this book, a child realizes how much he has learned from the time he was an infant blowing spit bubbles (your child will enjoy blowing them while you read) until now, when (wow!) he can go down a slide at the park all by himself. Every day your child struggles to learn skills he cannot master. Reading this book lets him savor the things he *can* do. As he turns 2, your child will love stories about naughty characters or small children or animals who get into trouble. Try *Madeline, Blueberries for Sal, Peter Rabbit,* the *Curious George* stories, and *Harry the Dirty Dog.*

The late 2-year-old, perhaps because she is discovering her own strengths and vulnerabilities on the playground, delights in stories of confrontation. *The Three Pigs, The Three Billy Goats Gruff,* and *There's a Nightmare in My Closet* may fascinate her, even if the adult reader is appalled at watching a wolf being boiled alive, a troll being tossed into a stream and drowned, or monsters being housed in a child's bedroom closet. A more pleasant, in fact funny, confrontation classic is *Caps for Sale* by Esphyr Slobodkina. A peddler of hats rants at monkeys in a tree who have stolen his caps. Finally the peddler, disgusted, gives up and flings his own cap to the ground, only to look over his shoulder and see the monkeys happily following suit.

In addition to stories about the naughty, the absurd, the fantastic, and the real world, a child enjoys being read to about any holiday, particularly Halloween. Hearing these stories helps make more sense of the hoopla parents indulge in from time to time. The seasons fascinate, too, particularly when viewed with wonder, as in *The Snowy Day* by Ezra Keats.

We suggest buying as many of the books described above as you can; they are listed, under the appropriate age category, in the No-Frills Shopping List at the end of this chapter. A silent message is delivered if you buy toys and clothes for your child but not books. At least some of the books you buy should be in hard cover. The color is usually more vivid, and the feel—even to a child—more substantial. Hardcover books last longer, up to the time a child learns to read himself. Then owning a few cherished books that he has almost memorized may make learning to read even more satisfying to a child.

"At the time, spending five dollars on clothing made more sense than spending five dollars on books. But I feel differently now."   *Mother of three / New Orleans, La.*

"I would buy the same number of books again, maybe more. At our house, reading to the children was part of the bedtime ritual. I don't feel it makes a great deal of difference which books you buy. If you like the pictures and stories you'll enjoy reading them. Usually it was Daddy who read to them while I did the dishes. It was their time and they all loved it. This ritual lasted until the children themselves learned to read (then *they* read the story to Dad). Today the kids are avid readers." *Mother of two / Wichita, Kan.*

"Books are the most used items among my children's 'toys.'"
          Mother of four / Boston, Mass.

Where should you look for children's books? The Dr. Seuss, Richard Scarry, and Mother Goose books are everywhere, but few bookstores are able to stock many of the rest on our list. Ask a children's librarian which store in your town has the best children's book collection; that store will probably be glad to order any book not in stock. Or order them through one of the school-supply stores listed in the Resource List.

If you live near a university with an early-childhood education department or a library school, ask whether it has a permanent noncirculating "model library" of children's books. Access to such a library provides parents with the opportunity to read books before they decide whether to buy them. Your local public library may not be helpful in this way because the most popular books are usually checked out.

The largest supplier of children's paperbacks is Scholastic Book Services, whose catalog lists more than 800 children's classics in addition to reprints of new children's books.

Don't overlook the inexpensive Little Golden Books (Western Publishing Co.), Wonder Books (Grosset & Dunlap), or Junior Elf Books (Rand McNally) in supermarkets and discount stores. Attractively illustrated versions of such classics as *Heidi* and *The Night Before Christmas* are available—along with, admittedly, some awful ones you'll get rid of quickly. These books cost so little that you can afford to buy a stack and allow a child to read and love them until they fall apart. Garage sales, thrift shops, public-library book sales, and used-book stores are other good sources of children's books.

Records

As with a book, you should sample a record before you buy it for a child to make sure you won't mind hearing it over and over. Somewhere around a child's second birthday is a good time to investigate this potential for entertainment and education (and fifteen-minute periods of free time for parents).

Unlike most television programs, records require imagination. They help a child learn to listen carefully, build his vocabulary, train his memory, and move his body rhythmically.

The catch is that many of the best children's records—the ones even the nursery-school pros don't mind hearing every day—are not stocked in discount or department stores. To find the best records visit your library, because many libraries have children's records. Or a friendly nursery-school teacher might lend some to you for taping or for listening before you buy.

Types of records to consider for children: folk songs, music of other cultures (African drums, Mexican mariachis), activity records that suggest exercises or play-acting, and story records—which are, essentially, books read aloud.

Among the artists popular with nursery-school professionals: Ella Jenkins, Hap Palmer, Pete Seeger, and Tom Glazer. One of our all-time favorites is Ella Jenkins' "Play Your Instruments and Make a Pretty Sound"; another is Hap

Palmer's "Getting to Know Myself." We have included these on the No-Frills List.

The Golden Records Division of Golden Books has many inexpensive LPs with storybooks attached to the album cover. One of them contains "The Three Bears," "The Ugly Duckling," "The Little Red Hen," and several other classics. And Scholastic Book Services offers more than forty book-record sets.

A mother of three preschool children in New York said, "I'm often too tired at the end of a day even to read a bedtime story. Instead we all sit close together on the couch listening to a story record and reading the book that goes along with it. What a boost these records can be."

A California mother of a 2-year-old says, "When Jennifer hears Ella Jenkins start singing 'Play Your Instruments and Make a Pretty Sound,' she runs to the kitchen for the electric-mixer beaters and the metal mixing bowl. We don't mind the banging. The look on her face is so hard to resist we end up joining her half the time."

Other popular records with practically all children are "Sing the Hit Songs of Sesame Street" by Children's Records of America and "Sesame Street Goes Disco."

Usually it is not until well after the third birthday, more likely the fourth, that investing in a record player for the child's own use is a safe idea—for the child and the machine.

IF I HAD THOSE YEARS TO LIVE OVER . . .

Some of our hardest decisions in these early years concern what to buy for the baby and young child. Many mothers we talked with would spend child-related dollars differently if they could start over again.

"If I had it to do over I would consider purchasing baby furniture and equipment secondhand. It's so easy to refinish cribs and chests and you can use your own ingenuity in matching these things to your personality."
Mother of one / Red Bank, N.J.

"What I'd do over is easy to say. Instead of spending that $125 we did on a chest of drawers, I'd spend it on twenty-five nights of baby sitting. We made the first couple of years too hard on ourselves!" *Mother of one / Denver, Colo.*

"The only thing I would do differently is in the equipment line. The sturdy, well-built wooden gym-type toys would be a must! As far as space for them, I wouldn't be as finicky as I was about cleaning up since they don't have a lot of parts to put away. Kids *do* love to climb, slide, and horse around on these toys." *Mother of two / Tampa, Fla.*

"I'd buy the best-quality things I could, especially in equipment, clothes, and toys. The 'bargains' I bought didn't last through even one child. Also, we'd budget more money for babysitting. Our whole family works better when parents and children have some time apart."
Mother of three / Ft. Wayne, Ind.

"If we have another child, it's going to be in a different apartment or house, I'll tell you! Instead of a glamorous view apartment, we'll have a ground-floor one with a play area outside that I can see from the kitchen. The yard or patio will have room to dig in and some paved area where the kids can ride tricycles." *Mother of one / Tucson, Ariz.*

"I was impractical when I bought things I thought the kids needed and wanted. We felt we had to buy them super gifts, better than we could afford. Now I know ordinary kitchen items make good, inexpensive toys. Oh, the money we could have saved." *Mother of three / Menands, N.Y.*

"I'd try to plan more carefully so I wouldn't waste money on toys and equipment that weren't appropriate to the child's age or interest. Because I was so busy, I made too many spur-of-the-moment decisions when shopping. I'd try not to fall for fads in toys or clothes."
Mother of four / Springfield, Mo.

"I'd get jackets with attached hoods. It's one less thing for them to put on and it keeps their ears and neck warm, too."
Mother of two / Burlington, Vt.

"I think buying 'convertible' baby furniture is like buying a dress you think will work for several occasions and then turns out not to be exactly right for any of them. In general, things such as a high chair that converts into a car seat and then into a carriage, a play table, a bar stool, and so on are more expensive and less handy than the 'real' thing every time."

Mother of two / Bismarck, N.D.

"I wouldn't have spent the money I did on toys. It's been my experience that children do more projects with everyday things found around the house, such as cardboard boxes, newspapers, old fabric, and old clothes. My youngest inherited tons of toys and they sit unused while she spends most of the day with her favorite doll and crayons and paper."

Mother of three / Laurel, Miss.

"I'd buy fewer toys, and I'd take the kids to the doctor less often. In retrospect, I would insist that my husband and I get away together, *alone*, once a week, even if only for an hour." *Mother of two / Eugene, Ore.*

"I wish I'd found out sooner about those metal poles that serve as extra closet rods that you can buy in some department stores. The one I have now hangs a couple of feet below the regular rod for about half the length of the regular rod. That means my daughter can reach her own dresses in the morning and, better yet, hang them up at night. And there's room on the top rod for clothes she doesn't fit into yet." *Mother of two / Pine Bluff, Ark.*

"We had no waste problem as there wasn't a penny to spare. Nursery equipment, toys, clothes, and books came almost entirely from thrift shops, gifts, and older cousins. Books are my special thing. I want my son surrounded by them but I can't help but flinch at the sound of a page being ripped. Because of this we buy tons of books at thrift shops at ten or twenty cents a shot, putting the valuable ones like *The Velveteen Rabbit* and *Peter Pan* up on an unreachable shelf to be brought down for the bedtime ritual."

Mother of one / Akron, Ohio

THE NO-FRILLS SHOPPING LIST: WHAT TO GET YEAR BY YEAR

Below are three shopping lists containing what we consider to be a sane minimum of everything—equipment, clothing, furniture, books, toys, and records—for each of the first three years of a child's life.

It's a list that we wish we had had before our first child was born, and has taken years to develop. In addition to our own experiences in buying for our children, the list takes into account the buying advice of the more than two hundred mothers we surveyed for this book.

Birth to 1 Year

CLOTHING AND BEDDING

Diapers (4 dozen prefolded cloth diapers or 3 boxes of disposables per week)

Pins (if plastic-head, should be metal-lined)

Bedding

3 fitted crib sheets
2 crib-size mattress pads
1 plastic crib mattress protector
2 crib-size rubber sheets

2 small washable quilts
1 set bumper pads for crib
6 lap-size flannelized rubber pads

Infant clothes

6 undershirts (the side-snap kind is easier to put on)
1 newborn-size stretch suit (in which to take baby home from hospital)
6 stretch suits (6-12 month size)
6 gowns (with drawstring bottoms)

1 hat
3 small plastic or cloth bibs
4 receiving blankets
6 waterproof pants (if you use cloth diapers)
1 bunting or snowsuit (depending on climate)
2 sets bootees

Crawler clothes

6 pairs overalls (with snap crotch)
6 tops
6 undershirts (depending on climate)

1 sweater
1 jacket with hood (depending on climate)
2 blanket sleepers

FURNITURE

Crib and mattress
Bassinet, cradle, or car bed
Portable crib (optional)
High chair or feeding table
Playpen and pad

Changing table
Chest of drawers (or shelves)
Plastic diaper pail with cover
Rocker with arm support for
    parents (optional)

MOBILITY AIDS

Infant seat
Car restraint for infant
Sling or wrap carrier

Backpack carrier
Diaper bag
Umbrella stroller

MEDICINE, TOILETRIES, AND HEALTH AIDS

Changing-table supplies
    Ointment for diaper rash
    Toilet paper (much better for plumbing than tissues or towelettes)
    Water
    Wastebasket
Rubbing alcohol
Nasal aspirator
Rectal thermometer
Petroleum jelly
Baby nail scissors with rounded points
Syrup of ipecac (replace every three years)
Baby aspirin
Pacifiers (orthodontic exerciser variety, optional)
Disinfectant (for diaper pail if you use cloth diapers)
Plastic garbage bags (to line diaper pail if you use disposables, optional)
Diaper liners (helpful in early weeks if you wash diapers at home)
Vaporizer (cool-mist type, optional)
Brush and comb

BOOKS FOR PARENTS

Baby and Child Care, Benjamin Spock
Child Behavior from Birth to Ten, Frances Ilg and Louise Ames (Gesell)
Mother to Mother Baby Care Book, Barbara Sills and Jeanne Henry
First-aid book

SAFETY AIDS

Gate(s) (mesh suction type is best because it can easily be adjusted to
    fit any doorway)
Plastic plugs for electrical outlets
Safety latches for drawers and cupboards (limit opening of cabinet
    or drawer to about one inch)

TOYS

Mobile (to hang over crib)
Small toys of different textures (cloth, wood, rubber) and shapes
Small cloth or cardboard books, magazines, catalogs
Ball(s)
Soft doll or stuffed animal
Activity toy for side of playpen
Sturdy photo album for family pictures
Mirror (nonbreakable)
Hinged box or other toy to open and shut

FEEDING IMPLEMENTS

Bottles or nursers
   8 oz.—8 to 10 for bottle-fed baby; 1-2 for nursing baby
   4 oz.—2 for water and juice; 1 for nursing baby
Nipples (use nipples, collars, and caps that go with brand of bottles
   or nursers)
Feeding spoons
   1 long-handled
   1 short-handled
Bottle and nipple brush (if you use bottles)
Bibs
   2 soft plastic ones
   1 molded firm plastic bib with trough bottom (for older baby)
Food grinder (optional)
Vegetable steamer (optional)
Set of plastic molds for popsicles (Tupperware)

1 to 2 Years

FURNITURE AND EQUIPMENT

Small, inexpensive chair, seat about 7 inches high
Small table, about 14 inches high
Car restraint for older baby and child
Open shelves (to store toys)

CLOTHING

Jacket (with hood if you live   4 pairs overalls (with snap crotch)
   in a cold climate)   6 undershirts
Sweater   4 tops
Snowsuit and boots   2 blanket sleepers

TOYS

Smallest tricycle, without pedals
Simple wood puzzle
Nesting boxes or ring toy
Doll
Truck or other push toy
Bath toys

Pull toy
Peg pounder (also called cobbler's bench)
Cartons or baskets in most rooms (for child's things)

BOOKS

Small ones child can handle

Anybody at Home?, H. A. Rey
Cat in the Hat Dictionary, Dr. Seuss
The Golden Song Book, Katharine Wessels
Goodnight Moon, Margaret Wise Brown
Look at Me Now!, Watson, Switzer, and Hirschberg
Mother Goose, any version
Pat the Bunny, Dorothy Kunhardt
The Rooster Crows, Maud and Miska Petersham

2 to 3 Years

FURNITURE

Sturdy table, about 23 inches high (work and eating surface for child)
2 or more sturdy chairs, seat about 13 inches high
Potty chair (inexpensive plastic, with pot that can be easily removed from top by child)
Step stool (for washing hands)

CLOTHES

15 to 20 pairs of training pants (collect from friends, if possible)
Shorts, pants, or dresses that pull up or down easily (for toilet training)
2 pairs shoes
Sweater
Jacket
Snowsuit and boots (depending on climate)
2 pairs pajamas (two-piece aid in toilet training)

TOYS/OUTING SUPPLIES

Pedal toy (it should be big enough so that child can use it for a while,
    but make sure he can reach the pedals)
Blocks
Colored markers (washable), crayons, paper
Plastic finger puppets
Lunch box (plastic doesn't rust) with plastic-lined thermos
Wagon or wheelbarrow
Hats (for pretending)

RECORDS

"Getting to Know Myself," Hap Palmer (Activity Records)
"Play Your Instruments and Make a Pretty Sound," Ella Jenkins with
    Franz Jackson and His Original Jazz All Stars (Folkways)
"The Three Bears," "The Ugly Duckling," etc. (LP Golden Book and
    Record set)

BOOKS

Are You My Mother?, P. D. Eastman
Blueberries for Sal, Robert McCloskey
Caps for Sale, Ezphyr Slobodkina
The Carrot Seed, Ruth Kraus
Curious George, Margaret and H. A. Rey
Harold and the Purple Crayon, Crockett Johnson
Harry the Dirty Dog, Gene Zion
Madeline, Ludwig Bemelmans
Play with Me, Marie Ets
The Snowy Day, Ezra Jack Keats
The Tale of Peter Rabbit, Beatrix Potter
There's a Nightmare in My Closet, Mercer Mayer
Three Billy Goats Gruff
Three Little Pigs
Who Knows the Little Man?, Walburga Attenberger

6

Feeding Your Baby and Child

In general, an infant (birth through about 5 months) needs only breast or bottle milk. A baby (6 to 12 months) gets milk but also eats traditional "baby" food in strained, puréed, or mashed form. A toddler (12 to 18 months) starts drinking from a cup and is in a transition stage with food, eating some baby food and some soft finger foods like bananas.

After that you're home free. The child nearing 2 will enjoy eating most of what the family eats. That is when you may want to take our quick refresher course in nutrition. Which additives and preservatives should a mother watch out for? What's the difference between saturated and unsaturated fats, between peanut butter kept in the refrigerated section of the market and that kept alongside canned goods?

We cover buying commercially made baby foods wisely in this chapter, along with a short course in nutrition describing foods to eat and foods to avoid. The next chapter covers how to make your own baby food.

COMMERCIAL BABY FOODS

"I used ready-made baby food. It was more convenient for me, and my child preferred it to anything I tried to make.

At about a year he was completely off baby food and bottles."   *Mother of one / Creve Coeur, Mo.*

In 1927, when a doctor prescribed puréed peas for his sick
daughter, Dan Gerber saw a need and filled it—some think
too well. But if you, as we do, sometimes have trouble getting even an adult meal on the table, ready-made baby food
can be a blessing.

Commercial baby food can be just as nutritious as the
homemade variety if you shop with the following guidelines
in mind:

● Read labels and choose foods that have little or no added
sugar, salt, preservatives, food coloring, or artificial flavoring.

● Buy plain vegetables, fruits, and meats—not combination
dinners and desserts, which sometimes contain empty calorie
fillers.

● If you want to buy some but not all of your baby's food,
buy meat, the most nutritious commercial baby food and
the one that is most time-consuming to prepare yourself.

● Avoid sweet desserts. Serve fruit instead.

In the past, critics of commercial baby foods have charged
that the salt and sugar added to such foods stimulate cravings
that last throughout life, contributing to high blood pressure
and obesity in later years. Nutritionists also objected to the
"modified starches" added to many combination dinners,
fruit and custard desserts, and all creamed vegetables. Added
starches quickly satisfy a baby's hunger, making it difficult
for a parent to know whether she is really eating enough nutritious food.

However, baby-food manufacturers have responded to
consumer demands to the point where most now claim that
their food contains no added salt and little added sugar and
has been improved in other ways. Many pediatricians agree.
In 1977 Beech-Nut brought out a new line of "natural" baby
foods containing no salt or other additives, in addition to
eliminating sugar from eighty-four items. The previous year,
Gerber had introduced a line of plain fruits and fruit juices
that did not contain sugar. Gerber has gone on to cut out
sugar in all of its products except for a few desserts and to

remove modified starches from meat-vegetable combinations, replacing them with combinations of natural grains and vegetables. Most baby foods have never contained preservatives, and since 1969 none has contained monosodium glutamate.

Baby food is likely to improve still more because better labeling is in the offing. Soon, if the Food and Drug Administration (FDA) has its way, the percentage of major ingredients in a junior dinner will be stated as part of the name of the food. Thus, a label might read: "Green Bean, Potato, and Ham Casserole—X% green beans, X% potatoes, and X% ham." Besides the main ingredients, infant labels would be required to include the percentages of any substance making up 5 percent or more of the food. (Ingredients comprising less than 5 percent would merely be listed.) The label on a jar of "Strained Egg Yolks" might read: "Egg yolk 80%, water 19%, salt."

If you want maximum nutrition you won't be affected by the changes, since most of the time you'll want to buy only the "plain" foods and add fillers of your choice—cottage cheese, yogurt, rice, or cereal—to please your baby's tastes. For even the busiest of us, it's just as easy to boil an egg and crumble the yolk as it is to buy a jar of egg yolk (at double the cost per egg).

Why add fillers? Many babies like a little rice or cereal or fruit to cut the taste of a meat or vegetable. Indeed, they may refuse to eat either meat or vegetables without such "doctoring"—hence the popularity of combination dinners. Also, manufacturers add fillers to make foods less watery and to keep the ingredients from separating.

Strained meats cost more than combination dinners and come in smaller jars. Nevertheless, they are better buys, both nutritionally and financially. A baby needs protein from meat, and a parent needs to know how much meat a baby is getting. As little as one third of a jar of strained meat a day may be enough for him, and it is easy to mix that at home with a little fruit, rice, or cereal—and you'll know how much meat he has eaten if you have mixed it yourself.

Most mothers appreciate being able to use commercially prepared baby cereals. They're easy to serve, and there's no messy oatmeal or cream-of-wheat pot to clean. Consult your doctor about which types of cereals he thinks are most nutritious and which are most appropriate if your child is allergy-prone.

We think that commercial "junior" foods are not necessary, except perhaps when you are traveling or visiting. By the time a child is a year old he can handle most table food if it is mashed or cut up for him. One possible exception: meat sticks. Although they have too many additives for us to feel comfortable about using them frequently, most children will eat them when they refuse everything else.

"The first word my children learned was 'EAT'! I thought that if they didn't eat at mealtime they would die. Ha!"
Mother of six / Redondo Beach, Calif.

"Any meal that was eaten outside and called a picnic was a success." *Mother of two / Phoenix, Ariz.*

"I always served my babies food at room temperature or cold. If a jar was just opened, I put some in a dish and never bothered to heat it further. If the jar was in the refrigerator, they got the food cold. It never bothered them and saved me a lot of time!"
Mother of three / Danbury, Conn

How Long Do Commercial Baby Foods Stay Good?

Most prepared infant-formula products, which are usually considered out of date after eighteen months, are dated clearly. As for baby food in jars, most producers claim that their food is safe indefinitely as long as the jar seal is unbroken. It is important to check this.

As sealed jars and cans cool down after heat processing, a vacuum forms at the top of the contents, ensuring that the food is wholesome and sterilized. The baby-food jar caps

button is sunken or concave, the vacuum is intact. If the vacuum is lost, the button will be raised or convex. *Parents should be watchful that every baby-food jar they buy and take out of storage to serve has a sunken safety button.* If you occasionally see a jar in a store with a raised safety button, give it to a store employee. To double-check yourself at home, when you remove a cap for the first time, listen for a definite "pop" as the vacuum is broken.

Because of consumer demand for a clearer guide to the age of baby food in jars than the confusing codes stamped on caps in the past, the major baby-food manufacturers have made some changes. Now Gerber, for example, marks a "for best quality use by" date on all products. It's on the lid of each jar. For most products, the date indicates a time three years from the packing date. (Some consumer groups say a shelf-life limit of eighteen months is better.) Even after three years, if the seal is intact and the container undamaged, the food doesn't suddenly become unsafe. But there may be changes in color and flavor and the levels of vitamins may be lower than the nutritional labeling indicates. Turnover in most stores is such that you don't have to worry too much about this, however.

Store baby-food jars away from steam and heat and avoid freezing them, which changes the texture of their contents. The same goes for boxes of baby cereal and cans of juice. Keep cereals away from soaps, detergents, and strongly flavored vegetables to prevent cereals from absorbing odors. Also, keep baby cereal away from other grain products that might be a source of insect infestation.

Dishing It Out

Each jar holds from one to three portions, depending on the age and appetite of your child. If you expect to use only a part of a jar, spoon only that portion into the feeding dish and return the jar to refrigerator immediately—with its original cap. The remaining contents can keep for up to three days. Note: (1) heating a jar repeatedly or not refrigerating it as soon as it is opened destroys nutrients and makes food spoil faster; (2) if you feed your baby directly from the jar, saliva from his spoon, when returned to the jar, may liquefy some foods by "digesting" them or cause the food to spoil more quickly.

A NUTRITION REFRESHER COURSE

Every health-conscious parent should know and put into practice a few basics about nutrition. Whoever does the family shopping by and large runs the show. Here are some hints—some of them, perhaps, surprises—that will help the family shopper fight the good fight:

The darker the color of starches, the better. The less that is done to food in the way of bleaching, cooking, and refining before it reaches the table, the more vitamins, minerals, and roughage you get. Whole-wheat or rye breads, graham crackers, and brown rice are better than their white counterparts, and whole-wheat and oat cereals are more nutritious than rice or corn cereals. Be aware, however, that many so-called "wheat" breads are made with refined flour and are dark only because of food coloring. Look for the term "whole grain" on labels to avoid this. And if you do buy refined-grain products, at least make sure they are "enriched." Also, when baking at home it is better to use whole-wheat or unbleached flour rather than bleached white flour.

The shorter the cooking time the better for vegetables and fruits. Steaming them is the best way to retain taste, vitamins, and minerals. Save the water that remains after steaming and use it again for cooking things like rice or for making soup. It can be kept in the refrigerator for about a week.

Fresh, frozen, canned—that's the preferable order for maximum nutrition. By "fresh" we mean *fresh*. Limp, wrinkled peaches are not as nutritious as peaches that were frozen or canned in water at the peak of the season. One advantage of canned vegetables is that they are not only cut and cleaned but cooked as well. They need only be puréed for infants, for example. Be sure to use the liquid in canned vegetables because it contains vitamins and minerals. But be wary of fruits packed in heavy syrup. Pour off as much as possible—or, better yet, buy fruits packed in water or in *light* syrup if you can't find the water-packed variety.

Don't forget roughage. Also known as fiber or bulk, roughage is the part of food that connot be digested—but it can still have nutritional value. All fruits and vegetables, brown rice, and whole-wheat bread contain roughage, which helps intestines do the work they are supposed to do.

Cloudy apple juice is better than clear. Pectin and starch have been removed from the clear juice because they tend to cause the juice to become cloudy during storage, and consumers supposedly like their apple juice crystal-clear. Nevertheless, juice containing pectin and the apples' natural starch is preferable, nutritionally. The pectin helps lower the body's cholesterol; the starch is slowly converted to sugar in the body, and is more easily digested than the sugar that is added to apple juice to compensate for the removal of the starch.

Watch out for additives. This umbrella term covers preservatives, artificial colors, artificial flavors, and minerals and vitamin enrichment. The average American eats about five pounds of additives every year. Their use has doubled in the last twenty years, and more kinds are approved for use in the United States than in any other country.

Some additives do good things. The addition of iron to bread and iodine to salt, for example, has made the nation healthier. Still, safety questions have been raised about many additives, and children, because of their small size, may be particularly vulnerable. Dr. Ben F. Feingold, a controversial allergy specialist at Kaiser Permanente Medical Center in San Francisco, has long studied the effect of additives and other foods on children. He contends that hyperactivity, for example, is directly related to sensitivity to particular foods or additives. He says bluntly, "If you are developing an optimal diet for toddlers, it is imperative to consider the problem of additives."

As of this writing, there is considerable controversy about the following additives, so you might be wise to try to avoid them.

Sodium nitrate. This is added to almost all hot dogs, cold cuts, bacon, and other cured meats to make them look redder and keep longer. Nitrates can react with chemicals called amines in foods to produce nitrosamines, very small amounts of which have been found to cause cancer in animals. Sodium nitrate is not, however, added to most brands of toddler meat sticks.

Red dyes. It took fifteen years for the FDA to ban Red Dye No. 2. Then Red Dye No. 4 was removed from the approved list. Now the dye used in place of both of them is suspected of causing cancer and also hyperactivity in test animals. Red dyes are used in maraschino cherries, hot dogs, soda, candy, cake, ice cream, and many other foods.

Yellow Dye No. 5 (tartrazine). This, the most widely used food dye, may, according to the FDA, cause allergic reactions, particularly in persons allergic to aspirin. It may be found in sodas, breads with a yellowish tint, instant puddings, and many other foods.

DES (diethylstilbestrol). Known to have caused vaginal cancer in the offspring of women who took the drug to prevent miscarriage, DES is still implanted in cattle to make them gain weight faster. Hearings are held periodically about the safety of this practice. DES may be found in liver.

BHT (butylated hydroxytoluene). The FDA has released a report on this common preservative that raises questions about its safety, particularly for those who take either oral contraceptives or steroid hormones. It may be used in margarine, gum, and in foods as diverse as enriched rice, instant potatoes, cereals, and dry soup mixes.

Saccharin. Recent experiments have established a potential link between saccharin and cancer. Although the results are still unverified, some authorities are adamant in their opinion that children, especially, should not be given saccharin-containing products—primarily "sugar-free" soda.

If you are concerned about additives or have a hyperactive or allergic child, check the Resource List for books containing more detailed information.

Know Your Fats

Fats are an important source of energy and vitamins, but eating too many saturated fats can raise the cholesterol level in your blood, which many medical experts consider a contributing factor in cardiovascular diseases. *Saturated fats* are found in dairy products, meat, egg yolks, chocolate, shortening, and some margarines. An easy guideline to remember: saturated fats stay solid at room temperature.

To avoid feeding your family too many saturated fats, serve more chicken, fish, and veal than beef and pork; if you do serve beef and pork, buy lean cuts, trim away any fat before cooking them, and drain away any fat you can during cooking; serve a vegetable or bean main course once in a while; skim off the fat that rises to the surface in soups and stews; buy skim or low-fat milk for adults and older children. Remember that prepared lunch meats may contain, by law, as much as 30 percent fat.

Unsaturated fats neither raise nor lower cholesterol level. Oils made from olives and peanuts contain mostly unsaturated fats.

Even better are *polyunsaturated fats*, which actually tend to help lower blood-cholesterol levels. White fish is high in polyunsaturated fat, as are the following oils: safflower, cottonseed, corn, and soybean.

Soft margarines are high in polyunsaturated fats. They are generally better than stick margarines, which are "hydrogenated"—put through a process of adding fats and oils to make a product that is more solid and will keep longer. The more hydrogenated the margarine, the more saturated fats it contains. (This also applies to salad and cooking oils; if the label describes the product as "hydrogenated," it is likely to be high in saturated fats.)

If you do use a stick margarine, however, check the label. If hydrogenated oils are listed first—meaning that they are the largest ingredient in quantity—look for another brand, one that lists a *liquid* vegetable oil first. Also check the "Nutritional Information Per Serving" on the outside package of the margarine. The higher the ratio of polyunsaturated fats to saturated fats, the better.

"For children past baby age you can save a lot of money if you use nonfat dry milk mixed with water. As long as it's really cold, my kids drink it as willingly as they do milk in a carton from the market. But be sure you buy a nonfat dry milk that's fortified with vitamins A and D. My pediatrician says that then it's just as nutritious as regular milk—maybe better for the kids, because the fat's removed."

Mother of five / Chicago, Ill.

Foods to Avoid

Some foods aren't very good for you or your children. Here are some of them.

Chocolate. Surprisingly, chocolate contains quite a bit of caffeine, which can kill B vitamins and contribute to hyper-activity. It can also cause allergic reactions in some people, and especially in young children. Caffeine has been associated with elevated blood-sugar levels, heartburn, and increased gastric secretions. Because of their lower body weight, children will be far more affected by a dose of caffeine than will an adult consuming the same amount. One study concluded that just one cup of chocolate drink can have the same adverse affect on a child as a bottle of cola or a strong tea.

Carob, which looks and tastes somewhat like chocolate, can be bought at health-food stores and may be a satisfactory substitute. As an added plus, it contains much less fat than chocolate.

Cola and other soft drinks. These, of course, are loaded with sugars, and are also full of caffeine—forty to seventy milligrams per twelve-ounce serving compared to about ninety in a cup of coffee, according to FDA figures. Instead of soft drinks, get your children accustomed to fruit and vegetable juices.

Salt. Consumption of salt has been linked to hypertension, which is said to affect one out of six American adults. Don't add salt to the water when cooking cereals, rice, and spaghetti. Salt food lightly and encourage your children to do the same. Avoid buying salty snack foods and go easy in using such high-salt flavorings as MSG, commercial bouillon, soy sauce, and meat extracts. Nutrition experts advise cutting salt consumption to no more than five grams a day, which equals about one teaspoon.

White sugar. Refined sugar has no nutritional value. It is nothing but empty calories. Some nutritionists actually consider it an additive poison. Sugar is not only a major factor in tooth decay, obesity, and diabetes, it may also be linked to heart disease and stomach ulcers. Dr. Doris Rapp, a pediatric allergist, has found sugar to be a major cause of hyperactivity in children.

Some persons who are dead-set against using refined white sugar suggest using dark molasses, brown sugar, maple sugar, honey, and "raw" sugar as substitutes. But be warned: these sweeteners should be used in moderation, too. Some authorities think the substitutes are really no better than white sugar they replace. Also, spores found in honey have been linked to botulism in babies. Some medical experts urge mothers not to use honey at all for children under 1.

Sugar-coated and presweetened cereals. These are bad for the teeth and may be less nutritious than plain varieties. The gum-like sugar in sugar-coated cereals can stick to the teeth for hours despite a casual brushing, whereas in unsweetened cereal the sugar that does not dissolve in the milk will collect at the bottom of the bowl instead of on the teeth. Many of the so-called "natural" cereals contain sugar in the form of honey and corn syrup used in processing. In general, hot cereals are more nutritious than cold cereals. Whole wheat and oatmeal have the most protein, vitamins, and roughage.

Peanut butter and jelly. Although peanut butter alone is a good, high-protein food, when combined with jelly it's bad for teeth. Most dentists urge parents to substitute margarine or applesauce for the jelly. Also, on the subject of peanut butter, it's better to buy peanut butter to which no preservatives or sugar have been added, and which has *not* been hydrogenated to make it solid and last longer. Nonhydrogenated peanut butter is usually found in the refrigerated-foods section of the market. At any rate, you can easily tell if it's nonhydrogenated because there will be a layer of oil on top that you have to stir into the rest of the contents, and there will be instructions on the label to keep it refrigerated after opening. If the texture of nonhydrogenated peanut butter causes your child to gag, add a little milk or orange juice to smooth it out.

Gelatin desserts. These consist mainly of sugar, along with artificial coloring and flavoring. Instead of buying the packaged variety, use unflavored gelatin and add your own fruit juices and fruit.

Nutritious Snacks

"I remember that the hour before dinner was always hairy. The kids were hungry and tired, so I would open a small can of green beans and—without heating—put them in a dish. It was something they could eat without ruining their appetites." *Mother of three / Montgomery, Ala.*

"After some trying times, I found that John tends to eat in cycles. When he's in a growth spurt, he eats like a horse. When he's in a relatively slow-growth period, he doesn't eat much. I don't keep candy, soda, or snacks in the house. When he wants a snack, he gets an apple, an orange, or a carrot stick." *Mother of one / Augusta, Me.*

Eating between meals is no sin. In fact, many doctors recommend eating five or six small meals instead of three big ones. If you are the family purchasing agent, make sure that the snacks available to the family are nutritious ones. Here are some suggestions, or memory joggers, for the shopper who, like us, gets into a rut:

Fruit. Cantaloupe, watermelon, oranges, strawberries, diced pineapple, tangerines, peaches, bananas, pears, blueberries, prunes, apples, plums, grapes.

Raw vegetables. Broccoli tips, sweet-potato chunks, jicama, Jerusalem artichokes, peas, carrots, tomatoes, cauliflower, asparagus, avocado, green beans, cucumber, celery (slicing across bias makes it easy for children to chew—no strings).

Cheese. Swiss, cheddar, cottage, string, cream. Avoid processed cheeses.

Popcorn. If you go easy on the butter or margarine and salt, this is a good snack for older children and adults. Keep it away from babies and toddlers, though; they might choke on it. Storing it in the freezer keeps the "pop" in corn long after the package is opened.

Seeds. Sunflower seeds, raw or toasted, are mild in flavor, chewy, and inexpensive. The kernels make a good addition to cookies, cakes, and bread. Roasted soybeans, usually found near nuts in the market, are another good snack of this sort. Like popcorn, keep these away from babies and young children.

Nuts. Almonds, peanuts, cashews, walnuts. (Buy broken nuts, if possible, to save money.) Nuts should not be given to babies or toddlers. Buy both seeds and nuts *unsalted*, if you can find them; most health-food stores carry unsalted varieties, but you may not find them in the supermarket.

"Cheese can be overused because it's so convenient. If your child is constipated, avoid it."
Mother of three / Lubbock, Tex.

"I always serve the supper vegetable as the afternoon snack. Being hungry then, the children are usually receptive even to new vegetables." *Mother of two / Manhattan Beach, Calif.*

"I have one child who eats everything, another who is very picky. The fussy eater is not as healthy as my good eater. I try and keep the poor eater's snacks very nutritious, so he gets some of his vitamins and minerals then."
Mother of two / New Palestine, Ind.

"My kids' favorite summer snack is frozen watermelon. I cut it into chunks, remove the seeds, purée it with a small amount of water, and pour it into ice-cube trays. When it's almost solid, I insert toothpicks. They go fast, and it's a lot less messy for little ones than the regular way."
Mother of four / Portland, Ore.

RONALD McDONALD AND YOU

To paraphrase Robert Frost, McDonald's is the place where, when you go there with a cranky toddler, they have to take you in. Quick service is essential when you are eating out with a small child, and McDonald's and other fast-food franchises offer it. The nutrition? Fine—if *you* establish the menu.

"We go to McDonald's for lunch once a week," says a California mother. "My son always has a carton of milk, a small order of fries, and a cheeseburger. He usually has fresh fruit later in the day. Going there has saved my sanity more than once."

Hamburgers and hot dogs are more nutritious than some health-food addicts claim, according to *Nutrition and the*

M.D., a monthly newsletter for physicians and nutritionists. One lean hamburger or two all-meat hot dogs provide about 10 percent of a growing child's daily needs for calories, protein, fat, iron, and riboflavin. Note, however, that a single hamburger has twice as much protein and twice as much iron as one hot dog. Also on the plus side for a hamburger: it contains only half the fat and two-thirds the calories of one hot dog. So unless your child can eat two hot dogs at a sitting, it's probably wise to choose a hamburger. And if you're concerned about food coloring and preservatives and calories, you'd better stick to hamburgers.

A few mothers even have some not unkind words to say for Mexican-style fast-food chains, too. "A beef tostada without beans isn't too bad nutritionally," says one. "It has fewer carbohydrates than a hamburger on a bun and includes some salad vegetables." And a nutrition consultant for the Family Practice Center at UCLA Medical School points out that pizza can be a complete four-food-group meal that has no more calories than a big steak, with the added plus that the crust is made with polyunsaturated fat while the steak contains saturated fat.

"I would not suggest trying to force a child to eat. Try to make meals a happy experience. If a child doesn't eat very much at one meal, I wouldn't give him any snacks until after the next meal. For snacks, I suggest food with nutritional value, such as fruit, graham crackers, cheese, milk, juice."

Mother of six / Wilmington, Del.

"Children eat when they are hungry. Avoid forcing food, filler foods, and candy. If you give children all kinds of nutritious foods to try in small amounts, they will gradually acquire a taste for all foods."

Mother of three / Troy, N.Y.

7

Making Your Own Baby Food

"I make all Sarah's food. We bought a baby-food grinder for under $10 and feed her the food we fix for our meals. The food's hot and we place it in the grinder. It's ready in one minute. If I make a lot at one time I use the blender and freeze the rest, but I usually prefer to fix one meal at a time."   *Mother of one / Blackwood, N.J.*

Using a few simple tools available in most housewares departments, many mothers process some or all of their babies' food. Preparing food at home costs about half as much as buying commercial baby foods. More important, you can avoid the excessive salt, sugar, and filler materials that are added to some of the commercial preparations. Surprisingly little time is required—particularly to "prepare" such excellent baby foods as bananas, cottage cheese, yogurt, and rice. We've included suggestions for more of these "no-work" foods in the recipe section at the end of this chapter.

ONE MEAL AT A TIME

If you are a one-meal-at-a-time type, a vegetable steamer and a hand-operated food grinder are all the equipment you will need.

A steamer is a collapsible metal basket that adjusts to fit

most pan sizes. Its function is to hold vegetables, fruit, and fish above water so that (with a tight-fitting lid on the pan) foods are steamed, not boiled. (Cooking in water destroys many of the vitamins and minerals in foods.) After steaming, food can be puréed or ground fine for an infant, mashed with a fork for an older baby, or served in chunks for a toddler. The steamer can be used for cooking all the family's fresh or frozen vegetables—and is also handy for reheating rice or other foods and serves as an extra colander. Save the water left in the pan for puréeing infant foods.

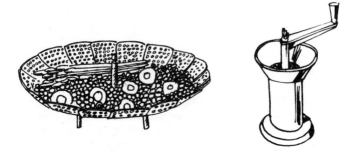

With a small hand-operated food grinder, you can make one or two meals at a time for the baby, using unspiced portions of your own foods. It's particularly useful when you're visiting friends or eating in restaurants because you can serve the baby only as much food as she wants, directly from the grinder. Portions of one night's meal can be refrigerated and worked through the grinder the next day.

A friend who has a 3-year-old daughter and a 6-month-old son agreed to test one baby-food grinder for us. A few days later we asked how the gadget had worked out. "We've been using that thing all weekend!" she reported. "Jamie likes the food—the only trouble is, Amy insists on grinding the food for him at every single meal." She immediately demanded to know where we had bought it.

"Don't have junk food in the house. Serve milk with all meals. A baby loves table food. Encourage a baby to eat by herself, using her fingers."   *Mother of four / Denver, Colo.*

"At the toddler stage, simple foods worked best for me: stewed fruit, hunks of cooked meat, pieces of cheese, chunks of bread. As soon as my children weren't interested in eating any more, I took the food away from them so they didn't throw it around."   *Mother of two / Portland, Me.*

"I made my own baby food, and found it saved me lots of money. For example, from a forty-nine cent package of frozen peas I could make twelve servings at a time when a single jar of puréed peas cost twenty cents and yielded only two servings."   *Mother of two / Palos Verdes, Calif.*

MAKE-AHEAD MEALS

If you want to prepare and freeze more than one meal at a time, a blender or food mill may be a good investment. Using a blender, you can quickly purée food fine enough for young infants; when the baby is older, switch to a slower speed to produce food with a coarser consistency. Blenders that open at the bottom are easier to clean. Small blender containers, useful for storing food in the refrigerator, are available with some brands.

Five steps are involved in preparing make-ahead blender meals for infants: (1) peel vegetables and fruits, trim fat and gristle from meats, and cut food into one-inch cubes; (2) steam the food until it is thoroughly cooked; (3) purée the cooked food in a mill or blender; (4) quick-freeze the food (in dollops on a cookie sheet or in an ice-cube tray); and (5) seal individual servings in plastic bags and store them in the freezer.

Never blend more than two cups of ingredients at one time. Meats and other thick foods should be blended only one cup at a time. Be sure to put in enough ingredients and liquid to cover the blades or the food will splatter up onto the sides of the container. Puréeing foods usually requires less liquid than chopping does, and the less liquid you put in, the less storage space you need. You can add orange juice or other liquid at feeding time if you want to thin out the consistency.

You can prepare enough food in advance to feed a baby for up to a month and then freeze it to be used as needed.

To freeze the food, either put portions into ice-cube trays (the plastic pop-out kind work best) or put dollops of food on cookie sheets. Cover the trays or sheets with plastic wrap, waxed paper, or aluminum foil and put them in the freezer. Freezing time will depend on the density of the food.

The frozen cubes or dollops of food can be stored in freezerproof plastic bags. ("Freezerproof" means not only waterproof but moisture- and vaporproof as well—an important consideration, especially if you have a self-defrosting freezer.) Sandwich bags will do in a pinch, but they—like waxed paper, milk or cottage-cheese cartons, and ordinary-weight aluminum foil—are not sturdy enough for long storage. Sturdy storage bags, though more expensive, can be washed and used again and again.

Other freezer storage possibilities:

Baby-food jars. Leave a little room for expansion when you fill the jars; let thaw in refrigerator before warming because immediate heating may cause jar to crack. Cover jars with freezer wrap and secure with rubber bands.

Foil tart pans. Cover with freezer wrap. These can go from freezer to oven to table and can be used over and over again.

Heat-in-the-pouch containers. These bags are similar to boil-in-a-bag frozen-vegetable pouches, and they offer similar advantages. You can thaw and heat the food quickly without dirtying a pot. The catch is that you need to buy a heat-sealer appliance. These gadgets are useful for freezing and storing fresh vegetables, spaghetti sauce, and other edibles as well as baby foods. One brand offers a six-by-eight-inch bag that is good for baby-size portions.

Properly packaged baby food can be kept in the freezer for at least a month. Foods that contain milk or smoked meats should be used within six weeks. Plain vegetables or fruits, blended and frozen in season, can be kept for several months. Don't forget to label each package with the contents and the date prepared.

As for thawing frozen baby meals, any way that works is fine. Among the possibilities: (1) remove cubes from the freezer the night before and let them thaw in the refrigerator until serving time the next day; (2) thaw and warm food in the top half of a double boiler or an aluminum egg-poacher food warmer; (3) steam the wrapped portions in a vegetable steamer. On a short trip, a frozen dollop or cube should be thawed enough to serve by the time you get to your destination. Frozen cubes can also be packed in a wide-mouth thermos.

Thawing is necessary, but warming is not. Many children are just as happy to eat foods served cold or at room temperature. Remember, don't refreeze food once it has been thawed.

NO-WORK BABY FOODS
(Or How the Human Race Survived Before Dan Gerber)

"I did a lot of mashing with the fork in those days," says one of the healthiest and most nutrition-conscious mothers we know. She made good use of the many foods that require little or no preparation other than steaming and mashing, particularly as her daughter made the transition from "infant" to "baby" at about the time she sat up.

Two things to remember: (1) by about 9 months, a baby can and should be having a few lumps in food; (2) cooked foods are easier to digest than raw food, although bananas, scraped apples and pears, and avocados are easily digested raw.

The no-work foods described here are the ones our grandmothers fed their children.

Banana. A banana for a baby should be so ripe that it has black spots on the skin. Peel half and mash with a fork. The other half can be stored, in the skin, in the refrigerator—or at room temperature if the room isn't too warm—for up to two days. Banana mixes well with baby cereal and makes some meats and vegetables more palatable to the baby. Another option: add 2 tablespoons of wheat germ and 4 tablespoons of yogurt to a mashed banana. If you have several bananas at peak ripeness, don't throw them away. Peel them, cut them into several pieces, wrap them carefully, and freeze them. Thaw and use quickly. Or don't thaw. A frozen banana makes a delicious treat for a teething baby or a hungry mom. It's somewhere between sherbet and rich ice cream in taste and texture.

Apple. Scraped apple is good for babies from 6 months on. Core an apple and cut it in half. Using fast, short strokes, scrape the side of a spoon across the apple, giving the baby a bite at a time. This is a handy and neat food, not only at home but also on trips or while waiting at a restaurant. Apple can help settle a queasy stomach. Some mothers prefer pears to scraped apples, as pears are easy for babies with no teeth to "gum," and don't have to be scraped.

Yogurt. If you are not a fan already, having a baby in the house is reason enough to investigate yogurt. In many Middle Eastern countries it has been a household staple for centuries, but in the United States it has only recently found popularity. What makes this cultured-milk product an ideal baby food is that, besides having a smooth texture, it contains less sugar and more easily digested protein than milk itself. In the intestinal tract, yogurt produces lactic acid, which helps control the type of bacteria that can cause diarrhea.

It may be helpful to give yogurt to babies who have been medicated with antibiotics. Antibiotics tend to kill useful intestinal bacteria as well as harmful ones, and yogurt helps replace the useful bacteria and clear up the diarrhea that often accompanies antibiotic treatment.

Buy unflavored yogurt to which no preservatives have been added and combine it with mashed bananas or other fruit. It can also be added to any other baby food. If you want to make your own yogurt (at one-fourth the price), there are handy commercial yogurt makers available.

Many babies, toddlers, and young children go through yogurt phases. Because it is so easy to spoon out and because it is so good for them, when children like it, many mothers push it. If your child temporarily tires of yogurt, freeze what you have on hand in the form of yogurt popsicles.

Cottage cheese. Because cottage cheese has little fat it is the most easily digested cheese and the first one fed to babies. Ten ounces of cottage cheese will supply the calcium equivalent of eight ounces of milk.

For a baby, mix half a cup of cottage cheese with half a cup of steamed, puréed fruit (or raw, mashed fruit for an older baby), and 4 to 6 tablespoons of orange juice. Blend quickly and serve. Half can be saved in the refrigerator for the next day. Some older children like plain cottage cheese as a dip for raw vegetables. Grating carrot into cottage cheese is a good way to get a vegetable hater to eat some.

Don't worry if your child isn't thrilled with cottage cheese at first—some babies don't seem to care for the texture. You can offer it again a few weeks or months later. Or you might try putting the cottage cheese in a blender, which produces a creamy-textured substance that still has all this food's beneficial qualities.

Egg. A handy source of iron, which is not contained in milk, eggs are so simple to cook that we sometimes overlook them. Despite their cholesterol content, many doctors think eggs are an ideal food that should be served once a day from 6 months on. Start by feeding the cooked yolk at about 6 months. By about 9 months, try the whole egg, scrambled or boiled. This is a fairly common "trouble food," so if there is a family history of allergies be careful about introducing it.

Scraped meat. Scrape raw beef or liver with a knife, the way our grandparents did it. What comes off is the soft, tender part of the meat. Put this into a custard cup and set the cup in a pan of slowly boiling water until the color of the meat changes. Prepare several meals' worth and freeze the extra. Babies may find it more palatable if it is mixed with yogurt or cottage cheese and fruit.

"I fed my children finger food from the moment they began to object to my feeding them. They got cut-up cooked vegetables, slices of soft fruit, little squares of bread, Cheerios, soft meats such as lean ground beef and finely chopped chicken. Both were eating finger foods almost exclusively by the age of 9 months, and all table foods by 12 months. On trips I took crackers and small cubes of cheese, green beans, or peas-and-carrots. They never had commercial baby food and are totally unpicky about tastes and textures."
Mother of two / St. Paul, Minn.

MOTHER-TESTED BABY-FOOD RECIPES

All the following recipes may be adapted for a single serving by using proportionately smaller amounts of ingredients and working them through a baby-food grinder or mashing them through a sieve. Each recipe as given will fill about two ice-cube trays or make about two dozen small dollops.

For the Infant Gourmet

Applesauce

12 medium-size apples
water
¼ c. brown sugar (optional)

Scrub apples but do not peel them (the skins are a store-house of potassium and vitamin A). Core and cut into eighths. Put into a large kettle and add just enough water to cover bottom of pan. Cover tightly and simmer, stirring once in a while, for 25 minutes or until apples are very soft.

For baby: Put half the apples and liquid into blender and purée. Repeat with the other half. Strain through sieve to remove difficult-to-digest skins. Spoon out dollops or pour into tray. Freeze.

For toddler and family: Dump into colander. Mash through holes using wooden salad bowl or spoon. Makes a delicious adult dessert when topped with a little honey and cinnamon and/or whipped cream.

Puréed Fruit

Most babies like bananas, pears, peaches, and apricots. (They also like plums, but experienced mothers know that plums stain badly.) The procedure for all these fruits is the same as for pears. Avoid berries, however, until the toddler stage, because they are more difficult to digest.

10 medium-size pears or other fruit
water
¼ c. sugar (optional)

Peel, core, and slice pears. Steam or simmer in small amount of water for 25 minutes or until tender. Add sugar and cool. For a baby, put half the pears and 1 tablespoon of cooking liquid (no more; pears get soupy) into blender and blend. Repeat. Spoon out dollops or pour into cube molds. Freeze. For a toddler, follow the same procedure as with applesauce.

Carrot Juice

4 or 5 medium-size carrots
4 c. water
½ c. nonfat dry milk

Wash carrots and cut into 1-inch pieces. Put all ingredients in pan. Cover tightly, bring to boil, then reduce heat and simmer for 1 hour. Cool and strain. Can be served in a bottle with an enlarged nipple hole or in a glass for toddlers. Store in refrigerator for up to a week or freeze in cubes.

Apple Juice

6 apples
1½ qt. water

Scrub apples, core, cut into eighths. Leave them unpeeled. Stew in boiling water. Strain off liquid and store in refrigerator.

Orange Juice

6 oranges
water

Squeeze and strain oranges. Dilute with boiled water, using two parts juice to one part water. Store in refrigerator.

Carrots

2 lbs. fresh or frozen carrots
water

Peel and cut carrots into 1-inch pieces. Steam until tender or simmer in 1 cup water for 25 minutes, or until just tender. Put half the carrots and ¼ cup water into blender. Purée or chop. Repeat. Freeze.

Sweet Potatoes

A favorite first vegetable of babies. Use large, round sweet potatoes; the skinny ones may be fibrous. Or you may use canned potatoes.

2 sweet potatoes
water

Peel and slice potatoes. Put in pan with just enough water to cover. Bring to rolling boil, reduce heat, and cook slowly for 30 to 40 minutes or until tender. Cool. Purée in blender or grinder or work through sieve for infant. Mash with fork for toddler.

Plain Chicken

2 chicken breasts
1 stalk celery, cut in half
1 carrot, cut in half

Steam chicken and vegetables, covered tightly, in a small amount of water until tender. Discard skins. Remove meat from bone and chop into cubes. Purée chicken with broth left after steaming. Freeze. (The advantage of making plain chicken is that you can keep track of how much meat the baby is eating. The following dinners are composed of roughly one-third meat.)

Chicken and Rice Dinner
(from scratch)

½ frying chicken, cut in pieces
3 carrots, peeled and sliced
1 stalk celery, chopped
1 cup fresh or frozen vegetables
1 t. parsley, chopped
½ to ¾ c. brown or white rice
water

Put chicken, parsley, and 3 to 3½ cups water in pan. Bring to boil, then reduce heat and simmer for 15 minutes. Add prepared vegetables and rice and simmer about 30 minutes or until all ingredients are tender. Let cool.

Remove chicken from bone. Purée half the chicken with ½ cup broth (if there's not enough left, use chicken bouillon or other stock). Repeat with the other half of the chicken. Do the same with vegetables. Mix all together in large bowl. Freeze.

Chicken and Rice Dinner
(from leftovers)

½ c. vegetables
2 c. cooked chicken, cubed
½ c. cooked rice (or cubed
   potatoes, barley, or
   millet)

½ c. chicken broth
½ c. milk

Steam vegetables until soft. Add other ingredients and purée.
Freeze.

Beef Stew

½ to ¾ lb. top round, cut
  into 1-inch cubes
flour
1 T. margarine or butter
water

3 medium potatoes, peeled
  and cut into quarters
1 stalk celery, chopped
½ c. beans or other vegetable,
  cut into 1-inch pieces

Roll beef in flour and lightly brown in margarine. Add 1½
to 2 cups water and bring to boil; then reduce heat and simmer 1 hour. Add vegetables and simmer 20 minutes more or
until both meat and vegetables are tender. Cool. Follow same
steps as in Chicken and Rice Dinner (from scratch). Freeze.

Other Meat Dinners

Favorites are chicken, veal, ham, beef, fish, and liver, in
about that order.

2 c. cubed meat
½ c. vegetable
½ c. potato or cooked rice

1 T. chopped onion (optional)
1 c. liquid (broth, milk, cooking water)

Steam solids until barely soft. Purée (or grind) with liquid
until smooth. Freeze.

Oatmeal Breakfast

1 1/3 c. rolled oats
2½ c. water

¼ c. brown sugar (optional)
1 c. applesauce

Grate oatmeal in blender, and then stir into boiling water.
Cook 3 to 5 minutes. Add brown sugar and applesauce.
Cook 2 more minutes. Remove from heat, cover, cool.
Freeze.

Easy-Fix Toddler Favorites

Scrambleburger

1/8 lb. ground beef
1 egg, beaten
¼ c. cooked potato, diced

Brown beef in skillet, crumbling it as it cooks. Add egg and potato and cook over medium heat until egg is done.

Chicken and Rice Soup Plus

1 can condensed chicken-   *leftover rice*
*   and-rice soup*   *1 hard-boiled egg, chopped*
leftover chicken

Mix all ingredients together and divide into meal-size servings to be warmed up as needed. This is easy to eat for a child who is learning to feed herself.

Chicken "Hot Dogs"

boned and skinned chicken   *cracker crumbs*
*   breasts, cut into strips*   *lemon juice*
flour   *margarine or butter (to grease*
1 egg, beaten   *   pan)*

Roll chicken in flour, dip in egg, coat with crumbs, sprinkle with lemon juice, and sauté or bake until done. Can be frozen before or after cooking. Good hot or cold.

Hamburger Packets

1 lb. ground round steak   *½ c. water*
*   or twice-ground chuck*   *½ t. Worchestershire sauce*
1 t. margarine or butter

Brown meat in margarine over medium heat, stirring until all the redness is gone. Add water and seasoning, cover, and simmer gently for 10 minutes. Cool. Divide into eight to ten meal-size portions and place them on small squares of aluminum foil. Wrap into packets and seal tightly. Freeze. Handy if child is to eat a different meal from that of the rest of the family. Thaw in refrigerator overnight and warm in oven (takes about 10 minutes) before serving.

8

Family Fun Recipes: Cooking with the Kids

No matter who is there—Mom, Dad, babysitter, friends—the kitchen is a wonderful place to have fun with children. The following recipes were shared with us by parents of pre-school-age children.

We want our children to taste some special things like orange juice squeezed from ripe oranges, corn on the cob eaten the day it's picked, maple syrup made from the sap of maple trees—and baked goods made with real butter and sugar. So, despite a policy of watchfulness over the use of sugars and fats, we include some recipes here that require sugar or butter or both. (See the warning about honey and babies under 1 year of age, page 187.)

The recipes are broken down into these categories: Drink Treats; Popsicles; Favorite Cookies; Birthday Desserts (That Aren't Too Sweet); Rainy-Day Ideas; and Holiday Celebrations.

DRINK TREATS

Soother Special

1 c. milk
4 T. plain yogurt
½ banana, cut into chunks

¼ t. vanilla
sugar to taste

Combine all ingredients in blender until smooth. Good for 6-month-olds on up.

Strawberry Shake

1 c. ice water
½ c. strawberries or
  other fresh fruit

½ c. nonfat dry milk
honey to taste

Combine all ingredients in blender for 35 seconds.

Orange Drink for an Army

6 c. water
2 6-oz. cans frozen orange
  juice, thawed

2 c. nonfat dry milk
nutmeg

Put all ingredients in your largest mixing bowl. Mix with
spoon or egg beater until juice has dissolved and all ingredients are blended. Chill in refrigerator for 30 minutes. Serve
in bowl with nutmeg sprinkled on top of drink. Let guests
fill their own paper cups with a soup ladle. Serves eight.

Peach Spoon Drink

1 egg
1/3 c. cold water
1 c. peaches, peeled and
  diced

½ c. nonfat dry milk
1 c. crushed ice
honey to taste

Combine egg, water, peaches, and dry milk in blender. Blend
two seconds. Add crushed ice and blend until smooth. Pour
into tall glass and serve with spoon.

Banana Frosted

One mother always has a supply of bananas in her freezer
for drinks like this. Once a month or so, she wraps chunks
of peeled bananas individually in foil, puts them in a freezer
bag, and then uses them when the mood strikes.

1 c. milk
1 scoop ice cream
1 ripe banana, cut into chunks

Combine all ingredients in blender until smooth. If you
don't have a blender, put ice cream in bowl and soften it
with wooden spoon; then add other ingredients and beat
with electric mixer or egg beater.

POPSICLES

A set of Tupperware popsicle molds is nice to have around the house. The relatively soft plastic "sticks" are safer for toddlers than the conventional variety. You can, however, for older children or younger ones who will eat the popsicles under supervision, use small paper cups and insert wooden popsicle sticks (available in hobby shops) in center of the cup when the mixture is slightly hardened.

Orange Yogurt Popsicles

1 6-oz. can frozen orange juice, thawed	8 oz. plain yogurt
6 oz. water	1 t. vanilla
	1 T. sugar (optional)

Mix all ingredients together and freeze in plastic popsicle forms. You may also use small paper cups; insert a wooden popsicle stick after liquid is partially frozen. Try the commercially made yogurt popsicles found next to ice cream in most markets to see how much children like them.

Peanut Butter Banana Pops

1 c. milk	½ c. creamy peanut butter
1 ripe banana, cut into chunks	½ t. vanilla
	chopped nuts (optional)

Combine milk and banana in blender until smooth. Purée. Add peanut butter and vanilla. Blend well. Freeze in popsicle forms. Roll in chopped nuts when unmolded, if desired.

Fudgesicles

3 T. instant cocoa mix	½ t. vanilla
2 to 3 T. sugar	2 eggs, beaten
dash salt	1½ c. milk

Mix all ingredients together. Freeze in popsicle forms.

Fruitsicles

1 ripe banana, cut into
   chunks
1/3 c. honey
6-oz. can frozen orange
   juice, thawed

10-oz. package frozen strawberries, thawed
2 c. apple juice

Combine all ingredients in blender until smooth. Freeze in popsicle forms.

Three More Good Pops

1. Equal parts cranberry, apple, and orange juices.

2. Grape juice and yogurt in equal parts.

3. Milk with carob powder (1 t. powder to 1 c. milk).

For each of the above, combine ingredients in blender until smooth and freeze in popsicle forms.

FAVORITE COOKIES

Note: When making cookies or other baked goods, be sure to preheat oven to temperature indicated in each recipe.

Super-Healthy Cookies

In a pinch, these cookies make an acceptable breakfast, along with milk and fruit. They freeze well, they are easy to throw together, and they get better as days go by.

½ c. margarine or butter
1 c. brown sugar
2 eggs
1¾ c. whole-wheat flour
½ c. rolled oats
½ t. salt

2 t. baking powder
½ t. cinnamon
1 c. raisins
1 c. walnuts, chopped
1½ c. apples, peeled and
   shredded

Cream butter and sugar. Beat in eggs. Combine all remaining ingredients and stir into creamed mixture. Drop by spoonfuls onto greased cookie sheets. Bake at 350° for 12 to 15 minutes or until done. Cool on racks. Yield: 3 to 4 dozen.

2-Year-Old's Sugar Cookies

You're likely to have all the ingredients on hand for these gems, which take no more than half an hour to make from start to cleanup. Your child will beam at the compliments she gets.

Beat together:

¾ c. sugar
½ c. soft margarine or
   butter
½ t. nutmeg
½ t. vanilla
1 egg
1 T. milk

Add:

2 c. flour
1 t. baking powder
1 t. baking soda
1/8 t. salt

raisins
nuts

Beat mixture with electric mixer until creamy and smooth. Drop by spoonfuls onto greased cookie sheets. Decorate with raisins and nuts. Bake at 350° for 10 minutes. Crisp on racks. Yield: 4 dozen.

Hint:

If you're short on time, most "drop" cookies can be turned into cookie bars by baking in an oblong (9 x 14") baking dish. No cookie sheets to grease and wash!

Pumpkin Cookies

2 c. sugar
2 c. shortening (using half
   butter improves flavor)
1 16-oz. can pumpkin
2 eggs
2 t. vanilla
4 c. flour
2 t. baking powder

1 t. baking soda
1 t. salt
2 t. cinnamon
1 t. nutmeg
½ t. allspice
2 c. raisins
1 c. chopped nuts

In large bowl, cream together sugar and shortening. Add pumpkin, eggs, and vanilla. Beat well. Sift together flour, baking powder, soda, salt, and spices. Add to creamed mixture. Stir in raisins and nuts. Drop dough by spoonfuls onto greased cookie sheets. Bake at 350° for 12 to 15 minutes. Cool on racks. Yield: 7 dozen.

Criss-Cross Peanut Butter Classics

Even a 2-year-old can enjoy making the criss-crosses with the tines of a fork.

1 c. butter	1 t. vanilla
1 c. smooth peanut butter	2 c. flour
1 c. brown sugar	½ t. salt
½ c. granulated sugar	1 t. baking soda
2 eggs, beaten	

Mix butter and peanut butter together with a wooden spoon. Add both sugars and mix until creamy. Add eggs and vanilla and mix well. Sift together flour, salt, and baking soda and add to other ingredients. Mix well. Drop by spoonfuls onto greased cookie sheets. Criss-cross with fork. Bake at 350° for 10 minutes. Cool on racks. Yield: 3-4 dozen.

Hint:
Grease cookie sheets with an *unsalted* vegetable shortening such as solid Crisco. It doesn't burn as easily as butter, margarine, and oil do.

Apple-Sesame Oatmeal Cookies

1½ c. rolled oats	¼ t. salt
¾ c. white flour	1 c. unpeeled apples, chopped
¾ c. whole-wheat flour	½ c. honey
¼ c. brown sugar	½ c. oil
¼ c. sesame seeds	1 egg, beaten
1½ t. baking powder	1/3 c. milk
1½ t. cinnamon	

Combine oats, white and wheat flours, brown sugar, sesame seeds, baking powder, cinnamon, and salt. Stir in apples. Combine honey, oil, egg, and milk and add to dry ingredients. Mix thoroughly. Drop by spoonfuls onto greased cookie sheets. Bake at 375° for 10-12 minutes. Cool on racks. Yield: 3 dozen.

Fortune Cookies

A preschool child will get a big kick out of these, particularly if he knows enough letters to recognize his own name. One mother, an artist, drew pictures of inexpensive toys she knew her children wanted and inserted *them* in the cookies. Whoever got the picture got the toy: a water pistol, a ball, and the like. Before you begin baking, write out the fortunes on eighteen ½-by-1½-inch pieces of white paper.

2 eggs	*1/3 c. flour*
1/3 c. honey	*1/3 t. banana or lemon extract*

Beat eggs with egg beater or electric mixer for 2 minutes. Add honey gradually and beat for 5 minutes more. Slowly add flour and keep beating until mixture is smooth. Add extract and beat 2 more minutes.

Warm a frying pan over low heat, grease it lightly, and drop cookie batter by tablespoonfuls onto it. Leave spaces between them. Toast the cookies about 30 seconds on each side, turning them with a spatula. Keep cooking and turning until light brown, which will only take a few minutes. Making these is like making pancakes. Be resigned to losing the first batch or two until you get the hang of it. While cookies are still hot, remove them and put them on paper towels. Place a fortune strip paper into the center of each and fold up the cookie. Cool on racks. Yield: About 1½ dozen.

Butter-Cutter Cookies

We find ourselves making these over and over again. One reason is that they taste even better after they've been frozen. Served with fresh pears or other fruit, they make a fine company dessert.

Prepare dough and chill it before you mention the word "cookie" to a preschool child. Just helping with rolling out the dough and cutting out the cookies is plenty for most 3-year-olds' patience *and* their coaches! If you have cookie cutters like the Hallmark plastic variety with indentations in the form of expressions on faces, roll the dough slightly

Butter-Cutter Cookies (continued)

thicker than the recipe suggests. Expressions will turn out fine. Any cookie or cake decorations you have around are fun for children to stick on the cut-out shapes.

1 c. butter	½ t. almond extract
½ c. sugar	2½ c. flour
1 egg	

Cream butter, gradually adding sugar, and beat until light and fluffy. Beat in egg and almond extract. Sift flour and gradually blend into creamed mixture. Chill dough for ease in handling. Roll out dough on lightly floured surface to 1/8-inch thickness. Cut into desired shapes with floured cookie cutter. Place on greased cookie sheets. Decorate if desired. Bake at 350° for 8 to 12 minutes. Cool on racks. Yield: 3 to 4 dozen.

Hint:

Freeze leftover cookie dough in frozen orange juice cans. When ready for more cookies, thaw slightly, push out, slice and bake.

Oatmeal-Raisin-Coconut Cookies

2½ c. flour	¾ c. margarine or butter, softened
½ t. baking powder	2 eggs
½ t. salt	¼ c. milk
1½ c. dark brown sugar packed	¾ c. raisins
½ c. granulated sugar	1 c. flaked coconut
2 c. rolled oats	

Sift together flour, baking powder, salt, and sugars in mixing bowl. Add oats, margarine, eggs, and milk; beat at high speed until well blended. Fold in raisins and coconut at low speed until well incorporated. Chill dough 30 minutes. Break off small pieces and shape into balls. Place on greased cookie sheets and flatten slightly. Bake at 375° about 15 minutes, depending on size of cookies. Cool on racks. Yield: 3 to 4 dozen.

BIRTHDAY DESSERTS (THAT AREN'T TOO SWEET)

If you're looking for an alternative to a sugar-filled bakery birthday cake, try one of the three cakes below with one of the six frostings that follow the cake recipes. We have also included one ice cream recipe and one sherbet recipe.

Carrot Torte

This delicious light cake can be baked in three 9-inch round baking pans for a traditional torte appearance, or it can be made in one 12-cup (standard size) bundt pan.

2 c. flour	4 large or 5 medium eggs
2 t. baking powder	2¾ c. carrots, coarsely grated
1½ t. baking soda	1 8½-oz. can crushed pineapple,
1 t. salt	drained
2½ t. cinnamon	¾ c. walnuts or pecans, chopped
1¾ c. sugar	1 c. shredded coconut
1½ c. oil	Cream Cheese Frosting

Sift together flour, baking powder, soda, salt, and cinnamon. In a large bowl, mix sugar, oil, and eggs. Add flour mixture a little at a time, mixing well after each addition. Add carrots, pineapple, nuts, and coconut, and blend thoroughly. Turn into greased and floured baking pan(s). Bake at 350° for 45 minutes. Cool about 10 minutes before removing from pan(s). Cool completely and frost (between layers and top for a torte) with Cream Cheese Frosting or, for no sugar, with Sugarless Cream Cheese Frosting, both given below. Keeps well in refrigerator up to a week.

Birthday Sponge Cake

1 c. honey
½ c. brown sugar
6 egg yolks
1/3 c. orange juice
½ t. cloves
¾ t. vanilla

¾ t. vanilla
1¾ c. whole-wheat flour
1 t. baking powder
6 egg whites
1 t. cream of tartar

Beat honey and sugar until smooth. Add egg yolks one at a time, beating until creamy and thick. Add juice, cloves, and vanilla. Sift and add flour and baking powder; beat well. Beat egg whites and cream of tartar until very stiff (at least 5 minuntes). Fold into sugar mixture. Bake in greased and floured angel-food pan at 325° for 50 to 60 minutes or until surface springs back when pressed lightly. Turn upside down on rack to cool for 2 hours. Remove from pan. Frost with Honey-Egg White Frosting or Sour Cream Frosting, both given below. (If a traditional cake appearance is desired, flatten a piece of bread with a rolling pin and place over hole before frosting.)

Pumpkin Cake

2 c. honey
1 c. oil
2 c. (1-lb. can) sieved
    pumpkin
4 eggs, slightly beaten
3 c. whole-wheat flour
2 T. cinnamon

3 t. baking powder
2 t. baking soda
2 t. almond extract
1 t. salt
1 c. chopped nuts or seeds
1 c. raisins or chopped figs

Mix all ingredients together in large bowl. Pour into two well-greased 9-inch layer pans or one 9-inch tube pan. Bake layers at 350° for 50 minutes. Tube cakes will require longer baking (test with toothpick).

Cream Cheese Frosting

½ c. margarine or butter
1 8-oz. package cream
  cheese

1 t. vanilla
1 1-lb. package powdered
  sugar

Soften margarine and cream cheese. Cream together with vanilla. Sift in powdered sugar and blend well.

Sugarless Cream Cheese Frosting

2 8-oz. packages cream cheese, at room temperature
2 T. honey
¼ c. heavy cream

Mix cream cheese and honey until well blended. Add heavy cream and beat with egg beater or electric mixer until the mixture is fluffy and holds its shape. Add extra cream if it is too thick. It's delicious this way or you can add 1 teaspoon lemon, orange, or almond extract for flavor. Store frosted cake in refrigerator.

Honey-Egg White Frosting

2 egg whites
¼ t. salt

1 c. warm honey
½ t. almond extract

Using rotary beater, beat egg whites with salt until peaks form. While still beating, add honey in a slow, constant stream. Add almond extract and continue to beat until mixture is thick and fluffy.

Sour Cream Frosting

2 c. brown sugar
½ c. sour cream

1 T. margarine or butter
1 t. vanilla

Cook sugar and sour cream in saucepan over low heat until it clumps together—not quite to the stage where it forms a ball. Remove from heat. Stir in margarine and vanilla and let stand until cold. Beat until frosting turns light and spread on cake.

Carob Frosting

If it's not a birthday cake unless it's got chocolate frosting, try this.

2 T. margarine or butter,
   at room temperature
2/3 c. nonfat dry milk
1/3 c. carob powder
¼ c. honey

1 t. vanilla
¼ c. heavy cream
¼ c. walnuts or pecans,
   chopped (optional)

Cream together margarine and milk powder until smooth. Stir in carob until well blended. Add honey and vanilla and beat until fluffy. Slowly add heavy cream and beat until mixture thickens. Sprinkle chopped nuts over top if desired.

Milk-Mint Frosting

This versatile frosting can be tinted with food colors, topped with toasted or plain coconut, or mixed with toasted chopped nuts.

1 c. milk
¼ c. flour
1 c. shortening

1 c. sugar
1 t. mint flavoring (or vanilla
   or almond extract)

In saucepan, combine milk and flour until smooth. Cook over low heat until thick, stirring constantly. Cool and set aside. In a mixing bowl, cream shortening, sugar, and flavoring. Beat in cooled flour mixture. Beat until fluffy and smooth. Makes about 4 cups or enough to cover and fill a two-layer cake.

Banana Ice Cream

1 c. milk
2 eggs, lightly beaten
2/3 c. honey

2 t. vanilla
1 c. heavy cream, whipped
1 ripe banana, mashed

Beat milk into eggs. Add honey and mix well. Stir in vanilla. Fold in cream and banana. Put mixture in an ice-cube tray and partly freeze until solid, about 1 inch from edges. Transfer to mixer bowl and beat until smooth. Return to tray and freeze again. Strawberries or other fruit may be substituted for bananas. Six servings.

Fruit Sherbet

¾ c. crushed fruit (pine-
   apple, strawberries,
   raspberries, apricots)
2 T. lemon juice
¾ c. honey

1½ t. unflavored gelatin
2 T. cold water
¼ c. hot milk
1 c. cold milk
1 egg white, beaten stiff

Mix fruit, lemon juice, and honey. Let stand until syrup
forms (about 2 hours). Soften gelatin in cold water, dissolve
in hot milk, and add to fruit mixture. Slowly stir in cold
milk. Pour into ice-cube tray and freeze until partly solid—
about 1 hour. Beat partially frozen mixture in a chilled bowl
with a rotary beater until creamy and frothy. Fold in beaten
egg white. Return to tray. Freeze until firm, stirring occasionally. Six to eight servings.

    For lemon sherbet, substitute ¾ cup lemon juice and 2
teaspoons grated lemon rind for fruit, and increase honey to
1 cup.

RAINY-DAY IDEAS

For the toddler with a cold, a cranky 2-year-old; for rainy
Sundays . . .

David's Banana Freezies

2 large bananas, cut into
   1-inch chunks
2 T. honey

Topping options:
¼ c. chopped peanuts
¼ c. wheat germ
½ c. chocolate sauce

Dip banana chunks into honey. Roll in topping. Freeze on
cookie sheets lined with waxed paper. When hard, store in
plastic bag. Serve frozen.

"Snow" Cones

crushed ice
1 6-oz. can frozen orange,
   grape, or other juice, thawed

Put crushed ice into paper cups, and pour juice over the ice.
Insert a straw into each cup of ice.

Snow Ice Cream

clean snow *brown sugar or honey*
milk *vanilla*

Pour small amount of milk over snow (small in proportion
to amount of snow). Stir in a little sugar and a little vanilla.
Mix up and serve immediately.

Homemade Peanut Butter

1 lb. peanuts (in shell)
2 T. peanut or other oil
salt to taste

Shell peanuts and remove skins. Chop nuts until fine in a
blender or put through the finest blade of a food grinder
three times. Mix together oil, salt, and ground nuts. Store
in refrigerator. (If a preschooler wants to eat some shelled
nuts, watch her closely. Very young children can easily
choke on nuts.)

Peanut Butter Candy

1/3 c. honey *½ c. nonfat dry milk*
1/3 c. peanut butter *¼ c. peanuts, finely chopped*
¼ c. toasted wheat germ *flour, if necessary*

If your wheat germ isn't toasted, place in a 350° oven for
about 10 minutes, or until lightly brown.

Combine honey and peanut butter until creamy. Mix in
wheat germ and milk powder, and then work in the peanuts
with your fingers. On a cutting board, roll mixture into a
sausage shape about ¾ inch thick, doing it gently so it doesn't
stick to your hands. (Flouring the board and your hands
might help.) Cut candy into one-inch pieces and wrap each
in plastic wrap, waxed paper, or aluminum foil, and store in
a covered candy jar. If you want it chewy, store it in the refrigerator.

Wheat Germ Zucchini Bread

A good way to use up those monster zucchini, if you have a garden. This recipe makes two loaves and freezes well. Let the kids shred the zucchini if you don't mind a mess. Better yet, let them make the whole thing.

3 eggs	2½ c. flour
1 c. oil	½ c. toasted wheat germ
½ c. granulated sugar	2 t. baking soda
1 c. brown sugar, packed	2 t. salt
3 t. maple flavoring	½ t. baking powder
2 c. peeled and seeded zuc-	1 c. walnuts, finely chopped
chini, coarsely shredded	1/3 c. sesame seeds

Beat eggs. Add oil, sugars, and maple flavoring and continue beating until foamy. Stir in zucchini. In separate bowl, combine flour, wheat germ, soda, salt, baking powder, and walnuts. Stir gently into zucchini mixture until just blended. Divide batter between two greased and floured 5-by-9-inch pans. Sprinkle sesame seeds evenly over tops. Bake at 350° for 1 hour or until toothpick comes out clean. Cool in pans 10 minutes. Finish cooling on rack.

Carrot Bread

A recipe for two loaves of bread that will please even the most confirmed carrot hater.

4 eggs	1½ t. baking soda
2 c. grated carrots	1½ t. cinnamon
½ c. oil	2½ t. baking powder
¾ t. margarine or butter	¼ t. salt
2 c. brown sugar	½ t. ground cloves
2 c. whole-wheat flour	½ c. raisins (optional)

In blender or with electric mixer, mix well the eggs, carrots, oil, margarine, and brown sugar. In a separate bowl, mix dry ingredients and add them to carrot mixture. Add raisins, if desired. Pour into greased and floured 5-by-9-inch pans. Bake at 350° about 1 hour.

Last-Forever Bran Muffins

This recipe makes dozens and dozens. Cut recipe in half if you don't have room in the refrigerator to store extra batter, which keeps up to six weeks. These muffins are wonderful for breakfast or with soups and stews.

1 16-oz. box brand flakes	2½ c. whole-wheat flour
1 qt. buttermilk (or 1 qt. milk plus 1 T. vinegar)	2½ c. white flour
1 c. oil	2 t. baking soda
1 c. molasses	2 t. salt
1 c. brown sugar, packed	raisins, dates, orange rind (to taste)
4 eggs, beaten	

Stir bran flakes and milk together. Add rest of ingredients. Refrigerate and use as needed. Fill muffin tins 2/3 full. Bake at 400° for 15 to 20 minutes (slightly longer if batter is cold).

Orange Gelatin Dessert

1 envelope (2 T.) un-flavored gelatin	1¼ c. freshly squeezed orange juice or other fruit juice
½ c. cold water	1 c. orange sections or other fruit, cut into bite-size pieces
¼ c. sugar	

Sprinkle gelatin over cold water in small saucepan. Place over low heat and stir until gelatin dissolves. Remove from heat. Add sugar, remaining water, and orange juice. Stir until sugar dissolves. Pour into individual molds or a 2-cup bowl, add fruit, and chill until firm.

Honey Tapioca

3 T. quick-cooking tapioca	1 egg yolk
1/8 t. salt	1 egg white
3 T. honey	¾ t. vanilla
2 c. milk	cherries (optional)

Stir together tapioca, salt, 2 T. of honey, milk, and egg yolk in saucepan. Let stand five minutes. Meanwhile, beat egg white until foamy. Cook tapioca mixture until it boils, turn down heat, stir constantly while it thickens (10 minutes or more). Add the remaining honey to egg white and beat. Stir into tapioca mixture. Add vanilla. Pour into small dishes, top with cherry if desired, and allow to cool. Refrigerate, covered with plastic wrap. Four servings.

Big Chewy Pretzels

These can be shaped in the form of snakes or in conventional pretzel shapes. They are delicious eaten warm.

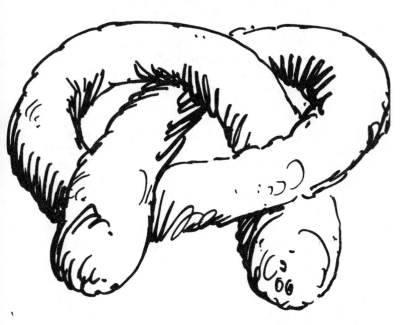

½ c. warm water
1 package yeast
¼ c. honey
1½ t. salt
1 13-oz. can evaporated
   milk plus enough warm
   water to make 2 c.
¼ c. oil

3 c. rye or whole-wheat flour
2½ c. white flour
¾ t. baking powder
2 qts. water
3 T. salt
1 egg white
coarse (Kosher) salt
caraway or poppy seeds

Pour warm water into bowl and add yeast. Stir until dissolved. Add honey, salt, milk, oil. Stir and slowly add half the rye (or whole-wheat) flour and 1 c. of white flour. When flour is well mixed in, cover bowl and let dough rise in a warm place for about 40 minutes or until bubbly.

    Sift together remaining 1½ c. white flour and baking powder and add it to dough, along with remaining rye flour. Stir well. Knead five minutes on floured board, or until dough is smooth. Break off pieces of dough and roll into long snakes about ½-inch thick and 20 inches long. Tie into loose knots for regular pretzel shapes or make into snakes. Place on three greased cookie sheets and let rise, uncovered, for 30 minutes in a warm place.

To give pretzels a shiny crust, bring 2 qts. water plus 3 T. salt to boil in a big pot. When pretzels have risen, dip each one in boiling water for two seconds. It's easiest if you use a large wire strainer or French fry basket to dip the pretzels in. Place pretzels on cookie sheets.

Add 1 T. water to egg white and beat lightly with fork. Using pastry brush, paint pretzels with this mixture, then sprinkle with Kosher-type (coarse) salt. Use caraway seeds or poppy seeds to make eyes on snakes. Bake at 400° for 20 minutes or until golden brown. Serve warm with butter or mustard or wrap well and store.

Cream Cheese Vegetable Dip

The kids might like their vegetables better with this dip—and it's great to have around when the adults are watching a football game.

*1 8-oz. package cream
  cheese, softened*
*1 small can minced clams,
  drained*

dash pepper
*1 medium onion, diced
  (optional)*

Combine all ingredients well and serve with crisp vegetables: carrots, celery slices, broccoli tips, cauliflower tips, green beans, etc.

Fried Banana Sandwich

1 firm, slightly green banana per person
1 T. margarine or butter per person

Peel banana and slice on an angle into pieces that are about ½-inch thick. Melt margarine or butter in a large frying pan over low flame. Put banana in pan and fry until lightly brown, turning occasionally with spatula. Serve warm between bread, plain or spread with cream cheese, sour cream, honey, jam, or a combination of these.

Kathy's Cream Cheese Cupcakes

A friend serves these cupcakes—which are actually miniature cheesecakes—at her annual Christmas buffet. She tops them with blueberry or cherry pie filling. Her children enjoy putting paper cupcake holders in muffin tins, putting wafers in the paper holders, and doing the garnishing when they're finished.

2 8-oz. packages cream cheese, softened	½ t. vanilla
	2 eggs
½ c. sugar	vanilla wafers

Combine all ingredients except for wafers and mix well. Using aluminum-foil cupcake holders arranged on a cookie sheet, put one wafer in the bottom of each and fill 2/3 with cream-cheese mixture. Bake at 350° for 12 to 14 minutes. Garnish with half strawberry or other fresh fruit if desired. Yield: 14 cupcakes.

If you can't find foil holders, use paper holders in a muffin tin. Baking time may be slightly longer. The paper comes off easily, leaving a cake that can be eaten with the fingers.

Easy-Way-Out Cupcakes

1 box cake mix
2 dozen flat-bottomed
  ice cream cones
1 box frosting mix (optional)

Follow package instructions for preparing the cake mix. Stand ice cream cones in muffin tins or on foil-covered cookie sheets and fill them ¾ full with cake mix. Bake them, following cake-mix package directions for cupcakes. Either frost when cool and/or serve with a scoop of ice cream.

English Muffins

When eaten fresh, these are a memorable treat, although they require a good deal of time to make. Even so, you may never again be satisfied with "store bought" English muffins.

1 c. hot water	*1 cake compressed yeast*
½ c. milk, scalded	*1 T. warm water (85°)*
2 t. sugar	*4 c. flour, sifted*
1 t. salt	*3 T. margarine or butter, softened*

In a mixing bowl, combine the hot water, scalded milk, sugar, and salt. In a separate bowl, dissolve the yeast in the warm water, let stand for 10 minutes, and add to the first mixture. Gradually beat half the flour into the milk mixture. Cover the bowl with a damp cloth and let the dough rise in a warm place for about 1½ hours, or until it collapses back into the bowl. Beat in the margarine and then beat or knead in the remaining flour. Let the dough rise, again in a warm place, until it doubles in bulk.

Place the dough on a lightly floured board and press or pat it until it is about ¾-inch thick. Cut into rounds about 3 inches in diameter (a clean empty 6-ounce tuna-fish or small cat-food can works well for this) and then let the rounds stand in a warm place until they double in bulk.

On a fairly hot, well-greased griddle, fry the rounds until they are light brown, turning them once. After cooling them slightly on racks, split the rounds in the traditional way with the tines of a fork and toast them. Yield: about 20 muffins.

Popcorn Storm

If you have an electric corn popper or an electric frying pan, this is a sure-fire idea to liven up a slow afternoon. The craziness is therapeutic for adults, too.

Place popper or pan in middle of a large old sheet. Put in oil and corn kernels as usual. Leave the lid on at first so the oil will heat up. When corn starts to pop, remove top. Stand at the edge of the sheet and watch the popcorn fly. Remember that the kernels will be hot! (Also, some of the corn may pop off the sheet, possibly getting grease on the floor, so do this in a room without a carpet.)

HOLIDAY CELEBRATIONS

Halloween

A nice, quiet ecology lesson can be taught in the house if
you use up the Halloween pumpkin. Below are recipes for
toasted pumpkin seeds and for a cooked pumpkin that might
then be used for the pumpkin cake or pumpkin cookie recipes
given in preceding sections. Make sure that the pumpkin is
still fresh. Also, when buying a pumpkin for cooking, as opposed to decorating, make sure it's a "sugar" pumpkin. Ask
the person selling them about this.

Toasted Pumpkin Seeds

pumpkin seeds
salt
margarine or butter

When cleaning out the pumpkin, separate seeds from fibers
and set the seeds aside, uncovered, to dry. Coat dried pumpkin seeds with melted margarine or butter. Put seeds, one
layer deep, in shallow pan. Bake at 350° until crisp and light
brown. Season with salt and serve warm or cooled. (Optional step for plumper seeds: soak overnight in salted water—
1½ t. salt to 2/3 c. water—and dry before coating with butter and cooking.) Pumpkin seeds have fewer calories and less
fat than peanuts, but about the same amount of protein.

Cooked Pumpkin

1 whole pumpkin
shallow baking pan

Cut top out of pumpkin, leaving stem on for handle. Set
aside. Scoop out seeds and fiber. Put top back on and place
pumpkin in shallow baking pan. Bake at 350° for 1½ hours
or until pumpkin is tender. Remove from oven and cool.
Peel skin off the pumpkin and mash pulp with a fork. It's
now ready to use for cake, pie, or cookies.

If you don't have a gingerbread person cookie cutter, trace this one, then make a pattern out of cardboard; place pattern on dough and cut around it.

Christmas

Gingerbread Men

Start this yourself the day before, as the dough needs to be chilled. These make good gifts for the children's friends.

3 c. flour
2 t. ground ginger
1 t. baking soda
¼ t. salt
½ c. milk

2 t. lemon juice
½ c. margarine or butter,
softened
½ c. sugar
½ c. dark molasses

Decorating Frosting (optional; recipe below)
red, yellow, green food colorings (optional)
raisins and nuts (optional)

Sift flour, ginger, soda, and salt into medium-size bowl. Combine milk and lemon juice in a cup and let stand several minutes. In a large bowl, cream butter and sugar until fluffy and light. Beat in molasses. Slowly beat in flour mixture, a third at a time, alternately with milk mixture, until blended. Wrap dough tightly and chill at least four hours or overnight until firm enough to roll.

On a lightly floured board, roll out dough, half at a time, until it is ¼-inch thick. Cut into shapes of your choice with a floured cookie cutter. Place shapes on lightly greased cookie sheet. Bake at 350° for 13 minutes, or until cookies are puffed and firm. Remove carefully with spatula to wire rack. Cool completely. Frost with Decorating Frosting or one of the frostings already given. Decorate with raisins and nuts if desired. Yield: about 2 dozen, depending on size.

Decorating Frosting

2 egg whites
1/8 t. cream of tartar
3½ c. powdered sugar, sifted
food coloring (optional)

Beat egg whites slightly in a medium-size bowl; beat in cream of tartar, then slowly beat in powdered sugar until mixture is smooth and stiff enough to hold its shape. Food coloring may be used to color portions of frosting, if desired. (If any frosting is left over, cover bowl with wet paper towels, cover tightly with plastic wrap or aluminum foil, and store in the refrigerator.)

Children enjoy the decorating. If you have a cake-decorating set, attach a writing tube and go to work. The children, however, may be just as happy with this simple device: snip a tiny corner off a small, clean envelope or a plastic baggie and fill it with frosting. Then the frosting can be squirted onto the cookies.

Chanukah

Yetta's Potato Latkes
(Potato Pancakes)

6 medium potatoes,
  peeled and grated
1 small onion, grated
1 t. salt

1 egg
½ t. baking powder
3 T. flour or motzo meal
½ c. oil

Press most of the liquid out of the grated potatoes and mix them well with the onion, salt, and egg. Add baking powder to flour and stir into the potato mixture. Heat half the oil in a frying pan. Drop the potato mixture by tablespoonfuls into the oil and fry until brown on both sides. Add oil as necessary. Serve warm with applesauce or sour cream.

Valentine's Day or St. Patrick's Day

Butter Hearts / Shamrock Cookies

The dough for these crisp cookies must be chilled for an hour
before cookies are shaped.

½ c. margarine or butter,
   at room temperature
½ t. vanilla

½ c. powdered sugar
1¼ c. flour
¼ t. salt

Combine butter and vanilla. Sift sugar into butter and mix
until creamy. Sift together flour and salt and add half of it
to sugar-butter mixture. Mix together with wooden spoon.
Add remaining ingredients and mix well. (If dough is very
crumbly, cut in 2 - 3 tablespoons of ice water.) Chill in refrigerator one hour.

On a lightly floured board, knead and then roll out
dough until it is ½-inch thick. Use cookie cutters if you
like, but this dough works fine with hand shaping alone.
A very young child can mash a piece of dough right on the
cookie sheet and work with it there. Shape hearts for Valentine's Day or shamrocks for St. Patrick's Day. If you feel
like it, shape an elephant! You can also make squares, tri-

angles, and circles. But whatever you make, try to keep
cookies the same thickness so that they all bake at the same
rate. Bake at 375° for about 8 minutes, or until cookies are
slightly brown around the edges but not in the middle. Remove with spatula and cool on rack. Yield: about 1 dozen.

Easter

Easter Monday Deviled Eggs

4 eggs, hard boiled

2 T. sour cream

¼ t. dry mustard

1/8 t. ground black pepper

1/8 t. salt

paprika and parsley (optional)

Remove shells from eggs. Cut eggs in half lengthwise. Remove yolks and, in a bowl, mash them with a fork. Add remaining ingredients and mix until smooth. Put some of egg-yolk mixture back into each egg-white half. Sprinkle with paprika and garnish with parsley. Refrigerate until ready to serve.

Mother's Day

Eggs-in-a-Frame

3 slices bread

margarine or butter

3 eggs

salt and pepper

Using a very small glass, cut a circle from the center of each bread slice. Melt butter in frying pan over medium heat. Fry bread and turn it over. Lower heat. Break the egg into the hole. Season. Cover the pan and cook 3 to 5 minutes. (The egg may be flipped if preferred.) Repeat with remaining eggs. Three servings.

Father's Day

What child is there who does not find the pancake-making process fascinating? This is a nice light pancake that a child can help to make for Dad.

Cottage Cheese Pancakes

1½ c. creamed cottage
   cheese

6 eggs

½ c. flour

½ t. salt

Sieve cottage cheese or beat until smooth, or put into blender. Beat eggs until light, add cheese, and blend. Add flour and salt. Blend until smooth. Drop by tablespoonfuls onto lightly greased preheated griddle and bake until bubbles appear on surface. Turn and continue to cook until lightly browned on the second side. Serve hot with butter and syrup, jelly, or jam. Yield: about 2 dozen 3-inch pancakes.

FAMILY RECIPE NOTES

FAMILY RECIPE NOTES

9

Basic Medical Care

"Let your own common sense be your guide—you'll be surprised at how well it comes through. Most illnesses are not of an emergency nature. Dr. Spock's *Baby and Child Care* is a good reference. If you're really concerned, call the doctor and put your mind at ease."

Mother of four / Barrington, Ill.

Our foremost job during the first three years is to take a body that is smaller than a Thanksgiving turkey and keep it flourishing until it reaches doorknob height and then some. Along the way there are moments of terror for us all. The terror will be minimized if you tackle it head on by being prepared.

This chapter covers what we consider to be the basics of good mother-variety of medical care: finding and using a good pediatrician; knowing ahead of time about the common illnesses you'll almost surely encounter; knowing something about the care of children's teeth; and learning to trust your own instincts about your child's health.

Starting on page 243 is an alphabetized section covering the common medical problems, the ones you'll most likely face before your child is 3. In this section we have summarized the experience of other mothers as well as our own reading, as mothers, of several books by pediatricians.

There is a chart of standard times for shots on page 241. Following it we cover what a parent needs to know about a child's teeth; we list medical supplies to keep on hand for routine care and emergencies; and we offer a few survival tips for the chief caretaker.

This chapter is not intended as a replacement for one's family doctor—or even for Dr. Spock's book. Rather, it reflects the experiences of many mothers handling common illnesses. This will give you a feeling for what to expect in most situations. The information presented here should be used along with the advice of your child's doctor.

"Find a pediatrician whom you can call for reassurance, one who has faith in your mothering. (Does your child *look* sick to you? Does your doctor value your instincts?) I'm on my third pediatrician, and it was worthwhile shopping around until I found one who has faith in me, who treats my concerns seriously, who is supportive about breast feeding, and who is interested in my children as total people."

Mother of two / St. Louis, Mo.

THE PERFECT PEDIATRICIAN

You probably can't be absolutely sure that a pediatrician is right for you until you've been through a couple of your baby's illnesses with him. (We say "him" because 85 percent of pediatricians are men.) However, you can maximize your chances of getting a good one on the first try by looking for a pediatrician who is:

Close to your home. Picture yourself driving ten miles to the doctor's office with a screaming child whose cut, while not emergency-room size, needs looking at.

On the staff of a good hospital. Usually this guarantees both that a doctor is respected by his peers and that your child will get excellent care if he becomes seriously ill. If the hospital is fairly close, so much the better.

Liked by other mothers whose opinions you respect. This indicates that he in turn probably respects the competence of mothers. It also indicates that he's probably been available when needed, or has provided a capable colleague to take over when he wasn't available. Ask other mothers about this. What happened when they needed a doctor on a Sunday morning?

"Boarded." This means that he has passed a stiff examination given by the American Board of Pediatrics. Besides "MD," he can write "FAAP" after his name, indicating that he is a Fellow of the American Academy of Pediatricians. If you choose a general practitioner, look for one who is a member of the American Academy of General Practice, an organization that requires members to take refresher courses to keep up with new medical developments.

How Do You Find Him?

Where do you look for such a paragon? Here are some suggestions:

• If you have a fairly sizable library nearby, telephone the reference desk and ask if it has a recent edition of the *Directory of Medical Specialists*, which is published every two years. By consulting this volume you can quickly determine the names of the pediatricians who practice in your area, whether they are boarded, where they went to medical school, when they went (and hence how old they are), where they interned, and where they did their residencies.

• Ask other mothers. If you don't know any other mothers of preschool children, the big users of pediatricians, find mothers in the nearest park on a sunny morning. Or stop by a nursery school at noon and ask the mothers waiting to pick up their children. Or ask the women waiting in your obstetrician's office. One mother says, "A friend liked her pediatrician so much that she suggested I go with her when she took her son for his six-month checkup. I was pregnant and pediatrician shopping. That's how I found mine. I can ask him any kind of baby-care question without feeling intimidated."

• Check with nurses, the real doctor experts. If you don't know any, telephone the children's section of your local hospital and ask for the head nurse. She probably won't give you the name of just one doctor, but she may give you the names of two or three. You might also be able to get knowledgeable advice about potential doctors from emergency-room staff members, who usually see several children's doctors in action on any given day.

• Ask your obstetrician, your dentist, and your lawyer which pediatricians they use for their children. Other professionals are likely to demand good medical care for their own families.

• Call a nearby medical school pediatrics department and ask who on the staff has a private practice in your area; then check to see if any of those doctors are accepting new patients. You might also ask if they know of any graduates who have recently established a practice in your community.

Selecting Your Pediatrician

After you've located a couple of good candidates, set up appointments to meet them and look over their offices. If possible, arrange for your husband to come along as well. Any good pediatrician welcomes an exploratory visit before the baby is born, and many doctors don't charge for such visits.

It's important to make sure that the doctor you choose is the sort of person you and your husband can easily communicate with and that he treats you, as well as your child, with respect and concern. Dr. Barbara Korsh, a professor of pediatrics at USC Medical School, has observed that many mothers feel shut out by the doctor-child relationship. After interviewing hundreds of mothers, she found that those who felt rushed, put down, or brushed off by their doctors were less willing or able to follow medical instructions. Often a doctor who is jolly and smiling with a child turns to Mom and becomes brusque and authoritarian.

Ask the doctor a few questions about topics that generate some disagreement among pediatricians: crying, breast feeding, colic, use of antibiotics. Try to determine whether his general attitude toward medicine and child rearing is in harmony with yours.

Remember that a pediatrician tends to serve as a first resort in dealing with learning and emotional difficulties as well as physical problems. Does the doctor seem sensitive to and perceptive about nonmedical issues? Would you trust his judgment in most areas of day-to-day living?

Remember too that your pediatrician may have to give you bad news from time to time. Does he seem like the type who would be willing to give it even at the risk of losing a patient?

Here are some other questions to ask the doctor (or yourself) during a check-out interview:

What are the office hours? Doctors with the longest office hours are, naturally, the most likely to be there when you need them. If a doctor regularly takes three-day weekends, you may want to look elsewhere.

Does he have a call-in time? Often you'll want advice on matters that don't require an office visit. Many pediatricians set aside a special hour, usually from seven to eight in the morning, for such telephone calls.

"I have a pediatrician with a regular morning telephone time," one mother says. "I find it a great source of comfort, especially with an infant whose symptoms I'm never sure warrant a visit."

What is the office atmosphere? Are there toys and comfortable chairs for toddlers and young children? Listen to the way the staff handles telephone calls—how would you like to be a distraught mother on the other end of the phone? If a mother with a really sick baby comes in, how are they treated? Do the nurses separate children with obviously contagious illnesses from the rest of the waiting room? Does it appear that there is a standard long wait, or is there an effort to keep things moving?

Is it a group practice? Even pediatricians need time off. In a group practice of three or more doctors, at least one is likely to be on duty or on call at all times. If you choose a good doctor, his partners are probably equally good.

What is the procedure if he is not available? Ask the doctor— whether he's in group practice or not—to spell out what arrangements are made when he and/or his partners aren't available.

When Do You Need Him?

Many pediatricians would like us to treat our first child as though she were a second child. Baloney! Nature surely is protecting the weak when new parents face a baby's illness with fright and insecurity. Insecurity is nothing to be ashamed of. As parents, it is our duty and right to learn how and when to seek medical care for our children. Good pediatric care requires close cooperation between parents and doctors.

The best way to make an ally of your pediatrician is to find out ahead of time how he wants you to handle mild cases of the four most common illnesses or symptoms of illness: fever, diarrhea, vomiting, and colds. He'll probably be delighted to give you explicit instructions. Then follow through, but don't hesitate to call him for moral support if you need it.

One mother ruefully told us, "My pediatrician gave us a one-page sheet of instructions. It told how to use aspirin for fever, gave a routine for vomiting and another for diarrhea, told how to give a nasal rinse to infants with colds, and listed things from the drugstore to have on hand. I pasted the sheet on a linen-closet door and forgot about it. Only now that I've been through every single thing on it the hard way, making and paying for calls and visits to the doctor, do I realize how very useful the sheet could have been." Be sure to ask your doctor if he has such a set of instructions— and if he does, be sure *you* remember to refer to it when necessary.

The second-best way to get the most from your pediatric dollar is to make good use of the telephone. The average pediatrician has hundreds of patients, and we suspect that most doctors would like to have a good night's sleep from time to time. If your baby has been running a fever all day, don't wait until midnight to call the doctor. In fact, don't call at night unless the situation seems critical enough to warrant a hospital visit (see box, "When to Get Help Fast," page 242). Use the morning telephone hour, if your doctor has one, for routine questions and garden-variety symptoms. "Use common sense," one mother urges. "I never just ran to the phone, but if I was truly worried about a situation, whether big or small, I didn't hesitate to call and get the doctor's reassurances or advice." Other mothers point out that pediatricians' nurses can also be very helpful over the telephone.

Reference Medical Books

Even experienced parents often have a hard time deciding whether a given situation warrants a call to the doctor or a visit to a specialist. After all, there's a large gray area between a stuffy nose and an obvious emergency. Here's where a good reference book, particularly Dr. Spock's *Baby and Child Care*, can be worth its weight in gold. You will find Spock and other reference books in the 649.1 section of most local libraries.

Another of our favorite books is *Childhood Illness: A Common Sense Approach* by Dr. Jack G. Shiller, a pediatrician and professor of pediatrics at Columbia University. Dr. Shiller explains that during the course of his practice he began to realize that many of his patients were being brought in by their mothers for reasons he considered unnecessary. He wrote the book in an attempt to teach parents enough about everyday illnesses so that they would have the confidence to muddle through on their own.

Despite its flippant title, another useful book is Dr. Marvin J. Gersh's *How to Raise Children at Home in Your Spare Time*. The medical sections are short, punchy, and helpful. Also helpful are *New Wives' Tales: Conversations with Parents About Today's Pediatrics* by Dr. Lendon H. Smith and *A Sigh of Relief: The First Aid Handbook for Childhood Emergencies* by Martin I. Green.

What Should You Tell Him?

A baby or toddler can't say where it hurts, so it's essential for parents to accurately record and report a child's symptoms. Be prepared to give the doctor the following information:

● *Fluctuations in temperature*. Keep a chart, and indicate whether the readings are oral, rectal, or armpit.

● *Whether the child's throat is red or shows white spots*. Use the flat end of a spoon or even a lollipop if need be to check.

● *Whether neck glands are swollen*.

● *Times of any vomiting bouts and what the child ate or drank between bouts*.

● *Frequency, texture, and color of bowel movements.*

● *Whether the child's breath smells foul.* This might indicate tonsilitis or a strep throat.

● *Whether the child is sleeping more than usual or otherwise "not himself."*

Jot down all relevant information and keep it near the telephone so that it will be handy when you finally reach the doctor. It's easy to become confused about important details when a baby is miserable and screaming. Also be on the lookout for other symptoms to describe when you think your child "looks funny."

Dr. Virginia E. Pomeranz, a professor of pediatrics at Cornell University and the author of several books on childhood illnesses, insists that it never hurts to tell a doctor too much. Seemingly unrelated facts, she says, may be important: a recent fall, a walk in the woods, a new dog, a trip to a strange country or a new city.

Just as you give the doctor good information, take notes when you visit him. Carry along a list of questions. When you're trying to comfort a baby who's just had a shot, it's hard to remember exactly what you wanted to ask the doctor—and what he says in response.

Tips for Easing Office Visits

Try to schedule appointments so that you won't have a long wait—usually for the first hour after lunch. In the morning, a doctor may be delayed by hospital rounds. Often it's worth postponing a child's afternoon nap to avoid lingering in the waiting room.

Carry along a selection of small toys or books. Pediatricians' offices are usually well stocked with such items but other doctors' waiting rooms may not be.

Take an extra bottle for the baby or a snack for an older child in case the wait is long.

Never lie to a child about what is coming. Any book you find describing a doctor's office equipment or his job can help even an 18-month-old understand what is going on and feel less anxious. You should also make sure that the doctor doesn't lie to or try to trick your child. For instance, some doctors will point to a picture on the wall or do something else to distract a child and then give her a shot unexpectedly, which doesn't make it hurt any less. Ask your doctor to tell both you and your child what to expect.

Ask the doctor if sample drugs are available when he is writing out a prescription. You can save money, and the doctor is usually happy to oblige. Also, ask that drugs be prescribed by their generic or chemical names instead of by brand names, so you can shop around for the best prices. Generic drugs are the same quality as brand-name drugs, but they tend to be significantly less expensive.

Also ask the doctor if he happens to know which pharmacy in your area has the lowest prices; often doctors do know. One mother mentioned how grateful she was when her pediatrician told her of a supermarket pharmacy that charged much less for all the family's medications than the one she had been going to.

"Doctors don't mind being questioned. Write their answers down immediately, as everything will become a blur when you leave and you'll be unsure and confused about exactly what was said." *Mother of three / Tucson, Ariz.*

When Should You Change Doctors?

"It's like taking your car to a new garage," groaned a friend who was considering changing her pediatrician. Switching to a new doctor isn't easy. After all, the effectiveness of a pediatrician hinges in part on familiarity.

If you're not happy with your child's doctor, finding a better one may be tough. However, you probably should start looking if:

• by the age of 3, your child still doesn't like the pediatrician.

• the doctor or one of his partners isn't available within a reasonable amount of time in an emergency.

• he has no set time for accepting or returning telephone calls, and if he acts annoyed when you do call about what you consider an emergency.

• his attitude is consistently patronizing, or if he makes you feel less, not more, confident about your mothering.

• the office is so busy that you can't be fitted in quickly when you feel it's necessary for your child to see the doctor fast.

• after a reasonable time, a potentially serious problem seems no closer to solution than it did at the start of the treatment.

• the doctor is so casual that he leaves everything up to you, or, conversely, if he allows no room for your own decisions and discretion.

SHOTS AND CHECKUPS

Besides finding a good doctor for your child and learning how best to make use of his services, it's essential to develop your own system for remembering shots and checkups. "My 3-year-old just got measles," one mother told us. "It was awful, and I blame myself because I realized she'd never gotten her measles shot. I thought my pediatrician would remind me but he forgot. And I forgot."

Doctors today strongly suspect permanent learning disorders may result from a severe case of measles, if not pneumonia and encephalitis, which are other complications. Yet, for lack of the shot, over 40,000 children a year, twice the figure of ten years ago, still get the disease, according to government figures.

It's foolhardy to leave it to a doctor to remind you when a child's shots are due. See the chart on the facing page which may help you remember when things are due. Also, keep your own immunization records, and file them so that you can find them quickly. Ask the doctor to sign or initial each entry (you may need to provide proof of immunizations when your child enters school).

Keeping your own medical records provides a safeguard against loss or misfiling in a busy doctor's office, and such a record is a handy thing to have when an emergency-room doctor wants to know when your child had his last tetanus shot. Moreover, since medical records are legally considered to be the property of the physician, not the patient, having your own copy can be a necessity if you move or decide to change doctors. This practice is changing in some areas,

IMMUNIZATION CHART

The American Academy of Pediatrics recommends the following immunization schedule for the preschool years. Use this record to jog your memory and that of your child's doctor, if necessary. If your child has any symptoms of illness when she's due for a shot, check with your doctor *before* bringing her in—usually you'll be advised to wait until she's better. Note: Your pediatrician's checkup and immunization schedule may vary slightly from the one below. Also, as new knowledge becomes available, recommendations for immunization schedules may undergo change.

Date of Birth: First Child_____ Second Child_____

Age	Immunization	Date Received First Child	Second Child
2 months	DTP diphtheria, tetanus, pertussis (whooping cough)		
	Polio		
4 months	DTP		
	Polio		
6 months	DTP		
1 year	TB test		
15 months	Measles		
	Rubella (German measles)		
	Mumps		
1½ years	DTP		
	Polio		
4 - 6 years (before school)	DTP		
	Polio		

242 / Mother to Mother

however; also, many doctors are perfectly willing to forward your records to another physician even if they won't give them to you.

If you suspect your child may be subject to allergies because of your or your husband's family history, ask the doctor about postponing shots. Some doctors maintain that a three-month delay in immunizing such babies helps prevent complications. (Others say that regulating the diet is more helpful.)

No matter how healthy your child seems, follow the schedule of checkups your doctor suggests. During these examinations the doctor has time to check for potentially serious diseases as well as observe a child's general development.

When to Get Help Fast

Call a doctor at any time, day or night, if any of the following symptoms exists:

- Pronounced difficulty in breathing.

- Bleeding that cannot be stopped.

- Severe abdominal pain that lasts for more than an hour.

- Convulsions.

- Unconsciousness after a fall, or difficulty in arousing a child from sleep.

- Prolonged diarrhea and/or vomiting. This can cause serious dehydration in a child under 3.

- Fever—of 101 degrees or higher in an infant under 3 months, or of more than 103 degrees orally or 104 rectally in an older baby or toddler.

- Poisoning, suspected or certain.

Know the location of the nearest twenty-four-hour emergency room. If you can't reach your doctor right away, take the child there.

HINTS ABOUT COMMON MEDICAL PROBLEMS:
AN ALPHABETICAL LIST

"Common illnesses are inevitable. Get a good medical insurance plan and a pediatrician close by. I'm a registered nurse, but we went to the doctor as much as anyone."
Mother of three / Larchmont, N.Y.

You'll probably feel like an old hand at coping with most of the illnesses and minor emergencies described in this section by the time your first child is 2 or 3. Still, it's hard for a new parent to remain cool and unflustered the first few times around. You may be able to minimize your panic (and perhaps, eventually, the number of your trips to the doctor) by reading what pediatricians and experienced mothers have to say about the home treatment of common ailments.

Colds

Most babies have two or three colds the first year, but a perfectly normal infant may have eight or nine, according to the U.S. Government publication "Infant Care." Our own pediatrician says that from 12 to 30 months, twelve colds—or about one every six weeks—is not unusual. Dr. Spock estimates that the average child of 2 or 3 in the northeastern United States contracts seven colds a year. A cold can last for a few days or, if a cough starts, a few weeks. Sometimes a child will pick up a new cold (your doctor will probably refer to it as an "upper-respiratory virus") before he has completely recovered from a previous one.

If you breast feed your child, you can usually expect fewer colds during the first year. Dr. Allan S. Cunningham, a pediatrician in Cooperstown, New York, found that breast-fed babies had only about one-third as many serious illnesses as a comparable group of formula-fed babies. If your child doesn't go outside your home for babysitting or day care, and if he has no older siblings, he'll naturally be exposed to fewer cold germs.

"With my first baby, every time she got a runny nose I was all uptight about it. Thank goodness I learned; my second baby had five colds in eleven months and I didn't rush to the doctor or get upset with any of them. They all pass."
Mother of two / Topeka, Kan.

The main reason to take colds seriously in an otherwise healthy child is that they lower resistance to secondary infections: ear infections, bronchitis, pneumonia, sinusitis. If, after a cold has been going on, a fever develops, if mucus from the child's nose looks yellow-green and very thick, if the child is obviously listless, or if his breathing seems labored, call the doctor.

Here are some suggestions from mothers for colds:

Runny noses. These usually start out clear and watery and later become thick and sticky. Some mothers use a nasal salt rinse. Ask your doctor about this—it must be done with care.

Coughs. A mixture of honey and lemon juice (one teaspoon every four hours for a toddler or small child) will do as much good as many fancy cough medicines. Watch out for wheezing (a rasping feeling and sound) when you put your hand on the child's chest. Call a doctor if wheezing develops, for it may signal the kind of congestion that leads to croup or pneumonia. A cold-mist vaporizer is helpful for an infant with a cough or cold, particularly in winter when the house is heated. However, our own pediatrician calls the vaporizer a "much-oversold" device. He suggests that parents try to keep an infant in an upright seat instead of using a vaporizer.

"When my child has a cold that settles in his chest, I improvise a croup tent by tying an umbrella to his crib or a chair, putting a cold-mist vaporizer on the chair next to the crib, covering it all with a sheet, and letting him sleep for a few hours under the tent. You may have to put the sheet up after the child has fallen asleep. It all helps a little."

Mother of two / Burlington, Vt.

"I've found that milk increases mucus. When there's lots of mucus in conjunction with a cold or an ear infection, I cut out milk completely for a while."

Mother of two / Roanoke, Va.

A normal diet is usually too much food for a child with a cold. Serve as many liquids as she wants: a normal amount of milk (skim, or none at all if she's prone to diarrhea), water, juices, and ginger ale. Fruit-juice popsicles are handy to have on hand. Serve grated raw apple, applesauce, gelatin, banana, cottage cheese, dry white toast, or yogurt.

When is it okay to let her go out? When there's no fever and your child is full of energy, let her go.

Croup. "Croup" is the term used to designate laryngitis in children. It usually comes on at night, with little or no warning. It may accompany a mild cold or slight hoarseness during the day, but there may be no other symptoms or warning. A child with croup will wake suddenly at night, coughing a harsh, raspy, "croupy" cough. He may heave, gasp, and be unable to catch his breath. Croup accompanied by fever is serious business, so take his temperature. If he has a fever, call your doctor immediately. If you can't reach him, take the child to the emergency room.

If he has no fever, take the child to the bathroom, close the door, turn on the shower, and run hot water at full blast to make as much steam as possible. Breathing the hot, moist air usually begins to relieve the croup. Once the cough subsides, put the child to bed and keep the air in his room moist with a vaporizer. Croup often recurs on the next night or two after an initial bout, so continue to use a vaporizer to keep the air moist.

"I vividly recall our first session with croup. I was suddenly awakened one night by a noise that sounded like a seal barking. At first I thought I was dreaming, but the bark came again—from my son's room. I rushed to him and found him in his crib, hacking and gasping for breath. Our health plan has twenty-four-hour emergency service, so I grabbed David and called the doctor. 'I can hear the problem,' he said. 'Your child has croup. Just take him to the bathroom, turn on the hot shower, sit on the toilet with him, and read him a little book.' It took three minutes for the croup to subside and five more minutes for David to get back to sleep. But it took hours for my terror to go away. I was awake the rest of the night." *Mother of two / Santa Monica, Calif.*

Colic

Colic is abdominal pain that tends to come at the same time each day. The baby draws up his knees and tenses his stomach, turns red, and cries a "hurting" cry. Colic is most common during the second and third months. It's just the result of an immature digestive system acting up, and will probably go away by the time the baby is 4 months old.

If you are sure that the baby is dry, clean, and well burped, try any or all of the following remedies but be aware that there is no sure cure.

• Walk the baby.

• Hold him face down across your knees and rub his back lightly.

• Give him a pacifier.

• Feed him a little warm water.

• Apply a warm hot-water bottle to his abdomen.

• Burp him again.

• If the doctor has okayed it beforehand, give the baby one-fourth teaspoon of your favorite liqueur in warm water.

• Wrap the lower half of the baby's body tightly in a receiving blanket.

• Borrow or buy a baby swing. The steady rocking soothes many colicky babies.

• Take the baby for a ride in the car.

• Put the baby in his crib, close the bedroom door, and vacuum the living-room floor. Remember that it is not your fault, not your baby's, not your husband's. It's just a condition that passes with time.

"I thought my month-old son was dying because his colic was so bad. Everyone just said, 'You're a nervous mother.' It really undermines your confidence. Since then I've learned that a little diluted anise-seed tea helps babies and toddlers pass gas." *Mother of two / Casper, Wyo.*

Constipation

Often constipation is caused by the introduction of a new food. "I always try a new food early in the day in case it disagrees with the baby," one mother says. "It ruins the afternoon maybe, but not the night's sleep for all of us."

For a baby, try apple juice first. Then try adding a table-spoon of one of the following to his bottle: prune juice, dark Karo syrup, molasses, corn syrup. Give a child of 2 or older one of the following: bran cereals, dark-green vegetables, or extra fruit. Or add a few tablespoons of prune juice to his favorite fruit juice. Do *not* use a laxative unless your doctor specifically recommends one. Be sure to notify your doctor if constipation persists.

If your child becomes constipated or retains his stools during toilet training, stop for a while and resume training a few weeks later.

Dehydration

Infants need five times as much fluid per pound of weight as an adult needs. If a baby or child has severe diarrhea or vomiting or both, he can quickly become dehydrated, a true medical emergency.

If a baby who normally is wet all the time is frequently dry (or if a toddler who generally has eight wet diapers a day suddenly has only two or three), if his urine looks slight-ly darker than usual, or if he acts listless and sleepy, call the doctor. If his eyes look sunken and the skin over his stomach has a doughlike quality, call the doctor *immediately*. (If you can't reach him, take the child to the nearest hospital emer-gency room.) Only a doctor can diagnose severe dehydration, and it usually requires hospitalization.

Diaper Rash

Almost every baby has a bout of diaper rash from time to time, especially if he has sensitive skin. Try the following remedies:

• Clean the diaper area carefully with soap and water at every change.

• Change the baby more frequently.

• In a young infant, check the mouth for the white patches of thrush, a mild fungus infection that may accompany diaper rash. Call the doctor about this.

• Apply whatever ointment your doctor recommends, par-ticularly before the baby naps or goes to bed for the night.

• Stop using rubber pants; instead, use double diapers during the day and triple diapers at night.

• Let the baby go without diapers for a few hours each day (put several diapers under her to catch the urine).

• Feed extra fluids, so that the urine is less concentrated.

• Since frequent bowel movements may cause (or at least irritate) diaper rash, give your baby less fruit if she's having movements fairly often—fruit, of course, loosens the bowels.

• If you smell a lot of ammonia at the first diaper change in the morning, ammonia may be building up in the diapers. Add half a cup of white vinegar to the second rinse when washing the diapers.

• Switch detergents, as your baby may have developed an allergic reaction to your regular brand.

• Switch to a different kind of diaper for a while—from cloth to disposable or vice versa.

• Ask the doctor for help if none of these remedies works after two or three days.

"A wonderful way to heal diaper rash is to put your baby out in the sun with no pants—if it's warm and sunny, of course. But be careful; my daughter's rash cleared up, but she got sunburned." *Mother of three / Corona, Calif.*

Diarrhea

Diarrhea is common in babies between 6 months and 2 years. It can be brought on by teething, a cold, too much fruit or fruit juice, a virus, an allergy, or food poisoning. Doctors say it's not a cause for great concern in an otherwise healthy baby, but then doctors don't do the cleaning up.

In a small baby, diarrhea can be serious because of the threat of dehydration. If an infant under 6 months has three or four watery stools within a few hours (or one huge, explosive, extremely liquid bowel movement), acts listless, and shows little interest in food, call the doctor. If diarrhea is combined with vomiting, particularly in an infant under 3 months, call the doctor *immediately*. It's a good idea to check with the doctor any time you think a child is losing more liquid than he is taking in.

Give only liquids to an older baby or child with diarrhea for twenty-four to thirty-six hours. Some doctors believe that clear liquids are best. Many mothers swear by yogurt, although some doctors say there is no proof of its value. At any rate, do *not* give foods that are hard to digest, such as ice cream, whole milk, boiled skim milk, orange juice, dark breads, vegetables, fruits. *Do* try water, flat cola, ginger ale, weak sweet tea, gelatin. If a child tolerates these, slowly begin to add bland foods that have little roughage and few fats —rice cereal, applesauce, bananas, mashed potatoes, cottage cheese. Waiting until the end of the day to give solid foods may let the child sleep through the night without hunger pangs. After adding one new food, wait two or three days before adding another so that you can identify the culprit if the child gets worse.

If you've had many bouts with diarrhea and constipation over the first couple of years, you may want to follow this mother's suggestion. "We just don't make our daughter flush the toilet after bowel movements," she said. "I like to be aware if she's had one and what it's like. It's usually the first clue I have that she's getting sick."

Diarrhea, like an ear infection, is most easily treated in the early stages. If it goes on for a long time, each succeeding bout seems to come more frequently, with less cause, and to last longer. To illustrate this point, Jeanne says, "Anne got diarrhea when we were visiting my family the summer she was 18 months old. It lasted, on and off, a whole year. Many mornings I started the day by changing sheets and scooping out a blanket sleeper. It was awful. Finally I realized how very careful you have to be when you start back on regular foods. I'm not a methodical person and I just hadn't been precise enough where it counted. I'd try orange juice the second day after she seemed better. Now I know that after a severe bout you have to treat a young child like a baby again and introduce new foods very slowly, a new one only after three days, to be sure the other foods are tolerated."

Another long-suffering mother says that when traveling

she learned to avoid all local water and to give her child canned juices, distilled water, and the like. But use restraint in this area. The most common failure in parents' treatment of diarrhea, according to one pediatrician, is that they give the child too much clear liquid. With diarrhea, he says, *anything* that is given must be given in *small amounts* at first.

Be prepared to tell a doctor how many stools a child has had in a given time period and about how many times he has voided when you call for advice about diarrhea.

Ear Infection

At one time or another this crops up in practically every child, most often after a cold and most commonly between 18 months and 3 years. It's one of the most painful of the common illnesses, and one of the few for which doctors can prescribe a lightning-fast cure—namely, an antibiotic.

Ear infections may be hard for a parent to diagnose at first, since they usually begin to occur before a child knows the words "ear" and "hurt" and there are no outward signs. Suspect one if your child is in the susceptible age group, if he already has a cold and starts tugging his ear, if he has a slight fever, if he becomes very irritable, or if he wakes up crying in pain in the middle of the night for no obvious reason.

Ear problems shouldn't be taken lightly because they can lead to hearing loss. Antibiotics work blessedly fast, but they work best during the early stages of an infection. A doctor must see the ear, so this is no time to postpone a trip to the pediatrician.

One caution: follow the doctor's instructions carefully and use *all* the medicine. The pain stops quickly, but the infection may linger. Many good doctors insist that you return for a checkup within two weeks to make sure the infection has been cleared up.

If your child has frequent earaches you may want to ask the doctor to prescribe drops, or he may suggest putting warm mineral oil or olive oil in the ear to ease middle-of-the-night pain. (Bear in mind, however, that some ear specialists forswear drops completely, fearing that they will mask a serious infection if parents assume less pain means less infection.) You may also want to have the child's hearing tested from time to time with a proper audiogram. (A "whisper" test does not measure perception of high-frequency sounds, which is the first to be lost in chronic and recurring middle-ear disease.)

One mother whose son had many ear infections says, "My advice to anyone whose child has had three ear infections within five or six months is to get him to an ear, nose, and throat specialist fast." There is a lack of agreement on this, however. Some doctors who have a conservative "wait and see" approach feel that specialists are overeager about inserting drainage tubes in the ears of children bothered by persistent ear infections. Since it is an operation requiring general anesthesia, it should not be agreed to without convincing evidence that it is really necessary.

Fever

One mother ruefully admits: "A fever is just a fever in a child next door. A fever in my baby is an emergency." An above-normal temperature indicates that an infection is present. Many germs are killed by heat, and fever is the body's natural defense against them. Ask your doctor ahead of time what procedure he wants you to follow to bring down a fever.

Up to the age of 1, most doctors encourage parents to take rectal temperatures for speed (one minute) and accuracy. After that children often object to the rectal procedure so most parents switch to underarm readings (four minutes). Not until the age of 5 or 6 can a child keep the thermometer under his tongue and his lips closed for an accurate mouth reading (two minutes). See Dr. Spock for precise directions on how to take all three kinds of temperature readings.

The degree of fever doesn't necessarily indicate the seriousness of an infection. Some children run very high fevers with very minor illnesses. Generally, however, a fever should be reported to the doctor if it persists for more than a day or so. (To get good help from the pediatrician, keep a careful record of the course of the fever.) Most fevers are viral in nature, respond to aspirin and time, and don't require antibiotics. But at the very least you should watch the child carefully and keep him home.

In the absence of any directions from your doctor, give a baby water or apple juice and an older child anything he

252 / Mother to Mother

will suck or drink, including lollipops, fruit juice, popsicles, crushed ice, flat soda, and gelatin. Do *not* give milk, which is difficult to digest. Do *not* bundle up the child in sweaters or blankets. Frequently sponge his face and body with a cool cloth.

If the fever is very high (103 or more) or if the baby is jumpy, shaky, or jittery, do the following to cool him down:

1. Bathe the baby in tepid water for twenty minutes. Leave his T-shirt on during the bath to keep his body wet, as just sitting in the tub is not sufficient.

2. Use aspirin if your doctor has approved its use beforehand in his general instructions to you. Maximum aspirin dosage is one grain per year of age every four hours. However, do not continue using aspirin for more than twenty-four hours.

3. Take the baby's temperature again after the bath and after giving him aspirin, allowing twenty minutes for the aspirin to take effect.

"In the middle of the night, you must remember that a fever is a symptom—not a sign of impending death. You must first break the fever, and then worry about what caused it. It sounds good here, but I still freak out when he's spiking 102 degrees at three a.m."   *Mother of one / New Haven, Conn.*

Convulsions may be associated with a sudden high fever. If your child has a convulsion, turn him on his side so he won't choke on his saliva. Wrap him in a wet towel and fan him to help bring down his temperature. Then put him in a safe place—on a carpeted floor, perhaps—and call the doctor.

"When my youngest was 2½ he had a convulsion from a sudden high fever. I knew nothing about convulsions and it might have been prevented if I had. I never bothered to take his temperature. If he felt warm I'd give him an aspirin. He had chills this time so I had a blanket over him on the couch while I did some housework. I was doing the wrong thing— keeping his body temperature warm."
      Mother of two / Atlanta, Ga.

Injuries (Minor)

"I used to be so embarrassed at my daughter's outrageous histrionics over a tiny cut," one mother said. "Then a friend pointed out that children, like adults, have very different pain thresholds, and somehow that helped."

An "Oooh! That hurts!" offered with a hug and a kiss is the best first step in dealing with minor injuries. Then try the following for:

Cuts. Stop bleeding with pressure, using a finger, a cloth, or an ice cube tucked inside a clean cloth or paper towel. Wash with soap and running water and protect with an adhesive bandage. Most doctors today advise against the use of iodine or other antiseptic.

Lips and tongues bleed more than other spots; wipe the blood away and you may be surprised at how small the cut is. A popsicle is a good thing for any minor lip or mouth cut when a child won't let you hold an ice cube on it. Check with the doctor if:

• the cut is gaping or there's a loose flap of skin.

• the cut seems more than a quarter-inch deep.

• there's any chance that a fragment of glass or other substance is still in the wound.

• the injury was caused by a dirty metal object or may have been contaminated by manure or other organic wastes.

• the cut is on the face, even if small (since scars there are noticeable). Speaking of scars, we know people who swear applying Vitamin E—one 100 I.U. capsule—three times a day to cuts and burns prevents scarring. Check with your doctor.

Burns. Apply ice or anything cold until the pain stops. Do not use ointment or grease. Cover with sterile gauze or adhesive bandage. If the burn is large, cover the area with a wet towel and take the child to the hospital. A child under 3 can become dehydrated fast from a large minor burn (see *Sunburn* below).

Bumps. Apply ice. Be particularly watchful after a head bump. Call the doctor if the child vomits, looks pale, seems sweaty, or acts sleepy—all of which may indicate a concussion. The doctor may suggest that the child skip the next meal, since it may cause vomiting.

Dirt in the eye. Usually the irritant will be blinked onto the lid, where it can be removed with the corner of a clean tissue. If the eye appears irritated and you can't see the speck, pull the upper lid gently down over the lower lid and hold it there for a few seconds. The tears that result may wash out the speck. If irritation persists, cover the closed eye with several gauze pads, tape them in place, and take the child to the doctor. In the case of foreign liquids in the eye, flush copiously with water and call the doctor.

Falls. Still your panic and wait a minute. If the child moves both arms and legs and cries loudly right away, she probably doesn't have a serious head or neck injury or broken limbs. If she's unconscious or if you think anything is broken, leave her where she is and call immediately for help. It's important not to move someone in this condition because you must be extremely careful of the neck. As one doctor says, improper movement could result in a quadriplegic.

If you suspect a head injury, run your hand over the child's head to be sure there are no lumps or depressions. Let him rest quietly. If he goes to sleep, awaken him after an hour and re-evaluate the situation. Keep an eye out for delayed symptoms such as vomiting, dizziness, soreness, and limping.

Puncture wounds. Press gently to encourage bleeding to wash out the wound, and then soak in warm water for ten or fifteen minutes. Cover with adhesive bandage. Check with the doctor if the wound gets sore or red, and if the accident happened outdoors check with your doctor as to whether the child's tetanus shots are still effective.

Scrapes and scratches. Wash with soap and running water. Use wet gauze or a clean washcloth to remove the grime, which can cause infection. Most doctors advise letting the wound heal in the open air unless it's an area likely to be hurt or dirtied in outdoor play. In that case, bandage the scrape before the child goes outdoors and take off the bandage when he comes in. As with cuts, most doctors advise against the use of iodine or antiseptics.

Slivers and splinters. Wash the area with soap and water and remove the sliver with clean tweezers, or scrape it out with a sterilized needle. Then wash the area again and cover with an adhesive bandage. Bear in mind that most splinters work themselves out anyway.

Sunburn. The main point is prevention. A baby should be kept in the shade with a hat on when you go to the beach or anywhere else in the hot sun. After he can crawl he should still wear a hat and shirt at the beach or other sunny place. If a child gets minor sunburn, wash the area with a vinegar-and-water solution and cover with a cold towel. If he acts lethargic, call the doctor. A good block-out sun screen really does protect the nose, cheeks, and shoulders of a fair-skinned child when he is at the beach or taking swimming lessons.

Poisoning

Call your doctor at once in any case of suspected poisoning. Don't delay just because your child seems all right. The effects of many poisons, including aspirin, take hours to become apparent

If you can't reach your doctor, call your local poison-control center (although some centers will talk only to doctors, not parents) or hospital emergency room. If you can get there in less than half an hour, Dr. Spock advises going directly to the emergency room when you can't reach your doctor. *Be sure to have the container with you* so that you can explain exactly ("Lysol Toilet Bowl Cleaner" not just "Lysol") what your child has taken.

Ask: (1) What do I do? and (2) What are the symptoms to watch for? Then write down the answers.

Corinne Ray, director of the Poison Information Center at Los Angeles Children's Hospital, is a mother of four and a frequent speaker on the subject of poisoning. She warns: "From 12 months to 3 years *everything* goes into the mouth. The time to be especially watchful is just before mealtime. That's when 90 percent of our calls come in." She also says that they hear from parents of boys twice as often as from those of girls.

Among the recent cases handled at the Center have been poisonings from: dishwasher detergent ("Two or three grains of it picked off the floor by a crawling baby can burn the lips or tongue"); toadstools; a mother's prenatal vitamins; powder dumped on a baby by an older brother ("It can be extremely dangerous if inhaled into an infant's lungs"); castor bean ("One could be fatal if a child chewed through the shell"); a new mouthwash left in mail boxes as an advertising promotion; fluoride vitamins; furniture polish.

"Always call the emergency room before inducing vomiting," Mrs. Ray warns. Usually induced vomiting is advised only for ingestion of plants or medications. In the case of products that could cause aspiration problems, that could get into the lungs, or that are acid, doctors do not recommend vomiting.

You'll want to have syrup of ipecac on hand in case you ever *are* told to induce vomiting. One doctor says that, in a pinch, raw egg is a pretty good substitute. Although she is a nurse herself, Mrs. Ray says that if there were time to get to an emergency room, she wouldn't try to induce vomiting in a child under a year old. "It's awful to see your own baby go through this. Personally, I'd rather have them do it in an emergency room instead."

Other mothers, however, say that they prefer to get the poison out themselves as quickly as possible once they've been told this is necessary. One mother said, "I had to give my daughter ipecac when she was 3. The doctor's advice was to have her drink as much water as possible at the same time. She took two doses of ipecac and drank twenty-four ounces of water without a murmur, although she hated to take medication and hated water. Then she threw up in the toilet like a lamb. Even at that age she sensed my fear and cooperated fully. I think kids know when things are serious and usually act accordingly."

To get an older child to take the foul-tasting syrup of ipecac, mix a little of it with a liquid the child likes. Then head for the bathtub so you can see what comes up and report it later.

Sore Throat

A child under 3 usually doesn't tell you that he has a sore throat. If he acts unlike himself but shows no other symptoms, get him to open his mouth wide enough so that you can tell if his throat is red. A red throat is often the first sign that you're in for a virus, a cold, or a strep throat. Any sore throat should be reported to the doctor, along with such other symptoms as cough, sneezing, headache, and fever. The doctor will help you decide whether you should make a trip to the office.

A sore throat may signal the start of an infection that can spread to the ears, tonsils, and lymph nodes. A "strep" throat, which can be diagnosed only by laboratory analysis of a throat culture, always demands immediate medical attention. If not treated, it can lead to rheumatic fever or nephritis, which in turn can permanently damage the heart or kidneys; thus it's not an illness to take lightly. If you suspect strep throat and can't get an appointment with your child's doctor, ask the nurse to take a throat culture.

Strep throat is rare in children under 3 unless someone older in the family has it, as it is very contagious. Thus if any family member's throat culture shows up positive for strep, the doctor may insist that cultures be taken from all other family members. The most common treatment for adult strep is a hefty shot of antibiotic, but most doctors prescribe a ten-day course of oral medication for children because the shot is painful.

Stomach Ache (Appendicitis?)

"My tummy's full of junk," Jeanne's daughter, Anne, confides from time to time. (Usually this means that she has filled it with junk.) An excellent stomach ache "treatment" for her and for most children, according to her pediatrician, is to have a bowel movement.

Most stomach aches go away fast, but in the back of a mother's mind always lurks the spectre of appendicitis. In a child under 3, however, it probably isn't appendicitis, which doctors say is most commonly seen in children between 6 and 12. Professors of surgery tell medical students that appendicitis may be the toughest diagnosis in the book. The only symptom may be mild discomfort; if it persists for hours and gets worse instead of better, *call a doctor.* Other possible indications of appendicitis: nausea; vomiting; pain and tenderness in the abdomen, usually settling in the lower right side; low-grade fever around 101 degrees.

Teething

A baby's first teeth usually appear when he's between 6 and 10 months old. By the time he's 2, he'll have most of his first set of teeth.

Your child may have some discomfort as a result of teething. He may seem irritable and show slight changes in his bowel habits. He may be spitting up or have a runny nose. Any symptoms more pronounced than these are probably due to something else, not teething. In fact, doctors say, a good general rule is to blame nothing on teething. After all, most of the time between 6 months and 2½ years a child is working on one new tooth or another, and it is unwise to automatically blame teething for what may be the start of something serious.

To ease the discomfort of teething, try massaging his gums gently, using the ball of your (clean) finger. Or let the child gnaw on a cold teething ring, a boiled cloth that doesn't shred, a yogurt popsicle, or a stale bagel. More than one doctor has suggested rubbing brandy on the gums; if your doctor approves, you might try this. To help the child sleep better, let him play outdoors more than usual while he's teething. If none of these ideas work, ask the doctor if you can give the child baby aspirin.

Viruses

It's estimated that up to 85 percent of all infections, including practically all upper-respiratory ailments and most gastrointestinal upsets, are caused by viruses. Antibiotics are not effective against viruses, and that is why, nine times out of ten, a doctor will tell you to "wait and see what develops" with your sick child instead of giving him an antibiotic.

If your doctor does suggest antibiotics for everything, get another opinion. Antibiotics have significant side effects, and there's no point in risking their use without a very good reason.

When a string of viruses gets you down, remember this: some doctors say that a child must get six or eight mild virus diseases a year in order for his body to develop systems for fighting more serious diseases.

Vomiting

We're not talking about spitting up, but about vomiting. You'll know the difference. Infants sometimes vomit after being overfed or overburped. Older children may vomit as a result of mild-to-moderate stomach upsets or gastrointestinal infections. Occasionally vomiting is a sign that something is seriously wrong.

If your child vomits, withhold *all* food and liquids for three or four hours. Then offer an infant apple juice or water —just one teaspoon every half hour. An older child may be given small sips of flat ginger ale or 7-Up. After three or four hours, offer small amounts of clear liquids such as broth or weak sweet tea. The next day, offer a "diarrhea diet"—a slow progression of easily digested foods. Follow this regime for two or three days.

Call the doctor about persistent vomiting that doesn't respond to this routine or if vomiting is associated with diarrhea or severe abdominal pain. Also call him about projectile vomiting in young infants. Aptly named, this is when food is vomited out with such force that it lands at a distance from the baby's mouth.

WHAT A PARENT NEEDS TO KNOW ABOUT TEETH

Before your baby has any teeth at all she can start a pattern that will cause real trouble. As mentioned in an earlier chapter, dentists have found thousands of very young children who have seriously decayed front teeth as a result of the "baby-bottle syndrome"' caused by prolonged sucking on a bottle, allowing milk or sweet juices to trickle slowly over the gums and new teeth. Dentists say that you should not let your baby suck on a bottle of anything for hours, and that you should *never* let him fall asleep with a bottle of milk.

Dr. Laurence C. Reichel, a well-known pedodontist (children's dentist), says that apple juice given in a bottle is "disastrous" because it has so much natural sugar. Dr. Reichel also says that a child more than 18 months old should be off the bottle, taking all liquids from a cup.

The Big Three: Sugar, Brushing, Fluoride

Sugar. Dentists agree that sugar is an important factor in tooth decay. Under ideal conditions, sugar should be consumed only at mealtimes, and teeth should be brushed afterward. But in the real world, children have been known to go to birthday parties in the middle of the afternoon and to have ice cream at the zoo. Encourage your child to rinse out his mouth with water immediately after having a snack. Provide plenty of nutritious snacks that are not artificially sweetened: fruits, vegetables, nuts, cheese.

The quantity of sugar eaten doesn't matter so much as the frequency and the form, Dr. Reichel believes, because sticky foods stay on the teeth much longer. Among such "sticky" foods he includes raisins and peanut butter—two supposedly "healthy" snack foods.

Brushing. Brush your child's teeth *yourself* thoroughly once a day. Dr. Stephen Moss, chairman of the pedodontics department at New York University's Dental Center, says, "It's not a good idea to send a 3-year-old in to brush his teeth by himself. You've got to be at least 7 before you have the skill to do it properly." Many parents include a good toothbrushing session in the nighttime ritual. You may want to follow the advice of another dentist who claims that simply wiping a child's teeth with a piece of clean gauze each night will prevent cavities in a child under 3.

"Candy at birthday parties, Halloween, and Christmas means an awful lot of candy. I let my kids have it at parties or on the holiday itself. If they bring candy home, I try to dump most of it out when they're not looking. For the rest, after they eat a piece, they have to brush their teeth. Often they get so tired of brushing they get bored with the whole idea of candy." *Mother of three / Hermosa Beach, Calif.*

Fluoride. Dr. Moss and most other dentists are enthusiastic about the effectiveness of fluoride in preventing cavities. After entering the body, fluoride becomes part of the tooth enamel, and it is said to reduce decay by 60 percent or more. If there is no fluoride in your drinking water, ask your doctor about making sure your children get it from pills or drops. One caution: some doctors who urge the use of fluoride believe that in liquid form it is absorbed too rapidly by an infant, eventually causing mottling and softening of tooth enamel. Ask your doctor about this.

The First Trip to the Dentist

Most dentists advocate that a child's first visit should be at around 3 unless you notice some problem beforehand. Since the condition of baby teeth affects the development of permanent teeth, it's not good to wait much longer.

If there's a pedodontist in your area, he may be your best bet because a regular dentist may not have the time or inclination to develop rapport with a 3-year-old. Furthermore, the equipment and furniture in a pedodontist's office is likely to be child-scale and thus less frightening.

Prepare your child for her first trip to the dentist by explaining, as clearly and truthfully as you can, what will be happening. (Ask the dentist ahead of time if he can give you one of the books or pamphlets written for this purpose.) If you have an older child who's relaxed and confident in the dentist's office, take the baby along to watch one of his regular checkups. Or let her watch while the dentist gives *you* a once-over. A good dentist or pedodontist will explain to a child ahead of time what he will be doing, show her how the equipment works, even let her hold the mirror. An hour or two of preparation and explanation may prevent a lifelong fear of dental procedures.

Questions Mothers Ask Dentists

What should I do if my child's tooth is loosened or knocked out in a fall? In the latter case, try to save the tooth, particularly if it is a permanent one. Wrap it in a clean damp cloth, or (if you will have a hard time reaching the dentist quickly) freeze it in salt water. "It's worthwhile to send other kids out to look for it," says Dr. Reichel. Many dentists today are artful about replacing original teeth. If a tooth has been loosened, it's important to have it checked and probably X-rayed by a dentist. A loose tooth can decay into nerve death without any evidence of pain or discoloration.

How dangerous is thumbsucking? If a child stops sucking his thumb by kindergarten or first grade, says Dr. Reichel, you shouldn't have much of an orthodontic problem.

What about pacifiers? Dr. Reichel recommends using one of the orthodontically approved brands in preference to thumbsucking. Otherwise nothing beyond breast or bottle feeding should be used.

When should a child's teeth be X-rayed? Limited X-rays are in order at about age 3, Dr. Reichel says, in order to catch such problems as an extra tooth growing up toward the nose. (He finds about one a week in his practice; this can cause problems for a lifetime if not treated early.) X-rays also give "growth guidance" in that they may indicate the need to do limited treatment early to prevent a need for orthodontics later. However, some medical experts are now insisting that X-rays should *never* be given routinely to very young children. Ask your doctor, as well as your dentist, about this.

Should I let my child chew gum? Sugarless gum is acceptable, Dr. Reichel says.

How and when is it determined that a child needs corrective orthodontics? Your child's regular dentist will recommend such treatment if and when he thinks it is needed. A retainer may be prescribed for a child as young as 3 or 4 to correct a "crossbite" (improper alignment of molars). Usually the eventual need for orthodontics is obvious as soon as permanent teeth start to appear. Dr. Reichel advises that conservative treatment early may lessen the need for more elaborate (and expensive) correction later on.

MEDICAL SUPPLIES TO HAVE ON HAND

The rest of the family will drink the last bottle of ginger ale just before you need it to help calm the queasy stomach of a toddler. Someone will eat the last yogurt popsicle. The thermometer will get broken and the adhesive bandages will disappear. Every mother should keep the following items in some safe place. They're all available without prescriptions in most drugstores.

Aspirin or an aspirin substitute—in liquid form for infants and children under 3; child-size tablets for older children.

Cough medicine—one recommended by your doctor.

Nasal decongestant or drops—if your doctor recommends their use; many don't approve of them.

Syrup of ipecac—to induce vomiting in case of accidental poisoning (replace every three years).

Thermometer—rectal variety.

Nasal bulb syringe—useful for removing mucus from the nose of an infant who is having trouble breathing.

Vaporizer—may be helpful for an infant's or baby's cough or a cold, particularly if your home is dry and a heater is going in the winter. Get a large *cold-mist* variety, one big enough so that you don't have to refill it more than once a day. It should have a safety feature that will let it go dry without burning out, and you should be able to direct the amount and direction of vapor. A substitute is a pan of water near a heater-blower.

Adhesive bandages—when your child hits 2 you may have to have an extra package to use for the real thing, because he will demand one for every small scratch.

Ginger ale or 7-Up—keep an extra six-pack hidden away for emergencies.

Lollipops—essential in diagnosing sore throats. A sick child may not let you open his mouth any other way.

First-aid book—available quite inexpensively from your local chapter of the Red Cross. See the Resource List for specific titles.

"Splinter kit"—clean, sharp needle, tweezers, sterile cotton balls or gauze, small magnifying glass, pill bottle full of isopropyl alcohol. These fit neatly into an empty adhesive-bandage box, so you won't have to waste a half hour searching the house for equipment.

SURVIVAL TIPS FOR MOMS

Knowing exactly what to do for a sick baby isn't much use if you're too emotionally or physically exhausted to do it. Here are some suggestions for making your life—and others' lives—easier when a bad bug is making the rounds, as well as a few suggestions about things you should know before-hand.

Let other mothers know when your child has a runny nose or comes down with anything contagious. (The more experienced the mother, the less afraid of contamination she is likely to be.) Colds are said to be contagious during the few days before any symptoms appear, and to remain contagious for one to two weeks after the first symptoms appear.

The point is that it's not worth the loss of another mother's friendship if she even *thinks* that you and your child are responsible for her baby's first or second cold. "I learned to put the decision on others no matter how badly we wanted to get out and see people," Jeanne admits. "I say, 'Anne's getting over a cold. If you want to postpone the visit, I'll certainly understand.' " The same general rule holds for babysitters and grandparents. We can't know, after all, what is coming up in another's life that coming down with a cold would interfere with.

"I believe that basically healthy children will stay that way despite what they do, like running around in 50-degree weather in shorts. It all depends on how much exposure they have to sick people. I keep my kids away from crowds and other people whom I know to be ill."

Mother of four / Canton, Ohio

Sleep when the baby does after you've been up at night with a sick child. Get outside yourself, literally and figura-tively, for at least a half hour every day if your child is go-ing through a long bout of sickness. (By that we mean any-thing longer than one day.) A tired martyr, after all, can't be a clear-thinking nurse.

"Since our health records sound like something from a soap opera, I guess what I'd pass along is 'talk about your prob-lems—don't hold them in.' It helps to keep one's sanity, to share the good and the bad. Presently I have three vomiting because of the flu. Never a dull moment here."

Mother of three / Watervliet, N.Y.

Know where the nearest emergency room is. Find out which hospital your pediatrician thinks you should use in an emergency, and know how to get there fast. Paramedic teams can be extremely helpful in real emergencies, and can get your child to an emergency room faster than you can because they can run red lights. Keep the paramedics' number near your telephone along with all the other emergency numbers.

Find a drugstore that delivers and accepts charge accounts. There's nothing worse than waiting in a drugstore for a prescription to be filled while your sick baby spreads screams and germs all over the premises. Know which pharmacies in your town are open all night. (Often a hospital pharmacy will be.)

"If you can't afford conventional private medical and dental care, the next-best thing is a well-baby clinic, usually run by your county health department. My children had all their checkups and shots at these clinics—and it was free!"
Mother of five / Denver, Colo.

"Only *after* Kristie had many ear infections did we more thoroughly read our medical insurance policy. We found that *all* visits to the doctor except routine checkups were 80 percent compensated. The same was true for prescriptions. My advice: *read insurance policies!*"
Mother of two / Boise, Ida.

"To get kids to take bad-tasting medicine, I chill it first, then mix it with a little *cold* juice the child likes. This seems to kill some of the bad taste. One time I even used it as an ice-cream topping!"   *Mother of four / Wilkes Barre, Pa.*

BUT IN THE END, TRUST YOURSELF

"I found that I was usually right when it came to diagnosing my children. After all, I was with them the most."
Mother of two / Tampa, Fla.

Minor illnesses, major illnesses—all of them are more often
sniffed out first by a mother than by anyone else. Time after
time when a baby or toddler doesn't "seem right" to us, he
isn't. Here the buck most truly stops with us.

"We can look at slides taken three years ago, and from
just the look around my daughter's eyes I remember they
were taken just before she came down with a bad virus," one
mother says. "And I'm the only one who could recognize
that look."

"I would never let my children be treated—in an emergency
room, say—without my being there. However much the doctors may disagree, a child needs its mom, and a mom owes
it to her child to remain cool and to be near at hand."
Mother of two / Flint, Mich.

"The best thing I ever did was take our first baby to *two*
doctors. My husband thought we should go to the county
clinic to save money but I wanted to choose our own doctor. So I did both. We got shots free from the county and
checkups from both. The valuable thing was that their advice was totally different on so many points that I learned
to rely on my own common sense. For example, our baby
weighed only 5½ pounds at birth and one of the doctors
said I should feed her every two hours and start cereal at four
weeks. The other said to feed her only breast milk and then
only when *she* wanted it. I tried the cereal but it went right
through her so I forgot that. Then, one doctor said she had
tight hips and that we should put four diapers on her at once
to keep her legs apart in the hope her hips would loosen up.
The other doctor said, 'Tight hips? What's that? No, I don't
see any problem.' I could go on and on . . . "
Mother of three / Charlotte, N.C.

When dealing with doctors and specialists of any kind,
a mother must be civil and courteous but at the same time
dogged and direct. Some doctors, for example, may never
bite the bullet and send you on to a specialist when your
child's lingering problem keeps lingering. If, to take just one
instance, you feel your child's hearing is not what it should

be, you ought to trust your instincts and take action. You may need to insist on a thorough checkup by a specialist or on taking your child to a hospital where there are more extensive testing facilities than can be found in most doctors' offices.

Elaine Heffner, who is both a psychiatrist and a mother of two, urges mothers not to abdicate their responsibilities to the "experts." But, she warns, the mother who disputes the judgment or refuses to accept the recommendations of a doctor, psychiatrist, or teacher can expect to be labeled "difficult"—if not crazy, irresponsible, or negligent—and to be regarded as a "patient" along with her child. That's too bad, because a child needs a strong mother, she says, a mother who knows—either instinctively or from her intimate knowledge of her own child—when the experts are not making realistic judgments. This doesn't mean you should challenge every opinion, of course, only that you should not be overwhelmed when an authority figure says something is so when you know it isn't so.

Almost every mother has a story of persistence—or of being continually observant—paying off when concern arises about a child's health.

"My first child tore up all his books even though he loved being read to," one mother related. "When he was 2, I had his eyes checked by an ophthalmologist. The doctor found him to be extremely far-sighted. Glasses made all the difference in him!"

Michael's mother was the first to realize that his feet turned in when he walked. At the end of a regular checkup with the pediatrician, she said, "Watch more carefully the way he walks." The doctor, six steps later, recommended a trip to an orthopedic specialist, who in turn recommended corrective shoes. Within a year Michael could walk a pretty straight line.

"I know I tend to blame the doctor when it's my own fault," one mother of three told us. "I'm not emphatic enough in expressing my own concern. But I'm learning!" So are we all.

BABY'S MEDICAL NOTES:

TEACHING

10

How to Discipline

TYPES OF DISCIPLINE

You don't have to go far to find advice about children and discipline: it's one area in which everyone has an opinion. Some people will tell you, "The only answer is to be firm. If parents weren't afraid to get tough, there wouldn't be so many delinquent teenagers." Others will warn you, "Toughness doesn't work in the long run. If you try to frighten a young child into good behavior, eventually that child may become a rebellious, hostile teenager." The problem for parents today is deciding which way is the *right* way. Should they opt for the authoritarian approach and risk repressing their children? Should they take a permissive position and risk spoiling their children? Or should they aim for something in the middle and risk confusing their children?

In *Between Parent and Child* Haim Ginott says, "Whatever grandfather did was done with authority; whatever we do is done with hesitation. Even when in error, grandfather acted with certainty. Even when in the right, we act with doubt." Many parents struggle with "doubt" until their children are grown, never certain they are doing the right thing.

In our opinion, there is only one right way of disciplining. That way is *your* way, tailored to your child and his nature and to your personality and life style.

271

Your own discipline formula should be influenced by four factors:

Your basic personality, life style, and outlook on life. Are your routines casual and easygoing or orderly and structured? Are you outgoing and gregarious or quiet and reserved? Are your social values radical, liberal, or conservative? Were you raised in a permissive, a middle-of-the-road, or an authoritarian atmosphere?

Your partner's basic personality, life style, and outlook on life. Does your mate lean the same way as you do or are there basic differences?

Your child's basic personality and outlook on life. Is he quiet and shy, amiable and easygoing, or assertive and active? Even more important, are there any extreme differences between the way your child approaches life and the way you do?

Your child's age, emotional and physical development, and general condition at any given moment. Has there been a sudden or slow change in your child's behavior? Has he just learned to crawl, walk, or talk? Has he become extremely negative, or afraid of strangers? Is he tired, hungry, sick, or just having "one of those days"?

If you take these four areas into account, whatever style of discipline you decide to follow should work fairly well. We say "fairly well" because even super-parents and super-children find that there are times when nothing seems to work.

The examples that follow show how four sets of parents handled discipline in ways that were natural for them and their children. We asked them to tell generally about themselves and to relate specifically how they handled bedtime.

Structured Parents / Structured Child

Mary and Don are well-organized people who lead a quiet life. Their only child, Andy, is also quiet and orderly. At a very early age he adjusted to the routines of the home, learning to nap, eat, and play at specific times of the day.

"We always respected the fact that there was a child in the house, but we also expected him to respect our rights as adults. He had places for his things; we had places for ours. We made an effort, at the beginning, to put his things away; he saw this and soon began to do it himself. We followed a regular bedtime routine. We told him it was time, bathed him, read him a story, tucked him in, and that was it.

Structured Parents / Unstructured Child

Like Mary and Don, Pat and Walt are quiet and orderly. Their daughter Jenny is, in Pat's words, "a real pistol!" There have been ups and downs all the way. "We've had to readjust our whole philosophy of child rearing to cope with her. We have to be consistent, and extremely firm. She is strong-willed. If I let down she takes right over. I have to keep my thumb on her. I used to condemn parents who spanked their children, but I've had to eat my words, since sometimes a strong smack on the rear has been the only way to control my daughter.

"Bedtime was battle time until we realized that Jenny doesn't need much sleep. We finally turned her room into a giant playpen, putting in a Dutch door that was open on top but latched on the bottom. We frequently go to sleep before she does. She has learned that she doesn't have to sleep but she does have to stay in her room."

Unstructured Parents / Unstructured Child

Val and Mike are easygoing and relaxed about life, and their son is also outgoing and full of fun. Val explains, "I hate to discipline anyone, so the only limits I set have to do with safety. I put responsibility on my son for his own actions. Toilet training, eating, picking up his toys—all these jobs were up to him. If he balks, I'd rather do it myself. Bedtime has always been a hit-or-miss thing. Sometimes it's six, sometimes it's eleven."

Unstructured Parents / Structured Child

Diane and Bill are energetic, fun-loving, always on the go. Their oldest child is quiet and shy. They have learned to tone down their own personalities with Billy, and to handle him gently. Diane says, "My natural instinct is to yell; I've learned to talk softly with Billy. He is leery of strangers, so we let him cling to our side, sometimes for the whole day

when we go to new places. Bill and I have very relaxed bedtime patterns, but Billy is a creature of habit. We put him
to sleep at his regular time, wherever we may be."

TROUBLE SPOTS OF DISCIPLINE

If your program of discipline is going smoothly, we suggest
that you continue with your present methods. If you are
having difficulty, however, you should closely examine your
child's basic personality and see how well it fits with your
basic way of discipline. If you are an outgoing, slap-and-hol-
ler type of person and your child is becoming more and
more withdrawn, then you may have to tone down your
personality and change your natural style of discipline to
see if such a change might be better for your child. If you
are quiet and loving and approach the problems of the
world with a hug and smile but your child is rough, aggressive, and becoming more so every day, then take a look at
your method of discipline. You may have to become more
assertive in order to control your child.

Dr. Robert Chamberlin, a pediatrician at the University
of Rochester, asserts that the form of discipline a parent
uses is just one small factor affecting a child's behavior. For
two years he studied two hundred 5-year-olds, some from
authoritarian homes, some from permissive homes, some
from middle-of-the-road or accommodating homes. He observed no correlation between the type of discipline used
and how well the children did in his testing. He concluded
that the child's innate temperament and how well suited that
temperament was to a particular family life style probably
had as much or even more impact than a particular method
of discipline. He also concluded that so long as nothing
dreadful was happening, authorities on child rearing should
not try to change the way a family is raising a child. We
agree. So long as nothing dreadful is happening in your home,
we urge you to do whatever it is that you are now doing.

We know, however, that everyone can use a little help
with some of the specific concerns in the "doing." How do
you handle temper tantrums? What do you do about biting,
hitting, kicking? How do you teach a child to respond to
the word "no"? How do you keep your child from crawling

into your bed at night? These and other questions are the ones women ask each other in the park, on the telephone, at the laundromat, and they're the ones we asked many mothers. Here we share some of their responses. Since each reader is different and each child is different, you can choose those solutions that seem most appropriate for your situation.

How do you establish routines with an infant?

"I established routines completely at my son's convenience. I fed, rocked, and held him whenever he needed it. He spent most of his waking hours in my arms. I gave him constant and loving attention for the first year, and I believe it has paid off, since the older he gets the more independent and self-reliant he becomes."

Mother of one / Salf Lake City, Utah

"I've noticed that people tend to spoil their children by doing things too fast for them, so I always try to wait before answering a request. It's worked very well. When my daughter first came home from the hospital I would wait at least five minutes after she woke up before going in to get her—unless she was screaming with pain or fear or something. It was good for my nerves; I was much more relaxed than if I had hurried in there every time. And she learned not to get frantic if I was a little late. She's a lovely person—all my friends say so—and maybe that's why."

Mother of one / New Orleans, La.

"From the day my daughter came home I put her on a schedule. I have continued this, since it was easy to set up a routine for her and best for both of us."

Mother of two / Seattle, Wash.

What did you do when your child started to crawl, climb, and get into things?

"One: Make it safe for baby. Two: Make it safe *from* baby. Three: Make it easy for me. I moved my few valuables out of reach and let them go!"

Mother of two / Des Moines, Iowa

"Since I feel it's a waste of time to constantly say no to a toddler, I put anything that might hurt my son or that I did not want broken out of reach. I had collected many beautiful objects and I did miss them. One night I put my son to bed early and brought out a few of my favorites. From that night on, the sight of my cut-glass bowl and crystal vase in their pre-baby place became the signal for my husband and me to dress, eat, talk elegantly, and forget for just one night that we were parents."   *Mother of two / Belmont, Mass.*

"I left a favorite plant on a low table. Whenever my daughter started for the plant, I told her 'no,' and removed her from it. When she learned that she couldn't touch the plant, I began to put back other possessions."
Mother of one / Arlington, Va.

"Anything that was dangerous to them was put out of reach. Anything that they must learn not to touch was a 'no-no.' If they touched it again they were told 'no' with a slap on the hand."   *Mother of two / Lawton, Okla.*

How did you handle tantrums?

"I believe that tantrums are a good outlet for tension—I say let the kids have them."
Mother of two / Flagstaff, Ariz.

"We had a 'quiet chair' in a corner of the living room. At first, I camly took her to the chair, leaving her there. She soon headed for the chair on her own. Wouldn't it be nice if we all had a 'quiet chair'?"
Mother of two / Miami, Fla.

"Sometimes I imitate her and get her to laugh. Sometimes I swat her on the fanny, but usually what works is picking her up and carting her off."
Mother of one / St. Paul, Minn.

"I almost got arrested once. I was in a market when my 2-year-old son demanded candy. I said 'no.' He threw himself to the floor, kicking and screaming. I calmly walked out of the store. A policeman had observed the whole scene and came after me, insisting that I couldn't desert a child that way. Teaching my son that I wasn't his slave was more important to me than the policeman. I kept on walking. Fortunately, my son trotted up to me a few seconds later and the policeman went off after more important criminals."
Mother of two / Santa Monica, Calif.

"You've hit a nerve. Tantrums make me crazy, and I only feel worse realizing such situations are almost always my fault. When my son is in a rotten temper it's usually because he's overtired or hungry, or has had little chance for decision-making that day and plain old rebels. However, just because it's my fault doesn't make it easier to stand his screaming.

"Once the stage is set and his act has begun, the only way for me to handle these situations is to bring down the curtain by leaving wherever we are and making sure he gets whatever it is he needs, be it sleep or food or just plain attention. But I never give in to the tantrum. Although at times it would have been easier to just buy the 'stupid ice cream' in the store, now I'm glad I didn't, since he's a pretty outstanding 2½-year-old who seemed a born tyrant at 16 months." *Mother of one / Providence, R.I.*

How about physical aggression, such as hitting, biting, or kicking?

"With very young children who perhaps are fighting over a toy, I found that most of the time I only had to get them apart and then try to interest them in something else."
Mother of two / Albuquerque, N.M.

"Sometimes I step in and break up a fight, but at other times—if the kids are evenly matched—I just leave them alone. I must admit that once or twice I've gotten so angry at my son being a victim that I've insisted he go right back and clobber the other kid."

Mother of two / Dayton, Ohio

"No one has the answer. It's sort of hit or be hit. It's embarrassing, but most children do it. We shielded our daughter when others hit her and expected other parents to do the same." *Father of one / Louisville, Ky.*

"I'm 5 feet 10, my husband's 6 feet 4, and at 3 our son is as tall as a 5-year-old. His size made it worse last year when he went through a terribly aggressive hitting stage. Since no one his age wanted to go near him, I found two boys a year older who live near us with whom he could play. Since then everything's much better." *Mother of one / Laramie, Wyo.*

How did you handle squabbling between children in your family?

"We minimized the problem. At one point we had three children under 5, and I never allowed a toy in the house, big or small, unless there were *three* of them. And whenever a fight developed I made the ones involved kiss and make up after a while. Invariably, there'd be so much giggling over the kiss that the cause of the dispute was forgotten fast." *Mother of five / Troy, N.Y.*

"There are days when I think I'll get rid of them. They fight continually, over everything. The more I try to be fair, the more they shout 'not fair!' Then, miraculously, they seem to get the hate and fight out of their systems and peace reigns for a while." *Mother of three / Atlanta, Ga.*

"I believe in letting them tell each other their feelings, but not in physical fighting. When my son and daughter fight, I make them sit in chairs facing each other. They can scream and yell abuses, but they aren't allowed to touch each other. Usually what happens is that they begin to laugh, and that effectively ends the fight."

Mother of two / Tahoe City, Calif.

What did you do when your child wanted to get into your bed at night?

"There is only one easy solution to this one. Just don't let him there in the first place. Once you start, it's almost impossible to stop!" *Mother of two / Billings, Mont.*

"There is one thing I'm grateful to my husband for every time I talk with a friend of mine who's exhausted half the time because her son often sleeps in her bed. My husband foresaw trouble breaking this habit if we ever started it, and he was adamant when I was tempted to give in. Our children get plenty of comforting if they wake up at night scared or sick, but it's done in their room and they don't crawl into bed with us." *Mother of two / Memphis, Tenn.*

"Both of my kids went through a long period of getting into our bed. Of course, it eventually wears out. If I didn't want them in our bed I found it worked well to pick them up, put them back in their bed and stay with them. But I can sleep anywhere and usually fell asleep in their room, so we slept together anyway."

Mother of two / Hartford, Conn.

"As a matter of fact, we enjoyed her coming in. In time, she preferred to go back to her own bed."

Mother of one / Madison, Wisc.

How did you teach your child to respect other people's rules and values?

"By first respecting *his* rules and values. Some adults act as if kids aren't people, but just little puppy dogs to be patted on the head and sent to 'their place.' When we visit, I make sure my sons are included in at least some of the activity, and not just shoved aside."

Mother of two / Austin, Tex.

"When a mother and child come to visit, I tactfully let them know that I set the rules and that I will enforce them. Conversely, when I'm visiting in someone else's home, I ask

if there are any special house rules. We have a variety of
friends with different customs and values. It has broadened
my son's view of the world to realize that people are different—that he has to behave differently depending on the
circumstances." *Mother of two / Springfield, Ill.*

"We don't visit people whose rules we're not comfortable
with." *Mother of one / Denver, Colo.*

"I've always taught my daughter to be nice to grownups, to
say 'please' and 'thank you,' to help clean up the toys. After
all, in the real world it's grownups—the boss, the teacher,
the principal—who count."
Mother of two / Cleveland, Ohio

**What do you do when your child's behavior drives you up
the wall?**

"Swear a lot under my breath and later write down the in-
cidents that cause it in my journal. I rant and rave and then
when I calm down I try to recall the facts. For three weeks
my son went through a whining period every day. When I
looked at the facts in my journal, I realized that he must
have been hungry. I gave him a snack the next time he
started the whining, and that ended the problem."
Mother of three / Bismarck, S.D.

"Sometimes it's hard to know. Is it you or is it the child?
If you're having a bad day and your child is acting up you're
going to come down fast and hard. That's when it's nice
to have a good friend or a babysitter and leave your child
to get an hour off by yourself."
Mother of two / Charleston, W. Va.

"The first year I ran the vacuum cleaner or went outside
with him in the park. The second year was the hardest. I
needed an hour away every day to stay sane, so I had a high
school girl come in while I went out for a walk. The worse
the day had been the faster I walked. But by the end of the
third year it felt like we were friends most of the time."
Mother of one / Birmingham, Ala.

"Changing the scene, if at all possible, can sometimes change the whole mood of the day. If you're out and your child is acting impossible, come home, lie down and read, watch TV, or listen to records with him. If you're in the house, then get out and talk a walk, go to the park, or visit a friend."
Mother of four / Eugene, Ore.

"Once in a great while when a child was impossible and unbearable, I would take her out for an ice cream sundae. It worked miracles!"   *Mother of three / Phoenix, Ariz.*

MAKING RULES AND SETTING LIMITS

Whatever their preferred styles of discipline, mothers and child-development experts agree that for the sake of his safety and your sanity you must set some limits, make some rules, and teach your child the meaning of the word "no."

In *Child Sense*, William Homan says, "Even to be a successful rebel against society it is necessary first to know enough of the rules of the society to be able to operate from within it." In her book *Your Child's Self-Esteem*, Dorothy Briggs says, "The family is a social group. And it is vital that it have rules enabling each person to meet his needs without constantly running roughshod over those of others." Briggs and Homan have different ideas on who should establish rules; however, both emphatically agree that rules and limits are necessary.

The Meaning of "No!"

The three steps in reinforcing the concept of "no" are:

1. At first, reserve its use for situations dealing with *safety*. "No, fire is hot!" or "No, don't chew the electric cord!"

2. Extend the use of "no" to include the *rights of other people*. "No! Pulling hair hurts me!" or "No! Hitting Robert hurts him!"

3. Start to teach your child to *respect the things in his environment*. "No! Vases are not for babies!"

One mother said, "During the first year I used 'no' very little—mainly for a few times when he was close to hurting himself. During the second year I used it much more, so he would not hurt himself or somebody else, and during the third year even more, so he would not hurt himself, somebody else, or some thing."

Another mother said, "For the first year there was no need for 'no.' During the second year I spanked her hand with a very firm 'no.' I used it only in an emergency, like playing in the street. Then, in the third year, the rule was that she would be put to bed if saying 'no' three times didn't suffice, and there were hardly any problems because she understood what was expected."

How to Discipline

Make rules and set limits on actions. You can make your child go to bed by physically putting her there; therefore, you can establish the rule that bedtime is eight o'clock. You can't make her go to sleep, however, so it's pointless to make a rule that says she must go to sleep at eight o'clock.

You can stop your son from kicking his baby sister, so you can make a rule that he may not kick the baby. You can't make him show affection for the baby, though, so it's a waste of time to make a rule telling him he must love his little sister.

You can say "no" when your child hears the jingle of the ice cream truck and demands a treat. However, you can't make him feel happy about your "no," or stop him from expressing his anger.

You can send him to his room and ignore him when he cries or has a tantrum. However, you can't make him stop crying at your demand.

You can and should make rules that limit actions. It's a waste of both your own and your child's time to make rules that you can't enforce, or rules to control your child's emotions.

Once is not enough. Most rules have to be stated over and over again. Young children have very short memories, and they honestly do forget. If you are teaching your child a new rule, calmly remind her of it before the event. One mother said, "When we go shopping I tell my sons 'Now remember the rules: you may have a treat when we've finished shopping.' Before we go to the park I remind them of the rules that they can't throw sand and must wait for a turn on the slide. I also try to let them know that bedtime will be 'in an hour' or that they'll have to stop playing 'in a while.' I've found that many problems can be avoided if I just take the time to remind them before, not after, the fact."

Show disapproval of the action, not of the child. Most people involved in child development and education believe that limits must be imposed on children's actions; they also believe that the action, not the child, should receive disapproval. When your child misbehaves let him know, in your own way, that you disapprove of the misbehavior but that you still approve of him. Your 7-month-old son, who is teething, bites your nipple while you're nursing. Stop feeding him and let him know that he can't use your nipple as a teething ring. Although he won't understand your words, practice "no-insult" discipline by saying, "No! You may not bite!" or "Ouch, that hurts! Don't bite!" Refrain from using such phrases as "You miserable vampire" or "Bad, bad baby."

Continue practicing this approach, even though your baby still won't understand your words. Your 12-month-old daughter pulls herself up and is playing with the knobs on the stove. Stop the action and let her know that stoves are very bad for babies, but don't make her feel that *she* is bad for reaching for the knobs. Give her something else to play with, put her in her playpen, or slap her hand if that's your style. Tell her, "You may not play with the stove" or "No, no, no!" But try not to say something like "You stupid kid— you want to burn yourself?" or "You're *always* getting into things! Why can't you be good once in a while?"

Your 2-year-old has just climbed to the top of the kitchen cupboard and is about to hurl your favorite coffee mugs to the floor. Stop him and let him know that while throwing dishes is bad, *he* isn't bad just because he was about to indulge in such an activity. Give him a ball to throw, smack his rear, or put him in his room. Tell him, "You may not play with mugs!" or "Those mugs are mine. They're not for throwing. Balls are for throwing!" Don't resort to threats ("I'll kill you if you touch my mugs one more time!") or lables ("You're a destructive brat!")

Your 3-year-old has just decorated the dining-room wall with magic markers. Let her know you're furious and that she may not draw on walls. Give her a sponge to scrub the walls, send her to her room, or throw the markers in the trash and say, "Look at that mess! You may *not* draw on the wall. You may draw on paper, but not on the wall." Try not to scream at her or indulge in sarcasm or dire warnings ("You're such a messy slob! Who do you think you are, Van Gogh? Just wait till your father sees this. You'll really get it!").

Babies and children are extremely trusting. They believe what you tell them. If you tell them often enough that they're bad or messy or impossible, they'll begin to believe you. And once a child thinks that he is messy or bad or impossible, he'll often fulfill that prophecy.

You're human, of course. At times you *will* label, threaten, or insult your child. With practice, however, you can learn to express frustration or fury at your child's actions while not attacking him as an individual.

In *The Wizard of Oz*, when Dorothy discovers that the Wizard has no power she exclaims, "You are a very bad man!" "Oh, no, my dear," replies the Wizard. "I'm a very good man. I'm just a very bad wizard." If you can learn to condemn an action without condemning your child, he will then be able to feel that some of his actions may be very bad but that he is still a very good person.

Don't be afraid to be an authority. No matter what your life style, as a parent you have the right—and the obligation— to be an authority. If you feel uncomfortable in this role think for a minute of the implication to your child. If you're searching for a doctor, you will certainly want one who is an authority in medicine. If you take a course in mathematics, wouldn't you prefer a teacher who is an authority in the subject? Therefore, don't your children have the right to expect you to be an authority as a parent?

Don't panic! Actually, with very young children it's very simple. There are only two things to remember:
1. Set limits on actions.

2. Be prepared to follow through physically in some way to stop the action if words alone don't work.

You may be unsure of your parenting skills, but you must realize—*always*—that you know far more about the matter at hand than a 1- or 2- or 3-year-old child. For example, if your 8-month-old is about to swallow a marble you'll automatically stop her because you know that swallowing a marble is dangerous. You can, and must, be authoritative about such dangers. Your 16-month-old has the cat's neck in his hands and is slowly squeezing the life out of the animal. You know that physical violence is not good for living things, so you can act authoritatively in stopping your toddler from hurting animals or other people. Your 2-year-old demands a cookie just before lunch. You know that cookies will ruin his appetite and thus you have the right to act authoritatively about things that you feel aren't good for your child. Usually you read a story to your 3-year-old daughter at naptime but today you're too busy. Here's another area where you have the right to be authoritative: when your concerns must take precedence over your child's concerns.

You can be a permissive authority, teaching your child only one or two rules, or you can be an authoritarian authority and teach him many more rules. You can enforce your authority with hugs and kisses or slaps and smacks. These choices are up to you. If you are going to teach even one rule effectively, however, you must do so with authority.

Offer praise when the rule is remembered. We often get so busy that we forget to compliment our children when they are behaving correctly. We just take it for granted when they're doing what we want them to do. Praise, in words accompanied by a hug or kiss, can be magic, especially when a child is really trying to remember a new rule or change a habit. Barbara reports, "There is a little boy in my class who is learning to use his voice instead of his fists in a conflict. If I remember to praise him at least once or twice a day, he usually remembers to use his voice. If I forget to praise him, he forgets and reverts to hitting."

A mother said, "My 3-year-old started the habit of spitting. I tried shouting, spanking, sending her to her room, and even spitting back to get her to stop. What finally worked was telling her over and over again, 'Gee, I sure like it when you don't spit.' At first I told her ten times a day. Now it's down to once every week or so."

TECHNIQUES THAT HELP

It's a lot easier to be authoritative about discipline when you've planned your day—when you're dealing with a healthy, rested, well-fed child. Mother is usually the one to think ahead so that family life works. Several mothers shared with us wheel-greasing techniques that have helped to make their days run smoothly.

"It's important to make a child look at you when you give a command. Young children truly seem to believe that if they're not looking at you they don't have to hear or heed you." *Mother of two / Palos Verdes, Calif.*

"The jar of meat sticks, the cheese, crackers, and oranges I threw in a sack before our trip to the zoo yesterday meant that our 2-year-old ate lunch in the car instead of napping on the way back. We didn't have to wait in long lines around the refreshment stands and we didn't have to face a crotchety child when we got home."
Mother of one / Washington, D.C.

"I ask myself whether an action will correct itself in time. For example, when my son accidentally spills a glass of milk, I don't get all excited. Instead, I calmly give him a rag and let him mop it up himself."
Mother of three / Omaha, Neb.

"My daughter was scared of the water, but it was essential that she learn to swim because we have a pool. When we signed up for swimming lessons, I made sure she was in the same class as a friend's child who loves the water. I knew darn well the excitement would spread in the right direction." *Mother of two / Little Rock, Ark.*

"I tried to keep my voice low and bend down to a child's level when trying to stress a point or command, looking directly in her eyes." *Mother of five / Troy, N.Y.*

"Prepare for the worst—hope for the best. One of my super-visors told me this when I started work at a community cen-ter, and it works as well for planning a day with my child. Nothing's brattier than a bored kid so I prepare several proj-ects a day to pull out of my sleeve as needed to keep my son occupied with something other than tying the cats' tails to-gether."   *Mother of one / Dallas, Tex.*

"My in-laws live two thousand miles away, and I very much wanted them to enjoy their visit with us when our son was 2. I was forceful about keeping Michael away from children with colds for two weeks ahead of time. I checked out sev-eral restaurants to find one where service was fast, since I knew they would want to take us out to lunch. I lined up a friend to watch him one day so I could take them to the museum. We worked around his naps so that he was always fairly rested and cheerful. It all paid off. It was a wonder-ful time for all of us."   *Mother of one / Concord, N.H.*

WORDS THAT WORK

Very often it's not what you say but how you say it that determines the results you will get. One mother we know usually gives a direction this way: "You may not throw sand! OK?" She is totally unaware of the question she leaves at the end of her commands. Another says, "Oh, I'm sorry, but you may not throw sand." Still others ask "Do you?" when the answer is a foregone conclusion, like "Do you want to stop throwing sand, dear?" All this amiability is di-luting the message.

In an interview Paul Wood, the author of *How to Get Your Children to Do What You Want Them to Do*, said that a parent should "demand what's critically important and keep quiet about the rest." He suggests that being straight and right to the point is the most effective way of giving a command.

Practice being direct in your commands. Stoop down, look your child in the eye, and say: "Don't throw sand!" or "Damn it, stop throwing sand!" or "You may *not* throw sand!" or "No! The rule is no throwing sand!" Any one of these, said in your own way and your own style, will clearly get across the message to your child that he must not throw sand.

After he has gotten your message, then you can explain why, or thank him for complying with your direction, or reason with him.

Barbara reports, "One of my own chronic dilution techniques is to say, 'I want you to . . .' Yesterday, I decided to try an experiment. Jonas was watching television. I warned him that dinner would be in five minutes. Five minutes later I went in to him and said, 'I want you to turn off the television and come and eat.' Jonas paid absolutely no attention, and it took a battle to get the TV off and him to the table. Today, Jonas was again watching television before dinner. I again warned him, and five minutes later I walked in the den, turned off the television, and announced, 'Jonas, it's time to eat.' It worked beautifully. He followed me right to the table without a complaint."

"I think a good rule of thumb is to be aware of what you're comfortable with. I'm *not* comfortable with whining, loud noises, harsh treatment of people or things, or lots of TV watching, for example, so these are the areas where I tend to be strict. I *am* comfortable with strong verbal expressions of feelings, even if that means standing toe to toe with my 3-year-old in a verbal free-for-all. I feel the need to control things like teeth brushing, kinds of foods eaten, and bedtime hours, but I don't feel the need to control how they dress. They can wear whatever they want three days in a row or sleep on the floor if they want to."

Mother of two / Downers Grove, Ill.

Little No's

Every mother has had the following experience. It's ten in the morning. Billy totters up and asks for his brother's blocks. Mom says "no." Five minutes later, Billy asks to water the plants. Mom again says "no." Ten minutes later Billy asks to go outside and again it's "no." First it's one thing, then it's another. Mom doesn't even hear the requests. She just automatically says "no" like a "no-no" recorded message.

If your tape is stuck in the "no" position, try one of the following suggestions to help get it into another groove:

"For nonemergency situations, I count to ten to give myself time to decide whether or not I really want to say no. When I do say it, I stick to it. How many times have I heard a child whine and scream for something and then wind up getting it?"   *Mother of one / Hawthorne, Calif.*

"When I'm tempted to automatically say 'no' without considering, I try to stop myself. I ask if this issue is really worth the time it might involve—either a ten- or fifteen-minute battle or the time I'll have to spend repeating and enforcing the 'no.' If it's really important, I say 'no' and that's it. But there are times when it's just not that important."
Mother of three / Jackson, Miss.

"When my children ask for something requiring a yes-or-no response and I'm too busy to answer, I tell them 'You'll have to give me time to think it over. If I have to answer now, the answer will be no. If you'll give me time, it might be yes.' "   *Mother of one / New York, N.Y.*

"I try not to overload my 2-year-old with too many 'no-no's at one time. I would rather he learn one or two very well than lots of them not well at all."
Mother of one / Fargo, N.D.

TRUTHS AND HALF-TRUTHS OF DISCIPLINE

In Victorian times there were certain truths about discipline that were accepted by many parents, such as "spare the rod and spoil the child" or "children should be seen and not heard." While these truths have been dispelled, new truths have taken their place, such as "always be consistent" or "parents must present a united front."

In this section we will discuss two of these modern-day truths and show that for many parents they are half-truths, or not even truths at all.

Consistency

"Be consistent" is a commandment every parent has heard or read at some time. Many books on child care tell us that in discipline we must be consistent. Many mothers told us that they always try to be consistent. Yet when we closely questioned some of these mothers, most of them admitted that it is impossible to be totally consistent.

"I'm only consistent about things that are important to me," said one mother. "Even then, I'm not consistent 100 percent of the time. Bedtime for my three children is eight o'clock. It's important to them—they need lots of sleep. It's important to me—I need time away from them. Yet even though it's important, I'll frequently let them stay up to play with their dad or watch a special TV show."

There are certain crucial times when we all try to be consistent. When you are teaching your child to avoid danger, you will instinctively be consistent. If he heads for a busy street or starts to pound his brother on the head with a hammer you'll naturally stop him every time.

You will also need to be consistent when you're trying to replace a bad habit with a good habit. If you're attempting to teach your baby to sleep through the night, you'll need to let him cry it out, every night.

You must be consistent when you're teaching your child a new rule. If you're teaching him to keep his hands off the stereo, for example, you'll have to stop him every time he touches it.

Except for matters of life and death, however, it's only human to be inconsistent sometimes. When your baby has learned to sleep through the night, it's only human to go to him if he wakes up crying. Once you've taught your child not to touch the stereo, let him get away with touching it occasionally.

One grandmother told us, "I learned to look the other way and just not see things when I didn't have the energy or the desire to enforce a previously stated rule. What I didn't see usually didn't hurt any of us."

Dad and Mom—A United Front

We hope you and your partner can agree on the major issues

of discipline, and it's probably best for everyone if major disagreements are settled without the benefit of your child's presence.

But no two people will agree all the time on every issue. It's not necessary, or even good, to keep up a "united front" at all times. Think of a small child who is faced ·vith two big people who always agree on what he should or should not do. He's bound to feel overwhelmed at times. It's good for him to realize that people, even parents, sometimes have differences of opinion, and that some of the time one of them will side with him. Murray Bowen, director of the Georgetown University Family Center, says that parents often feel they must present a united front even if one of them feels the other is not acting in the child's best interests. An insecure mother, for example, may go along with her husband's method of discipline even though she's convinced it's not good for the child.

One mother said, "In my opinion, it's sometimes beneficial if parents have opposing views in their feelings on discipline. My husband and I are very different—we balance each other." Another mother commented, "When we're faced with a disagreement sometimes we compromise; sometimes I give in, sometimes he gives in, and sometimes we battle it out right in front of the kids."

"We followed one person's way in one area and the other's in another," said a third mother. "Whoever started first usually got to follow through. My husband has a thing about toys on the floor, and he figured out a way to get our daughter to pick them up and put them away. I have a thing about bedtime, so it's my responsibility to put our daughter to bed. When Dad is in charge, our daughter often stays up till ten or eleven. When I'm in charge, she leaves her things around. She's learned our ways—that we're different, that we expect different things from her. Most of the time our method works beautifully."

"My husband and I are both basically permissive," said still another woman, "but he's more pushy than I am. I tell our son to do whatever he wants about eating; my husband says, 'I want you to eat your peas!' I stay out of their relationship. It belongs to them, not to me."

PACIFIERS, SECURITY BLANKETS, AND THUMBSUCKING

Some mothers feel guilty if their children suck their thumbs or have a pacifier or security blanket. "It's as if she's showing the world that I don't give her enough love, that somehow she's missing something," said one.

Instead of feeling guilty, try turning that feeling into pride. Pat yourself on the back for having a child who is bright and precocious enough to have found such a harmless way to help protect himself from the insecurities of this world. One well-known pediatrician says he feels a little sorry for the child who begins to discover that the world isn't the most marvelous of all places and wishes he could give the child "some other way of comforting himself in addition to—not in place of—the solace of finger sucking that he has discovered for himself."

If your child has a blanket or a pacifier he'll give it up on his own when he doesn't need it any more. One mother recalled, "When my son was about 1½ we were at his grandma's (she lives on a boat) and he threw his pacifier overboard. Well, a sea anemone that was on the gangway grabbed it and was sucking it. We just said he needed it more, and that was it!"

No mother we talked with has found a way to force a child to stop sucking his thumb, at least not before the age of 3. Your child may stop on her own, but there is nothing you can do to force the issue.

One friend, however, did find a way. "For years, we've been putting money in a jar," she said. "Every year we told our daughter she could have the money on her next birthday if she would stop sucking her thumb. She stopped. She was 10 last month. We gave her the money. I tried everything before that: yelling, painting yucky goo on her thumb, making her fingernails pretty, putting a glove on her hand. Believe me, nothing worked!"

In general, then, in these situations the rule is: leave your children alone, don't draw attention to their behavior or make a fuss about it, and eventually they'll stop when they're ready to.

SPANKING

To spank or not to spank? That is the question. Some mothers swear by spanking as the quickest way to get across a point of discipline to a young child. Others spank only in an emergency or when they've been pushed to the wall. For some parents, spanking is effective; for others it is not. There is no agreement among parents, or for that matter among experts, about the value or the harm of spanking.

Almost every parent we questioned has spanked her child for some reason or other at some time during the first three years. The parents who feel comfortable about spanking say, "It works." The parents who feel uncomfortable about it say, "It doesn't work."

One mother told us, "Spanking works great for me *and* for my daughter. Sometimes reasoning is lost on her but when I spank her she knows that's it. It definitely relieves my tension and she knows where she stands. She pushes and pushes at the limits, and when I spank her, finally, she becomes a different person."

Another woman expressed a different view. "I can't stand spanking for me! I feel I've lost when I resort to spanking. I can't think of any time when spanking has effected a long-term change in behavior."

"I only spank when I'm absolutely furious," said a third mother. "For dire emergencies, like running into the street, or when I've had it and can't tolerate even minor misbehavior. My 2- and 4-year-old sons both know that whatever behavior brought about a spanking had better cease, immediately!"

"Spanking doesn't accomplish anything for me," said still another. "I get angry, and occasionally spank. But my daughter never remembers a previous spanking. It's as if the slate is wiped clean, and a half hour later she'll do the same thing over again."

Should you spank your child? You, like most of us, will probably make this decision based on your emotions rather than on principle. Rationally, most of us agree that there are better ways of teaching a young child; emotionally, all of us get angry with our children and spank. No, we probably shouldn't spank our children, but yes, we probably will.

MASTURBATION

Just as your baby discovers his fingers and toes, he or she will eventually discover and begin to handle his penis or her vulva. He or she will find that touching the genital area brings pleasurable sensations. And occasionally you may find your children, blissfully in their own world, handling their genitals.

Most pediatricians and most mothers feel that the best way to handle this natural exploration is to ignore it. One mother commented, "When my 3-year-old son sits in the tub fingerir : his penis, I start to blush and feel hideously embarrassed. However, intellectually I know that my feelings are *my* hang-ups, so I calmly look away and begin to fiddle around in the bathroom, finding something else to do."

"I must admit that I'm tempted to say, 'No, no, don't touch,' when my daughter rubs her genital area. But I know these words aren't mine, but just an echo of my mother, who made me feel so guilty about my body," another mother told us.

"My son is beautiful," said a third mother. "Every part of him is precious. I want him to feel that his genitals are as important and nice as the rest of his body. So when he reaches for his penis, I say, 'That's your penis,' just as I say 'That's your nose' or 'Those are your eyes' when he touches those parts."

JEALOUSY AND SIBLING RIVALRY

Jealousy and sibling rivalry are facts of life. Even an only child is not totally exempt from these feelings—often an only child will have a surrogate brother or sister, a close friend with whom he will act out feelings of jealousy. When you bring a new baby home from the hospital, your older child will feel jealous, and these feelings will continue, to some extent, throughout his childhood.

To help you identify with your child, put yourself in the following situation. Your husband comes home one night, politely asks you to sit down, and explains, very nicely, "Well, dear, in a few weeks I'll be bringing home a second wife. I still love you, but I feel there's enough room in our house, and in my heart, for two—a big, grown-up, responsible old model like you and a beautiful, brand-new, up-to-date model like Gail." Unless you're a saint, there's no way you wouldn't have some feelings of resentment in this situation. Unless your child is a saint, there is no way she isn't going to feel resentment toward a new brother or sister.

How do you handle these feelings? Accept the fact that they exist and encourage your child to express his hostility. In Judith Viorst's book *I'll Fix Anthony*, a younger brother dreams of the day when he'll be 6, and therefore magically older and braver and stronger than his older brother. Anthony continually tells his little brother "You stink." The mother says that deep, deep down in his heart Anthony loves his brother, but Anthony still asserts that his brother "stinks."

Barbara says, "The children in my preschool class immediately identify with the feelings in this book. It opens the floodgates of their own emotions, and they discuss their brothers and sisters, both older and younger, calling them abusive names like 'old b.m. head' or 'dum dum.' They scheme and plot about how some day they'll get even with their siblings. They express feelings of hate and dislike, and yet when their brothers and sisters come to visit they show feelings of love and friendship."

"I give each child a special time alone with me each day. When the youngest, Molly, was a baby I had my special time with Johnny while she slept. Now that they're older (2½ and 5) each respects the other's private time with Mom."

Mother of two / Newark, N.J.

RESPONSIBILITY

Just how much responsibility do you have for your child's behavior? Bertram J. Cohler, a psychologist at the University of Chicago, says, "Parents are not responsible for their children's outcome to the extent to which we've been taught. Children are independent creatures who create their own lives."

Intellectually, Dr. Cohler's words make sense. You know you can spend a fortune for art lessons, but your child won't become a Georgia O'Keeffe unless she is born with artistic ability and inner drive. You can start your baby swimming, but he won't be a Mark Spitz without inborn ability and self-determination.

Each mother, whether new with an infant or old with grandchildren, knows that her child is a unique individual. Yet each mother, new or old, feels responsible when it comes to discipline.

"My 2-month-old son has colic and cries for two hours every day. It's certainly not my fault; I'm doing everything I can. So why do I feel so guilty?" asked a teenage mother.

But it's not just teenage mothers who feel inadequate. "When we got home from a shopping trip, my 3-year-old took a purloined pack of gum out of his pocket," said an experienced mother of five. "My first reaction was 'Oh my lord, I've failed as a mother. I haven't taught him not to steal.' "

"I received a note from my daughter's high school principal asking me to come by to discuss a problem," another mother told us. "I spent the afternoon worrying about what she might have done wrong, and what I might have done wrong in raising her."

The truth is, as a parent you will always feel somewhat responsible for your child's actions. The trick is, however, to keep those feelings from getting in the way of intelligent action—or intelligent *inaction*.

Your 6-month-old baby is addicted to his pacifier. You meet a friend and her baby, sans pacifier. You may feel guilty, but don't let your feelings cause you to take away your child's pacifier before he's ready to give it up.

You take your 18-month-old to the market. He demands a treat and has a tantrum when you refuse. You may feel responsible, but don't let your feelings cause you to give in to the tantrum.

You and your 2-year-old are visiting a friend. Your child clobbers your friend's child. Although you may feel embarrassed, don't let your feelings cause you to overreact and abuse your child.

Dr. Cohler says that all a child really needs is love, clothing, food, shelter, and some guidance. The rest, he says, is up to the child. This is an oversimplification, but a parent can take comfort from it. Relax—it's *not* all up to you. If you discipline your child to the best of your ability, then the rest is up to him and his natural tendencies.

11

Toilet Training

You've been teaching your child ever since he was born. You held him and fondled him, teaching him that the world is a safe place. You helped him learn to crawl, with smiles and encouragement. You helped him learn to walk by clearing a path for him. You helped him learn to feed himself by giving him bite-size pieces of food and not worrying about the mess. You have provided a suitable learning environment and offered praise and encouragement. He has learned to walk, talk, and feed himself in his own way and at his own pace.

The same holds true for toilet training. You will teach him by providing the materials and place for toileting. You will suggest a method and offer encouragement. Your child will then train himself in his own way and at his own pace.

"I know it sounds strange, but I got closer to my child through toilet training. I was thrilled to help her learn something so important so fast. It was the first time I realized there was a person there, someone I had to treat with real sensitivity." *Mother of one / Dallas, Tex.*

TIMING AND APPROACH

Your child's maturity is the first thing to consider, since it's the most important factor in successful training. Toilet training is for *children*, not babies. Most mothers and child-development experts agree that attempting to train a baby is a waste of valuable time. A baby needs time to practice and perfect all the tasks and skills of babyhood. You, her mother, need time to baby her. Over and over again, mothers who tried to train their first-born children before their second birthdays said they would wait until later if they had it to do over again. One mother reported, "Grandparents on both sides told me how intelligent Mary was and that she could easily learn. I began training at 1½, tried for a month, and gave up. I tried again a few months later and gave up again. Finally, when she was 2½, I was successful. I didn't start my second child until that age, and I have not yet started my third, who is now 2½."

We strongly recommend that you do not begin training your child until he is at least 2. And even 2 may not be old enough unless he's showing other signs of readiness. He should be walking. He should be retaining his urine for several hours—occasionally waking from his nap, and even in the morning, dry. In general, he should be consistently keeping his diapers dry for periods of two or three hours. He should also be able to understand and respond to simple directions. He should be talking well enough to use and repeat a few simple words associated with toilet training. All these factors will indicate to you that your baby is becoming a child, and that he is ready for toilet training.

In addition to maturity, your child should be in a generally calm period of her life. If she automatically says "no" whenever you make a request, it's better to wait until she's in a more agreeable stage. Hold off training if your child is making an adjustment to a major change such as a move or a new baby, or even to such a seemingly undisturbing event as a visit from Grandma.

"With my first, I started training at 18 months, which was ridiculous. She wasn't ready, so it became a frustrating hassle. In fact, she continued wetting her bed periodically until she was 6. I firmly believe that toilet training should not begin before 2, or even 3, if a child isn't ready. I also advise ignoring any pressure from outsiders, especially grandparents. My mother kept insisting that Beth should be trained before my second child arrived. My mother-in-law kept telling me how all her children were trained before they were 1. I tried to please both of them, consequently causing many unhappy experiences for my daughter and myself.

"On the other hand, my son (supposedly boys are more difficult to train) was no problem whatsoever. One day when he was 2½ he asked me when he could go to school. My answer was: as soon as he stopped wearing diapers. At that point, he told me he had to go potty. I put him on the toilet, he went, and the diapers never went back on."

Mother of two / Palm Springs, Calif.

"With the first one, twenty-four years ago, I started out like the books said, as soon as he could sit up. But I had trouble with him until he was well over 4 years old. The second one, also a boy, I started a little later. But I also had trouble with him until he was 4. The third I started at about 2, but he also had trouble. So when Joe came along, five years ago, I forgot about it until he showed interest, and it worked out just fine. He was going by himself at 2½, and even staying dry at night." *Mother of four / Springfield, Mo.*

Take a look at your child's personality. Does she require firm handling or does she respond best to gentle coaxing and a smile? A teacher knows that children are individuals. When she wants three different children to put away their blocks she tells them in three different ways. Johnny, for example, is active and boisterous, constantly testing classroom limits; he needs to be told firmly that he *must* put away his blocks. Susan is quiet, introspective, and shy; she needs only a whisper and a pat to accomplish this same result. Relaxed and easygoing Mike may respond best to being jollied along with such words as "Mike, if you don't get going and put away these blocks, the ants will eat them all up." In toilet training, your child may need firm but friendly directions, a whisper and pat, or to be jollied along.

Your own temperament is important too. How do you feel about your child's bowel movements? Some mothers who have changed thousands of soiled diapers without flinching find themselves utterly repelled by wet or messy pants. One mother said, "Changing diapers never bothered me. But the first time I had to take off a pair of 'full' pants, I started gagging and almost threw up. After this happened a few times, Jimmy began gagging too. I realized I had to do something different, so the next time I breathed through my mouth, helped Jimmy take off his own pants, and let him slosh them in the toilet. I also let him wipe himself, although he used almost a whole roll of toilet paper doing it."

Are you facing any major changes or problems in your own life? If you start training while you're in a state of disruption, your child may pick up your feelings and toilet training will become a battle that no one wins. "My husband and I were separated when my daughter was 2," one mother told us. "I had to return to work, and it certainly would have been easier to find a babysitter if my daughter had been trained. However, I decided that with so much disruption in our lives, this definitely wasn't the time for training. I finally found a sitter who understood, and together we trained my daughter a few months later when our lives were calmer."

A second mother didn't wait. "We were planning a move across the country when my son was 2," she said. "Since we were going to visit my in-laws and I wanted to prove how great I was, I felt I had to train him before the move. I bribed, threatened, cried, and cajoled. Nothing worked, and for years afterward he had frequent accidents."

"I think the most important aspect of toilet training is to make sure *you're* ready to go through with it. After observing several friends I realized that when the mother set her mind to do it the child cooperated, and when the mother dithered around and got upset so did the child."

Mother of two / Macon, Ga.

One final point. You will naturally feel good about both yourself and your child when toilet training is successful. You will just as naturally be inclined to feel bad about yourself and your child when it is unsuccessful. Being aware of these potential feelings before you begin training may help keep them from overwhelming you and making you feel like a failure if your child doesn't train herself with ease. One mother told us, "The year I spent training my oldest son was one of the worst in my life. He was the right age, 2½, and I think I did everything right. But it just didn't work. He wasn't trained until 3½. The whole process was so long and drawn out that all I want to do is erase it from my mind. When I start training my daughter, I'll be certain to quit if everything doesn't go smoothly. Better to send her to school in diapers than put either of us through the struggles that I had with my son."

PREPARATION

"Before my daughter was trained, at 2 years, we spent a few weeks talking about the potty seat. We then practiced, and sat down together. It was kind of a fun time to visit with each other—I sitting on the big seat, and my daughter sitting on her own seat. She succeeded a few times, but with no regularity. I didn't push, because I realized that she now knew what to do, but she simply chose not to do it."

Mother of two / Spokane, Wash.

"My son had a doll he taught to go 'wee wee on the potty.' After he taught it, then he learned himself. However, I found that he had to give up training the doll when it was his turn, because he spent all his time playing with the doll while he stood and wet his pants."

Mother of two / New York, N.Y.

Before your child can train himself, he needs some pretraining experiences and skills, so start getting ready a few weeks before you actually begin toilet training.

Get an inexpensive plastic potty chair, the kind that sits on the floor and has a bowl that lifts out from the top. Leave it in the bathroom for a week or so before you even mention toilet training so that your child will get used to it being there. When your child shows an interest in the potty, tell him that in a few weeks he can learn to use it just like grownups, and big kids use the big one. Let him play with the potty when he chooses, sitting on it and getting up, with clothes off or on.

"After the first few days, I got rid of the deflector on the potty seat for my son. It was easier to mop up the urine on the floor than to have to worry about his amputating his penis every time he sat down or got up."

Mother of one / Lincoln, Neb.

It's helpful, at this point, to invite your child into the bathroom whenever you, your husband, and particularly other children use it. Allow your child to sit on his own potty and watch while you tell him, "Mommy is wetting in the potty" or "Daddy is making a b.m." Even the family dog can be used for a toilet model. One father told us, "When my wife went to the hospital for a varicose vein operation, I asked her if there was anything special I could do for her while she was gone. She told me that it sure would be nice if our boy was out of diapers. And by the time she got back, he was. The dog would go out and do a wizzie and my boy would go out and do a job too. My wife was pretty pleased. She'd been puttering around, you know, and it hadn't worked for her."

"My second daughter watched as her sister used the toilet. She also watched her father and me. When she was ready to be trained, she wouldn't have anything to do with her own safe, comfortable potty chair. From the very start she insisted on climbing up on the regular toilet, just like the rest of the family."

Mother of two / New Haven, Conn.

"My daughter idolizes her brother. Because of this, she is having difficulty with toilet training. She insists on standing facing the toilet, pulling down her panties, and while leaning slightly forward she fills up her shoes. She even remembers to lift the seat. It works for brother and she's always tried to grow into his routines."

Mother of two / Portland, Ore.

Decide what toilet-associated words you are comfortable with. Remember, these words will be used for a long time. What sounds cute at 2 may not sound that way when your child is 4 or 5.

Buy or borrow as many training pants as you can. Ask your friends for their used ones—they may not think to offer unless you ask. One mother said, "The thing that helped most was a sack full of training pants from a friend. They were all different sizes, but it didn't matter. I didn't tense up when on the first day my daughter went through eight pairs."

If at all possible, train your child during warm weather. The whole process is much simpler if she can wear only training pants and a shirt during training.

During training, some children want to do everything for themselves. Therefore, you might want to teach your child to take off and put on her own pants before you begin training her. (This is a lot easier if her training pants are nice and loose on her.) Unless your child can do this with ease, don't make it a part of toilet training. It's not a good idea to teach two skills at one time.

Plan to begin training on a day that is relatively free of outside activities and interruptions so you and your child can spend some relaxed time together. One working mother we know began training her child on a Saturday. By Monday, when he went to the babysitter, he was well on the way to being trained. Another mother said she began to train her daughter on the day after her second birthday. "She got to start this great adventure as an extra birthday present. I also put away some of her real birthday presents, and got one out whenever she succeeded in using the potty. It worked beautifully."

TRAINING

"My daughter started using a portable floor potty at around 23 months. It was springtime and warm so she wore training pants and no outer pants. The first week or so I used an automatic timer with a bell and set it for every hour. When the bell rang, she was reminded to think whether or not she felt the urge to go. At first, if she went potty she got a piece of sugarless gum. After a month she no longer needed the gum. I'd forget on purpose to give it to her and soon she forgot. She was delighted with herself."

Mother of two / Richmond, Va.

Our favorite method of toilet training is based on behavior-modification techniques. Wetting or making a bowel movement in the potty (positive behavior) is rewarded with praise, hugs, and a treat (positive reinforcement). Wetting or making b.m. in the pants (negative behavior) is discouraged by saying to the child, "Next time, we'll use the potty," asking him to show you where the potty is, and finally by withholding the treat (negative reinforcement).

When your child wakes up on the day you've decided to start training, say to him: "Guess what! Today is the day you can learn to use the potty, just like Daddy and Mommy. We're all so proud that you're such a big boy now."

Take him from his bed and check his diapers. If they're dry give him a treat and tell him, "Here's a goodie because your diapers are dry. You can have lots of treats today if you wet in the potty and keep your pants dry."

Take him to the bathroom immediately and help him sit on the potty. If he wets, show your delight and pride and give him a treat. Call in Dad and the rest of the family if they're home. Even favorite animals, live or stuffed, might be invited to share this proud moment. After celebrating, help your child to pick up the pot, carry it to the toilet, and dump it. Some children are frightened of flushing; if yours is, you might wait and do it yourself later.

"I still remember my daughter's shining face when she gingerly carried the wee-wee all the way to the big toilet and poured it out slowly, as though it were liquid gold."
                    Mother of one / Boise, Ida.

"When each of my seven children took their first step I stood on the sidelines giving them applause and praise. When they fell down, I encouraged them to get back up and try again. During toilet training, I tried to give the same kind of support. I gave applause and praise when my children succeeded. I gave encouragement and guidance when they failed. And I helped them to try over and over again."
                    Mother of seven / Boston, Mass.

After your child dumps the urine, help her put on training pants, again emphasizing that she won't have to wear diapers anymore now that she's old enough to wear pants. Do not put on any outer clothing, even shoes or socks. If the house is chilly, turn up the heat.

If your child wakes up wet, don't give her the treat but repeat the same dialogue, taking her to the potty shortly after she wakes. If she begins squirming around and wants to get up, tell her, "I guess you just don't need to wet. Let's put your diapers away, and put on potty pants. You're getting to be such a big girl, I'm sure you'll remember to wet' in the potty when you have to."

Give your child all kinds of fruit drinks during the first few days of toilet training. This will encourage frequent wetting and give her lots of chances to practice.

About every half hour, check your child's pants. If she's dry, give her a treat, praise her, and again explain, "You're getting this cracker because you're such a big girl with dry pants." Ask if she needs to use the potty and go with her if she needs help. Remember to reward successful attempts and to encourage her to try again later if she doesn't need to use the potty yet.

When your child wets his pants, remember that everyone

makes mistakes. Tell him calmly, "Oh my, you wet your pot-ty pants. Remember, today you're going to wet in the potty. Let's take off your wet pants. Now show me where you will wet next time." Gently take him to the bathroom. If he asks for a treat, tell him that treats are for dry pants, not wet pants. Allow him to put his own wet pants in the dia-per pail and get his own dry ones.

During the first few days, your child will make frequent mistakes. If you find that you're getting frustrated or angry with yourself or your child, step back, count to ten, and re-member, "He's learning, he's learning."

"I never punished my boys or got angry when they had ac-cidents. Each time they started to have an accident, we'd make a game of hurrying to the bathroom so they could get to the toilet. If they wet the floor, I'd always say, 'Oh, that's your pee-pee. It goes in the toilet, remember?'"

Mother of two / Manhattan Beach, Calif.

"My wife and I shared this responsibility, taking care to give our son the same calm, relaxed instructions each time. Too many parents confuse their children by not being specific and consistent in their instructions."

Father of three / Des Moines, Iowa

Bowel training should happen simultaneously with urine training if you follow this method. However, many mothers said that urine training came first, then bowel training.

After the first few days, gradually lengthen the time span between "dry-pants checks" and rewards, and also lengthen the time between "go-potty" reminders. Within a few weeks your child should be fairly well trained. He'll be so proud of his new skill that you can easily take away his treats.

One mother who tried this method with her 2-year-old daughter said, "I was very resistant to the idea of using a bribe. However, I agreed to try. I was amazed! My daughter was trained in three days. I was afraid she'd keep asking for her potty treat until she went to college. But, to my amaze-ment, she forgot all about it in two weeks."

If, after a week or so, your child is having little or no

success with training, we urge you to stop the whole procedure. We can't give you an exact "stop the show" date, since it will vary. If you find that you or your child is getting nervous and uptight, continuing after two or three days is just not worth it. Better to accept that neither one of you is ready than to turn training into a struggle.

A mother of five emphasized this point: "With my number-one son, I was *so* nervous about toilet training. Everyone kept reminding me how brilliant he was and people would drop hints to the effect that a 2-year-old as smart as he was ought to be out of diapers. So I started training him. And even though it didn't work, once I started I kept on trying. I got more and more upset and he got more and more obstinate. Ten years later I still remember with horror those six months of battles.

"With the other four children, I just waited until I thought they were ready (between 2 and 2½). You know, it's funny, but I can't remember training any of them. It was all so easy; it just seemed to happen."

"Toilet training—my first experience was: ugh! When my first son was 2, all my well-meaning friends kept asking, 'Isn't he potty trained yet?' Well, he wasn't, so I read up on it, bought training pants, and we started. What a mess! One accident after another, even to the point of hiding to avoid the toilet. Then one day, I said 'I quit!' Back we went to diapers, and what a relief for me and my son. To make a long story short, one day about three months before Bobby's third birthday, I heard this little voice saying 'Mommy, I have to go potty.' From that day on, he trained himself. It was *his* way when *he* was ready, and it was a quick, pleasant experience."   *Mother of two / Cleveland, Ohio*

POST-TRAINING

Staying dry at night or during naptime isn't really a part of toilet training. Some children start staying dry at night and during naptime before they are trained, some shortly after, and others not for a while. If your child is consistently dry in the morning, let him give away his diapers to a new baby who will need them more. If he still wets at night, allow him to wear his diapers to bed. Many 3- and even 4-year-old children still need a diaper at night.

If your child isn't wearing diapers at night or for naptime and is going to sleep in someone else's bed, take along a rubber sheet to slip under his sheet because nighttime accidents occur more frequently in new situations. Friends and motel owners will be very appreciative of this courtesy.

Even after your child is well trained, she may still have accidents. Don't let these worry you—or her. You'll have to keep on reminding her, occasionally, to go potty. One mother says, "My 6-year-old son still needs reminders. He'll wait until the last minute, and sometimes just not make it."

Another mother said, "When my daughter wakes up from her nap in a crotchety mood, she says 'no' to everything. The conversation then goes, 'Do you want to go potty?' 'No!' 'Mommy wants to.' That usually does it. She runs for the toilet. If the words don't do it, she watches me go and the power of suggestion does."

Let your child begin using the regular toilet as soon as he is comfortable with it. A boy might be encouraged to sit on the front of the bowl facing the tank. If you put a few scraps of brightly colored tissue in the bowl and let him "shoot" the tissue down, he may be encouraged to wet in the bowl, not spray the floor. As soon as he's tall enough to stand up, suggest that he do so; a step stool kept nearby for your son to stand on will help his aim immeasurably. If you have a daughter, encourage her to sit far enough back so that the urine falls into the toilet, not over the rim.

After your child is trained, let him use the toilet facilities wherever you go. A few children become so attached to their own "potty" that they find it difficult to go in strange places. One friend recalls a story from her childhood. "I vividly remember one vacation just after my younger brother was toilet trained. We stopped at three motels and investigated the toilets before we found one that had white seats. My brother just wouldn't accept a black-seated john!"

"We encouraged our children to discreetly use the outdoors if necessary. And, in fact, my second child trained himself while we were out camping. He watched his older brother. It was great fun to pick a tree, and 'go wee' on it."

Mother of two / Hyattsville, Md.

"I found that letting my son use a coffee can instead of a potty chair worked out well at times. We still carry a can in the car with us, in case of emergency. It can be closed up until you can empty it."

Mother of four / Boulder, Colo.

We hope that you can adapt these suggestions to your child and that you'll find training easy. Most of all, we hope that both you and your child will remember toilet training as a happy learning time.

12

Touch and Teach Your Baby

Child-development experts agree that the first three years of a child's life are tremendously important in determining the patterns she'll follow for the rest of her life. Thus parents and educators are continually looking for ways to encourage intellectual and personal growth in very young children.

This chapter describes some of the ways you can help your child learn and grow. Like the rest of this book, however, it is intended only as a general guide, not as a set of instructions for raising a brilliant child. Some parents, we've found, tend to be overanxious about their children's first three years. One mother expressed this anxiety: "I was afraid that unless I stuffed as much knowledge as possible into my child during those years he would be doomed for the rest of his life to remain at the foot of his class. I read every new book, I bought every new toy, I spent hours stimulating him, and still more hours worrying because he didn't react to all my games. Fortunately, I had a second child when my first was 2, and I didn't have the time to worry about educating any more."

It is true that if you leave your baby in his crib all day with nothing to do you'll be depriving him of his right to learn. It is just as true, however, that if you spend all your time and energy trying to educate and stimulate him, you'll be depriving him of the right to develop on his own, and yourself of the right to a life of your own.

In an article in *Mothers Manual,* Robert Strom, director of the Parent-Child Lab at Arizona State University, says, "The typical adult beginner can handle only about ten minutes of fantasy play with a preschooler. This fact means it is unreasonable to participate beyond our point of disinterest." If parents do continue beyond this point, says Strom, they may give the child the impression that the activity is not worthwhile, or that it's boring. So, consider your interests, your child's interests, and both of your abilities. Then use those suggestions that seem worthwhile for both of you.

"Playing 'learning games' with my kids drives me nuts. I never could stand analytical games, toys, or puzzles. But I'll read stories any time and go outside with them at the drop of a hat. I do what I do and refuse to feel guilty."
Mother of two / New York, N.Y.

"Most of all, just being with my child—just playing with him the way *he* likes to play—is fun. We share the things we enjoy and don't worry about the rest."
Mother of three / Riverdale, Md.

"What did we do just for fun? We had a little hill outside our apartment that we used to sit on every night and watch for Daddy's car to come home. When they were babies, I sang songs and ended with a rousing rendition of 'Daddy's Car Is Here' sung to the tune of 'The Farmer in the Dell.' As they got older, we named the color of cars and types of trucks as they went by while we waited."
Mother of two / Milwaukee, Wisc.

"At this time of my life, I've come to one conclusion: productive people are happy people. So I tried to bring up my baby with the enjoyment of being happy doing her own thing. When she was an infant I didn't try to entertain her every moment; I worked and did my own things while she played and enjoyed herself alone. We did have times together, but I felt it was important for her to explore and find enjoyment in herself, and we were both happy seeing each other busy."   *Mother of two / Boston, Mass.*

"After dinner our kids enjoyed roughhousing with their father; then I read them a goodnight story after the 'on the floor' playtime. Looking back, it was this nightly routine that made for happy memories later."
Mother of three / Hawthorne, Calif.

"Just for fun, we put all the mattresses on the floor and did tumbling on them. We went out, at midnight, in just-fallen snow. We dug in the dirt and planted a garden. We took daily walks, in good weather and bad, and when it was too miserable to go out we set up ten to twenty large grocery bags on the kitchen floor and my sons ran in and smashed into them, trying to knock down as many as possible. Then we'd set them up again and start over."
Mother of two / Eugene, Ore.

BUILDING BONDS OF COMMUNICATION FROM BIRTH

Before you teach your baby anything else, it will be helpful if you and she can share your thoughts and emotions, through both spoken language and body language. Many parents of teenagers complain that their children never discuss anything with them, and this is a gap that you can start closing in *infancy;* that's when communication begins and can become a deep-seated, important part of both your lives. We offer here some guidelines that will help you foster a climate for real communication, and real teaching, both when your child is a baby and in later years.

Reflecting Your Child's Feeling

Give your baby the right to his own emotions, both negative and positive. Listen to them and repeat them to him in your own words. When he's unhappy, assure him that it's okay to feel that way sometimes.

Suppose your baby has fallen down and is screaming at the top of her lungs. First check to see that she isn't seriously hurt, then pick her up, hold her, and say, "Oh, dear, you fell down. It looks like you hurt your knee. Oh, boy, that must really hurt! It sure hurts to fall down." Don't get too mushy; just affirm the obvious truth—that she's crying because something hurts. You'll find that children of all ages often stop crying very quickly if you accept their right to feel hurt.

Or suppose your baby is happily sloshing one of your best guest towels in the toilet bowl. You take it away from her and she howls with rage. Reflect *her* feelings. Say, "Boy, you're really mad at me because I took that away from you." By handling her response this way, you're showing her that it's all right to express her anger even though it is not okay to slosh your things in the toilet. She may not understand your words yet, but both of you will be getting practice in expressing feelings.

Finally, suppose your toddler is driving you bananas with his negativism. "No" has become his favorite word. If you responded to all his negative feelings, you'd get nothing done all day. Don't feel guilty about ignoring some of his negative feelings. However, occasionally say to him, "Boy, it's not easy growing up, is it? One minute you want to be a little baby; the next minute you want to be big. One minute you want a cracker, and the next minute you throw it on the floor." These words may not help your child right now, but they may help *you* if you say them.

As time goes by, you'll have many occasions to reflect your child's feelings. Your baby is 13 months old and takes his first step. Enjoy his satisfaction. Your baby is 15 months old and scribbles a picture. Reflect her pride. Your baby—now becoming a child—is 18 months old and climbs to the top of the slide. Share his accomplishment. The more you share from day to day with your child, the stronger and richer the bonds of communication will be.

Communicate Your Own Feelings

You will sometimes feel angry with your child; all mothers do. Anger in itself is not destructive, but how you handle it may be. Some mothers take it out on themselves; they never yell at their children, but they may become depressed or sick. Others act out all their anger with their children even when they're angry about other things; they yell at the kids and blame them for everything. Still others label their children "just plain bad, like their Uncle Oscar," and decide that they're not worth getting angry at.

None of these ways of handling your negative feelings does anyone much good, and they may do great harm. It's not always easy to express your own anger in a way that doesn't damage your child's self-esteem. Two examples may aid you in venting your anger without hurting yourself or your child.

Suppose you've just finished scrubbing the kitchen floor when the phone rings. You leave the room for a moment to answer it and when you come back your baby is smearing soapy water all over the floor. Although you're annoyed with yourself for leaving him alone, you're angry at him too. Tell him, "I am furious! I am mad! I just finished scrubbing the floor, and now I'll have to mop up the whole mess all over again." He'll get the idea that you're angry. In fact, he'd probably be able to "read" your anger even if you didn't express it. But he won't get the feeling that he's a slob, that he can't be trusted, or that he's basically no good.

Or suppose you're taking a walk with your toddler when she suddenly darts into the street and is narrowly missed by a car. First you feel frightened out of your wits; then you feel guilt, and then anger. First swat her on the bottom, if that's your style, and tell her, "No! Streets are not for babies." But then tell her how frightened you were, that you were afraid she was going to be hurt. She'll probably start howling, and you'll want to howl with her. Keep on communicating your feelings until you're both feeling better.

ENCOURAGING SELF-ESTEEM

Nurturing a sense of self-esteem is a must at all stages of your child's development. A child who has very few material advantages or "enrichment" experiences can overcome these limitations if he has been raised with the gut-level feeling that he is the most marvelous child in the world. On the other hand, a child who has all possible material and educational advantages may have a difficult time as both child and adult if he has not received nurturing in self-esteem from his parents.

Some parents confuse self-esteem with self-centeredness. One mother said, "I know some children—and adults, too, of course—who are egotistical and stuck-up. They go around bragging about how great they are. I don't want my child to act like that. Won't he act conceited if I tell him he's great?"

Certainly, your child may show off and brag at times; almost every child does, occasionally. But if he develops inner self-esteem he is much less likely to have to look outside himself for approval or to continually feel that he must prove he's the greatest. If he has true self-confidence he won't have to prove anything—he'll just know that he's okay.

Nurturing self-esteem begins when you first bring your baby home from the hospital. Most parents don't need much coaching in how to give their new baby the feeling that she's marvelous and much-loved; there will naturally be lots of cuddling and oohing and ahing. The new baby will surely be the focus of your life, at least until the novelty wears off. However, some parents may not realize the importance of seemingly mundane everyday interaction with their child, right from the beginning.

An excellent teacher once said to us, "So many modern mothers rush around trying to make time for 'special times' with their children. If only they'd realize that caring for a baby—changing his diapers, bathing him, feeding him— is the best kind of special time." We agree. The attention you give your child is total at those times, and you're teaching him what *caring* is all about, which is one of the most valuable of gifts. Yet some parents hurry through these tasks so they can get on with something they consider to be more educational, or more important.

It is the simple, everyday care that you give to your baby that will give her the feeling that you care for her. And because you care, she'll know she's worthwhile.

When you rock, pat, snuggle, and croon to your baby you let her know that the world is a safe place. When you make every effort to respond to your baby's cries, even if you can't figure out what's wrong, you show her that you're listening and trying to understand what she's saying. When you roughhouse, roll on the floor, and end up hugging and kissing your older baby, you're telling her that she is precious. When you occasionally rock your toddler to sleep, you let him know that his world is still safe. When you share the pride and pleasure of big events, like the first time he rolls over by himself, and the small events, like taking a bath, you're telling your baby that he is great and life is good.

In a recent article in the *Los Angeles Times*, Herbert Kohl, author of numerous books on education and parenthood, discussed his grandmother, who had a "terrible" life in Europe before coming to this country and whose early days here were also difficult. Yet Kohl's grandmother said, "Expect trouble and then learn to enjoy," and she did just that, joking and singing while she cared for her children. And she never stopped enjoying herself or her children, no matter how difficult life became. "The most sensible way to experience the joy of having children is to give up the idea of a life free of conflict and learn to celebrate the joy as it comes, and to minimize the grief, disappointment, and trouble," Kohl concluded.

This, we also believe, is the best way to encourage self-esteem in your child. Play down his faults and the problems of day-to-day life; encourage him to develop his inborn assets and acquire new strengths, and then enjoy.

ENCOURAGING YOUR BABY TO TALK

For most new mothers, baby talk comes easily. You'll naturally talk to your baby from the very beginning even though she can't respond—you'll tell her how much you love her, how beautiful and wonderful she is; that she has her father's eyes and your nose. You'll talk to her when you're changing her, bathing her, feeding her. And as you talk, you'll be giving her the best possible start in learning to speak herself.

"I think talking with my children was and still is our favorite form of play. I encouraged them to talk by talking to them, enunciating every word carefully, and repeating things over and over. I tried to teach them the idea of using words properly to express their desires, and I never talked down to them. As early as a year, verbal communication is an important thing between parent and child. By telling them 'hello,' 'goodbye,' 'I love you,' 'Yes, you may have a cracker,' or 'No,

don't touch the stove' you establish a sense of what is happening and how you feel about it in their day-to-day life."
Mother of two / Springfield, Mo.

Your baby's first language is crying. And although his cries may sometimes drive you to distraction, you'll respond as often as possible to this language, doing your best to answer his requests.

Babies learn to talk by imitating what they hear. You can help your baby start this process by imitating *her*. When she begins to coo, bleat, blow bubbles, or make any kind of baby sounds, imitate what she's doing. This will assure her that she's important and that what she's saying is important. "When he was 3 months old, my son began imitating me imitating him," said one mother. "We carried on long two-way conversations this way, and usually finished our talk with smiles of delight at our cleverness."

After your baby is vocalizing frequently and is able to imitate sounds with some degree of accuracy, experiment with new sounds. Make war whoops. Try a few "da-da-da-das" and "ma-ma-ma-mas." Your baby's later fluency in imitating real words will be greatly facilitated by these sessions.

Tell your baby the names of the things in his world. When you see something new, say, "That's a dog." One new father instituted a nightly ritual. "I was so delighted with my baby," he said, "that I wanted to introduce him to all the things in our home. I took him around and said 'hello' to the dogs, the lamps, the pictures, the chairs. We kept that up for years."

A mother let her son name some of his favorite toys. "The first sound he made was 'aga,' so we called his stuffed dog Aga, and when he later said 'aba,' we called his bear by that name."

Another mother said, "I crept into my daughter's room in the morning before she woke up and turned on a cassette recorder. She entertained herself by talking, and later I entertained her by playing for her the tape she had made. I also saved several tapes as a permanent record of her voice at 3 months, 5 months, a year, and so on."

During her second year, your baby will begin to speak in strings of gibberish and will sound as though she's speaking complete sentences in a foreign language. Continue to share her language with her, but also be sure to continue speaking *your* language with her.

Simplify your language when you want her to clearly understand what you say, but use complete sentences—for example, "Throw me the ball" or "Sit down in your chair" or "Look at that dog." Keep directions and explanations very brief.

At other times use your normal vocabulary and speak to your baby just as you'd speak to your husband or a friend. Squat down to his level and tell him your opinions about an upcoming election, your feelings about the beauty of nature, or your thoughts on a book you've just read. If you do this, your child will not only pick up new words but will also respond to the sound and cadence of adult language, and will soon be fluently using it himself.

When your child begins to use actual words, he'll mispronounce many of them. At this point, don't imitate his baby talk, but gently tell him the correct pronunciation by repeating the words. For example, when he says "Me want buc," you say "Oh, you want a *cup*."

"I made a special point to use big words when I talked with my 2-year-old daughter. When she was 3 she amazed friends and relatives by using words such as 'enormous,' 'attention,' and 'primarily.' " *Mother of two / Seattle, Wash.*

"I played a game with my son to teach him the meaning of little words like 'in' and 'on.' I told him 'Here's Bunny, sitting *on* the table. Now I'm putting Bunny *under* the table. Now he's *on* the table again.' Then I gave him his stuffed rabbit and *he* did the putting. By the time he was 3 he knew the meanings of all kinds of little words."
Mother of one / Miami, Fla.

"I always tried to find some time to listen to my children, but when I was too busy to listen, I was honest and told them that I wasn't really listening. They usually went on talking, but I didn't have to respond. However, later I'd make it a point to block out my own concerns and listen to what each child had to say. They're teenagers now, and we still talk together often. I think my efforts to communicate with them when they were young were really worthwhile."

Mother of four / Chicago, Ill.

DEVELOPING MOTOR SKILLS

More and more often, nursery-school and kindergarten teachers are noticing that children are coming to school deficient in their physical, or "gross motor," skills. One teacher said, "Children come to my classroom knowing how to read. They can do puzzles; they can string beads; they can count. Some 4-year-olds can even add and subtract. But many of these same children are afraid to try and catch a ball. They can't ride a tricycle. They have trouble with balance. I used to spend most of the morning teaching children reading-readiness skills; now I find I have to spend time teaching them gross-motor skills. They don't need these things for academic success, but they *do* need them for social success during recess, where it really counts."

If your baby is active and on the go from birth, you won't need to help him to use his body. But if he's basically inactive and content not to move much, try some of the following suggestions to get him moving.

When changing your baby during infancy, gently stretch her arms out, then fold them back over her body in a hug.

Gently "bicycle" your baby's legs. One mother has made a game of this. "My 2½-month-old son's favorite activity is 'Run Down to the Beach.' I take his feet in my hands and I say really slowly, one word at a time. 'Do . . . you . . . want . . . to (I bicycle his legs slowly) run down to the beach?' (I bicycle his legs quickly.) He just smiles, and is so tickled by the surprise ending."

When your baby's legs are curled up, put your hand or stomach against them. When she naturally kicks out, pull away. Eventually she'll automatically kick you back when you exert the slight pressure.

"I loved dancing with my son," said one mother, "and it meant we both got exercise. I held him closely in my arms, turned on some music, and moved. I waved his arms, wiggled his ears, kicked his legs in time to the music. When he was 3 or 4 months old he began to bounce around and do these things himself, on his own, whenever he heard any music."

Another mother told us, "A beanbag chair was one of our best investments. It was useful not only as a chair but also as a climbing surface for my daughter. When she was an infant, I'd put her nude in the middle of the chair, and then push on either side to cause her to move up and down. When she got older, I'd toss her into it; she quickly learned to wiggle out, and then I'd toss her back again."

Learning to swim may be the least of a mother's reasons for taking a baby to Mom and Me swimming lessons. One mother said, "My child was so antsy and energetic that, somehow, I had to get her as tired as I was. Swimming did it!" Another mother commented, "My son was easygoing, relaxed, content just to sit around. I signed him up for swimming lessons when he was 9 months old so that he'd get *some* kind of exercise."

As your baby grows and begins to walk, make sure she has space in which to walk, run, and climb safely in your house or yard or at a park. If you live in a one-story house or apartment, take her to places where there are stairs. Going up the stairs is much easier for most babies, so let her crawl up at first, staying right behind her. Then help her learn to crawl down. Many babies will attempt to crawl downstairs head first. To save her from a possible skull fracture, help her learn to scoot down, on her belly, feet first.

Once she has learned to crawl up and down stairs, help her with walking up and down. Again, up is easier for the first attempts. She'll begin by putting one foot up and then dragging the other one up. Hold her hand until she gets the hang of this new accomplishment.

One mother said, "We live in a small apartment. I try to get to the park every day, but don't always make it, so I gave my son his own climbing chair. It's an old upholstered chair. He jumps on it, climbs on it, and does whatever he wants on his chair."

"Boxes were my son's favorite toys. I kept several on hand, and whenever he needed to be entertained, out they came.

He climbed in them, crawled through them, pounded on them. When he demolished them, they were easily replaced."
Mother of three / Burlington, Vt.

"One piece of equipment I bought for my first and used for all three of my children was the Creative Playthings Slide. My children loved it! From the age of a year up, they played under it, hid from Mommy, crawled up it, slid down it. As they grew older it became a fort or an observation tower for imaginary games played with friends. A neighbor now has our slide for her toddler, and although it's ten years old, it's still in great shape."
Mother of three / Sioux Falls, S.D.

Balls

A ball is an essential toy for a baby or child. Give your baby several different-sized balls, making sure they're too large to put into his mouth. He won't be able to catch a ball, but you can roll it to him and teach him to roll it back. Sit on the floor with your legs stretched out and have him sit opposite you with his feet touching yours. Roll the ball back and forth. If it goes "out of bounds," let him retrieve it. Gradually enlarge your playing field by sitting farther and farther apart.

As he grows older, teach him to catch a ball. First, stand facing him and ask him to hold out his hands. Hand the ball to him and encourage him to bring it up to his body in a hug. Ask him to hand it back. Gradually move farther apart, tossing the ball very gently. Children as old as 4 have trouble catching, so don't worry if your child can't do this yet.

"My child was hit by a ball when he was 2 and developed a strong fear of them. We got him over his fear by playing with balloons. He discovered that balloons didn't hurt, and eventually learned to like balls," said one mother.

"We played basketball with our 2-year-old daughter," said another mother. "To start, I gave her a ball and asked her to drop it in a wastebasket. Gradually I moved the basket farther away. She was absolutely thrilled every time she made a basket."

Some other miscellaneous suggestions for getting your child moving come from other mothers.

"Tug of war is a favorite game in our house. We use a piece of stretch fabric. I hold onto one side, my daughter grabs the other. I pull her, she pulls back. At first, I always had to let her win, but now that she's 3 it's sometimes a real battle."
Mother of one / Cedar Rapids, Iowa

"My daughter learned to catch by grabbing at toilet paper rolls that I tossed to her while unpacking groceries. After catching them, she would put them away in the bathroom."
Mother of one / San Diego, Calif.

"We play the old-fashioned game of follow the leader. I stretch my arms; my 2-year-old stretches his. I get down on the rug and crawl; he crawls after me. Sometimes I'm the leader, sometimes he's the leader. We both get lots of exercise and have lots of fun. The only problem is, he can outlast me every time."   *Mother of one / College Park, Md.*

"As soon as they could toddle, all our kids loved to join in our after-dinner family 'disco' sessions. Sometimes we danced with each other but mostly we all did our own thing and everybody had a ball." *Mother of three / Boulder, Colo.*

SENSORY DEVELOPMENT

Here are some suggestions that may be fun for you and at the same time will help to stimulate your baby's senses of sight, sound, and touch.

"When my daughter began batting with her arms but still wasn't able to sit up by herself, I put her in her infant seat in the playpen and strung all sorts of objects on a line across the pen she could wallop things to her heart's content. I also put a small metal mirror and a few objects on a two-inch piece of elastic band so she could pull against that. My husband used the playpen outside so the children could watch him fixing the car or gardening without crawling around and putting all kinds of obnoxious things in their mouths."　　　　　*Mother of two / Little Rock, Ark.*

Rattles

You can help your baby use his ears and eyes with the following rattle games.

Stand behind your baby so that she can't see you. Shake a rattle over her head until she looks for it. Continue shaking the rattle and circling it over her head. If she reaches for it, let her have it.

Another time, move the rattle in a curve, from one side of your baby's head to the other, so that she follows it with her eyes.

Still another time, stand where he can't see you. Shake the rattle near his feet and give him time to track the sound and look at the rattle. Then, still staying out of sight yourself, change the position of the rattle, shaking it to the right of him, to the left, over his stomach, or over his head.

When your baby enjoys holding his rattle, shake it close to him. Give it to him as soon as he touches it. Another time, gradually shake the rattle close to him and then lift it so that he has to reach for it.

Drop the Toy

At some time between 5 and 7 months you will notice that your baby has learned a marvelous new skill: she can drop things. She'll be thrilled with this new ability and will practice it over and over again. You may not be quite so thrilled by this game, since you'll also spend hour after hour picking up the things she drops.

But remember, when you're bending down to pick up a toy for the hundredth time, that your baby needs to develop the muscles in her hands. Grasping and letting go of objects is the first step toward later facility in using her hands for drawing, cutting, knitting, typing, and thousands of other things.

One mother we know turned "drop-the-toy" into a game. "I set my kitchen timer, gave my son his favorite stuffed animal, and put them both in the high chair. 'Drop Dog,' I told him. 'Come on, let Dog fall.' The first time, I showed him how to sweep the toy off the tray. Then I picked it up, he dropped it, I picked it up, over and over, until the timer went off. Then I took him and Dog down and stopped the game. We played 'Drop Dog' at least once a day. Turning it into fun seemed to help keep my son from dropping so many other things."

"I took the cushion from a low chair and put it in front of the chair. Then I put my 10-month-old daughter's favorite animal, Pooh Bear, on the chair and told her to go and get Pooh. Next I encouraged her to drop Pooh, and finally showed her how to climb off the chair and retrieve the bear herself. After a few times with me supervising, she was able to play this game all by herself."

Mother of one / Alliance, Neb.

Peeking and Hiding

All babies naturally start playing peek-a-boo at around 4 months. Hiding games help teach your child that things go away but then they come back. Every mother we talked to had her own favorite version guaranteed to bring delighted laughter from her child. You will develop your own peek-a-boo games; one mother shared her version with us:

"I hid my child's rattle under a blanket, leaving part of it sticking out, and told him, 'Go find your rattle. Let's look under the chair. Is it there? No. Maybe it's under this blanket.' Then I pulled the blanket up and we found the rattle. I immediately hid it again and let my son find it himself. We repeated this game over and over.

"A few weeks later I hid the toy behind the drapes, first leaving part of it out so he could easily spot it, then hiding the whole thing. Eventually, my son liked to hide some things himself, but I had to find them quickly or he would immediately show me the hiding place."

If you and your baby enjoy hiding games, make them more sophisticated. Let your baby watch you hide a toy in a can. Then encourage her to find it, showing great enthusiasm at her success. After she can find a toy hidden in a can, wrap it loosely in paper and encourage her to find it. You can extend this game indefinitely, hiding a toy in a can,

wrapped in paper, covered with a blanket, under a pillow. Of course, if your child gets frustrated, stop the game.

Another version of this game is to get three containers of different sizes. Hide the toy under the smallest container and tell your child, "Go find your toy. It's in the smallest can." Keep hiding it in the same container. After a few tries, your baby will probably go right for it. Then change its position, hiding it in the largest can several times, and finally in the middle-sized one.

Change the game, and let your baby hide the toy for you to find. To make it more fun, occasionally guess incorrectly. Even very young babies love to see Mommy make a mistake.

Other Games

Several mothers told us of other games that stimulated their babies' senses, providing learning experiences:

"I made a collection of some safe small things for my baby after I discovered he had a passion for unsafe small things like stray pins and cigarette butts. I gave him jar caps, juice cans, rocks, clothes pins, and any other things small enough to pick up with his hands but large enough so he couldn't swallow them. Then I gave him a coffee can. He played with these things for hours, looking at them, tasting them, putting them in and dumping them out of the can."

Mother of two / Arlington, Va.

"I bought a set of natural-colored hardwood blocks for my daughter's first birthday. It was the best investment I made. At first, I gave her six or eight blocks and let her do her own thing. Then I showed her how to make a tower and knock it down. I lined them up on a low table, and again let her knock them down. She played with these six blocks for hours. When she grew bored with six, I gradually added more."   *Mother of one / Redondo Beach, Calif.*

"I heard somewhere that even new babies like to have human faces around them, so I drew simple happy faces and sad faces and made a picture gallery for my daughter, taping them to the wall above her bed and over her changing table."
                    Mother of one / Phoenix, Ariz.

"When my daughter was born, her grandmother gave her a music box. This started a collection of music boxes, and I've gotten her one on each birthday. Since birth, she's treasured them. Not one is broken, and now she's about to have a baby herself and start her child a collection of music boxes."
                    Mother of three / Cleveland, Ohio

"My daughter loves to be outside, to touch the wet grass, the rough bark of a tree, the sand at the beach. When I couldn't be out with her, I put her in her playpen on the back porch with her toys so she could be outdoors anyway. She has learned what birds are and to recognize different animals such as cats, dogs, and rabbits."
                    Mother of one / Altantic City, N.J.

SOCIAL RELATIONSHIPS

Your baby's first smile at you is her first real social contact. New parents do ridiculous things to inspire those early smiles and chortles. Remember, however, that each child is different. Take your cue from your child. If she is easily startled, take a gentle, low-key approach to early social play.

At some time during the second six months, your baby may show her devotion to you by screaming bloody murder whenever you leave her. She may pick a very inconvenient time to experience what the experts call "separation anxiety."

(The day Barbara's mother arrived for a month's visit, Jonas decided that he hated everyone but his own mother. He wouldn't go near his grandma for the whole month.) Only time will solve this problem, but you may be able to avoid it to some extent if you start early to expose your baby to friends and sitters outside your immediate family. Try to engage a steady babysitter during this period, if you can.

A child doesn't really need friends his own age until he's 2 or 3. However, you may notice that your baby is much happier when other children are around. If he has no brothers or sisters, occasionally take him to the park or invite older children into your home to play with him. Stay close by at first. Eventually you may find that older children from the neighborhood will spend hours entertaining your baby, while you sit nearby reading or doing needlework.

Most mothers we questioned agreed that inviting a playmate in means more, not less, work until a child is at least 3. However, most of them also agreed that the benefits were worth the extra work. Early exposure to other children helps toddlers learn that they can't always have their own way. This is especially important for "only" children, who don't have opportunities within the family to learn to give and take without a lot of stress.

Few 2-year-olds are able to share very well. A child that age has just begun to realize that he is himself and that his things belong to him. To avoid constant battles, put away his special toys when friends come to play and try to provide activities that don't require much sharing. Invest in *two* of a few of his favorite toys—like two sets of crayons or two identical dump trucks—so that he can share them with friends.

If there are no suitable playmates in the immediate neighborhood, take walks with your child and look for signs of children. When you see some evidence of a child the right age, be assertive: knock on the door and introduce yourself and your child. Who knows? Maybe inside that door is another mother going crazy with her 2-year-old. If not, try again—at a different house, on a different day, on a different block.

13

**Teach Your Child
Through Work Play**

Your child will have to perfect many skills before she can
learn to read, write, add, and subtract. We have labeled these
skills "work play." Included in this section are some games
and activities that will help your child prepare herself for
formal education. These activities should be fun for you
and your child, but they are also your child's serious work,
since the old saying "Play is the work of childhood" is as
true today as it was when it was first uttered many years ago.

"My 2-year-old most enjoys doing useful things, so I try
very hard to let her do things for herself. I let her feed herself, even though she makes a mess. I let her help dress and
undress herself, help set the table, pick out cans at the market, stir the batter when I'm cooking. A few days ago she
was trying to play with a toy that was a bit difficult for her.
She tried very hard and worked on it a long time. All of a
sudden she shouted, 'I did it! Yea for Sara!' "
Mother of two / New London, Conn.

"Sometimes I feel guilty because I don't enjoy playing with
my children. I'll find things for them to do, but I can't
stand to sit down and build houses, or play games, or work
with puzzles. My husband, however, loves to play with the
kids. So I do my part by reading books and collecting games

328

and materials so the kids can have these special times with Dad. When other mothers talk about the fun they have playing with kids, I sometimes wish I were different. But these have been happy years anyway."

Mother of two / Little Rock, Ark.

"Child's play is work. If the adult knows that, then there is integrity and purpose in every activity, in every moment of a child's day. And this can keep a mom's spirits high, this sense of integrity she has about her job."

Mother of two / Kansas City, Kan.

SORTING AND MATCHING

A baby who is starting to walk is old enough to begin to be aware of similarities and differences. This is an important factor in reading readiness, since reading is merely a sophisticated method of recognizing similarities and differences. Some of these activities are suitable for toddlers; others are better postponed until your child is 2 or 3. Start with the simplest ones and introduce more complicated games when your child shows he's ready to meet new challenges. Remember to praise his successes. If he can't get the hang of a new game, put it aside for a few weeks and try again.

To start, make two different sets of three similar items—for example, three milk containers and three soup cans. Put the set on the floor and let your toddler play with them for a while. Then ask him to bring you all the cans. After he's given you all of them ask him to bring you all the milk containers.

On another day extend this simple game by pasting a soup label on one grocery bag and part of a milk container on another bag. Tell your child to put all the soup cans in the bag with the soup pictures and the milk containers in the bag with the milk picture. Play with her long enough to get started and then let her do it any way she wants.

After your child can sort things that are grossly different, try sorting things that are slightly different. Sort cans of peas and cans of corn, red blocks and blue blocks, square blocks and curved blocks. Don't expect your child to master concepts of color or shape, just give her experiences in seeing similarities and differences.

"I turned cleaning up into a sorting game. I got several heavy-duty shopping bags and decorated them with pictures of each type of toy in my son's collection. He had a bag for stuffed animals, one for blocks, one for balls, one for miscellaneous junk. At the end of a play session he helped me put the toys into the appropriate bags. I hung lightweight items from a hat rack in his room. I put heavy items on his toy shelves."   *Mother of two / Hyattsville, Md.*

"Although I didn't know it was 'reading readiness,' I constantly gave my daughter sorting experiences. I encouraged her to sort or separate sticks and stones at the park, to put large shells in one pile and small shells in another at the beach, to help sort the laundry, putting my socks in one pile, her dad's socks in another, and her own in still another."
Mother of one / Manhattan Beach, Calif.

"Every once in a while I made a hand-and-foot puzzle for my 2-year-old son. On a large sheet of paper I traced around my son's hands and feet, my husband's hands and feet, my hands and feet, and occasionally around the hands and feet of dolls or stuffed animals. My son would then attempt to match everyone's hands and feet with the correct outlines. Finally, he'd put his own hands and feet where they belonged. Later we traced around the entire body. We usually had a hilarious time and ended up all jumbled together on the floor laughing and kissing and hugging."
Mother of one / Portland, Ore.

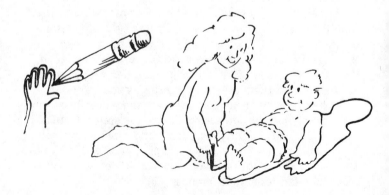

"I made a 'thing puzzle' for my 3-year-old. I scrounged around the house for ten or twelve small items—a key, a block, a spoon, a can opener—and traced the outlines of all these things on a large piece of cardboard. I put the actual things in a shoebox and gave it to my daughter, who had a marvelous time matching all the objects with their outlines."
Mother of four / Decatur, Ill.

When your child has had experience recognizing similarities and differences in things, you can begin to teach him to name and recognize shapes. Use descriptive words about shapes throughout the day. Talk about the round ball, the square box, the rectangular door. After some general use of vocabulary, buy a box of magnetic shapes. Using your refrigerator as a board, let your child manipulate the shapes. First make random patterns. Then take out one shape and say, "This is a circle. I'll put it up here. Can you find some more circles?" Help him locate all the circles. After a few sessions of circle talk, do the same thing with other shapes.

"We went on 'shape walks.' I'd announce, 'Come on, Sue, let's go find some circles.' We'd walk up and down the streets pointing out wheels, doorknobs, hula hoops, and other circles to each other. Sometimes we'd finish our walk with a quiet session at home drawing pictures of all of the circles we had seen."   *Mother of one / Cambridge, Mass.*

"I made my son a flannel board by covering the back of a small bulletin board with a large piece of flannel, stapling it securely, and then binding the board with heavy carpet tape. I then went to a school-supply store and bought an inexpensive box of felt shapes. My son is now 5, and he still plays with his flannel board."
Mother of two / San Antonio, Tex.

"I keep all my plastic bowls and containers in one low drawer, all the tops in another drawer. When I'm busy in the kitchen, I dump all these items in a jumble on the floor. My 1-year-old daughter has become amazingly adept at putting the lids and containers back in the correct drawers."
Mother of one / Blackwood, N.J.

"The Tupperware shape ball I bought when my son was 9 months old has been one of his most-used toys. At 1½ years he could begin to put some of the shapes into the correct holes. By the time he was 2 he was able to match up all the shapes with all the holes. And by the time he was 3 he could name all the shapes."   *Mother of two / Detroit, Mich.*

"I bought a couple of simple wood puzzles for my daughter, and she put them together over and over again. When she got bored with her puzzles, I traded with friends rather than spend money buying more."

Mother of four / Wilmington, Del.

COLORS

Try some of these activities if you want to help your child distinguish colors and learn their names.

The first step is to use color talk, pointing out and describing things by their color. A few obvious examples are green grass, a red stop sign, blue sky, a yellow daffodil. Once your child is familiar with the names of colors, play some games with her.

Give her four red objects and four green objects. Put them in a pile. Show her the red object and ask her to give you all the other red objects. Once she's sorted things that are red, ask her to give you the green objects. When she recognizes the differences between two colors, gradually add more and more colors to the game.

If you can involve the whole family, it might be fun to designate one day of the week as a "color day." Start with red. Wear red clothes, cook red food, make pictures with red crayons or red paper, take a walk and look only for red things, put a few drops of red food coloring in the bath water, and read or tell "Little Red Ridinghood" at bedtime. Schedule "color days" during those "blah" months when there are no holidays to add spice and excitement to life.

Barbara reports, "Color Days in my prekindergarten classroom come very close to Halloween and Christmas in importance. We made butter on yellow day, and we imported snow (crushed ice from an ice company) to sunny Southern California on white day. On purple day each child created his own version of the 'Purple People Eater' and then put on a play for parents, who were also dressed in purple. Mothers have told me that children are so excited by school on these days that they pick out the appropriate color-coded clothes the night before and wake at the crack of dawn asking, 'Is it time for purple day yet?' "

"I gave my 3-year-old some experience in mixing colors. I bought a few eye droppers at my local pharmacy. First, I let my son squeeze a little water into the eye dropper and drip it out. Then I gave him a polystyrene egg carton, filling each cup half full of water. I dropped some red, blue, and yellow food coloring into three of the cups and let my son be a 'magician' and mix the colors. Eventually all the colors turn brown, but meanwhile my child has a marvelous time."
Mother of two / Montpelier, Vt.

SCIENCE

During their first few years all children are natural scientists. Your child will want to get into everything and learn all he can about what makes his world work. He will use his hands, his ears, his mouth, his eyes, and his nose. You will have to thwart some of his scientific curiosity for safety's sake, but if you follow a few of our suggestions he'll have opportunities to safely touch, taste, smell, hear, see, and investigate much of what's happening in his world.

"To see my children's faces when they begin their trek into the unknown is, for me, the most delightful part of raising a family. Right now, my 8-month-old is enraptured as he crawls from one end of the room to the other, knocking on furniture, pulling leaves off plants, opening drawers. It's a total job watching him, but we have a ball."
Mother of two / Reno, Nev.

"As soon as my son really learned to walk we began to go on nature walks. All you need for this is a pail or some other easily carried container. A magnifying glass, a jar for stray bugs and critters, and a pair of clippers are handy to have, too. Craig always enjoyed collecting things, and 'found' items are often more precious to him than bought toys. It's sur-

prising what you can find just around the corner or up the
block."   *Mother of two / Tampa, Fla.*

Give your child an ice cube. Let her feel it and lick it,
then encourage her to put it in a dish and watch it melt. Use
the words "liquid" and "solid," but don't expect her to be
able to say them or remember them for very long.

Help your child collect some objects such as rocks,
pieces of wood, cloth, a pencil, a jar lid, a sponge, a toy
boat, a small piece of aluminum foil. Let her experiment
and find out which things float and which things sink.

Make your own bubbles. Squirt liquid detergent (we've
found that for some reason Joy works best) into a bowl and
gradually add water, stirring with a spoon. Keep trying out
the solution with your bubble blower until it's just right.
Add a few drops of glycerine for longer-lasting bubbles. For
blowers use the plastic rings that hold together six-packs of
beverages, plastic hair rollers, or thin plastic-coated wire
twisted into a hoop. If your child can't blow bubbles by
himself, do it for him. He'll have a marvelous time chasing
and popping bubbles.

Water is in many ways the best and cheapest learning
toy for a toddler. Give your child plenty of opportunities
for water play—in the tub, in the back yard, in a shallow pan
on the floor. Be sure to stay with her, though—children
have been known to drown in just a few inches of water.

"On those awful days when nothing seemed to work and my
son and I spent our time growling at each other, I would
plop him in the tub and he would become instantly tranquil.
He splashed, squirted water out of an empty liquid detergent
container, filled and emptied cups, and squished sponges
while I sat on the floor nearby with a good novel. There
were some days, during the early years, when he took two
or three baths a day." *Mother of one / Gary, Ind.*

Sand is probably the second-best, and second-cheapest,
learning toy for a toddler. An inexpensive plastic pool with
a large piece of plywood for a cover works fine as a sandbox,
although it will have to be replaced occasionally. A pit dug

in the back yard is even better, except that the sand tends to spill out into the rest of the yard. A pit dug in the ground and lined with bricks or weatherproofed wood is probably best. However, make sure to keep a sandbox covered when your child is not playing in it or the neighborhood cats will think it's for their convenience.

Buy clean sand at a building-supply store and get a large plastic container. Fill it with spoons, cups, pots and pans, a large salt shaker, a strainer, a sifter, a funnel, plastic cars and trucks, plastic animals, and pieces of wood. Put your child in the middle of the sandbox and let him do his own thing. If your child should get covered with sand, sprinkle some baby powder on him; then you can brush the sand off more easily.

"We live in an apartment, so we couldn't possibly have our own sandbox," one New York mother told us. "To improvise, I made an inside sandbox. I poured a few containers of cornmeal into a large dishpan and set the pan on newspaper-covered floor. My children have a marvelous time playing in the meal."

If you can stand the mess, mix water and dirt and let your child play with mud. In fact, even if you can't stand the mess, let him have a little mud occasionally. His future nursery-school teacher will bless you—she won't have to spend months telling him it's okay to muck around with fingerpaints, clay, and all the other messy things he'll find in a good nursery school.

Growing Things

Watching things grow is a fascinating if often frustrating activity for preschoolers. They are fascinated once something begins to grow but frustrated because the process takes so long. Here are a few projects to try at home.

You probably already know how to grow a sweet potato vine. But to refresh your memory, this is how it's done. Fill a quart-size mayonnaise jar with water. Stick three tooth picks in the sides of a sweet potato to hold part of it out of the water. Suspend the potato from the mouth of the jar by the toothpicks. Roots will grow first, then vines will sprout from the top.

Line the inside of a plastic glass with damp paper towels.

Put dry lima beans between the wet paper and the glass. Watch them sprout.

Cut a potato in half and sprinkle it with grass seed or bird seed. Watch the seeds take root and grow.

Sprinkle bird seed on a damp sponge and watch it grow.

"Dig some dirt from your garden, and then mix in lots of cheap rye-grass seed and add water until it turns to mud. Find a few pine cones, and glop the mud and seed mixture on the pine cone. Spray the cones with water once a day, keeping them moist. In a few days grass will begin to grow, and in a few weeks the cone will be covered with grass."
Mother of three / Salt Lake City, Utah

"My children start growing their own Easter Basket grass a few weeks before Easter. They help dig up some mud from the garden, put it in a plastic bowl or basket, and plant some grass seed in it. Every day they water it, and by Easter it's full grown." *Mother of four / Sioux Fall, S.D.*

Cooking

Cooking counts as "science" because by doing it your child will learn that he can make things change. Here are some cooking activities that many 2- and 3-year-olds can handle:

• Practice measuring and pouring with water or sand.

• Dip liver or chicken into flour.

• Scrub raw vegetables and fruit with a brush.

• Snap beans or shell peas.

• Make a quart of frozen orange juice.

• Pour from a child-size pitcher into a cup.

• Stir and beat such things as instant pudding, cocoa, scrambled eggs.

• Spread soft butter, cheese, or peanut butter on toast.

• Roll out cookies with hands or flatten them with a plastic cup.

• Crack and peel hard-boiled eggs.

"As soon as they can stand on a chair, my children help

me in the kitchen," said a mother of two boys and one girl. "Stirring an egg in a deep bowl is a good job. Pouring ingredients from a measuring cup into a bowl, washing dishes, putting cookies in the cookie jar, and wiping woodwork with a damp cloth are other jobs we share."

Making butter is a good kitchen activity. Pour about an ounce of heavy whipping cream into a baby-food jar and add a dash of salt. Put the cap on tightly. Then play a record with a strong beat and let your child shake the jar until it turns to butter. "No matter how often we make it or how expensive the cream," said one mother about making butter, "it's worth the time and money to see the awe on my 3-year-old daughter's face when the cream changes to butter."

Another mother shares her recipe for playdough. "This is without a doubt the best playdough recipe in the world," she insists. We've tried it, and agree!

Playdough

2 c. flour	2 t. cream of tartar
1 c. salt	2 T. cooking oil
2 c. water	food coloring

Mix all the ingredients except the food coloring together in a saucepan. Stir vigorously. Cook for approximately 3 minutes, stirring constantly. The mixture will congeal, and you'll immediately know when it's finished. When the dough is cool enough to handle, knead the food coloring into it. This recipe will keep for several months if stored in a covered container.

Some Other Good Ideas

Here are some other thoughts from mothers on enriching
their children's lives in the scientific area.

"I think we enjoy one special thing the most. During the
summer we collect acorns and refrigerate them. Then when
winter comes, we feed the squirrels from our kitchen window sill."   *Mother of two / Cincinnati, Ohio*

"When I'm tired and need a few minutes' rest, I tell my
daughter, 'Lie down, honey. Let's close our eyes and just
use our ears and listen.' My 3-year-old will lie absolutely
quiet for about five minutes, trying to hear the sounds of
birds, an airplane, water dripping, footsteps, or bees buzzing."
                              Mother of three / Seattle, Wash.

"A cheap card of magnets from the hardware store was
one of my son's favorite toys. At first he just played with
the magnets. When he got bored with that, I gave him paper
clips, nails, a thimble—things a magnet would attract. On another day, I dropped paper clips into a pie pan filled with
water and let him use a magnet to pick the clips out of the
water. On still another day, I buried the paper clips in a dish
of rice and let him play detective and find the clips with his
magnet."   *Mother of four / Shreveport, La.*

"My 2-year-old son has enjoyed the garden I planted. While
I was planting it he would dig in the garden with me, using
his own bucket and shovel. When it came time to harvest our
crop he was always excited about going along with me and
helping pick the vegetables and put them in his bucket."
                              Mother of one / Raleigh, N.C.

"Perhaps the thing I did best was encourage a lively sense
of curiosity and creativity. The children had an old typewriter, a magnifying glass, all kinds of paints, crayons, huge
drawing pads, clay, and musical instruments to experiment
with. We gave my son models and good tools as soon as he
showed an interest (at about 3). My son and I used to have
an 'opera' going when he'd come home from school. I'd an-

swer the door singing, 'Who is it?' and he'd sing back, 'It is Ro—bert!' And we'd go on singing arias through lunch until we were both hysterical. I hate a sober household!"

Mother of five / New York, N.Y.

"When my boys were toddlers and we went on mountain trips, my husband would take sticks, stones, bark, or whatever was available and make elaborate Indian villages, using stones to make fences, sticks for tepees, houses, campfires and lean-tos. I was amazed at some of the villages they created. The kids were so proud of them."

Mother of two / Casper, Wyo.

NUMBERS

To help your child learn to say the numbers from one to ten, use them a lot yourself. Say, "I'll count to ten while you go get your doll." Or "Let's count to five and then we'll go outside." Or "When I count to eight, your dinner will be ready." Or, "You'd better get over here before I count to three!" Just as your child learned to talk by copying you, he'll learn to say numbers by copying you.

Understanding the concept of "number" is much more difficult than learning to recite their names. To help your child begin to understand the concept, start with the number two. Say, "Show me your hands. Let's count them: one, two. You have two hands. Now show me your feet. Let's count them: one, two. You have two feet." Count ears, eyes, Daddy's feet, Daddy's ears, etc. Next, count objects: two dolls, two trucks, two balls, etc. Point to the objects and say the number. Once your child has grasped the idea, let her point while you count, and finally see if she can point and count.

Let your child practice wherever you go. In the park ask her to bring back two sticks; in the supermarket ask her to get two cans of dog food; at home ask her to bring you two spoons. Once you're sure she understands the concept of "two" go on to "five," since she has five fingers and five toes, and follow the same procedure. Many children as old as 4 or 5 have difficulty counting, so don't push it. If your child doesn't readily grasp these concepts, try again a few months later—or delegate the job to Big Bird. Many children learn to count by watching "Sesame Street."

If your child is a mathematical genius and you need more information, read *Give Your Child a Superior Mind* by Siegfried and Therese Englemann. This book has an excellent section on teaching mathematics to young children.

READING BOOKS AND STORIES

Introduce your baby to the pleasures of reading before he's a year old. Buy one or two cardboard books. Sit with your baby in your lap, holding the book slightly out of his reach. Turn the pages and point out the pictures, telling him the names of the characters or objects.

David's first book was Gyo Fujikawa's *Baby Animals*. Barbara read it to him this way: "David, look at the puppies. Puppies say 'Ruff, ruff.' Look at the ducks. Ducks say, 'Quack, quack.' Oh, look at the elephants! Elephants say 'Eeeeeeeee.' "

After a brief trial reading session, leave the book with your child. He may chew on it, try to turn the pages, or ignore it.

When your baby gets older, play "What's That?" with *Dr. Seuss's Picture Dictionary* or a Sears catalog. Let your child turn the pages. Point out objects and tell him their names. After a while you'll be able to tell your child to find the cat, or the monkey, or the cup. He may miss occasionally, but after you do this several times you'll be amazed at how many things he will recognize.

As your baby grows, he'll become interested in listening to stories with simple plots. Every now and then try out a few storybooks with your baby, like Margaret Wise Brown's *Good Night Moon*. Take your cue from your child's interest. Some love the sound of stories from the very start; others are only slightly interested, and still others aren't interested in books at all. Their urge to move and explore overshadows everything else. If your child isn't interested, forget all the reading for a while. Come back to it later and try again.

When we asked mothers to tell us what they did for fun, over and over again they said "Read." "I think the quiet times were the most fun. At night, after a bath and while they had their snack, we would lie across the bed and I would read to them," said one mother.

"We believe in books, *lots* of them, for children—books to own and books to borrow," said another mother.

"Even babies love the cadences of poetry. Mine love *Poems to Read to the Very Young,*" said still another.

Unbelievably soon—perhaps just after her second birthday—your child will welcome a changing variety of books. The library is the answer at this time. If your child is boisterous, go alone to pick out books for her. A few hours invested in exploring the books available will help you choose good ones.

It may seem like a nice idea to take your child with you to the library so that he can choose his own books, but until he has some concept of "library" and some familiarity with books he'll be more of a distraction than a help. Do, however, make an effort to select books you think he'll find interesting. Jeanne wasn't able to spend time alone in the children's section until Anne was 2½, but then—because she *was* alone—she had plenty of time to look for books that reflected what was on Anne's mind that week: making pancakes (*Little Bear's Pancake Party* by Janice and Mariana); sharing toys—or, more precisely, not sharing them (*It's Mine!* by Crosby Bonsall); telling time (*What Time Is It, Jeanne Marie?* by Francoise); getting dirty (*Mary Ann's Mud Day* by Janice May Udry). All were hits.

For a list of children's books we consider too good to miss, see the section on books in Chapter 5.

"Although babies are supposed to ruin books, ours seldom did. Whenever my boys accidentally ripped a book, I substituted an old telephone book for it and told them, 'Good books are not for ripping. Here is your ripping book.' They ripped away on their telephone books and almost never ripped a regular book."   *Mother of two / Atlanta, Ga.*

"My daughter's favorite book was her own pocket-size photograph album containing snapshots of her, her friends, her grandmother, our dog, and even her favorite toys. I saved this book as a treat for riding in the car or waiting in the doctor's office."   *Mother of one / Ft. Worth, Tex.*

"Rather than keep a regular baby book, I bought a composition book and made a book about my son. I wrote in it once or twice a week and illustrated it with very crude line drawings. This was the first book I read, word for word, to my son. When he was 18 months old he memorized it and 'read' it back to me. I stopped writing in his book when he was about 2 and still regret it, since he's 8 and he still gets out his 'Baby Book' to refresh his memory about what he was like when he was a baby."   *Mother of two / Joplin, Mo.*

"My children love to listen to 'told' stories. I made them up myself, using the kids as the heroes. I told them real stories about their activities and make-believe stories featuring them as courageous, strong heroes. By the time they were 3 they helped me tell the story. Plot was totally unimportant, by the way. I think I could have interested them in the telephone book if I had occasionally inserted their names and recited it with drama and gusto."

Mother of two / Eau Claire, Wisc.

TEACHING YOUR CHILD TO READ?

Educators have heated disagreements about the subject of teaching the very young child to read. Some feel that the earlier the better, citing studies which seem to prove that the child who reads before she begins school does better in reading throughout her school career. Others feel that  later is better. *They* cite studies which seem to prove that early readers lose their head start by the second or third grade and that early reading may cause psychological damage.

Both groups agree on one thing: a child should not be forced to read before she is ready. Educators use tests to determine reading readiness. As a parent, you can use a simpler method. If your child comes to you demanding to be taught to read, then you can safely teach her. But unless she asks for instruction, we suggest that you concentrate your efforts on other areas.

"I wouldn't try to judge the potential of a child too early. I knew Sue would be intellectually gifted because she was reading at 3, but I kind of put Patty down (she was two years younger) because at 2 she didn't seem to have a long attention span. What a mistake! Today both girls are in medical school, and Patty is the dogged student, not Sue. Giftedness has a much broader spectrum than IQ tests show. There are kids who are socially gifted, and it doesn't show up on any scale." *Mother of five / Bellerose, N.Y.*

"When my daughter was 3 she began asking me to tell her what the words in her books said. At 4 she was reading picture books fluently. By the time she was 5, she could read the *Los Angeles Times*. But I didn't teach her. All I did was tell her that the letters c-a-t said cat, and the letters a-n-n-o-u-n-c-e-m-e-n-t said announcement. When people ask me how I taught my daughter to read, I tell them I didn't do anything except read to her a great deal and answer her questions." *Mother of two / Los Angeles, Calif.*

One mother, a first-grade teacher, had an instructive story to tell us. "Surely, I thought, as a teacher I should give my son a head start and teach him to read," she said. "When he was 3 I borrowed some materials from a friend and proceeded to teach him phonics. He learned to read, and he's reading above grade level in the fourth grade. But I regret giving him formal instruction because he never picks up a book on his own, without pressure from his teacher or me.

"When my second son was 3 I went back to work, and I was much too busy to even think of teaching him to read. Instead, I read to him, for relaxation, at the end of the day. He also learned to read before going to kindergarten, but he did it on his own, listening to his brother's reading assignments and mimicking him, and asking me to pronounce and define some of the words in his books.

"I taught my older son to read, but I also unintentionally taught him that reading was hard work, and he still avoids that work. I read to my younger son for pleasure and fun. He's 7 now, and he still reads all the time—for pleasure and fun."

Barbara reports that she doesn't teach reading in her

prekindergarten class because, she feels, there are too many other important skills for a 3- or 4-year-old to learn. Occasionally a child learns to read in the class, but only on his own.

However, they do a lot of reading. Barbara reads to the children, and mothers read to them. Also, there is a continually changing library of books available to the children throughout the morning.

"Read me a story," Barbara asks a child.

"I can't read," she replies.

"Yes you can," Barbara says. "Just look at this picture. Now tell me what's happening."

"The monkey's putting a big yellow hat on his head."

"That's right. See? You're reading."

Barbara also helps her children learn the pattern of words by giving each of them a "word book"—an unlined notebook with a fabric binding. "I sit down with a child and say, 'This is your very own book. I'm going to write your name in it,'" Barbara says. "I print the name in large letters at the top of the first page and then I read the child's name, running my fingers under the letters as I say them. 'Brian—these letters say Brian,' I ask the child to read the name back to me. And finally he draws a picture of himself."

The next day they get out the word book again, and Barbara asks the child to read his name. Then she asks him to tell her a beautiful word, an ugly word, a funny word, or a scary word, the only rule being that the word must have an emotional impact for the child. As the children read they add words to their books every few days. Some children easily learn to read hundreds of words, some only a few; the number of words they learn, and the rate at which they learn, varies from child to child. Some books are filled with pretty words like fairy and flower, other with the names of super heroes like Superman and Luke Skywalker, and still others with scary words like ghost and Darth Vader.

"In my first year of teaching," Barbara says, "I read Sylvia Ashton Warner's book *Teacher*. In it she describes her methods of teaching Maori children to read. I adapted her methods to the children in my New Jersey kindergarten. In my twelve years of teaching, I have found word books to be the best way to prepare children for reading.

There's no pressure, and each child truly reads his own words in his own way and at his own speed."

The Alphabet

● Sing the alphabet song so that your child will become familiar with the names of the letters of the alphabet.

● Buy magnetic, felt, or sandpaper alphabet letters. While your child plays with them she will become familiar with the shapes of the letters. Then play "What's That?" Pull out two or three letters and ask your child to give you the A or bring you the C. When she gets two or three letters correct, give her a few more.

● Look for letters of the alphabet when you go for a walk. Point out and recite the letters in stop signs, school-crossing signs, and so on.

● Decorate your child's wall with one of the many available alphabet wall hangings or sets of decals.

● Watch "Sesame Street" with your child. Most children who consistently watch this show learn the alphabet.

"My children learned the alphabet using blocks. When I thought they were ready (my oldest was ready before she was 2, my youngest not until 4), we played a block game. I had one block with each letter of the alphabet. I would show my child a block; if she could tell me what letter it was, she got the block. If not, I kept it. We'd keep this up until she got all the letters. I started with a few familiar letters like A and O and X. Once she learned these, I added a few unfamiliar ones, until she had learned all the letters of the alphabet. I used the same game for teaching numbers."

Mother of three / Lincoln, Neb.

ART

There are only a few essential materials you will need to keep around the house to provide your child with the stimulation he needs to be creative through art. In fact, a child with a box of crayons and lots of paper has all he really needs.

The first time you give your baby a crayon and a piece

of paper, remember this: *the process, not the product, is important.* There probably are many potential Picassos who were turned away from art because unthinking parents or teachers told them they should try to paint a "pretty picture" or color more neatly. Provide your child with a few simple materials and a place to work, and then let him do whatever he wants.

Crayons and Markers

Buy a box of large size crayons and then throw away the box and put the crayons in a coffee can or some other sturdy container. Settle your child at her table and give her the crayons. She may dump them out of the container; she may peel off the paper; she may try to eat them. She probably won't color anything with them at first.

When she loses interest in using the crayons as playthings, take a crayon and make a few lines on a large piece of paper. Give her a crayon and see if she wants to copy you. Then stand back and watch her delight when she discovers what she can do.

Marking pens are also fun for children, but make sure you buy washable markers—the permanent kind really are permanent! Take off the cap yourself, since your child could easily swallow it. Be prepared for a little marker on your child, and beware: once your child discovers what crayons and markers can do, any surface is fair game. So keep the crayons out of her reach unless you want everything in the house redecorated. Also, be patient about expecting a child to recap felt-tip markets. Few children under 5 can remember to do it, much less understand the need for it.

"I've given my children plenty of paper and crayons ever since they were infants. Drawing their own pictures is and has always been their favorite pastime. They're seldom without a pen or pencil in hand."

Mother of two / Memphis, Tenn.

Paints

As your child grows, you might want to buy a few large jars of powdered tempera paint at an art-supply store. While you're there, buy several water-color brushes, preferably with short, wide handles. Then go to the supermarket and buy a roll of plain white shelf paper or a large roll of butcher paper (available from the butcher himself) and a gallon jug of liquid starch. These basic supplies should last for a couple of years. You might also invest in a sturdy, adjustable easel— but a stiff piece of cardboard propped against an upside-down chair works just as well.

Before your child's first paint session, set up his paint area carefully. Mix only one color of paint, following the in-structions on the container. (One hint: add liquid carefully; if you make it too runny, throw out the paint and start over.) Cover the floor with newspapers or a piece of oilcloth and cover your child with one of Dad's old T-shirts. Give your child a small container of paint and a brush for each color and show him how to put paint on the paper. Then stand back and let him do whatever he wants.

At first he'll probably just smear the paint on the paper, but eventually he'll begin to make simple designs with cir-cles or lines. When this happens, he'll want more than one color. Supervise paint sessions carefully to make sure the paint goes on the paper rather than on your walls or carpets. Baby oil is great for removing paint and marker from your child's hands and face. Cover the leftover paint and store it in the refrigerator.

"My children love to fingerpaint," said one mother. "It can be a giant mess, but it's really not any worse than any other kind of painting." To set up fingerpainting, spread out a large sheet of shelf paper and dampen it slightly with a sponge. Pour a blob of starch in the middle of the paper, then sprinkle on a little powdered tempera. Let your child mix in the color and mess in the paint. After a few experi-mental sessions you can show him how to make a design with his fingers.

"I set up fingerpainting in the bathtub," one mother told us, "and end the paint session by hosing down my kids and everything else that needs it."

"On a warm day, water-painting delights all of my children, from the youngest, who is 13 months, to the oldest, who is 8. I give each child a bucket of water and a variety of old, large paint brushes and paint rollers. They have a marvelous time painting the walls of the house, the sidewalk, and the driveway with water. One day I found some painters' hats on sale, and what a thrill to suddenly turn squabbling children into real painters." *Mother of five / Boise, Ida.*

"I started a hand- and footprint gallery when my baby was just born. I painted my child's hand and foot, then pressed them firmly on a piece of cardboard. Each year we make new ones and compare the sizes with previous years'."
Mother of two / Peoria, Ill.

If you don't mind a colossal mess, try this suggestion. Roll out a long piece of shelf paper on the kitchen floor. Paint the bottoms of your feet and your child's feet and then walk up and down the paper until the paint disappears. Repaint your feet and again walk on the paper. The results will make a marvelous mural for your child's room.

Be sure to ask your child to tell you about some of his drawings and paintings, and write down exactly what he says—poor grammar, mispronunciations, and all. Correcting him will inhibit future creative-writing sessions. Besides, in later years you'll chuckle over his mistakes and marvel at his growth.

You can encourage your child to express his feelings about his drawings if you're patient. Say your child paints a crude picture of a person, with a big circle for a head, eyes, mouth, and arms and legs coming out of the circle. Say to him, "Tell me something about your picture." If this doesn't bring any response, ask him, "Who is that in your picture?" "Mommy." "Oh, and what is Mommy doing?" "Mommy cried." "Oh, my. What happened?" "Mommy hurted arm." "And then what happened?" "Mommy all gone. Me cry." Keep asking "And then what happened?" until either you or your child has created enough. But you'll probably give out long before your child does.

Barbara recalls, "David was born on Lincoln's birthday, and so he was interested in Honest Abe at a very young age. He created one of my favorite stories right after his third birthday. 'This is Lincolnhan,' David said. 'He eated birthday cake. He died. Then he grew very very old.'"

Once your child begins to draw or paint, both you and

he will want to display the results—the refrigerator makes a good bulletin board for an array of art. Date your child's drawings and save a few representative samples in a box in your closet. Or, if you have time, put them in a scrapbook, adding to it from year to year, to have an ever-changing record of your child's work.

One mother covered a wall of her child's room with corkboard and let him continually redecorate the room with his own art. Jeanne hammered in two sturdy nails at either end of Anne's room, looped a clothes line between the nails, and hung artwork on the rope with clothes pins.

"I bought an attractive frame and hung my son's first efforts in our living room. I once got an offer of twenty-five dollars for one of his first paintings when I told visitors it was an abstract work by a new but soon-to-be famous artist."

Mother of two / Roanoke, Va.

Collage

Start an old-fashioned scrap bag by throwing bits of ribbon and fabric, strips of shiny wrapping paper, old buttons, and bottle caps into a special box or basket. Look for intriguing collage materials when you and your child go for walks. On a rainy day, give her a large sheet of construction paper or piece of cardboard and show her how to put glue on a piece of fabric or paper and push it down on the cardboard. Once she has the hang of gluing, let her create her own designs.

"Since they were 2 or 3, one of my children's favorite things to do is a 'gluing.' We collect items specifically for this, so we're always prepared. String, glitter, yarn, old buttons, small wood chips, plastic caps, styrofoam packing materials, and other miscellaneous objects are dumped into a box in the broom closet as they're collected. Old magazines get a thorough going-over by my son, who clips out special pictures for collages. We buy white glue in large containers at the hardware store, where it's inexpensive, and then keep refilling the smaller, more manageable containers the children use. Last year at Christmastime my 4-year-old made collage books. Then I wrote stories in them, and we took them to a local old people's home, where they were really appreciated." *Mother of two / Oakland, Calif.*

"We love to make scrapbooks. I tear interesting pages from magazines and let my child cut or tear out shapes and pictures and glue them onto construction paper. We staple the pages together, and if I have time I ask my child to tell me about the pictures and I write down what he says. We started making scrapbooks when he was 2. Now that he's 5 he enjoys making books about one subject, such as cars or zoo animals." *Mother of two / St. Cloud, Minn.*

Another suggestion is to buy a package of tissue paper in assorted colors. Give a few pieces to your child to tear into small shapes and sizes. Then pour some liquid starch into an empty cottage cheese container, lay pieces of tissue on a square of cardboard, and paint over them with starch, using a large watercolor brush. Cover the cardboard with several layers of tissue paper. A design or picture emerges as your child keeps adding scraps.

"A play group with five 3-year-old girls meets at my house once a week. One project stands out from all others, because it was like magic to the children. I gave each child a paper plate, some liquid paste, and a container full of beans and macaroni. They pasted these things on the plates. While they were resting, I sprayed the plates with gold paint. To those five little girls, it was like a miracle to see something they had made turn to gold." *Mother of two / Boston, Mass.*

Cutting

Learning to use a pair of scissors is complicated. Some children have excellent control over their small muscles and can easily manage scissors by 2½ or 3. Others have poor coordination and may still be having trouble at 5. If your child isn't adept at using his hands at first, take it very slowly. Eventually, when his small muscles develop, he'll learn to cut, just as he learned to crawl and walk.

Before you begin to teach your child to cut, give her some experience using her hands. Buy a container of large stringing beads. Tie a bead to the end of the string so they won't all slip off. You may have to show your child how to pull the beads all the way to the end, but after that it's free play.

Let your child make necklaces from Cheerios or straight macaroni. To stiffen the ends of the string, dip them in fingernail polish.

Give your child a pair of small tongs and some cotton. Show him how to close the tongs on a piece of cotton and then open them and drop the cotton in a bag.

Before you start cutting, buy a good, fairly sharp pair of small sewing scissors. Buy left-handed scissors at a school-supply store if your child appears to be left-handed. You'll have to watch carefully at first to keep your child from hurting herself with sharp scissors. But the risks are worth it, since it's almost impossible to teach a young child to cut with the cheap scissors designed for young children. Once she's learned to cut with sharp scissors, your child will be able to handle the dull scissors designed for this age range.

Start by having your child hold the scissors in both hands. Hold a straw or a thin piece of stiff paper in both of your hands. Show him how to close the scissors and snip through the straw or paper. When he is proficient at snipping straws, let him cut wider pieces of paper. Show him that he must keep opening and closing the scissors to get all the way across.

To teach a child how to cut with one hand, go back to straws. Let her watch as you cut and then stand in back of her and position her hand on the scissors. Help her open and close the scissors, first with a single snip, then two or three times. When this is easy for her, draw straight lines on a piece of paper and guide the paper for her as she cuts on the lines. Finally, let her cut around a figure, and don't worry if she strays from the lines. Give her only one object at a time to cut out.

Some children like to cut just for the joy of using scissors. Others get bored quickly and want to make something with their results. If your child wants to make things, save his snippings and let him use them for making a collage or chains or whatever else he wants.

Warning: Once he has learned to use scissors, your child may decide to cut his hair, or the dog's hair, or a bedspread, so keep an eye on cutting activities until he completely understands what he may and may not do with scissors.

SPECIAL GIFT PROJECTS

As every mother knows, children love receiving presents. They can also learn to love giving presents, especially if they can give something they've helped to make.

Most materials appropriate for small children to use to make gifts are simple and inexpensive. We've discovered, however, two commercial kits that are so much fun for everyone in the family that we can't resist sharing them.

Shrink Art. This kit, available at hobby stores, consists of a package of special plastic sheets. Following the instructions on the package, you draw on the plastic with permanent marking pens, cut out the drawings, and bake them in the oven. The drawings shrink into hard, permanent miniatures of the originals. As soon as your child can scribble, he can make shrink-art pendants for necklaces, Christmas tree ornaments, book marks, or hundreds of other baubles. If you can't find this kit, write to the manufacturer: Artis, Inc., Solvang, California 93463.

Picture Plates. Texas Ware makes a kit that lets children (and grownups, too) design their own dinner plates. The kit is not terribly expensive. Write to Texas Ware, 2700 So. Westmoreland Ave., Dallas, Texas 75224. Barbara reports, "My boys have been making plates for the last five years. They each make one a year. I'm putting away their plates, and when they get married I'll give each one a set of his own personalized dinnerware."

Portraits. Buy an inexpensive glass or mat frame, a package of good white paper, and some watercolor markers. Cut the paper to fit the frame. Ask your child to make a picture of Daddy (for Father's Day) or Grandma (for Christmas). He may just scribble, he may draw a primitive head with arms and legs jutting out, or he may draw a remarkable likeness. Accept his art as is. Ask him, "What does Daddy like to do?" and write down his responses. Repeat this portrait session each year until your child is grown. One father we know has eight portraits hanging on his office wall. His son is now 10, and still makes a picture of Dad every year. And although this dad now chuckles, he admits to some embarrassment when his son was 4 and dictated the words, "This is Daddy. He likes to drink booze."

Tin Can Holders. Glue strips of felt or construction paper onto juice cans to make pencil holders. Let your child decorate the felt with buttons, macaroni, sequins, glitter, rickrack, or any other "precious" scraps. Tuna fish cans make excellent coasters, large coffee cans make lovely cannisters, and large juice cans make beautiful vases.

Ice Cream Containers. Go to an ice cream parlor and ask for several discarded five-gallon containers. Your child can paint or decorate these containers to be used as gifts—wastebaskets. Or cover the container with wallpaper, felt, fabric, construction paper, or anything else that comes to mind and give it away to be used as a toy bin, a sewing basket, or anything else that comes to the receiver's mind.

Russian Tea. Assemble the following ingredients:

2 parts instant tea	*½ part instant lemonade*
1 part Tang	*shake of cinnamon, cloves, and nutmeg*

Let your child spoon the ingredients into a baby-food jar. Encourage him to taste, smell, and watch the changing pattern of the layers. Finally, put the lid tightly on the jar and let him shake it all up.

Cookies, Gingerbread Men, etc. See Chapter 8, "Family-Fun Recipes," for many edible gifts to be made with your child.

Plants. Let your child grow some of the plants already discussed in this chapter and pass them on as gifts. One teacher told us, "One of the children in my class brought me a sweet potato vine for Christmas two years ago. It's still in my den bookcase, and still growing."

Rocks. Make paperweights from large rocks, decorating them with paint, felt scraps, and bits and pieces from your scrap bag. Make "pet rocks" from small rocks, adding tails, eyes, noses, whiskers, etc.

Apple Sachet. For this you'll need a few apples, a large box of whole cloves, about a half yard of brightly colored nylon net, and one yard of ribbon. Help your child poke cloves into the apples. This may take four or five sessions, depending on your child's persistence and dexterity. When the apple is covered with cloves, set it in the center of a square of net.

Gather the net together and tie it securely with a piece of ribbon. Tie on another piece of ribbon to make a loop so that the sachet can be hung in a closet, bathroom, or kitchen.

Wrapping Paper. Sponge paint, potato-print, fingerpaint, or draw with markers on large pieces of butcher paper. Then use this very original paper to wrap all kinds of presents. One mother told us, "I haven't bought wrapping paper for years. I save the comics from the Sunday paper and use them to wrap gifts for birthdays and Christmas. In a pinch, I've also used newspaper decorated with colored ribbon and tape."

Paper Chains. Chain-making is still an all-time favorite of children from 2½ to 12. Make chains for Christmas, by all means, but also make them for Halloween, Valentine's Day, birthday parties, or just any old day. Almost every adult in America has made chains as a child. And once learned, it's a skill you never really forget. Just get some construction paper, start cutting and pasting, and have fun.

GETTING HELP

14

Father and Child

"My husband was from a family where fathers pat the children on the head, play with them but don't bathe them, feed them, teach them. I wish I had tried to involve him more."   *Mother of two / Minneapolis, Minn.*

All the information given in this book won't be of much use unless we have zest for our job. An important part of maintaining this zest is getting help from others in the work of child raising. The best potential helper of all, of course, is the child's father. (For single parents or those in a situation where there is only a part-time father, a grandparent, or a good friend for relief, the other sources of help discussed in the remaining chapters become even more important.)

Certainly it is not only for their own relief that getting help from fathers is a basic concern of many new mothers. Father, by sharing the joys and responsibilities of child raising, can be enriched. Our child will surely benefit from another human being's visceral involvement in his life. And a marriage will grow, not falter, through a sharing of child care—whatever the day-by-day arrangement—that feels reasonably fair to both parents.

Yet, if we face facts, we realize that some perfectly good men take longer than others to become truly involved in their children's lives. We realize that you can't *make* anyone else be involved in anything. Father involvement comes from inside father and inside child, not from inside us. But what a mother *can* do is not get in the way of such involvement. She can try to create a climate in the home that encourages involvement by both parents. In this chapter we give some ideas on fostering such a climate and pass on what other mothers have told us fathers do in the early years of their children's lives.

Before we list specific things other mothers told us that fathers do in their homes, we have a few specific caveats for Mom:

Don't insist things be done your way. If you want help you have to let your helpers use their own judgment, at least on non-life-and-death matters. One mother told us that she fought with her husband for days because he refused to use cloth diapers on the baby—he "went through Pampers like water." Finally, she said, "I realized that he did, after all, change the baby. That was what was important."

Allow room for choice on the part of the helper. There are countless ways a father can choose to show his commitment to his children. The inventiveness that some men display in playing with their children, for example, makes their wives fall in love with them all over again. Perhaps he may choose to be more solicitous of *you* during the early years rather than do the actual physical tasks of bathing and changing and feeding the child himself. One mother mentioned that what her husband did that was the most help of all involved no direct contact with the baby. "We don't have a washer or dryer," she said. "So my husband does the laundry in the basement of our apartment house when he comes home from work each night. Anyone who knows the clothes you go through with an infant and a toddler knows what a big help that is." Wise was the old pediatrician who once said the very best thing a father can do for his children is to love their mother.

Realize that compliments are the best motivators. "I always praised my husband when he did something innovative with a child and he often did the same with me," one mother of five wrote. "As the children grew older I encouraged him to take them with him to his evening courses. It's amazing what they got out of it."

Keep Dad aware of how you are feeling and encourage him to do the same. "I think fathers often just don't realize how important their support is," one mother said. "It helps if you tell him, 'I really need your moral support. I want you to come with us to the pediatrician tomorrow.'" Another mother said, "When our boys were 2 and 4 I remember my husband, a magazine reporter, took an extra job with an old buddy writing a radio show two nights a week. We needed the extra money very badly. But one day I said to him, 'I think we should borrow money from your parents if we have to instead of risking our marriage. We all need you here too much every night.' He was flabbergasted. 'Are you serious?' he asked. I was. And I was right."

Here now are some ideas from other mothers on how— before the baby is born, during the first year, and later on— to create a climate that encourages involvement by both parents, as well as some specific things they mentioned that other fathers are doing.

BEFORE THE FACT

"With the last two children, my husband was more involved earlier than he was with the first two. I think it was because he was *there* at the last two births."

Mother of four / Schenectady, N.Y.

"Often when I look at my daughter's face I notice the almost imperceptible scar caused by her forceps delivery. Invariably I then think warmly of my husband. He was right with me all through labor and at her birth. It feels like he's been helping just as much ever since."

Mother of one / Modesto, Calif.

"With natural childbirth, fathers don't feel like it's just the mother's baby, but *their* baby, too."

Mother of three / Cambridge, Mass.

If your husband is enthusiastic about parent-education classes, books and films on pregnancy and birth, and visits to friends with babies, great. But if he's not interested yet, it's not worth making a fuss over. A prospective father's sense of urgency, after all, is not the same as yours.

But, as noted in Chapter 1, what *is* worth taking a stand on is having your husband help you in the labor and delivery rooms. Whatever it takes, it is enormously worthwhile, according to all the mothers we questioned, to work toward having the father there at the birth. Nothing else quite gets him off to the running start that helping out at and seeing his own child's birth does.

Certainly prospective parents may consider having the new father be the chief helper at home when mother and baby arrive there from the hospital.

THE FIRST YEAR

"We have a house rule: whoever sees it first cleans it up. That goes for messy diapers, spilled milk, broken toys, and fights. Everything."   *Mother of two / Austin, Tex.*

How do you swab a newborn's navel? How do you give a slippery baby a bath? One mother of a 2-year-old made sure her husband was involved in such matters from the very beginning by refusing to let herself be the *sole* family authority on child rearing. "It wasn't hard," she laughed. "I'm an only child and I never did much babysitting in high school." The basic approach, she says, was "What do you think?"

"It started out by my thinking out loud, 'Do we dress her in a snowsuit or in a sweater and blanket? Should we move the cradle to her room now? Should we let her cry longer? Who can we trust to babysit?' Now it's 'Why does she act so nasty when she plays with Amy? How can we keep her from running away from us in parking lots?' " She adds, "My husband has a lot of good ideas I'd never think of. And the great thing is we both feel confident on our own and about each other. We both know where the books are and we both read them."

A baby needs to learn to feel secure in getting food from someone besides Mother and a father needs to enjoy holding and feeding his baby. Be sure to let him give her some feedings. If you nurse, get the baby accustomed to an occasional bottle of whatever formula the doctor recommends or use a breast pump and fill a bottle yourself. A father needs to be able to offer a screaming baby something more than a ride on his shoulder.

"I remember a night when our daughter was two weeks old and I couldn't get her to stop crying after supper. It was the end of my first full week indoors in winter taking care of an infant—I was going bananas. My husband and I snapped at each other and I started bawling. I yelled that she was all his and went out in the dark for a walk. Gradually I calmed down and after half an hour I went back. The baby was *still* crying and my husband was really upset. 'I can't *do* anything for her!' he said. I took her, unbuttoned my blouse, and she started nursing, making those slurping noises. He looked crushed and I felt awful. The next day I started giving her a little sugar water in a small bottle so she'd get used to it and from then on I always had a few bottles of something in the refrigerator so he could be able to try feeding her during the rough times." *Mother of two / Flagstaff, Ariz.*

Early in the first year, a couple working together can avoid what one mother calls the "Saturday Night Crazies." To do all the things required for one tiny baby to spend a short evening with someone else, a person would have to start "getting ready to go out" at night in the *morning.* There is food for the sitter, food for the baby, messages for the sitter about where you will be, messages about the baby's schedule, often a pass at tidying up the house, showering and dressing and picking up the sitter. "My husband used to go out and run two miles at six p.m., come home, shower, and then wonder why I wasn't ready to go with bells on at seven," one mother said. The two talked it over and now her husband runs at five, helps with the preparations, and they go out the door together at seven.

LATER ON

In some homes Dad takes care of the bath and serious toothbrushing because that's what fits best into the routine. In others, fathers supervise breakfast and getting dressed or

take their children outside during the hour before dinner
when many children and parents seem to be at their worst.

It's important for a child to have his father do some of
the hands-on work each day, if possible. "All I really left
for my husband to do all week long," one mother related,
"was read a bedtime story. I think my son would have been
better off with a little more contact. His father has a good
deal shorter fuse than I do about whining and dawdling,
and maybe our son would have done less of it if my husband
had been responsible for more day-to-day care." If both parents do some of the hands-on work, neither one falls into
the trap of being just the "fun" parent and the other the
"work" parent.

Try to relieve each other even when you and your husband are both at home. The temptation to spend every weekend as a merry threesome is strong, but it doesn't work out
as a steady diet. You need some time alone in the house,
and so does a father.

"Pete has been very involved with the baby from the beginning, and that has eased my life a lot. We take turns with
'baby duty' during evenings and weekends, but we also
spend time with all of us together reading, wrestling, playing, or whatever. We plan 'private time' for each other, both
separately and together, because we function as better parents if *our* needs are met, too."

Mother of one / Minneapolis, Minn.

Here are some other, more specific pointers (many of them
obvious but worth checking yourselves on if you sense a
problem in this area) from other mothers about things fathers can try in the second and third years of a child's life.

Dad and child usually enjoy shopping together. After a child
is walking, she needs new shoes or sneakers every three or
four months. Ask Father to buy them. Also ask him and the
child to stop at the bakery, the shoemaker's, or the toy
store. One or two errands at a time are plenty, however.
"At the savings bank they gave her a plastic piggy bank, at
the bakery she got a free cookie, and at the shoe store a red
balloon," one amazed father told his wife after a Saturday-

morning foray with his 2-year-old. The smiles he and his daughter got from strangers were pretty nice for him to witness, too, he admitted.

"My son sits there and waits while my husband gets his hair cut on Saturday morning. He'd never do that with me! They're just happy to be with each other then."
Mother of three / Philadelphia, Pa.

Dad can join other parents and children on play outings. "We live near a park where children and parents congregate," one mother said. "My husband gets a kick out of going there with our 2-year-old on weekends. I think he finds it just as comforting as I do when I go there during the week to see that other kids his age also throw sand and whine and have a fit when it's time to go." Also, fathers, just like mothers, can often learn more about discipline from watching other parents in action than they can from books or courses.

Dad can get involved in the children's schooling. For most of us, this happens naturally, since a large part of the family discretionary income may be involved. But that's not the most important thing. "I'll never forget the day we visited a co-op nursery school during a Saturday-morning open house," one father said. "There were all these people doing all the right things with these kids, but I got depressed. It just wasn't somewhere I could see my wife and myself fitting in." Other fathers, however, enjoy participating in cooperative nursery schools, cleaning up, building things, going to meetings. After your child is enrolled in any kind of school, let her father take her there or pick her up whenever possible. Encourage your husband to visit the school and go to school programs. No professional performance equals the thrill of watching your own 3-year-old be a troll in a presentation of *The Three Billy Goats Gruff*. And the children invariably feel great pride in showing off "their" place to Daddy, and Daddy to their friends.

Father can help on the special occasions. When your child is invited to a birthday party, maybe Dad can go with him to buy a present and then they can wrap it together. When it's your child's birthday, consider having the party when

Father is home. "My husband dreamed up this game of filling balloons with water, knotting them, then having the kids toss them at a board on which he'd put a big nail." one mother said. "The yard was littered with busted balloons and the kids got wet but they all had a wonderful time."

Sharing the bedtime reading. Many fathers don't have the time to choose books themselves, but they can read them to the children and enjoy the cozy camaraderie that results. Seek out humorous and beautiful children's books at the library. Fathers will enjoy the reading far more if there's often a fresh pile of good books handy. "My husband remembered having the Babar books read to him as a child," one mother said. "It was wonderful to watch him intently reading the same stories to our daughter."

Share the nighttime "check." "The last thing I did before going to bed each night was check the baby," one mother wrote. "I can't remember exactly when my husband eventually began to join me. Our son now is 3, and we still 'check the baby,' smiling at the way he sleeps in the midst of his army of favorite animals. He's so beautiful to us then. It's the one time each day when we can be sure of savoring him together, sure of savoring each other as parents."

Let the child see where Dad works. Particularly for fathers who spend long hours at work, it's good for both father and child if the child can picture where Dad is. Even a 2-year-old will benefit from knowing "this is the road Daddy takes to work, this is the building, this is where he has lunch," and so on. "My son saw two of his pictures tacked on the wall in his father's office," one mother said. "I'll never forget the look on his face."

Dad can help by building things. A father who is good at carpentry can do many things for his child, from building a cradle on. Most homes are not set up for preschool-age children. Sinks are high. Tables are high. Door knobs are hard to turn. A father who is so inclined will find a grateful child (and wife) if he can build step stools, low bookshelves, gym sets, or play houses. A father good with a hammer—or a mother, for that matter—may enjoy looking at books like *Children's Spaces* by Molly and Norman McGrath, in which there are photographs of indoor and outdoor "spaces" for young children created by fifty architects and designers. Most of the projects were done by people for their own children. One particular project: a four-section mobile storage wall that neatly defined a child's play area at one end of the parents' large living room in a New York City apartment. One side of the wall faced the parents' part of the living room, serving as a display area for art. The other (invisible from the adults' part of the room) held shelves for toys and a desk for sit-down projects like puzzles.

As a child grows older, most fathers find their own ways to father. Often they find a way to involve their children in things they themselves enjoy doing. A 4-year-old will be thrilled to go to a miniature golf course. A 5-year-old can marvel at developing pictures in a home photo lab.

As these pages are typed, in our own houses fathers are finding their own ways to "father." Fred Henry, whose daughter watches him shave and has breakfast with him at six-thirty every weekday morning while her mother sleeps, has just spent two months of Saturday time building a doll house with Anne. Together they chose the color scheme: peach for the living room, pink for the children's room, lavender for the bathroom, and bright red and green for the exterior. Wild colors or not, Jeanne says, it's now the first thing she'd grab after Anne in a fire.

In *Give Your Child a Superior Mind*, now in its tenth printing, the Engelmanns describe the lives and training of many geniuses, a large percentage of whom had fathers who devoted much time to teaching their children during pre-school years. As the poet George Herbert noted in the early 1600s: "One father is more than a hundred schoolmasters."

Abstract artist Joe Goode says he began drawing as a young child in Oklahoma with his father, a portrait artist. Every Sunday for a year he and his father went to the woods to draw the same log. He says, "In the summer it was dried out, brown with a dying color. In the fall it was covered with dead leaves, in the winter with snow, and in the spring with mold. We followed its appearance and color through the four seasons, because my father wanted me to see how much something changes even though it's essentially the same."

Children can learn even from a man who seems obsessed by work. Writer May Sarton, now in her 60s, looks back at her childhood and realizes what she had read between the lines of her father's actions: "Through my father I witnessed that if the vision were there, a man could work eighteen hours a day, with joy, and never seem to tire. I understood that a talent is something given, that it opens like a flower, but without exceptional energy, discipline, and persistence will never bear fruit."

This chapter was written at the end of the four years it took us to do this book. Because of that, we suspect that it has a different tone, a calmer one, than it would have had if it had been written when we were still in the most-demanding birth-to-3 period. It's next to impossible to do, but we wish there was a way to help new mothers realize how few the years are when the minute-to-minute demands of a child are so great. But we never listened to people who told us that either.

In our own homes we have watched our husbands grow and develop as fathers, just as they have watched us develop as mothers. Along the way we realized that the best thing you can do is to toss out the score book. Ideally, you both will be willing to do more than half of the child care when you're both home. But whatever you work out, anything that works in your own house is great.

Here are some thoughts from other mothers:

"When he comes home, I usually want very much for him to take over, but I know it just doesn't always work."
Mother of three / Flint, Mich.

"Jerry needs to be pushed. I used to feel he was doing it grudgingly when I'd ask him to try to stop the baby from crying. So I'd say to myself, 'What the heck, I'll do it myself. It's not worth the effort.' Then I realized the baby wouldn't die if he cried five minutes straight. And I realized his father didn't know how to stop the crying because I'd never left him alone to really try it."
Mother of two / Boise, Ida.

"A few years ago I felt most loved when I was watching my husband cook us a gourmet dinner. Now real bliss is when

I'm broiling the steaks and *he's* reading the kids a story before putting them to bed."

Mother of two / Middlebury, Vt.

"I think the hardest thing about raising a child alone must be that there's no adult there to laugh with at the funny things they say or to be proud with you when they learn something new." *Mother of six / Omaha, Neb.*

"My husband makes a birthday ceremony out of the 'measuring door.' It's the one in the dining room. Every birthday from the time they could walk he has lined the children up against it and marked off their height. If we ever move I think I'll have to take it with us."

Mother of three / Providence, R.I.

"What my husband does? One small thing almost brings tears to my eyes every time. When we're out late for the evening and our daughter needs to be waked up for the drive home, my husband does it. He picks up Jennifer—who's now thirty-eight pounds—as if she were a cloud. He does it so carefully you'd think he was carrying emeralds. She doesn't ever really wake up. It's the same when we get home. I put the car in the garage while he tucks Jen in her own bed."

Mother of one / Jackson, Miss.

"I think of us as bookends as far as the overall well-being of our children is concerned. We do different things for them. We have different strengths and they know it. I handle most of the day-to-day care but he provides the financial security that lets me do this. And he lets me know he thinks what I'm doing is important. That makes all the difference."

Mother of three / Portland, Ore.

"I work full-time as a teacher and my husband sells insurance from his office at home. His schedule is so flexible that, as I look back, I realize he's spent a lot more time with our son than I have. He toilet trained him. He chose the nursery school. He buys the toys and arranges for our son's friends to come over and play. I'd guess you'd say he's the 'mother.' It works fine for us." *Mother of one / Hartford, Conn.*

15

Babysitters

"Every time I get in the car to go out with my husband alone I breathe a sigh of relief so loud it's audible to him, too. It's a lot of work to get a sitter, but every time I do it I'm glad. We have *got* to have some time to ourselves to survive as a couple."   *Mother of two / Lexington, Mass.*

Ingenuity and persistence in finding and using good babysitters: it ought to be packaged and given out at baby showers. Most of us don't realize how necessary sitters are until our first baby is no longer a baby. Many mothers regretted, as has been mentioned in an earlier chapter, that they had spent money on expensive furniture and toys that might better have been spent on sitters. Part of the problem is that new parents aren't always aware of the possibilities for using sitters, or of the different kinds of sitters that are available to meet various needs.

Consider early on using sitters for times other than Saturday night. For example, some regular time free of the baby during the week is a boon both to a mother's sanity and to a couple's relationship; Mom doesn't feel trapped, and a tired dad, longing for home, doesn't get met at the door by a companion raring to go out. One woman with children now in college told us that the free Tuesdays her own mother gave her in the form of a combination sitter-cleaning lady when her children were babies was the single best thing her mother ever did for her. "*Ever*," she says, "even though I didn't quite realize it at the time." Other mothers mentioned that young neighborhood girls who came over to play with toddlers allowed them time to complete projects that otherwise would have taken months. And more than one set of parents has found out that Saturday night is not always their favorite time to go out. "Our best teenage sitter comes regularly from three to six on Sunday afternoons so that my husband and I can go out together," one mother of two preschoolers said. "We may take a walk on the beach, look at houses for sale, or go to the library. Those Sunday afternoons of freedom make us feel that we have had a 'weekend' together."

At the same time as you continually try to be imaginative in the use of sitters, realize that you will need a repertoire of types, all of whom need to be selected with care. Cost varies greatly among the types, of course. Even more important, the high-school-girl sitter useful for Saturday night when your child will sleep the whole time is different from the one you need for six hours during the day in the middle of a school week and different still from the reliable older person you may need for a whole weekend. Persistence comes in when you learn that "finding" your types is rarely done once and for all. Teenagers grow up; a favorite mother-sitter in the babysitting co-op may move away; the older woman may decide she's not up to sitting anymore. Also, astonishingly soon your own child develops preferences. The, most available sitter may not be the one she likes best.

The challenge, however, is worth it. There's the obvious advantage of getting out of the house for a while and coming back refreshed. Then, too, getting to know sitters of different ages can be a pleasure in itself. A mother whose children are now teenagers and babysitters themselves told us, "We've kept in touch with several of our fomer sitters. Some are in college, another is working, one is married—and my daughters were junior bridesmaids at the wedding. One said in a letter, 'When I tell my roommates I'm writing to *my kids* they look at me sort of funny. But I do think of them as being partly mine.' And I feel, in a way, as though I have several grown-up daughters."

Using sitters well is part of mother-as-manager, providing one more source of self-esteem and even self-knowledge. "I honestly think I've learned more about myself through finding babysitters," one mother said. "Whatever it was that motivated me to go to the trouble of finding a good sitter—going out with my husband, seeing friends, going to a class—was something truly important to me. I'd only worry if I *didn't* want a sitter sometimes."

"Because we had neither family nor a competent older person on whom we could depend, I seldom left my baby for the first six to nine months. I feel that this was unfortunate, as I began to resent being so tied down. I'd advise a new mother to take the time to find someone experienced with young ones and to definitely get out on occasion as early as four to six weeks after your baby arrives. It not only does the mother a world of good but is ultimately better for the baby and their relationship."

Mother of three / Seattle, Wash.

"The most dreaded task of my week used to be getting sitters. I felt like a boy asking a girl for a date or as if I was asking a big favor of somebody."

Mother of one / Lakeland, Fla.

FINDING SITTERS TO MATCH YOUR NEEDS

The hard way, we learned that the time to pile up telephone numbers of sitters is *before* your father has a heart attack, *before* an old friend comes to town and wants to meet you for lunch, *before* you are offered a part-time job you need to accept. And believe us, good babysitters in every price bracket can be found for every hour of the day. "If you kept your eyes open for eligible men when you were dating you've got the idea where to look for babysitters," one mother said. "Everywhere."

The basic categories of sitters, where to find them, and other mothers' experiences with them are described below.

Teenagers

"Our best babysitters have always been young people in the neighborhood who like small kids and are willing to do puz-

zles, go for walks, push swings, read stories, and so on."
Mother of three / Chapel Hill, N.C.

Girls between 12 and 15 are the best, according to many
mothers. By the end of their sophomore year in high school
most teenage girls are going out themselves on weekend
nights, and many have regular jobs. If you find and train a
mature 12-year-old neighborhood girl, your sitting problems
may be solved for three years. However, for a long day—say
from eight in the morning until after a child's bedtime—be
especially careful about considering the maturity of the teenage sitter. And don't overlook teenage boys as sitters, especially if you have boys. The Sills boys have male sitters most of
the time.

"A good teenage sitter is likely to have a good mother,"
one mother said. "I always talk in advance with the mother
on the telephone, and pick up the sitter myself the first time
I use her. I figure that since she lives nearby, the sitter's
mother may be a good source of help if her daughter needs
it and can't reach me." Courtesy to the parents of your teenage sitter (for example, getting her home when you say you
will) pays off, usually, in the sitter's *parents'* willingness to
let her work for you again.

"We hired a teenage sitter for every Saturday evening on a
contractual basis—she's paid whether we go out or not. We
found her through the high school counselor. We also use
a retired woman, a grandma who spends two days a week
at our house so I can get out to be me."
Mother of two / St. Louis, Mo.

In choosing a teenager you want to sit for you regularly,
it helps to learn, as subtly as you can, whether she really
needs the money. If she does, she's less likely to cancel because she decides she'd rather go to a party or a movie. Frequently using one sitter has advantages. "I saved myself a
lot of time on the telephone," one mother said. "When we
found a good teenager we used her enough so that she considered us a part-time job. It was also a lot easier than having
to explain everything about our child and house every time
we went out."

Sources of good teenager sitters: other mothers in your neighborhood, high school and junior high guidance counselors, an ad in your church bulletin, local Girl Scout troops, graduates of babysitting classes sponsored by the Red Cross or local hospitals. Find out the going rate in your area and always pay *at least* that much per hour. Sometimes it is customary to pay more if there is more than one child in the family or for daytime sitting as opposed to the easier nighttime variety. For a good sitter, it's probably not a bad idea to raise the rate after a few months.

Co-ops and Exchanges with Other Mothers

"I'm in a sitters' club, and I think it's great. With one call to the secretary I'm assured of a sitter who is an experienced mother. Also, I'm meeting the neighbors on a meaningful basis at last." *Mother of two / Schenectady, N.Y.*

Co-op and exchange sitting groups are proliferating all over the country. The benefits are more than just financial: your children will develop a built-in circle of friends and, best of all, you know you're leaving your children with another experienced parent.

How do co-ops work? The "gadder," or person going out, calls for a sitter a day or two in advance, notifying a secretary who is usually paid in free sitting. The secretary job may alternate each month. If you can't find an existing co-op, form one of your own with other parents who live nearby.

"Our sitters' club has meetings every three months. First we have a business meeting to announce the secretaries for the next three months and discuss any problems that have come up. Then we have a party. Most of the members really enjoy the meetings because it gives them a chance to visit without their children along." *Mother of one / Richmond, Va.*

Less complicated—and perhaps the easiest way to get daytime sitters for very young children—is to exchange with another mother you like. Taking care of two children under 3 is, do not be surprised, twice the work. But being able to go to the dentist or the doctor alone, or even to have uninterrupted time to work at home, is for many of us well worth the extra work on other occasions.

Mothers who can rely on each other to care for their respective children often end up forming lasting relationships. One of the most affecting parts of Jane Lazarre's *Mother Knot* concerns such a friendship. Lazarre's son and the children of her neighbor bathed together at night before their fathers came home, and the children ran to greet each other in the morning with giggles and hugs. "Trusting each other, seeing how much we were alike, we began to take care of each other's children," she wrote. "And leaving them with each other, we were able to concentrate on something besides the moment of reunion." The day the friend moves from the apartment house is as wrenching to the reader lucky, enough to have enjoyed such a friendship as it is to the author.

A disadvantage to using other mothers with children is the risk of either your child or theirs becoming ill, so it's usually best to hire a sitter for important appointments or plans. But if you must go out when your own child is sick, a friend who also has a sick child can save the day. Bundle up your child and take him over. Other sitters will avoid you because, naturally, they don't want to get sick themselves.

Sources of exchange sitters and potential mother friends: other mothers in your Lamaze or parent-education classes, an ad in your local shopping paper, or nice faces at the park or supermarket.

Drop-off Sitters

"Through another mother, when my younger daughter was 18 months old I found Mrs. Mullins, an older woman who cares for her grandson and several other children, mornings only, in her own home. There are rarely more than five children there at one time. Mrs. Mullins is pure gold. She doesn't do housework when the children are there. The only TV allowed is 'Sesame Street.' In her big yard, which has a concrete sidewalk for tricycle riding, I saw a tortoise sunning one day. She also has a dog, an aquarium, and a stock of toys acquired from grateful mothers. My daughter loves to go there!"   *Mother of two / Walnut Creek, Calif.*

There are many excellent sitters to be found in local neighborhoods everywhere. Usually they are women who are already caring for their own preschool-age children, or perhaps for their own grandchildren. For a few years in their lives they may welcome a little extra money along with companionship for their own charges.

This kind of sitting is different from licensed day care in private homes (see Chapter 16) because of its more casual, unbusinesslike nature. In this kind of sitting, the sitter usually prefers to care for children of mothers who don't work full-time; that way she can more easily shut her doors for a while if her own personal life requires it. Also, this kind of sitter simply chooses not to work the nine-hour day that licensed family-day-care providers must.

One mother of a girl, 4, and a boy, 2, uses such a sitter for both children the two mornings a week her daughter doesn't go to nursery school. The mother drops her children off at nine-thirty in the morning and picks them up at one-thirty. She says, "It's an unwritten rule at Maura's that if your child is coming down with something, or is even slightly ill, you stay away. Maura doesn't want her own toddler sick and I don't blame her. She's super with the kids and I'm not going to kill the golden goose!"

"When I went to a weekly morning class I took my 9-month-old baby to a sitter's house. Leaving was painful because Amy always cried, and I knew she didn't understand what was going on. She caught many colds after I stopped nursing her at 8 months and I feel she caught most of them at the sitter's. I stopped using that sitter when the course ended and, instead, for the next year or so I got a high school girl to come over to our house after school three days a week so I could get out." *Mother of one / St. Paul, Minn.*

"Know your drop-off sitter well. Be very selective—not about the cleanliness of the home, but about the sitter's personality." *Mother of three / Barrington, Ill.*

Most often you hear about daytime sitters from other mothers. Don't be afraid to suggest doing such work to a neighbor whom you feel is energetic and a good mother and who has adequate space. One mother said, "When our drop-in sitter moved away, my friends and I advertised in the local paper for someone who loved children, had a yard, and could use fifty dollars a week. We found a wonderful woman with two preschool-age kids of her own. She's become our friend and a friend to our kids. It couldn't have worked out better."

One caution: Before setting up such an operation yourself or before encouraging someone else to do so, check out any legal restrictions covering such work in your community.

Agencies

"My son found a surrogate grandmother in a lovely woman sitter we found through an agency."
Mother of one / Atlanta, Ga.

Using an agency sitter—usually an older woman who is supplementing retirement income—is probably the most expensive but also the most convenient way to get sitting help. Most of these women have their own cars and will drive to your home, and with many agencies it's possible to request a favorite sitter time after time.

Agency sitters can be very good, or not so good. When one woman asked Jeanne if Anne could nap on the living-room couch instead of in her own room because "stairs are a problem for me," Jeanne realized that the sitter was not up to handling a robust 2-year-old.

Sources: Ask other mothers about agencies, or look in the yellow pages of your telephone directory. Agency sitters charge by the hour, with a four-hour minimum, plus a transportation fee. Many agencies also offer live-in vacation sitters for a flat-fee daily rate, regardless of the number of children.

Other Possibilities

"All my friends and I are jealous of the only woman we know who has a wonderful set of parents who sit for her any time she likes." *Mother of three / Phoenix, Ariz.*

Of course, grandparents—if they're willing—can be marvelous sitters. Carrying a heavy baby or keeping up with a toddler or 2-year-old can be too much for some older people, however, no matter how willing they may be, so it's a necessary kindness as well as a prudent precaution to evaluate your own parents' health and strength before asking them to sit for you. Another likely sitting possibility may be your child's aunts and uncles. "My sister and I take all the children for each other once a year for a long weekend so we can get away with our husbands alone. What bliss!" said one mother.

College students, nursing students, wives of students, mothers of school-age children, teachers on vacation, the wives of men who work at home—these were some of the other categories of sitters mentioned by mothers. Ask around, and maybe you'll find a gem. A married student couple may be the best solution of all to the vacation-sitting problem, especially as your children get older. If you live near a college or seminary, check with the student employment office. Also, some nursery schools offer a "babysitting option" following the regular class sessions.

LEAVING YOUR BABY

The earlier the better, your baby must learn that you go away sometimes but that you'll eventually come back. An infant should see the face of a new sitter while you're still there, so make sure the baby is still awake the first time you use a new sitter. After all, how would you feel if you woke up at night and saw a strange face hovering over your bed?

Once your child learns to talk, never lie to him about the fact that you're going out or about how long you'll be gone. Your child is learning to trust you, and it's important not to destroy this growing trust, even if you have to start an evening of fun by leaving behind a screaming child.

As your child grows older, you can teach her about time by explaining, "Mommy's going out for a while. Betty will get you up from your nap. She'll give you a frozen banana and let you watch 'Sesame Street.' She'll give you dinner. Then Mommy will come home."

A good book on the subject is *My Friend the Babysitter*, a Golden Press children's book by Jane Werner Watson. This cheerful book is presented as a flashback: a 3-year-old recalls how he got to know several different sitters and to learn that he could trust all of them.

"I had a child who at 6 months, 9 months, and a year went through crying spells when I left him. Sometimes it happened when I left the room; sometimes when someone else tried to hold him; and sometimes when he was left with babysitters. I had to go ahead and leave for his sake and mine, because I knew if I didn't the situation would get worse. As time went on he got over the crying. Now at the age of 2 he likes his sitters and even looks forward to my leaving."

Mother of one / Detroit, Mich.

HOW TO HANDLE A NEW SITTER

"We never asked sitters to do any work other than give the children their undivided attention. We always had the baby in bed, if the time was right. In the evening, the children were fed and in their pajamas. Our children were taught to show respect for their sitters and to be on their best behavior. As a result, they all enjoyed each other.

Mother of four / Denver, Colo.

It's important to take the time to familiarize your child with a new sitter, and vice versa. Many mothers say they allow from half an hour to an hour for this before they leave the first time a new sitter comes. Others say that if a neighborhood teenager is to be the sitter, they ask her to come over earlier in the week for an hour or so to become acquainted so that everyone will feel more comfortable later. It's not unusual for a teenager who has no younger siblings in her own family to require a little instruction in diaper changing and bottle feeding. But even with a familiar sitter, try not to tear out the door the minute she walks in.

Part of the extra time spent with a new sitter can be used to ease her natural misgivings about being in a strange house with a lot of responsibility. Some teenage girls have active imaginations and won't sit for you a second time if they're frightened in your home. Take the time to show your sitter—teenager, older woman, or anyone else—that all the windows and doors are locked, and how to lock them. Also explain how to *unlock* them. Plenty of sitters have inadvertently locked out both themselves and their charges—or only themselves, which is even worse.

One mother said she never forgot to show new sitters how the thermostat worked after arriving home one evening to find the sitter shivering and wrapped in a blanket. And show new sitters how to work the television set, the record player, and the stove.

Most important, give every sitter a few moments alone to read through your "babysitter information chart" (see next page), which you should keep posted near the telephone or on the wall in the kitchen. Be sure to print in a prominent place on the chart your own home address. Few sitters would be able to rattle off your street number from memory if they needed to telephone for help in an emergency, and you don't want them to have to run outside to find it.

Other useful information to include on the instruction sheet (in addition to emergency phone numbers and the address and number of where you'll be): children's names and birthdates; details of medical insurance coverage; location of such medications as syrup of ipecac; name and phone number of children's legal guardian(s) in case of your death; directions to your house (may help firemen or a teenager's mother to get there faster); daily schedule of children.

We expect our babysitters to be reliable. "Only twice in five years has it happened to me but, boy, do you get angry when a sitter isn't home when you get there to pick her up," one mother said. Reliability goes both ways. "If we cancel a sitter at the last minute, we always drop off some money the next day or make up for it the next time we see her," another said. "After all, she can't work elsewhere if she's saved the time for us." If you know you'll be more than a half hour late, call.

Set the ground rules early, such as no visitors, no smoking, no sleeping. Explain your policies on television watching (for both child and sitter), snacks, bedtime, picking up toys. "It's a lot easier to explain the first time I use a sitter that when I get back I expect the house to look reasonably like it did when I left than it is to fuss about it after she's sat for me for six months," admitted one mother. "I learned that after one girl we really liked left the sink full of dishes and toys all over the place on a night we unexpectedly brought friends home for a drink."

Insist that the door be opened to no one, that telephone

BABYSITTER INFORMATION CHART

We may be reached at:
(Tack or tape on phone number, address
of people or place you are visiting.)

Our Names_____

This Phone Number Is_____

This Address Is_____

Child's Name and Birthdate_____

Contact in Case of Emergency:

Children's Doctor_____
(Name, phone number, address)

_____

Fire, Paramedics_____

Police_____

Hospital Emergency Room_____
(Phone number, name of hospital, address)

_____

Nearby Friends (Names, phone numbers, addresses)_____

_____

_____

Children's Legal Guardian (in case of parents' death)
(Name, phone number, address)_____

_____

Father at work _____ and/or Mother at work_____
(Phone Number)

Directions to house_____

_____

_____

Information on Medical Insurance Coverage_____

_____

Consent to Emergency Medical Treatment (Either include actual consent here, signed by parent, or indicate at which hospital consent forms are kept on file and in which doctor's name).

Special Notes:
Medications (including syrup of ipecac, to induce vomiting) are on the top shelf of the bathroom medicine chest.
Make sure screen door onto deck is kept locked; she isn't allowed on deck alone.
Make sure bolt at top of downstairs front door is engaged; otherwise she can get out this door since she knows how to unlock it.
If she locks herself in the bathroom, the key to the bathroom door is in upper left-hand drawer of desk in living room.

Child's daily schedule: For trips of a whole day or more, prepare a daily schedule chart listing, in part, time to get up, breakfast, lunch, nap time, dinner time, and bath and bed time.

calls be kept short, and that the telephone be answered in such a way that the caller does not know how long it will be before you and your husband return home. ("They're busy and can't come to the phone right now. May I have them call you?")

To many sitters an evening can seem very long. Provide some food for a mid-evening break, and show her where you keep the books and magazines. For a long afternoon, suggest an activity that both she and your child might enjoy. "I leave all the stuff out for making cookies once in a while," one mother told us. Spell out the fact that you want a bedtime or naptime story read.

"My husband always takes the kids to the bakery on a Saturday morning when we're going out that night. They pick out treats for their dessert and also one for the sitter."
Mother of two / Billings, Mont.

SOME FINAL THOUGHTS ON SITTERS

"I would not, if I could do it over, feel guilt-ridden about hiring babysitters during the day, because often the exclusive attention of a sitter for an hour or so is more fun for a toddler than a round of errands with Mommy."
Mother of three / Albany, N.Y.

"With my first two children I never had enough babysitting. Then with child number three I had a mother's helper for a month after I'd been home from the hospital for two weeks. It was fantastic! I also learned, finally, to get sitters for some times when I was home but just needed to nap or finish some work or get ready to go out or just to escape."
Mother of three / Akron, Ohio

"For important occasions you can't have a sitter come too early, because something always comes up at the last minute. I learned that the time we were late to the wedding of a very good friend because of having to explain something complicated to the sitter before we could leave."
Mother of three / Iowa City, Iowa

16

Day Care
for Working Mothers

Tread lightly in this area, we tell ourselves. Most of the one-third of American mothers with children under 3 who work full-time do so because they *have* to, and no one wants to add worry about the quality of day care to their financial pressures. Others may toil at full-bore careers or hard-won jobs that they don't want to lose or to interrupt.

Yet the work of *mothers* is what this book is about. If we were to imply that paid outsiders can care for our children in the same way that we do we would be lying, but we would also be lying if we implied that babies don't need fiercely devoted care.

The truth is that finding care for a baby when you work deserves more effort than any other subject in this book. A new personality is at stake. Our own gut feelings tell us this as strongly as does the flood of child-development literature that shows a child's future ability to love others is greatly affected by the care he gets in the first years of life.

You *can* find good care. Writer Charlotte Painter, whose husband died shortly after their son Tommy was born, called finding day care "one of the sweeter problems life offers, because there are good human solutions to it."

"Good human solutions" to the problem of day care aren't always easy to come by, however. This chapter is *not* written for someone who needs a babysitter for next Monday morning. It is, rather, designed for parents who are willing to do whatever digging it takes to come up with a substitute parent for the hours when both mother and father are at work. It is also written for new mothers who, although they may not need or want to work right now, are mulling over the idea of working in the future. The death or disablement of a husband, divorce, financial setbacks, or the screaming meemies from too many hours of baby care can all occur before a child is of school age, plunging any of us into the day-care search.

Basically, in this chapter we try to give you an idea of what a baby needs and what in reality is out there to fill that need, along with some directions for finding parent substitutes. We also include ideas from other mothers on making day care work.

THE CHILD'S NEEDS

No matter what the care situation, the *needs* at the stages from birth to 3 are universal:

• The *infant* or very young baby needs *quick responses* and the right amount of stimulation and cuddling. Put simply, you want that diaper changed when it's soiled. You want the baby hugged once in a while, but not smothered all day long.

• A *toddler* requires *constant watchfulness for his safety* but also *gradual exposure to the everyday world and to language.* You want the child protected from the hot oven and you want him to learn that the word "hot" means what the oven feels like when it is on.

• A *2-year-old* requires someone with *patience, stamina, and humor* to handle the normal aggression and curiosity of this age, and he also needs, at least occasionally, *other children* to play with. You want someone who won't yell "Don't touch that, you'll get splinters!" when the child picks up a piece of scrap wood, someone who won't think a child is incorrigible if he goes through a period of biting younger children, someone who will handle toilet training in a manner you approve of.

• A *3-year-old* needs *other children to play with nearly every day* and will develop self-confidence by doing a few things away from home and/or away from the chief caregiver. In other words, you want a care situation where your child gets the benefits that come from doing something like attending a good nursery school.

A mother almost automatically sees that these changing needs are met. She can grow from a baby nurse to a language teacher to a child-safety expert to a friend-finder depending on her child's age and level of development. Some parent substitutes cannot do this. A grandmother, for example, may be smashingly good at one stage but not be strong enough, physically, to cope with another stage. This is why finding good day care for the early years is a sticky problem, and one that is rarely solved "once and for all." These changing needs are also the reason many mothers as well as some child-development experts think the optimum mother substitute in the early years is best represented by two different kinds of care: during the first year or so, someone who comes to the child's home; thereafter, taking the child to be cared for by someone who runs a family-day-care operation in her own home.

WHAT'S OUT THERE: THE FOUR BASIC TYPES OF DAY CARE

According to the U.S. Department of Labor, almost half the preschool children of working mothers are cared for at home; about a third are taken care of in someone else's home; roughly 5 percent are in day-care centers; and the rest have other arrangements. If you expect to work after your baby arrives, you need to learn as much as you can about all the alternatives. The four basic types of child care available in the early years are: (1) a person who comes to your home, (2) family-day-care homes, (3) day-care centers, and (4) relatives. We will discuss each of these options in some detail.

1. A Person Who Comes to Your Home

"When I worked, an older woman came to the house. I found her by chance when she answered a friend's ad but decided not to accept that job, which included cooking. I

hated to leave Becky at all but it was economically necessary. I felt very strongly that the best situation was keeping her in her own home so that she wouldn't have to com-
pete with other children for attention. It's worked out su-
perbly—never any separation anxiety."

Mother of one / Braintree, Mass.

The best substitute mother for an infant or toddler may be
a grandmotherly type of person who will care for your child
in your own home.

Such caregivers will probably always be around for those
families lucky enough to find them and value them. Winston
Churchill erected a memorial plaque to his nanny, Elizabeth
Everest. And we recall seeing a warm picture of Jimmy Car-
ter, smiling broadly, with his arm around an elderly black
woman, Rachel Clark. The caption described her as "the
woman who helped raise him during his boyhood days in
Plains."

The advantages to this arrangement are easily apparent:
no early-morning frenzy to get your child fed, dressed, and
packed for the day; less exposure to other babies' illnesses
than in a group-care situation; less stress on your child from
unfamiliar surroundings. If you have several children on different time schedules for schools and lessons, this may be
the only practical answer for child care. It is, however, undoubtedly the most expensive alternative.

A possible disadvantage here, beyond expense, is that
you will be responsible for seeing that the person is covered
by social security and that she has two weeks' paid vacation
a year, both something of an inconvenience. Also, in this
type of care, TV and sweets can be used in excess for "pac-
ifying" youngsters instead of the outdoor play and exposure
to other children that they may need. You have to spell out
your requirements and preferences early and insist that they
are followed. Another possible disadvantage is that you need
to check up on this type of caregiver often at first, particularly if your baby can't yet talk and tell you about what his
day is like. A caregiver in your home, after all, is by defini-
tion an unsupervised worker.

If price is no object and you have an extra room, you
may consider live-in help for the early years. At Albermarle

Nannies in London, managing director Sheila Davis told a reporter: "The British nanny is becoming Britain's new twentieth-century colonizer abroad." At that agency, a prospective nanny is selected after a long screening process and signed to a year's contract with an option to renew. If she decides to leave prematurely, she must pay her way back. But if the family is dissatisfied, they pay for the ticket back to England.

English nannies, of course, are not likely to be within the budgets of most of us, nor would they necessarily fit easily into our life styles. There are agencies that arrange for live-in help of various other kinds, from mature women to *au pair* girls—young women from foreign countries who do domestic work as their first employment in the United States. (Check both the yellow pages of your phone book and the help-wanted section of your newspaper to locate such agencies—in addition to asking friends for recommendations, of course.)

Au pair girls, however, may not work out for the mother who works forty hours a week. Many mothers say that these girls—because of their youth, their inexperience with the English language, and their frequent homesickness—simply do not offer the solid security and experience that most working mothers need to be able to depend on. As one mother of three who tried this arrangement said, "I felt like I had a fourth child in the house!"

"I'm an airline stewardess and my husband's in business for himself, so his income is unpredictable. We need the benefits like health insurance from my job, so I went back to work a year after our twins were born, flying nine days a month from ten a.m. to eleven p.m. We hired a live-in English girl, and it's working out beautifully."

Mother of two / Baltimore, Md.

"When I was divorced I went back to work as a nurse. Setting it up has been a logistical nightmare, but I feel I've got the best possible care for my children now. My 3-year-old son goes to a nursery school near our house five mornings a week. When it's over at noon, my live-in woman picks him up and oversees him at home until I get there at five-thirty. My daughter gets out of school at two-fifteen, so she's also cared for at our home."   *Mother of two / Dallas, Tex.*

Other places where you may find help who will come to your home are senior-citizen groups or church groups in your area. Your best bet might be to do some serious exploring in your own neighborhood. "I wanted people to call after my ad was in the paper and say they were dying to care for our child," one mother said. "Instead I got calls telling me 'I was just laid off at Taco Bell. How much do you pay?' Others couldn't give references or had no qualifications. Finally we asked a woman in our neighborhood who stays home with her retired husband. We have the ideal set-up now."

Placing an ad in the newspaper is the most common way of locating a caregiver who will come to your home. Be specific in what you want. Here are two ads from a local newspaper:

Full-time housekeeper, live in/out. Private room, bath. Professional couple, infant. Telephone 555-4321.

Child Care, enthusiastic and responsive individual needed to plan and supervise activities for two girls ages 8 and 3 from 8 a.m. to 6 p.m. Some light housekeeping. Must have own trans. Hollywood Riviera area. Telephone 555-5147.

The first ad is much too vague. In fact, one isn't sure from reading it whether child care is involved at all. The second is better, obviously written by a parent who has done some soul searching about what kind of care her children need.

"Consider having your most likely candidate work in the house for a weekend. Watch for signs of common sense and warmth. We did this and realized our first impressions during interviews were sometimes off base. A woman who smoked turned out to be a regular Mary Poppins for our kids, while another—who was a wholesome-looking health-food enthusiast—turned out to have a rotten disposition."
Mother of three / San Francisco, Calif.

After you have found someone who seems, on the basis of the interview, to be a good caregiver, check up on her. Particularly during the early weeks it's a good idea for you

Interviewing a Caregiver

Talk about your family and work situation briefly, but be specific about what duties and responsibilities you expect the caregiver to assume. Then, in a general way, ask her about her background. Follow up with more detailed questions, such as:

- What is your previous experience caring for children?

- Why are you changing jobs?

- How do you think children should be disciplined?

- How do you think a child should be toilet trained?

- Do you drive?

- Have you had a medical checkup lately?

- If my child had a serious accident, how would you handle it?

- Are you willing to be outdoors with my child for a couple of hours during the day in good weather?

- Are you willing to take my child to a park or playground occasionally so that he can play with other children?

- Are you looking for a long-term job?

- What are the names and telephone numbers of at least three persons who know you well and/or for whom you have worked before?

Be sure to introduce the sitter to your child and allow time to see how they react to each other. Before the sitter leaves, show her around your house.

Spell out any restrictions you may have about such things as smoking, drinking, television, food, using the telephone, and visitors.

Find out if the sitter will do tasks (laundry, cooking, cleaning) other than child care if you want them done.

Discuss work schedule and salary. Be sure to get a medical release form so your child can receive care in an emergency if you can't be reached. Be absolutely certain to check all references.

or your husband to go home unexpectedly during the day. One mother said, "I worked a forty-five-minute drive away and couldn't check on things myself, but I asked my daughter's godmother, who lived nearby, to pop in every few days to see how things were going."

Another mother mentioned that she took the time to introduce her caregiver to nearby friends with children the same age as hers, which resulted in play exchanges that the children enjoyed as well as another set of eyes and ears to judge the sitter's performance. She also introduced the caregiver to another woman on the street and the two became friends. Many mothers mentioned that they made time to telephone home at least once every day because it reassured them and gave moral support to the sitters.

2. Family-Day-Care Homes

"I babysat at home so I wouldn't have to go out and work, watching from three to four children plus our two. We had a marvelous time, with order and plenty of love. My own children were happy, as they each had a playmate or two their own age." *Mother of two / Buffalo, N.Y.*

There are lots of women like the one quoted above, many of them gifted with calm dispositions and more than average energy, who care for young children in their own homes. At their best they can provide the very finest care, even though the cost is usually *less* than any of the day-care sources already discussed. Our own preference, as well as that of many mothers we talked with and of some child-development experts, is for care in such a home for the child of 2 and 3, although a caregiver who comes to your own home is probably best for the first year or so (and even longer if she is particularly good).

The big advantages: a clear idea for the child who the parent substitute is; another normal home to explore and learn about; other children to play with, providing the child in a small nuclear family with some of the pleasures and pains of a larger extended family.

The disadvantage to such care from the parent's point of view is that usually, and realistically, the caregiver doesn't expect to support herself through this work. She does it not as an occupation but as a source of extra money and, often, for companionship for her own children. Family-day-care mothers do substitute mothering when it fits into their own life styles and needs. This, of course, can make you nervous if you must work fifty weeks a year from eight-thirty to five. You need the caregiver more than she needs you.

But, to many, it's worth the nervousness. Time after time mothers mentioned that once such a caregiver became committed to a child she stayed committed, and that's the beauty of this kind of care. When it works, it truly provides substitute mothering. "It's worth having to worry about my sitter getting sick or her kids getting sick or her husband wanting to go on a vacation once in a while to have my child so happy in a house on our own block," one mother said.

"I had a woman with children the same age as mine taking care of my daughter when I worked. Since I was a teacher, my time schedule was ideal. When my daughter turned 3, I enrolled her in a nursery school two mornings a week and kept her at the woman's the rest of the time. If possible, I feel the individual attention of a mother substitute is better than a day-care center or full-time nursery school. I know how tired teachers get. Mornings are fine, but by afternoon they tend to be tired, so they may not always be able to give warm, loving care." *Mother of one / Tampa, Fla.*

A good overview of this sort of care is given in *Family Day Care: A Practical Guide for Parents, Caregivers, and Professionals* by Alice Collins and Eunice Watson, two social workers who have studied the subject under a grant from the Ford Foundation. They point out that today's caregivers want to look after children who are well cared for by their parents. Not only does this make the caregiver's day easier, it means the children will probably be good companions for her own children and aren't likely to be brought to her house when they're ill. The authors cite studies showing that a leading reason for the day-care-home mother ending an arrangement is parental neglect of the child. (Close behind was failure of parents to pay on time or to stick to agreed hours.)

Take your child with you to any day-care home you're

considering and watch his interaction with the caregiver and the other children she cares for. Ask her the same questions you'd ask someone you're interviewing to come to your home (see box—"Interviewing a Caregiver"). Find out how many children she's caring for. And also find out if there will be other people in the house during the day (a grandmother, a teenager coming home from school, a boyfriend) and make sure none is the sort you wouldn't want around your child. Ask if she ever takes the children out in her car during the day and, if so, if she has enough seat belts and car restraints to go around. Other things to check for:

- Are the rooms well lighted and cheerful?

- Where will the children nap? Will each have his own cot?

- Is there space for each child to keep his own things?

- Are there footstools for children to reach faucets/toilets?

- Are there books/toys around that look as if they're used?

More important than these points, of course, is the day-care mother's personality. All the personality factors mentioned in the section headed "What Is a Good Mother Substitute?" (page 399) apply here, but a parent seeking a day-care mother has a way to check out this kind of care that isn't possible with most other forms of care: she can observe the caregiver on her home ground. Neatness doesn't matter, although cleanliness does. You'll want a reasonably clean floor if you have a crawler-age child. Look for other things that tell you what kind of person you're dealing with. Many particularly good child caregivers are also good with other growing things, like plants and pets, so there may be a dog or a cat around.

"If you use a family-day-care home, try to find out first as much as you can about the stability of the woman's home life. I found a wonderful woman my daughter just loved, but the arrangement only lasted six months. It turns out she was going through a divorce at the time and eventually moved out of the neighborhood."

Mother of one / Des Moines, Iowa

Check the "situations wanted" section of the classified ads for something like this, which we found in a recent edition of our local paper:

> LICENSED loving day care in my home. Lomita area. Arts/crafts, hot lunches, fenced yard. 14 mo. to 4½ yrs. 555-7893.

Call your local Department of Social Services to obtain a list of persons who are licensed to care for babies and children in their own homes. The licensing agency limits the number of children (usually six, including those of the caregiver) who may be cared for at any one time and insists on minimum standards of safety and cleanliness.

But don't stop there. Some figures show that as many as 90 percent of day-care homes are *not* licensed. A good argument is made by many caregivers that they do not want to put up with the hassles involved in licensing. Parents, too, may object to licensing, insisting that they are more capable of deciding what a safe, good home is than is a spot-checking government inspector.

"With my son I worked full time until he was 2½, so I had to have a sitter nine hours a day five days a week. My best babysitters were friends or family of a friend. I also tried a licensed babysitter. I thought because she was licensed by the state that meant something, but I found out differently. I'd be much more careful now who I left my children with. I left the licensed babysitter because if my son spilled his food the sitter would hit him. One day she hit him in the mouth with a spoon, and I found out because it kept bleeding and bleeding. I'd say make sure you *really* know the person who has your child." *Mother of two / El Paso, Tex.*

The problem is not so much licensing as getting giver and user together, and licensing agencies do offer this service. Still, word-of-mouth or a diligent search of the neighborhood is the way most parents find out about day-care homes.

3. Day-Care Centers

Certainly, day-care centers are more reliable sources of care than any other in the sense that if one of the people who run it gets sick the center doesn't shut down. And, unlike the other sources of day care, they're fairly easy to find.

Before going into the possible disadvantages of this, the most controversial type of child care, some general information is in order. Most private and publicly operated day-care centers accept only children over 2 who are toilet trained. However, some of the increasing numbers of commerical day-care chains accept babies. Mini-Skools Ltd., for example, operates more than eighty centers in eight states for children from 6 months to 6 years old.

In government-supported centers fees are based on family income, and children of one-parent families are usually given preference. In the few centers subsidized by industry, universities, or churches, fees are a little higher than those charged by government-supported centers. Finally, the fees at privately operated or "commercial" (for profit) day-care centers can be as high as those you would pay to someone who came to your home.

Feelings about day-care centers vary dramatically. Children's advocate Selma Fraiberg, a mother and professor of child psychoanalysis as well as the author of *Every Child's Birthright: In Defense of Mothering*, asserts that most centers set up for the convenience of parents and for a business profit, *not* for providing all-important substitute mothering to babies. Well-known pediatrician William E. Homan, in a new edition of *Child Sense*, calls centers that care for children from infancy to kindergarten age "inventions of the devil, conceived as a second-class and expedient solution to a deeply rooted societal problem."

On the other hand, Susan Stein, in *Child Care—Who Cares?*, points out that while commercial operations can be operated at a profit if staff and salaries are kept at a minimum and enrollment at capacity, the care may not be as bad as that in some nonprofit centers that have no interest in good public relations. She asserts that the care may also be a good deal more stimulating than the "TV care" many children receive at home. "The general bias against profit-making child care does not seem to be founded on a comparison of quality, but rather on the ideological notion that business doesn't belong in child care at all," she claims.

There are some nonprofit day-care centers set up on a cooperative basis by several mothers in a neighborhood.

Since the people who run these centers are intimately involved in their day-to-day operations, such centers tend to be very good. In her book *Working Mothers*, Jean Curtis praises them for their grass-roots type of energy, their flexibility, and their emphasis on caring, as contrasted with more conventional kinds of day care, which she characterizes as "custodial." She says that most people who have seen well-run cooperative nonprofit centers agree that they offer a positive alternative to the hassle of finding and paying for housekeepers, nannies, or other mother substitutes who come to the home.

"I tried a day-care center for a while. My only real objection was that it seemed so noisy and crowded—I'd get exhausted myself if there were so many people zooming around me all day long. Instead, I found a lady nearby who watched my daughter, and we were a lot happier with that arrangement."
Mother of one / Scranton, Pa.

Whatever your general feelings about commercial day care, you should be aware of several inherent problems in day-care-center settings for the very young.

One is communication between parents and staff—not just about how each day goes but also about differing approaches to care. It sounds easy to achieve, but you don't always get communication in vital areas, such as how discipline or toilet training is handled at the center. It's tough at the end of a day to make time to check on such things with staff members who are just as anxious as you are to go home, but a child can become confused if there is great disparity in approach to care between home and center.

"The job is fatiguing and requires a lot of stamina on the part of the caretaker, and unless the parent makes an effort to establish constant communication, he may not know what is happening with his child," says Rosalind Silver, Day Care Licensing Supervisor for the New York State Department of Social Services. Observers at most centers note that the more parental involvement, the better the care. In fact, some children's advocates are urging legislators to make parental participation a requirement in federally funded centers. What's more, they're urging that businesses be required to give parents time off from work to spend a few hours a week at the centers with their children.

Another problem is high staff turnover. "Someone must know each child well enough to decide when he needs to be held, to be taken for a walk alone, or simply to play quietly in the presence of an adult or another child," says Dr. Sally Provence, who with others tried to set up the very best day-care center she could at the Yale Child Study Center. While everyone—including us—tells you to make sure that *one* person is responsible for the major amount of care for each child, we can't tell you how to make sure that a usually low-paid staff member stays at the center long enough for your child to build up an attachment to him or her.

Then there's sickness. Mrs. Silver notes a high incidence of upper-respiratory illnesses. "The children's needs are not paramount sometimes," she says. "The parents' needs are overriding. At what point does the parent remove and return an ill child?" However, a recent study in Sweden followed three groups of children: the first went to day-care centers that had between sixteen and sixty-eight children; the second to family day-care homes that had a total of four children; the third group of children stayed in their own homes. Results showed that, as might be expected, the children who stayed home had the least number of respiratory infections. But the other two groups had the same number of infections. Once you leave home for group care, the size of the groups does not appear to affect the illness rate.

"I worked from the time my daughter was 6 months old. I found a great sitter through the newspaper. At 2, she was put in a day-care center operated by the local school district with federal money. Since I'm a single parent, I only have to pay a certain percentage of my income, and this has made it possible for me to work and have good care for her. It's a great school." *Mother of one / Chicago, Ill.*

"Instead of a day-care center near my house, I chose one a block away from my office. That way I can visit at lunch-time, and my child and I also spend half an hour in the car together going and coming."

Mother of one / Dayton, Ohio

Thoroughly investigate any center you're considering for your child. Many of the evaluations relating to atmosphere and physical plant described in the nursery-school chapter apply here as well. It's particularly important to get a feel for whether or not the center is excessively regimented. There were days at the Yale day-care center described by Dr. Provence, for example, when the children couldn't seem to cope with planned learning activities, so staff members might take some of them for a walk or a ride in the shuttle bus, or into another room with one adult for a quiet period. On other days, when some of the children were tired or slightly ill, lunch would be served early and the children would be given a longer rest.

Adequate staff-to-child ratio is crucial. Most states require a minimum of one adult to four infants, one adult to six 2-year-olds or eight 3-year-olds, and two adults to fifteen children of mixed ages between 2 and 6. However, many mothers and more than a few child-development experts are convinced that a staff ratio of one adult to two children is necessary for the best care of children to the age of 3.

There should be one person (or at the most two) who is responsible for your child during most of the day. If your child is cared for by a bewildering variety of people, there is little chance that she'll develop a true substitute-parent child relationship with anyone at the center. As we have already noted, however, high staff turnover can be a problem at some day-care centers, so try to get a frank assessment of the turnover situation when you talk to the staff. Also, you should read "What Is a Good Mother Substitute?" (next section) and keep those questions in mind as you talk to the person(s) at the center who will have the most to do with caring for your child.

Do not be timid when you visit the center! A young mother anxious to get her child into a federally funded program with a long waiting list may be deferential to the point of not finding out everything she should about a day-care center. Instead, she should realize that good caregivers welcome and respect evidence of parental concern. Ask as many questions as you like; make sure you see everything you want to see; and insist on meeting the person who will be most responsible for your child's care.

To sum up, a good parental investigation of a day-care center will answer the following questions:

• What will the child's day be like? Is there excessive regimentation?

• How is communication between parents and staff handled?

• Is there any parental involvement in the center? Does center policy allow you to visit whenever you can be there, particularly at a time of special stesss for your child?

• Is there high staff turnover at the center?

• What is the policy on sickness? What is done with the child who gets sick while at the center? Since babies, especially, can get very sick very fast, a nurse or someone else well versed in signs of illness should always be on hand.

• What is the current staff-to-child ratio? What will it be in the future?

• How many people will be responsible for looking after your child? (If it's more than one or two, you should probably look elsewhere.) Be sure to meet and talk to these people.

• What about the center's program in education in the sense that a child's developmental needs at each stage are recognized—as, for example, in play opportunities, toilet training, feeding methods?

• What are the working conditions? Would *you* like to work at the center? What provision is made for the staff to take breaks from direct child care?

• What kind of information does the staff get from you? Questions relating to the child's medical history, feeding patterns, typical day at home, favorite types of toys and games, how he lets you know what he needs and the way he likes to be comforted all indicate that the center makes allowances for individual characteristics and preferences.

• What is the physical plant like? Are bathrooms set up for use by children, with low sinks and toilets? Is there a yard or other outdoor play area? How safe is the front entrance or area where parents park before picking up children?

4. Relatives

One of the most frequently mentioned sources of day care was relatives. Undeniably they qualify as people who will give the child the feeling his welfare is important to them. For parents, good care by relatives often makes it possible to work without the bouts of guilt that may accompany other forms of care.

Every relative-care situation is unique, but there are a few things that should be carefully considered before you enter such an arrangement. One is willingness to communicate with each other and work out inevitable areas of disagreement. If you feel you must handle the relative with kid gloves, it may not work out.

For example, many women in our mothers' generation, who didn't have disposable diapers and often didn't have automatic washers and dryers, tried to toilet train children as early as possible. Today most parents prefer to wait until they see signs of their child's readiness before beginning toilet training. If there's a difference of opinion on issues like this, you both must be willing to hear each other out. In matters you feel very strongly about you should insist on your way, but in anything else it would probably be wise to let the caregiver, who will be dealing with problems on a day-to-day basis, use her own best judgment.

Then there's discipline. One mother of a feisty 2-year-old boy told us that even though her own recently widowed mother was eager to care for her grandson, she took him to a day-care home. "Some women soften up with a grandchild and my mother is one of them," she said. "I'd never leave my son with her all day every day. She'd say, 'Please, Robert, don't do that,' and he'd run all over her anyway. Now my *husband's* mother—if she lived nearby, I'd leave my son with her for sure. When she says something's wrong, it's wrong and that's it. That's what my son needs."

Another mother with children now in grade school cheerfully admits that her own mother, who cared for the children during the week when they were young, is more effective at disciplining them than she is. "The week when my 10-year-old son knew his grandmother was coming for an overnight visit he picked up all his toys and stuffed them in a closet," she told us. "He made the bed and dusted around a ceramic horse collection. When my mother went into the room she picked up one of the horses and said there was too much dust there. Then she went to the closet and all the stuff fell out. She put it all in the middle of the room, went out and got a garbage pail, put it at the door, and told him he'd better clean everything up in half an hour or it was going in the pail. He knew she meant it. In half an hour that room was more orderly than it had been in six months."

There should be some agreement about pay. Most situations work out best if the relative is paid the going rate, or close to it, but even if a relative refuses to accept money for care, something should be done in return. One mother said she balanced her mother's checkbook, did her taxes, and often took her out to lunch while the child's father did all his mother-in-law's yard work and some house repairs in return for the weekday care of their child. It's important not to take advantage of relatives in ways you wouldn't with a stranger.

"I had to go back to work when Robert was 3 months old and worked until he was 15 months. He stayed with one grandma twice a week, another grandma once a week, and with his dad twice a week. I felt good about this since his babysitters not only cared for him but loved him. But, still—I missed him so much."   *Mother of one / Tulsa, Okla.*

"I'm very fortunate to have a mother who's always willing to help me out with the children, and my mother-in-law is just the same. So from the beginning, when I went back to work I felt at ease about leaving the baby."
Mother of one / Charlotte, N.C.

"My mother was willing to take care of our son and she needed some extra money. But it didn't work at first. Rusty would go on energetic rampages that left her apartment messed up and her neighbors angry at the noise he made. Now my mother comes to *our* house and it's better all the way around."   *Mother of one / Glendale, Calif.*

WHAT IS A GOOD MOTHER SUBSTITUTE?

"I have a wonderful woman caring for my toddler. When she puts clothes on the line to dry and has John follow along holding the basket of pins for her, he looks so proud. Now he's at the door waiting to go in the morning instead of fighting it like he did with our other sitter."

Mother of one / San Diego, Calif.

The personality of a mother substitute—whether it is a relative, a live-in or live-out person, a woman caring for children in her own home, or a person at a day-care center—is all-important.

"I look for warmth and an easy-going nature when I interview someone to care for my children," one working mother said. "Everything else is secondary."

Another description of what a good caregiver for young children needs is given by Dr. Sally Provence of the Yale Child Study Center. "The unobtrusively watchful eye, the ear attuned to the sounds of contentment or distress are universal and essential qualities of those who nurture well," she says. The woman described above who can hang clothes and keep a child safe and happy at the same time surely has this quality.

A baby needs "attuned" watching by *one* person. The reason so few day-care centers accept infants and young babies is that caring for them is so labor-intensive—or, in other words, it's *expensive*. Babies need attention all day long, and the person giving the attention must truly care whether it is coos and gurgles or irritable cries coming from *that* baby.

A mother and father need to put out all their personality feelers when sizing up a person to care for their child. "Have the baby there and even an older child or two if you can borrow them for the interview," one mother advises. "It's amazing how fast you can tell how people feel about kids when they're in the same room with them."

In a family-day-care home, try to get a feel for whether the woman listens when children talk and answers their questions patiently. Do the children seem fond of her and able to express themselves freely? If she's caring for children of her own at the same time, does she seem the sort to be able to handle the inevitable conflicts wisely? One caretaker we know insists that her own school-age son's room and toys be off-limits to the children she cares for, and only if he invites them into his room to use his things do they do so. This makes sense to us. A woman considerate of her own children is likely to be the same with those of others.

Does the woman seem as if she would take the time to teach the children the same things you would, like washing hands before eating and saying "please" and "thank you"? Does she have a fairly good idea of how the day will go for your child with routines that include rest, snacks, outdoor playtime?

Try to find out her ideas on discipline, toilet training, feeding and eating patterns. All should be fairly similar to your own. Don't be timid about asking the names and telephone numbers of other parents who have used her.

"If I had it to do over again I'd worry more about the baby and less about the boss. Instead of using the handy day-care center that's right on the way to work, I'd hire someone to care for my baby at home for about the first year. Then I'd find a good mother in the neighborhood who could use some extra money and ask her to watch my daughter at her house along with her own kids."

Mother of one / Seattle, Wash.

Beyond the personality of the caregiver, another factor in good care is continuity. Many mothers we talked with mentioned sleepless nights, eating problems, increases in thumbsucking and the like when day-care arrangements had to be changed.

Pediatricians warn of depression in a baby as young as 6 months if the parent or other person who cares for him leaves. "It's important that the . . . person who has taken the major part of a child's care not give it up during the first two or three years, or give it up only after a substitute has very gradually taken over," says Dr. Spock, and we agree.

Day care can work for the very young only if the goals—providing parenting—are clear, says child psychiatrist Richard A. Felch, director of children's services at the Capitol District Psychiatric Center in Albany, New York. "If it's strictly a hyped-up, souped-up 'Sesame Street' I question its worth," he told a newspaper reporter. "You can have all the geniuses in the world teaching them but if the kids don't know the intimacy of good parenting they're not going to learn anything. The child who's curious and questioning and exploring and sociable is the child who knows that if anything goes wrong his parents (and caregiver) will support him." Dr. Felch insists that if caregivers see themselves as significant parental figures and demand an intimate emotional relationship with the infant, they must be prepared to honor and sustain that commitment. Stability, he says, is a must.

Paradoxically, after you consider the stability of the caregivers, in the back of your mind *you* always have to remain flexible. The child-care decision—a "human" one, subject to human frailty—is rarely made once and for all. Your family-day-care mother may move away or decide she no longer wants to do this kind of work. Or the person who is a fine caregiver for an infant may not be up to chasing after the 2-year-old who darts into a busy street. A child changes dramatically during her early years, and the caregiver's day changes right along with it.

At the Yale Day Care Center described by Dr. Provence in her book *The Challenge of Day Care*, it was harder to provide good care for children from 14 or 15 months to about 2½ than for babies or older children. The staff for this age group needed to have "flexibility and a sense of fun along with an ability to remain reasonably mature in his or her own behavior." The pediatrician and author admits drily, "Adults having such qualities are, in our experience, especially hard to find."

So, sometimes you have to grit your teeth and change caregivers even though you realize that a child needs the security of one chief caregiver at this age.

"Instead of backing day care centers, why doesn't the government just allow the woman who cares for a few kids in her home to keep all the little money she makes instead of having to pay taxes on it?   *Mother of three / Santa Monica, Calif.*

CONDUCTING THE DAY-CARE SEARCH:
A BATTLE PLAN FOR PARENTS

Where do you find this warm, flexible person with the watchful sixth sense who will be around for two, three, or more
years?

You may not have the time or the inclination to do all
of the following, but the more ground you cover the more
confidence you'll have that the decision you make is the
right one. And the more thoroughly you investigate all the
options, the easier it will be later if the bottom falls out of
the type of care arrangement you have chosen and you have
to start looking all over again. Steel yourself. Faint heart
never won fair lady—or a good mother substitute.

1. *Get your money facts straight.* There are exceptions, but
roughly speaking these are the basic types of care in order
of cost, with the most expensive first and the least expensive
last: a person who comes to your home who is of housekeeper quality; commercial day-care center; *au pair* girl; federally funded or otherwise subsidized day-care center; family-
day-care home; relatives.

Before you discard some alternatives out of hand because
you're sure you can't afford them, you should realize that
you may have more economic flexibility than you think.
Mothers who work or go to school full-time can now claim
significant tax credits to offset necessary expenditures for
child care or household help, regardless of family income.
A tax credit is a direct reduction of your tax bill after you've
toted it all up, while a deduction only gives a partial reduction based on income. You don't have to fill out the long
tax form to get it, nor do you have to claim the child as a
dependent.

Child-care wages paid to a relative—say, a grandparent—
now qualify, as long as he or she is not your legal dependent.
To be eligible you must rely upon the relative to be responsible for the care of at least one child under 15 or of an in-
capacitated adult. Consult the nearest Internal Revenue Service office for more details.

2. *Ask other working parents,* both at work and in your
neighborhood, what they do about child care. What would

they advise a new parent to do? Get an idea from them on the going rates in your area for the four basic types of child care.

3. *Check out child-care information and referral agencies.* In more than twenty-five cities private agencies have been established to give parents facts about care options for every age and income level. They offer information about after-school care, parent co-ops, group home care, and other alternatives that fit under the umbrella term of "day care." One such agency is the Child Care Switchboard of San Francisco. Ask at the public library whether such an agency exists in your city.

4. *Study the "situations wanted" classified section of your local paper.* Take a deep breath and call any likely candidates.

5. *Put an ad in the local paper* most likely to be read by the sort of person you'd like to care for your child, either in your home or hers. Even if you're not certain you want this type of care, it's a good learning experience—and a comparatively inexpensive one. Find out as much as you can on the telephone and then set up interviews with the most promising prospects. Don't bother seeing them if they are even a little vague about supplying you with references.

6. *Call the local Department of Social Services to get a list of persons licensed to care for babies and children in their own homes.* Visit at least one so that you can get a feel for this type of care option.

7. *Check the yellow pages under "nursery schools" for day-care centers and investigate at least one of these* after finding out if they offer care for children the age of your child.

8. *Use your imagination.* One mother told us she called the local elementary school to get the name and telephone number of the PTA president and then called this woman to get the names of some mothers in the area who already did or might like to do child care in their homes. "PTA presidents are invariably competent, gregarious types who know what's going on in their neighborhoods," this mother explained. Another woman said she had called neighborhood churches to ask if they maintained a file of members who did child

care. Another put an index card describing her needs on the bulletin board of a senior citizens' center; she got several responses. Keep a watchful eye on your neighborhood for signs of other women with children your child's age or for women with big, happy families. You might consider asking them if they're interested in doing child care for you.

9. *Check references.* As has already been mentioned, this is an absolute must. Nothing is worth taking a risk of leaving your child with an alcoholic or a drug addict. Even if it requires a long-distance call, do it by telephone rather than by letter. People are usually more willing to give a frank opinion verbally than they are to do so in writing.

10. *Start a file box or other record-keeping system* with sections for each of the four basic types of child care. Make notes on all likely prospects who, even though they may be busy now, might be available in the future.

MAKING DAY CARE WORK

"When the three of us walk in the door at night, I take the telephone off the hook and it stays off for at least the first hour we're home. That's the baby's time. Period."
Mother of one / St. Paul, Minn.

Connecting the Two Worlds

Many mothers told us they didn't know what planning and organization were until they tried to combine parenthood with marriage and a full-time job. The choice of a good daytime caregiver for the child is just the start of making it all work. Like the mother above, you must take an aggressive approach to life.

Right off the bat, ways must be found to ease the separation pain that both parents and baby feel.

To a baby who has learned to feel comfortable with one particular face and voice, separation from that voice and face for even an hour is terrifying. Unlike an adult, a baby simply doesn't have the mental equipment to know that Mother will *ever* come back. Some psychologists say a child doesn't have this ability until 18 months. At the same time, many mothers told us it was very difficult for them to leave their babies with someone else. They felt they were missing beautiful moments that would never come again.

Anything that can lessen the feeling of two separate worlds for baby and parents is good.

One mother said she eased into the day-care situation by having her baby go to a family-day-care home for only a few hours each day the week *before* she went back to work, and she herself spent an hour at the day-care home on each of the baby's first two days there. Many day-care centers encourage a similar arrangement. Don't be timid about asking others to let you do this, and if you feel your child needs you to stay a while with him before you leave, at any time, try to do it.

At the Yale Day Care Center parents who worked nearby were urged to park their cars across the street from the center so that the toddlers and older children could look out the window several times a day and say, usually happily, "Mama's car" or "Daddy's car." This tangible reminder of parents seemed to comfort even those children whose parents did not park there. Employees pasted family photos at child height on lockers belonging to each child. Favorite toys and blankets were brought from home to the center, something that should be done in all outside-the-home care, then put in the lockers to which children were allowed free access. Older children at the center were allowed to receive telephone calls from parents and, within reason, to have an employee place a call to parents for them.

One mother said she made a cassette tape recording for her 2-year-old son. "I sang his favorite songs, told two favorite stories, and said several times, 'Ricky, this is Mommy. I love you, and I'll see you soon.' He took it with him to the babysitter's and listened to it off and on during the day when he seemed lonely for me."

Another way to connect the family members' worlds is to show your child your office or place of work. Even a child as young as 2 will recognize and be proud of seeing his own artwork on your desk or wall. You might also provide a red-letter day for your child by inviting a special friend from his day-care center or family-day-care home over to play on a Saturday.

When possible, visit your child in the middle of the day.

It will be a pleasure for you both, usually, and in addition provides you an opportunity to check on your child's care situation.

"I work for a company that's on flextime. The hours I work are seven-thirty to five-thirty but I take a two-hour lunch in the middle of the day to go home and be with my son."
Mother of one / Flagstaff, Ariz.

Besides trying to connect the two worlds, help the toddler and older child acknowledge and master feelings about separation. Teach her to say hello and goodbye to relatives, neighbors, dolls. Give her a chance to play games in which she controls her own coming and going and directs the coming and going of others, games of hiding and rediscovering, games of losing and finding.

Communicating with the Caregiver

The biggest single thing parents can do to make it go smoothly is to communicate often with the caregiver. Even at a day-care center there should always be one person with whom you can talk easily and comfortably about your child's day, someone who will warn you that you might be in for a rough night because the toddler's been irritable and pulling at his ear all afternoon.

"I spend a half hour a day chatting with the sitter," one mother told us. "We discuss our own personal lives as well as what's happened that day or that night with my daughter. Like this week my daughter learned to do puzzles and the sitter let Kathy do them there, too. The sitter knows Kathy loves to put on her own shoes after her nap even if it takes forever."

Many times, particularly at bustling day-care centers, such communication is hard to achieve. With many parents coming and going at five-thirty or six and a baby overjoyed to see you and anxious to go home, it's not possible to have any kind of talk. Early mornings may not be much better. "With one sitter, I had to leave my son at her doorstep at seven a.m. in order to get to work on time," one mother said. "The sitter was still in her robe and just coming to. At night the after-school kids she sat for were there. You've got to talk to the sitter, but sometimes they don't have time."

One mother's solution was to take her sitter out to lunch on Saturday once in a while. Another, who had a flexible work schedule, made a point of dropping in on the sitter occasionally during the children's naptime. Ask your sitter when she'd prefer to talk with you or what she thinks can be done. Even if it means dropping off your child before the others get there, it's worth it.

Another parent who was particularly pleased with the woman who had been caring for her 3-year-old for two years said she knew things would go well almost from the start: "The day-care mother asked me to write her a letter at the beginning telling her everything I could think of about my son. It was a pleasure to write and I know she found out things that it would have taken her weeks to learn any other way."

It's a good idea to have your child's caregiver visit you at your home at least once when your child is there, too. Many good nursery schools encourage such visits as a way to encourage the child to talk to people at the school about his house, his pets, his room, his toys.

"When we had our sitter and her own children come to Peter's third birthday party, he was thrilled."
                    Mother of one / Kansas City, Mo.

If you have a good rapport with the caregiver, you'll be better able to cope with the very normal jealousy that occurs when your child, particularly your baby, shows affection for her. If things are going properly, the child *will* feel warmly toward the person you choose to care for him during the day, but that doesn't mean you'll be supplanted in your child's heart. One study showed that when children were hurt physically or emotionally and both mother and caregiver were in the room, the children invariably turned to the mother for comfort. Babies, like anyone else, recognize primary emotional commitment.

"I know I shouldn't mind it, but when I make a lot of arrangements so that I can take a vacation with the family, I don't like it very much when the children say they can't wait to get back to see if the sitter's puppies have their eyes open yet." *Mother of three / Atlanta, Ga.*

More likely you will feel like the mother who told us, "I can't accept even constructive criticism of my child from my relatives, my friends, and barely even from his father. But the few times our sitter mentioned some problems, I listened with all my heart." You may also, like us, agree with the psychiatrists who say people with rich personalities have "internalized others"—grandparents, friends, teachers, sitters—who have been very interested in them. One Los Angeles child psychiatrist asked, "Do you know any kids who are spoiled because they have too many real positive emotional responses from people?"

Arranging Your Time

Besides taking pains to connect the world of home and daycare, it is very important for working parents of very young children to arrange their time carefully.

One divorced father with custody of two children under 5 said his days started off horribly until he realized the children didn't have to eat breakfast at home. Now the children eat at the sitter's and the household is much better off. An unorthodox illustration of standing back and trying to figure out how to make the day easier came from a mother of two who returned to her job as an elementary school teacher when her younger son was 2. The only way she could make it to school on time, she said, was to let the children put on clean clothes after their baths at night and then sleep in them. "Now all we have to do in the morning is slip on some socks and shoes, eat, grab toys and we're off."

When you're reunited at night, see that the baby gets attention, not the pile of dirty laundry or the couple waiting to hear whether you'll go to their party Saturday night. Pediatrician T. Berry Brazleton has written several moving accounts of the early evening hours in homes of children with working parents. In one case we feel sympathy for a child who seems in the way of two career-oriented adults. In another, the children seem to get *more* than their share of attention from a tired single mother. Somewhere, common sense tells us, there's a middle ground—but solid attention should be paid to the child first.

Where it all hits the fan is when either the sitter or your child gets sick. Few of us have the kind of work situation where there is any understanding of the agony we face when our child, on the one hand, is miserable and wants to be in bed and the boss, on the other, wants a report out. All we can say of help in this area is that you must picture yourself in this situation before it happens. Compile a list of agencies that have sitters who will work for sick children. Perhaps you're fortunate enough to live in a town like the one in Northern California that has an agency staffed by women with nursing experience who handle nothing but the sick children of working parents.

If the child's sickness involves a trip to the doctor, you or the father will have to take time off from work. "It helps us to allow for this when figuring out vacation time for the year," one mother said. "We take less than the maximum allowed for our 'official' vacation so that we can have several vacation days left to take when we *need* to, with a clear conscience." Another help, particularly if you have a young baby, is to choose a pediatrician who has regular Saturday office hours. Just to get the child's shots and regular check-ups involves several trips to the doctor the first year alone.

"I'm always trying to figure out how to cut corners so we can enjoy more time together. Like we were always running out of milk until I learned that even in this big city you can still have milk delivered. Between that and hiring a cleaning service to come in twice a year and *attack*, I'm getting squared away."   *Mother of two / Brooklyn, N.Y.*

Instead of blaming yourself, your spouse, or your child when snags develop, it helps to bear in mind what Berkeley sociologist Arlie Hochschild has pointed out. You're trying to fit three jobs to two people: his, hers, and the equally demanding job of raising children and running a household. Work is still set up for the traditional man with the tradition-al wife who stays home, Hochschild says, not for the man with a working wife and young children, and certainly not with the wife and children in mind. "So in assimilating into this male work culture," she says, "women are trying to crunch and fit and squeeze themselves into roles that weren't designed for their needs."

SOME OTHER ALTERNATIVES

If the crunching and squeezing is too much for your child or your family and you have a choice, perhaps the best of all possible worlds for child and mother is one in which she works part-time. Certainly it's far easier to find good care for part of a day or part of the week than it is for a normal forty-hour work week. So even though the pay may not be too generous, it's worth thinking about this possibility and checking out the part-time job situation in your community.

There are other options; one is flextime, which allows some workers flexibility in scheduling their thirty-five or forty hours a week. Also, there are go-getters out there drumming up work through things like job sharing. One woman who has been sharing a receptionist's job with a friend at a company in Palo Alto, California, told a reporter, "I have a little girl, so I was interested in a job that would allow me to be a mother at the same time. It works out famously. You're here for four hours and it doesn't get drawn out." Teachers in many areas have been active in trying to convince school boards to allow them to share one teaching position.

One of the critical issues for women today is balancing career and family. We have to help each other through this unique period of history, says Barbara Wilson, director of career services at Wellesley. She criticizes the "queen bee" syndrome in which women executives at the top identify with male management models and are unsympathetic to the problems of working women. Women in positions of authority should be willing to consider flexibility of scheduling, she says. Among her own thirteen employees are some who work three days a week and a night at home, some who work four days a week, others who work from seven a.m. to three-thirty p.m.

We think much of the world needs to change its way of thinking about what is work and what is a good life for men and women *and* children. In the meantime, maybe a half a career at least for a few years, is the best bet for many of us.

"You don't know what desperation is until your husband is laid off, the mortgage needs to be paid, and you've got to look for a job and a babysitter at the same time. Finding work is simple compared to finding decent care for the kids."
Mother of two / South Bend, Ind.

For women who must work full time, like the one quoted above, the child-care alternatives available in the United States are, in our opinion, inadequate. Too often they're unreliable, too expensive for the average family, or may even endanger a child's mental or physical health. It seems to us that there should be some kind of day care—subsidized by federal and/or state government, industry, or private institutions or groups—that would make it possible for mothers who need to work to do so and still be assured of at least a *minimum* standard of care for their children. In fact, the United States is the only industrialized nation in the world without a national day-care program.

We favor increased government funding for day-care facilities and we support legislators who are trying to get such funding or who are working in other ways to alleviate the problem of inadequate day care. But government can't and shouldn't do it all. We salute parents who work to set up neighborhood cooperative-care centers and we would encourage any move that made family day care in private homes more attractive to the women who do this work. The biggest boost of all may come, inch by inch, as business and industry recognize the need for flexibility in working hours.

It is up to parents to work to bring about these changes —our children cannot plead for good day care for themselves. Just as we have had to push for more control in childbirth, for women's rights in general, and even for healthier baby food, we are going to have to push for decent day care for all of our children who need it. No one else is going to do it for us.

You may be fortunate and find a splendid caregiver quickly. More likely, as you grow into being a mother and the bonding takes place, you will agonize over the choice of a substitute mother. Eventually you may quit your job, work part-time, run a family-day-care home yourself, or even go on welfare if you must work but can't afford to pay for good care during the crucial early years.

It isn't forever, after all, that a child needs so much attention. A friend who went back to work full-time when her son was 5 confided one day that she knew her son was strong inside, that he could cope if anything happened to her. At the time our own child was only 2 and still very dependent. We thought our friend was crazy. How could a 5-year-old be that confident? Now we know. If a child gets the security of good parenting in the first few years, whether from a biological parent or a substitute, he'll usually be raring to go at 4 or 5—to nursery school, to day care, to life away, for part of the day at least, from his primary caregivers.

"I went to work part-time when one child was 1 and the other was 4, and was lucky enough to find a sitter who had two kids of her own the same ages as mine. I felt great about working. It gave me a lot of self-confidence and positive feelings about myself. My husband has a job that lets him be with the kids during some afternoons so I never felt guilty about working. I'd do the same again, but I'd still advise a new mother to stay home as long as she was happy and didn't feel hopelessly trapped. For some women, however, working is a blessing for all involved: wife, husband, and kids."   *Mother of two / Burlington, Vt.*

"If I had it to do over again, I probably wouldn't be a full-time homemaker and mother during those early years. I'd work part-time or go to school part-time. In no way do I feel now, with my children at ages 16 and 13, that they would have suffered if I'd done that. Working mothers, part-time at least, feel less trapped and seem to enjoy the time at home so much more—and the children take so much less for granted. Also, another big reason is that children with part-time working mothers tend to be much less dependent, a great asset later, in the teen years. They make better decisions."   *Mother of two / Charleston, W. Va.*

17

Nursery Schools

Although we know there are plenty of pros and cons to any given aspect of child care, a good nursery or preschool can be a boon to both children and parents. Thus, we are writing this chapter from the pro-nursery-school position. If you have decided against nursery school, this chapter may help to change your mind or help you to understand why many other parents value it. If you have decided for nursery school, the information given here should enable you not only to choose a good school for your child, but also to help her to have a valuable learning experience.

WHY SEND YOUR CHILD TO NURSERY SCHOOL?

There are many reasons to enroll your son or daughter in nursery school. A child around the age of 3 needs to spend time with other children. She's usually ready for some independence and for socializing on her own without Mom's continual presence. She needs to get to know that she can trust adults other than her own relatives, that she can learn from them and ask them for help. Also, no matter how many toys and materials your child has, there is bound to be more expensive and creative equipment in the average nursery school than there is at home. Finally, no matter how much you enjoy teaching your child, you can both use a break. Remember, even if you put your child in school for two hours and forty-five minutes (the usual school day) for two days a week, she'll still spend over *ten* waking hours at home with you on those days. The time you spend away from your child will be as good for you as it is for her.

"Mike wasn't quite 3 when I enrolled him in nursery school. I did it as much for me as for him. I had just had another baby and Mike was difficult to handle—he was too rough with the baby, too rough with his friends, just a bundle of energy. So I enrolled him in a nursery school—to give me a break and, I hoped, so that he'd learn to get along with others. He did fine in school, and after Christmas he went through a personality change; he went back to school a calmer boy. I always thought of him as a high-spirited horse whom I wanted to train but not take away his spirit."

Mother of two / Philadelphia, Pa.

WHEN SHOULD YOU SEND YOUR CHILD TO SCHOOL?

The average age for starting nursery school is between 2½ and 3, but your child may be ready before 2½ or she may not be ready at 3. There are several factors other than age to consider in deciding when to send her.

Is your child fairly strong and healthy? She'll be exposed to many new viruses when she starts school and she's likely to bring them home—a consideration if you have younger children.

Is she toilet trained? Some schools accept children in diapers, and a few even offer programs of toilet training, although, of course, you have to be willing to go along with their methods. This might be all right—but the school has your child only a few hours a week, and you have to deal with the problem the rest of the time. Most schools, however, ask that children be trained, or close to it.

Is your child ready to let you leave her in nursery school? Some children are totally bereft if their mothers leave them; it's as if their mothers had died. But if your child has spent some daytime hours away from you, at the home of either a friend or a babysitter, then she's probably already learned that Mommy goes away and Mommy comes back. She may not be overjoyed, at the start, but she should be able to accept your absence during nursery-school hours. If, however, you have never left her, she may become so terrified at being left at the school that her time there may be totally wasted.

Are *you* ready to have your child go to nursery school? Every mother feels a little sad when she leaves her child at the schoolroom door for the first time. Her baby is growing so fast, and she sometimes wishes she could slow her down, just a little. This is a natural feeling. But some mothers are *over*anxious about leaving their children. It's easy to recognize a "clingy mother" symptom in someone else, but extremely difficult to recognize it in oneself. If you feel overly upset when you're separated from your child, it might be a good idea to talk over your fears with a doctor or counselor before sending her to nursery school.

Are you finding it increasingly difficult to keep your child busy and happy with the resources at home? In nursery school she'll make new friends, and may want to bring these friends home to enrich her life there. And in nursery school she'll use new materials and learn new ways of playing with old materials. Naturally, she'll want to continue this play at home, so all the old resources will have new possibilities.

"Two of my children attended an excellent university-sponsored nursery school at a teacher-training center, and it was a marvelous experience for both of them. A photographer took pictures of Melissa, at 4, ecstatically painting with a large brush at an easel. The pictures were arresting, and were later displayed at a college photography exhibit. Today Melissa's an art major at that college—still painting ecstatically."
Mother of four / Rutgers, N.J.

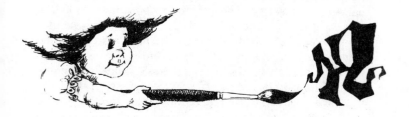

HOW TO CHOOSE A NURSERY SCHOOL

"For several years before I sent my son to school, I heard other mothers talking about schools. I listened carefully all that time, and the school I finally chose was the only one they had never criticized. It turned out that it also cost the least, so I really lucked out."

Mother of three / New Orleans, La.

If you live in a small town with one or two nursery schools, your decision will be easy. If you live in a big city, however, you may have to do some research. In the South Bay area of Los Angeles, for example, the yellow pages list more than ninety entries under the heading "Nursery Schools," and this listing doesn't include all the recreation programs, adult-school programs, and church programs offered in the area. Since most of you don't have time to visit every possible school in a metropolitan area, you'll have to narrow the field before you begin.

Other Mothers. Probably your best resource is other mothers. In fact, some mothers told us they had picked schools they hadn't even visited, based only on the recommendations of friends and neighbors. Talk to every mother you know. Button-hole mothers in the market. Check with your pediatrician, with kindergarten teachers, with the children's librarian. Fairly soon you'll begin to hear the same schools mentioned over and over. Then visit the most frequently recommended places.

The Telephone. The telephone can also be used to investigate schools and to narrow the field. For a handy list of questions to ask about nursery school, see the headings on pages 426-433 of this chapter. Then check the yellow pages and start calling. Stop calling when you find two or three schools that seem to meet your needs, and try to visit at least these schools. If this isn't possible, ask for the names of one or two parents at each school and call them to ask if they and their children are happy with the school.

It's important to observe the schools yourself, of course, but it's just as important to talk to the parents of children who have attended those you're most interested in. A lot depends on specific teachers, and if you have to make a choice between two teachers who both seem good, other mothers can undoubtedly help you decide which one is best for your child.

Location. Many mothers choose schools primarily because they're in their neighborhood. So—especially if you're sending your child to school to learn to socialize and make friends with other children—you may want to check out nearby schools so that your child's classmates will live close enough for afternoon visits and birthday parties. Visit schools closest to home, to see if one might be appropriate for your child.

"I chose a school close by because I was anxious for my kids to get to know children from the neighborhood, and it paid off. They made lasting friends in nursery school. Then when they entered kindergarten they were totally relaxed, because they had some friends to go with."

Mother of three / Cambridge, Mass.

Your Child's Needs

"I visited three schools before choosing one for my 3-year-old daughter. The first thing I did at each school was try and find a student who most resembled my daughter, and then I observed the school day through the eyes of this child. When I enrolled my daughter in school, I was amazed to discover how similar she was to my 'model child.' "

Mother of one / Boulder, Colo.

The most important person in your school decision is your child. Therefore, before you look at schools, give some thought to him. Is he boisterous and active or quiet and shy? Does he have lots of friends and enjoy being with a large group, or does he prefer playing with small groups of children? Has he shown early abilities in music, ball playing, block building, or art? Are there signs of any disability, either physical, emotional, or social? In the area of discipline, does he respond best to a tight or loose rein? Is he happiest in a structured environment with set mealtimes, bedtimes, and rules, or does he prefer flexible schedules and rules?

If your child has any special needs, either positive or negative, there's probably a school that will suit him. The ideal school for your child is one that will encourage him to develop his strengths and at the same time overcome his weaknesses. So, in choosing a school, continually keep your child in mind.

One California mother chose a school that met outside, in a local park, for her physically active son. "He could run, play with balls, climb, and do all of the things he enjoyed the most," she said. Another mother, suspecting that her daughter might be musically gifted, looked for a school with a great deal of music in its curriculum. Still another woman feared that her volatile daughter might be hyperactive. "I enrolled her in a small, structured, but low-key nursery school, where she could learn some inner controls," this mother said. "My fears of hyperactivity were unfounded, and my daughter thrived in this calm atmosphere."

Type of School

Another way to narrow the range is to decide ahead of time what type of school would best suit you and your child. For a brief rundown on types of schools, see the accompanying chart. Consider your child, your financial situation, and your own philosophy before determining a type of school for your child. For example, if you're new in town and like working with children, a cooperative school might be best for both you and your child, since both of you will meet new people. If finances are a problem, look into recreation programs, co-ops, college or adult-school programs, or church schools. If you'd like your child to have a head start with reading and other more academic subjects, then check out Montessori schools.

Although we can't go into detail about every kind of nursery school, we do want to discuss at some length two types: first, the Montessori schools, because they are so prevalent and because Maria Montessori's ideas have influenced so many school activities in both preschools and grade schools; second, cooperative schools, because Barbara Sills teaches in a parent-participation program similar to many cooperative nursery schools and we feel a look at how her school is run will be interesting as an example of this kind of school.

Montessori Preschools

"In the other preschools I visited, I came away marveling at the patience and cleverness of the teachers. In the Montessori schools, I came away marveling at the children, at their diligence and concentration."

Mother of two / Cleveland, Ohio

Maria Montessori was an Italian physician and educator who worked with children in the slums of Rome in the early 1900s. She was the first person to dramatize the importance of the early years in a child's life, and also the first to see the significance of early education.

To the average adult who knows nothing about how a child learns, Montessori's ideas make astonishingly good sense. Her basic concepts were that teachers should pay attention to the *children*, not the other way around, and that children should learn at their own pace. She also believed that children should learn in a controlled environment using the imaginative teaching materials that are the heart of her program.

Many nursery schools are influenced by Montessori's ideas and many of them use some of her materials, but most of them don't use them in the same way as they are used in Montessori schools. Montessori schools *are* different. In many areas of the country Montessori preschools are the only ones that offer a structured learning environment rather than an unstructured play atmosphere. Socialization is just part of daily life in a Montessori classroom; it comes about naturally, without any encouragement from the teacher.

In a Montessori school, children must attend five mornings a week, even though they begin when they are only 2½ or 3. The children may choose pretty much what they want to do and when they want to do it from among any of the projects—which are known as *work*—that have been demonstrated to them by the teacher. They take any equipment needed from its place on a low shelf, use it, and then return it. The work involves five areas:

● Practical life. Scrubbing floors (the children draw circles on the floor with soap and then scrub inside the circle); washing windows, complete with professional squeegees;

NURSERY SCHOOLS

Type of School (Relative Cost)	Possible Advantages	Possible Disadvantages
Church affiliated (Moderate)	— Tend to have small enrollment, hence good teacher-pupil ratio. — May have more outdoor play space than private schools, which must pay high taxes. — Offer religious alternative to secular public schools. Atmosphere may be especially caring.	— Teachers may not have degrees. — Parents may have to get involved in fund raising. — Religion taught may not coincide with your beliefs.
Commercial plus day care* (Expensive)	— Day-care option (allows parents to work without changing child's pre-school.) — Whole-day option. — Open all year. — Some have kindergarten programs of good quality and after-school care for older children.	— Children of working parents predominate; hence there may be more children who come when ill. — Teachers may work full day and be tired. — Little chance to meet other parents. — May have less outdoor play space than other schools.
Cooperative— parent participation* (Low to moderate)	— Parents can meet other parents, learn about child-rearing skills, see own child in perspective. — Fathers are more likely to get involved, if only in weekend work sessions.	— Conflicts are possible with other mothers who are reprimanding your child. — Child may be self-conscious when you are there.

Type (Cost)		
	— Children get to know many different adults. — Parents are encouraged to understand and even control philosophy of school.	— May be less structured than other schools. — Parents must participate.
Montessori (AMI) (Expensive)	— Emphasis on learning process that gives child the idea that school is earnest business. — Good ones follow Montessori philosophy, not individual teacher's leanings. — Atmosphere of quiet and order may carry over to the home. — Academic help useful to slow learners.	— Socialization and imagination may not be encouraged as much as at other schools. — May follow public-school holidays (Working parents must make other arrangements for care). — May be too many hours and/or days a week for some children.
Private (Moderate to expensive)	— May have distinctive educational philosophy reflecting views of owner. — May have impressive physical plant and equipment.	— Expense — Academic-oriented schools may overemphasize testing. — Not much socioeconomic mix.
Public supported (Low)	— Broad socioeconomic mix. — Inexpensive—in fact, some are free. — Location—most are in immediate neighborhood.	— Classes may be large. — Entrance requirements may be very specific, requiring residence in a certain neighborhood or parental income under a certain amount.

* Discounts available for more than one child in family.

cutting carrots, piercing them with toothpicks, and then serving them to other children; grooming themselves or friends; etc.

• Sensorial exercises. Using a variety of materials, the children isolate one defining quality, such as odor, weight, shape, or texture. For example, with eyes closed the children examine objects they take from a paper bag and try to figure out what the objects are.

• Language and reading. Letters of the alphabet are cut out of sandpaper and glued to cards. As the children learn the phonetic sounds, they see the shapes and feel them with their fingers. They build their own words on a mat with the cut-out letters. They begin reading only when they are ready and proceed at their own pace.

• Math. The concept of quantity and symbols for quantity—the numbers 1 to 10—are introduced by a series of rods that the children can count and compare. They match sets of symbol cards with the rods.

• Children are encouraged to learn about the world around them. The concept of "island," for example, may be taught through the use of clay forms around which water is poured.

Usually all Montessori teachers are college graduates, with degrees in elementary or preschool education, but there are two kinds of schools. At AMI schools teachers are graduates of a rather expensive course given under the auspices of the Association Montessori Internationale. This nine-month course includes taking classes and observing at Montessori schools. The AMI affiliation is reviewed yearly. Teachers at AMS schools, on the other hand, have been trained in an American Montessori school only. The students spend three months in school and then intern, while paid, at American Montessori schools.

For books on Montessori schools, see the Learning and Enrichment section of the Resource List.

"My son spent a year in a Montessori school, but it just wasn't for him. He's creative, outgoing, and loves to socialize, and there was too little emphasis on these characteristics in his school. Also, he's extremely emotional, but was given no help in trying to express his negative or positive feelings."

Mother of two / Wilmington, Del.

"During my daughter's first month in a Montessori school, she polished brass endlessly. It was something she felt comfortable doing while she sized up the situation. When first presented with the math material she did the first exercise over and over for weeks. Then she took off like gangbusters and is now doing a lesson a day. For a long time she completely ignored the beginning reading materials, but now she's beginning to show an interest in it.

"The great thing about Montessori is that if kids are interested in academics the most fascinating material is there to teach them. The teaching is totally individual. There is no competition or comparison. Four children will sit together socializing for all they're worth, but each is doing something different. Some people think that academics are stressed in a Montessori school. From my experience, the only thing that's in any way stressed is independence. And that's been great for both of my children."

Mother of two / Palos Verdes, Calif.

Barbara's Cooperative Preschool

The South Bay Adult School has a thriving parent-education department, with classes for parents and for children from birth through the teenage years; Barbara's program is specifically for parents and prekindergarten children. The children may attend school up to five mornings a week, and each parent works in the classroom one morning a week, as well as attending other regularly scheduled planning meetings and lectures. The cost of this tax-supported program, in cash, is relatively low. The cost in time is high, however, since each parent puts in an average of eight hours a week in school.

In this sense, the program is similar to many cooperatives, since parents actively participate in the planning and implementation of each day's activities. But it is also a little different. In many co-ops the parents actually own the school, hiring and firing teachers and establishing policy that the teachers carry out. Barbara, on the other hand, works for the local school district. Since it is an adult school, her main job is to assist parents with the jobs and problems of being parents and to teach them how to work with the students. The teacher establishes policy and then the parents carry it out in the classroom. Her secondary role is to work with the children.

The curriculum for parents is flexible and depends on the needs and desires of the parents in the class. Both major issues (such as how to be a mother without losing one's identity) and minor problems (such as how to get children ready for school without any hassles) are discussed.

The children's curriculum is similar to the typical nursery-school curriculum described in this chapter. What's special about the program, and about many other parent-participation schools, is that each parent brings his or her own talents and interests to the classroom. This enriches everyone—parents, children, and teachers.

One year everyone learned a little Spanish from a mother from Mexico. Another year, inspired by a class member who was a musician, they studied classical music. One mother commented, "I'm amazed! Donny actually turns to the classical music station and listens to Beethoven and Bach. And he can identify all the instruments in an orchestra by both sight and sound."

Another year, when they were learning about community workers, a father who was a doctor visited class with his bag. The children got to listen to one another's heartbeats, take blood pressures, and examine the syringes and needles used for shots—and in the process they overcame many of their fears about going to the doctor.

That year, like each year, there were many other such examples of parental involvement and learning about real-life situations, and by the end of the year every member of each child's family had come to school. They had Fathers' Days, Grandparents' Days, Brothers' and Sisters' Days, and even Pet Days on different Saturdays. Family members painted, played with clay, used building blocks, or did whatever activity the children had planned.

A cooperative provides an extended family for many parents and children who do not have relatives living nearby. In her year-end evaluation one mother said, "This class is like the one-room schoolhouse of years gone by. We're really a family. Like many families, we've had our squabbles, and we've fought—but we've also hugged and made up, and emerged closer for the skirmishes."

"The South Bay Adult School preschool class helped me more than anything else during these past few years. I was tied down in the house with two young children and had little opportunity to meet other mothers or observe other children. In this class I talked with other mothers and found that many of my problems were not unique. I also learned so much from speakers, from discussions, from working with other children. It all helped me understand my own children."
Mother of two / Manhattan Beach, Calif.

"A co-op experience seemed perfect for us, since I longed to be part of my daughter's early schooling. We found a school where the atmosphere was cluttered but supportive, a free-choice environment that pretty much left the child alone. My daughter gave indications of perception difficulties, and I now feel that those two years were not well spent because she often seemed confused. She chose to run, to ride bikes—to do the things she could do best—but she never chose, or was encouraged to choose, any of the tasks that might have helped her to overcome her problems.
"I chose that school because it basically met *my* needs. If I'd given more thought to my daughter's needs, I would have chosen a different school, one with a more structured environment where her difficulties could have been explored."
Mother of one / Jackson, Miss.

VISITING A SCHOOL

"My oldest daughter was 3 when she started school," one mother told us. "I visited the school before she started and talked with the director, but because I knew nothing about nursery schools, I didn't know what to look for, what questions to ask. I checked on cleanliness and personal hygiene, but didn't look for more important qualities, like atmosphere, curriculum, or teacher qualifications."

If at all possible, try to visit a school before you enroll your child and, ideally, to spend a full morning at any school you're seriously considering so you can get a realistic picture of what your child will be experiencing. Visit alone if you're considering a school for the next year; take your child if you're planning immediate enrollment. In either case, call ahead to alert the school to your visit and ask if a teacher or the director can be available to talk to you. If you wish, you can use the following questions as guidelines for what to ask—either in person or on the phone if you screen the schools by calling a number of them in advance.

Are the children involved?

Nursery school should be a joyful place, so look for happy children. If you look for total joy, however, you may be forever disappointed. One child may be frowning with concentration as he paints, trying to express his thoughts on paper; another's whole body may be tense with effort as he learns to pump himself on a swing; and still another may be crying with frustration if a block tower she's trying to construct has just tumbled to the floor.

Look for children who are engrossed in the work or play of the school day, and look for a warm, accepting atmosphere where the children can comfortably express all their feelings, whether of happiness, sadness, or frustration.

Also look for children who are involved with each other. Two children may be sitting together sharing a picture book or a large group of children may be chattering away as they dig in the sand or play in a doll corner. On the other hand, several children may be working alone, either because they're not quite ready to make friends or because they just wanted to be alone. And sometimes some children may just be sitting, gazing into space, in their own dream world. At some time during the day you may see a child hit, kick, grab, or even bite another, but all these things, even the fighting, are signs that children are interacting and learning to deal with one another in a group situation.

"One thing about nursery schools—cliques are formed when kids are together a lot, and a child who goes only two days a week will be left out if the rest of the group goes five days.

So if possible, make sure your child is in a program the same number of days as all the other children in the class."

Mother of two / Bayshore, N.Y.

Is the teacher effective?

Nursery-school teachers come in all shapes, ages, colors, and genders. Some have master's degrees in education, others have only a high school diploma. The best teachers have only one quality in common: they love children. They enjoy working with kids, talking with kids, disciplining kids, teaching kids. They respect each child in their classes and feel that even though a child may be only 3, he is already both extremely valuable and vulnerable.

There is no rigid set of rules by which you can tell if a teacher loves children. In this area you have to go by the "feel" of things. There are, however, some tangible qualities to look for that will demonstrate effective teaching. Watch the teacher as she talks with and instructs both individuals and groups. An effective teacher often assumes a squatting position or sits on the floor so that she's on the child's level. Listen to her voice. An effective teacher controls it like a musical instrument; she'll speak quietly at times, if the child or situation needs quiet, or she may raise her voice, and even occasionally yell, if the need arises. Observe her sense of timing. An effective teacher has special insight, and she can often step in and avert disaster before it starts by stopping an activity and switching to something else if she senses that the children are about to get out of hand. She will stop reading a story or singing a song if she senses that the children aren't with her.

An effective teacher has learned that each child is different. She may firmly tell one child, "Jimmy, you must paint a picture before you play with blocks," because she knows that Jimmy needs firmness. She may touch and pat another child, gently leading her to the easels. She may even completely ignore a child whom she knows needs to watch a while before getting involved in an activity.

Watch for a teacher who knows how to listen. An effective teacher knows that children quickly tire of "teacher talk" and encourages a great deal of "kid talk." Look for a teacher who accepts a child's right to his own feelings, be they negative or positive. An effective teacher allows a child to express anger or hurt verbally by saying to her something like "It sure does hurt when you fall down. Go ahead and cry. Now tell me how much it still hurts!"

And, finally, give a seemingly ineffective teacher the benefit of a doubt. All teachers are human, and their problems and moods occasionally cause them to operate at a less than optimum level. If you think this might be the case, ask something like, "Was this a rough day for you?" An effective teacher will probably reply, "It sure was. It always happens! When a visitor comes and you want to do your best, you fall flat on your face."

Is the curriculum varied and are the materials appropriate for young children?

Most nursery schools provide activities that help the children progress in the following areas:

Gross Motor Skills. Most nursery schools use balls, ropes, wheel toys, swings, monkey bars, tumbling mats, and balance beams to get a child moving and developing his body.

Fine Motor Skills. Beads, pegboards, scissors, crayons, pencils, hammers and nails, screwdrivers, nut and bolts, and things to take apart are commonly available to help children use the muscles of their hands.

Art. Lots of paint, clay, crayons, markers, scissors, paper, paste, and collage materials should be available to encourage each child to do his own thing.

Science. There may be animals, plants, magnifying glasses and magnets, mud and sand, sensory materials to touch, taste, and listen to, and a variety of other materials to allow children to explore and discover how people, animals, plants, and mechanical things work.

Math. Felt, sandpaper, or magnetic numbers and lots of objects to count are the only materials needed to help a child learn that "2" is 2, "4" is 4, and perhaps that $2 + 2 = 4$.

Reading Readiness. Books are the mainstay of a reading-readiness program, but cut-out letters of the alphabet, games like Lotto or Bingo, sorting and classifying materials such as buttons and beans, and many other homemade or purchased games may also be available as resources to help a child in this area.

Language. Having children and adults to talk with is the prime prerequisite in this area, although puppets, tape recorders, and record players may also be available.

Literature. A variety of good books—some to be read by a teacher, some to be looked at by the children—is a must.

Music. A teacher who likes to sing is the most important part of a good music program. A phonograph, records, tape recorder, autoharp, guitar, piano, and rhythm instruments will make good music even better.

Drama and dance. A phonograph and records or a tape recorder can provide the music—or someone playing the piano or guitar. Does the teacher suggest that the children move like elephants or snails—or do whatever the beat inspires them to do? If so, this encourages creative dance and gives the children an opportunity to pretend. Occasionally they may make up plays about familiar stories, like "Little Red Ridinghood," or everyday events in their lives, such as getting dressed in the morning. These seemingly mundane subjects make for superb preschool drama.

Nutrition. Vegetables, fruit, cheese, milk, and a variety of other nutritious foods are offered at many schools to teach children to enjoy—and even prefer—good food. Other schools have stoves, electric frying pans, toaster ovens, and cooking utensils to help children learn how to prepare foods and simple meals.

Socialization. All of the above activities encourage socialization. Dolls, dress-up clothes, a corner that is a store one day, a fire station the next, blocks, and Legos are just a few of the many other materials that encourage one child to work or play with another child.

Some of the preceding materials and activities may be missing from some very good nursery schools, and we may have left out other activities that good nursery schools offer. For example, we purposely left reading out of the above discussion, but in Chapter 13, "Teach Your Child Through Work Play," we do cover reading and the young child. If

you choose a school that offers reading, make *certain* that
your child is ready for it. Also be sure that it's an individual
reading program, such as is found in Montessori schools, and
that it's offered only for children who are either already
reading or are definitely ready to read.

How are the day's activities structured?

Most schools follow a fairly typical schedule of alternating
quiet times and active times throughout the day. A few
schools, however, allow the children to establish their own
schedule, and there are no formal "times"; each child is free
to rest and be active whenever she chooses. We feel that
most young children thrive in a school with some set struc-
ture, that 3- and 4-year-olds can't always decide for themselves when they need to rest or need to run. But there are
people who feel differently, and only you know your child
well enough to determine which would best suit him.

Are the activities geared to the individual child?

Each child is on her own level of development, with her
own set of interests, abilities, and skills. A good nursery-
school program takes these individual differences into account, providing a variety of materials and activities and
allowing the children to express themselves in their own
unique ways.

Take a look around the room at the displays of paintings or crafts. If each one is different, showing varying skills
and abilities, you can be certain that the school is geared to
the individual child. Observe an activity period. If there are
three or more activities in progress at the same time, it's a
good sign that the children's individual needs are being met.

How does the school handle discipline?

There is a wide range of philosophies on discipline, from
permissive schools where anything goes to schools with authoritarian policies. Most schools, like most parents, fall
somewhere in the middle. What seems to work best with
most children is a few clearly stated and easily understood
rules, with consequences for breaking them that teach the
child, or give him a chance to cool off, without punishing
or ridiculing him.

If you want to know about classroom rules, ask the teacher to explain the school's policy. Or better yet, ask the children. At one school we visited the children eagerly told us the rules: "No running." What happens if they run? "Go back and walk!" "No throwing sand, puppets, chairs, apple juice, stones." And if they throw things? "You get benched for a long, long time." "No hitting, pinching, pushing. No hurting nobody." And if they hurt someone? "You sit on the chair. Then you talk with the teacher. Then you talk with the kid. Then you say sorry." When the teacher or another child is talking the rule is: "Sit on the edge of the rug and be quiet, or it's goodbye, Charlie." And finally, "No dilly-dallying in the potty, 'cause some kid might pee in his pants."

"When he was just 4, I enrolled my son in a permissive non-structured nursery school. Greg is small, and was the youngest in his class. He was often overwhelmed and had to fight to survive among children much more aggressive than he was. He began to withdraw into himself, and at school he clung to the teacher and usually did nothing. I decided to keep him out of kindergarten, and enrolled him in a more structured, less permissive preschool this year. At this school, children are kept so busy and seem so happy that there's little to fight about. My son is now outgoing, self-confident, and friendly, free to get on with learning and enjoying new things."   *Mother of two / Memphis, Tenn.*

How large is the school?

The size of the school may or may not be important to you. Many parents prefer a smaller school, if they have a choice, even if it means not sending their children to the most popular or best-known school in their community. One mother complained of an assembly-line feeling when the children were dropped off and picked up that allowed her no time to get to know and talk to other mothers and their children. Also, you may feel that, because of its size alone, a really large school lacks warmth and intimacy—and this may be important to you.

On the other hand, a bigger school may have more equipment and a wider range of activities, as well as more opportunities—in terms of sheer numbers—for your child to make friends. It may also, although not necessarily, make available students and teachers from a wider diversity of backgrounds than might be possible in a smaller school. This may be important to you, too.

Only you can make these judgments and rate schools from these points of view—and size is something you may want to take into account.

"I've had experience with about five different schools, some fancy and some plain. I liked the small ones that were homey-looking, the ones with pots, pans, spoons, a regular yard, some grass, some dirt, and where ropes were tied to trees for climbing and for swings and there were metal barrels and boxes that could be moved around."

Mother of two / Springfield, Ill.

Some Other Questions to Ask
About School Policy and Procedures

• Does the school offer a mid-morning snack? Are the snacks nutritionally sound?

• What is the cost and what are payment procedures? Will the school refund money if you withdraw your child?

• Is there an extra charge if you want to drop your child off early or pick him up late?

• Does the school offer day care after regular school hours?

• What is school policy on illness?

• How does the school handle emergencies? Does it require the names of two friends who could care for your child in case of an emergency? Does it want you to leave a number where you can be reached if you're not at home? Does the school recommend that you have an emergency-treatment form on file at a local hospital?

• Does the school require proof of immunizations? Does your child need a doctor's permission form?

• Is the school (and/or staff) certified by the state?

• What sort of training and experience has the staff had?

• Is there an established procedure for teacher-parent contact? Are there opportunities for informal visits and chats?

• Will there be chances for parents to get acquainted with each other?

• If you have a special talent (music, art, a foreign language, etc.) could the school use your services, and possibly give you a break on tuition in exchange?

• Is there a fairly even ratio of boys to girls in each class?

• Is there a ratio of one adult to ten or fewer children?

• What is the school's policy on toilet training? How is a child handled if he has an "accident"?

• Does the school encourage children to bring toys or other things from home for "Show and Tell" or "Sharing"?

• What is the school "first-day policy"? Are parents encouraged to stay the first day? If a child is reluctant, are parents permitted to stay for a while on subsequent days?

"My 3-year-old daughter's school has a perfect first-day-of-school policy. There's only one day of school, for about an hour and a half, the first week, when about five parents and five children come to school for a brief orientation. The children have a chance to get to know each other, the teacher, and the school day, and so do the parents. It's such a relaxed and easy way for both children and parents to get acquainted with school that I'm surprised more schools don't try it."
Mother of three / Kansas City, Mo.

PREPARING FOR SCHOOL

"Only once before—when a love affair ended, in fact—have I had the lost feeling I had the day I left my son at nursery school for the first time. He kissed me happily and joined some boys playing with a big fire truck. As I drove off I couldn't think of one thing worth doing by myself. It took me weeks to find my own 'fire truck.'"
Mother of two / Ithaca, N.Y.

Talk about school beforehand. Tell your child that you're proud she's growing so fast and is ready to go to school just like some older child on the block. Don't make any rash promises like "You'll just love this school" (she may hate it at first) or "You'll make *so* many friends" (she may not make any) or "You'll have such fun" (she may have a lot of misery, at least at the beginning) or "Mommy will stay with you until you want her to leave" (she may want you to stay forever).

Be just a little guileful—stress the part of the school day you know she'll like best, and if you know she hates something, like resting or washing hands, conveniently leave that out of your explanation. One mother said, "I felt I should be completely honest with my daughter, so even though I know she hates to take naps I told her she'd have to rest at school. She worried about resting for a full two weeks before school started, and was so apprehensive about it that she didn't enjoy any of the activities preceding this horrible event. Once rest time actually came and quickly passed, she perked up completely and never mentioned it again. I could have spared her that initial worry."

Ideally, you should plan to stay with your child on the first day of school. If school policy forbids this, then exert a little parental pressure, and try to change the policy. Tell your child, "I'll stay with you the first day, if you want me to, so we can share it together." If she asks about the other days, tell her, "Maybe I can stay for a few minutes and help you find something to do," and then add something like, "I'm so happy that you're growing so fast and can go to school by yourself, just like your big friends Brian and Sue."

It would be nice if your child had at least one friend going to the school because even an adult feels more comfortable going to a strange place with a buddy. If you don't know anyone attending the school, however, you might ask for the names of a few children who will be starting when your child does so that you can arrange to get your children together before the start of school.

Buy your child something new to wear or take to school the first day to make it special: a new lunch box, a backpack, a new shirt, a new pair of sneakers. On the subject of clothes, be sure and dress your child in play clothes and sneakers or rubber-soled shoes. The bane of every nursery-school teacher's existence are sandals or boots. They're a nuisance and as much of a safety hazard as an unfenced play yard or an unblocked electrical outlet.

"I still remember the bookbag my mother bought me to take on the first day of school thirty years ago. I don't remember school at all, but I can still remember the feel and the look of the green plaid bag I so importantly slung over my shoulder."   *Mother of four / Hyattsville, Md.*

SCHOOL PROBLEMS

Occasionally, a school isn't right for a child or a child isn't ready for school. There is no one perfect solution if your child is unhappy in school. If you stick it out a while longer it may work out—or it may not.

If your child is unhappy about school, talk with him and try to find out what's happening. One mother we know took her 4-year-old to McDonald's, and when he was happily eating, she brought up the subject of his unhappiness with school. "I don't like that dumb school," he told her. "I hate it! I don't like it when you leave me at the gate, and they lock us up!" His mother knew the gate was latched to keep children off the busy street in front of the school. Since she couldn't do anything about that, she decided to go through the gate and into the classroom with her son for the next few days and stay until he found something to do. That solved the school problem.

If you can't find the reason for your child's unhappiness, talk with her teacher. One little girl started refusing to get ready for school in the morning. This went on for two weeks before her mother talked to the child's teacher, who told her that Amy was happy at school. "We continued to talk," the mother told us, "and together we came up with the problem: the car pool. Amy just didn't feel comfortable going to school with a stranger and so many other children. So I continued taking her myself a while longer."

Some teachers will give you a straightforward opinion and will work with you and your child to come up with a solution. And if the problem can't be solved, they may recommend that you take your child out of school.

Other teachers may not be so helpful, however. A teacher's ego is involved, after all, and she may feel that she has failed if she hasn't made school a happy place for your child. One mother told us, "My daughter was very unhappy with school, but when I talked with her teacher she told me that Sue 'seemed fine' at school, although she was 'clingy' and a bit 'overdependent on adults.'" The teacher said she'd make a special effort to make school a happy place for Sue, but the problems continued. Finally the mother talked with the school director, who told her, "Sue's testing you. If you give in she'll always try to manipulate you." The mother tried it for a few more weeks, but then, she says, she gave in to her "gut-level feeling that Sue was just too unhappy to derive any benefit from school. So I took her out. Three months later I enrolled her in another school, where she had no problems."

If the problem continues, visit the school yourself and try to observe your child without letting him see you, since most children act differently when Mom is in the room. And if you're still uncertain, ask a friend—someone your child doesn't know well—to observe for you and be an impartial witness to what is going on in school. One mother went through all these steps but, she said, "I still didn't know what to do. Danny's behavior changed at home. He followed me around the house, never letting me out of his sight. He cried whenever he was left with a babysitter, something he hadn't done since he was a toddler. I finally asked a friend who was a former nursery-school director to visit the school. She did, and said, 'Take him out. He's so miserable, it's just not worth it.' We did take him out, and it was the right decision. For whatever reasons, he just wasn't ready for that particular school. The following September he entered a different preschool, and he loves it. That's because he's ready and it's the right school."

Once you do decide to take your child out of school, it's probably best to wait a while before enrolling him in another school. When it all works it's certainly worth the money and effort.

One mother said, "We were so fortunate in our nursery-school choice. My daughter went to the same one for three years—from 2½ to 5½. She not only got to know her friends there very well, but also the teachers. Several of the other mothers have become my good friends and we're at the point where my daughter and I actually share a daytime 'social life' together. I think the benefits of sticking with one school if you have a good one are great, particularly for an only child like ours."

"I can't believe it. Since my son started nursery school he's a different child," another mother told us. "He wakes up at six in the morning and asks every ten minutes, 'Is it time for school yet?' He rushes into the classroom and will hardly give me a goodbye kiss or wave. My mama's boy pushes me out the door. I must admit that I feel a little hurt at losing my baby, but I also feel a lot of gladness seeing my boy so happy in his own school world."

At 3 your "baby" is disappearing and a child is rapidly taking his place. A banner event around a child's third birthday may be his entry into nursery school, and when that happens your child learns to function outside the home. The wonder of it—you can actually let go a little. It's wonderful for your child, and it's just as wonderful for you.

18

Mothercare:
Taking Care of You

This chapter is about taking care of you. Not the baby, not the father, but *you*.

We asked the mothers in our survey, "What were those years like for you?"

" . . . too tiring. With children 22 months apart, it was crying, diapers, and inadequate sleep. I enjoyed my children much more after they turned 3."

Mother of two / Troy, N.Y.

"My first reaction to this question was that they were close, loving, relaxed, and uncomplicated. And then, later, I remembered all sorts of negatives: concern about the kids' development (I remember watching Steve walk shakily at a late 15 months and thinking, 'He'll never be able to run'); worry over the noise they made, because we were in an apartment and I hated to bother the neighbors; the tremendous feeling of responsibility during the day and how relieved I felt when my husband came home to share it; feeling tired; the beginning of soap-opera days (something to watch while I fed the baby); trying too hard to keep the apartment neat; and guilt, guilt, guilt if I didn't take them out twice a day every day of the year. I remember trying to take a rest while they were napping—the minute I'd feel like sleeping, one would wake up. I remember thinking that if I had a hundred dollars I'd give it away if I could just take a nap. I can understand the battered-child syndrome, because a couple of times I know I was out of control. (For me, being out of control means yelling like a shrew.) I think we block out some of these times. Somehow the close, loving, relaxed moments are better remembered." *Mother of two / Essex Junction, Vt.*

"Those years were great! A number of factors made it so, primarily luck and planning. Luck: doting grandparents close by, only too happy to take a child for as long as a week; good friends who were having their first child at the same time; enough money so that I didn't have to work and so that we could afford short trips and nights out and sitters. Planning: only two children, and those reasonably spaced; living in areas with lots to do."
Mother of two / Santa Ana, Calif.

During the years when you have a child under 3, the demands on your time and energy are enormous. It's easy to spend most of this time and energy taking care of others' needs all day, every day. What is left is not much of a *you*—not one who can really enrich the lives of the people you love.

Any mother who complains at the end of a day, "I can't get anything done!" is really saying, "I'm not taking very good care of *me*, and nobody else is, either."

From our own experience, we know that it's insidiously easy for new mothers to feel overwhelmed by forces that, in combination, can turn a reasonably happy woman into a wretched witch. Here are the forces, as we see them:

Isolation. There is little effortless camaraderie to be found in most kitchens or most neighborhoods in the daytime anymore. Housewife networks are fast disappearing as more and more women are holding down full-time jobs.

Ego shock. It can be extremely demoralizing, when a woman becomes a mother herself, to realize how little the world values a mother's job. Even if her husband is very supportive, it can also be a blow to do without a paycheck for a week of hard work.

"Houseitis." Day after day, the mother of a young child is faced with two responsibilities that come into direct conflict: the more she encourages her child to explore the world, the more house "work" she has to do. The result can be feelings of futility and depression.

Physical demands. Full awareness of the physical workload of those first three years often comes only when they're over. Lifting babies and equipment, chasing toddlers, and doing extra laundry—it's all hard physical work.

The guilt trap. As the people who have the day-to-day responsibility for their children's growth, mothers can buckle under if they blame themselves for every problem from thumbsucking to temper tantrums or if they expect (if they only try hard enough) to produce a brilliant athlete who can also play the piano and master theoretical physics.

Each of us must find our own ways of coping with these destructive forces that can hit us so fast and so hard when our first child is born. But there's a hidden bonus: if we work to understand these forces and deal with them honestly, our own personal growth may be as great as that of our children during these years. At the very least, we may be able to avoid taking out our frustrations on our families.

ISOLATION

"Kids under 3 are adorable, and it's exciting to watch them enjoying things for the first time and learning things every day. But for me it has also been the most frustrating and unhappiest time of my life because of the lack of freedom and the lack of contact with other adults during the day."

Mother of two / Houston, Tex.

Nearly two-thirds of all the mothers of children under 3 in the United States stay home to raise them. Most are grateful to be able to do so. Nevertheless, it is hard to believe—until you actually find yourself cooped up with a baby day after day—what it is like. There are no ready-made routines, no colleagues, no supervisor. If you want to talk to someone, you have to go out and find her. For shy women, this experience can be devastating.

Philip Slater, former chairman of the department of sociology at Brandeis University and author of *The Pursuit of Loneliness*, points out that many housewives and mothers have to do without "community life," which he says exists "when one can go daily to a given location at a given time and see many of the people one knows." Whenever domesticity seems to have worked well for women, he says, there has been considerable community life and a sharing of household and child-rearing responsibilities with other adults. He calls the idea of expecting the average mother to spend most of her time alone with her children in a small house or apartment "a relatively modern invention, and a rather fiendish one at that." A few men may have jobs that are as tedious as domestic work, he says, but usually they do not have to do their work in isolation.

Although one may disagree with Slater's view of housework, we nevertheless need to be aware of the reality of isolation and how much of it we can take.

It is not only Mother who needs others. By the time a child can sit up, he is very much aware of other children. Watch how fast infants and young children make eye contact with each other in a crowded restaurant.

But what do you do if you have no friends nearby? If your child has no playmates? You go out and find them.

Barbara Sills remembers marching down the block and knocking on doors, trying to find playmates for David. In the process, she met another mother who is still a good friend. Jeanne Henry went to a local park almost daily when Anne was small, partly because she enjoyed the contact with other mothers.

A friend who can make you laugh at the events of your day is worth her weight in gold. Find one.

One experienced mother also advises others to maintain or develop friendships with people who are single or childless: "You need to be able to communicate with that portion of the world that doesn't give a waking thought to children."

If you're shy, remember that mutual need (somebody to talk to!) and a common interest (babies) is the stuff of friendship. Most new mothers are very receptive to other new mothers and their babies, who are potential friends for their children.

Find out which park in your area is the most popular with toddlers and their mothers. Investigate babysitting co-ops, story hour at the library. Join one of the mushrooming numbers of parenting classes offered for parents and toddlers by community adult schools, city parks and recreation departments, or the YWCA.

One determined young mother found a solution that works for some—creating a play group for the children. But it took some doing. "I was in one at first that was terrible," she says. "I answered an ad, and boy, was I sorry! The mothers were not like me at all and that bothered me. Furthermore, all the women stayed and drank coffee and ate cake while the kids hung around their respective mothers' feet. So I quit."

But she persisted in trying to find a good arrangement. "I waited until I got to know some mothers and children in the sitters' club. Then I picked out the ones I liked best and made sure they liked each other too. What we have now is great—a group of four mothers and their children. Only one mother at a time is there, the one whose house it is. We rotate, but switch if the hostess' child is sick. The kids love it." She adds, "We find it doesn't work as well if the mothers stay more than a few minutes when dropping off the children. We visit when picking them up."

When you have made a few friends whose children are the same age as yours—or, better still, who have older children as well—you are only a telephone call away from understanding and support, even when you are marooned with a sick child.

One mother of a 2-year-old boy says emphatically, "I'm always learning—like what to take seriously and what to ease up on. There is no doubt that my friends who are more experienced mothers have helped me more than any doctor, book, or article ever could."

When you have developed a babysitter repertoire, you should make a point of occasionally getting out *without* your child during the day. A former social worker reports that she made herself hire an agency sitter once a month so she could have lunch with her professional colleagues. "I came home feeling wonderful—and I kept up, even if in a small way, with my field," she said. More than one mother told us that she had learned of the "ideal" part-time job for herself simply by maintaining ties with old work friends.

The darkest side of the new mother's isolation is the lurking possibility of child abuse. The crying binge of a colicky baby may seem easy enough to cope with when your husband or a good friend or your own mother is with you to help and give you moral support. But when you're alone, prolonged crying, dawdling, whining, or contrariness can seem like part of a plot aimed at destroying your sanity.

Sociologist Jessie Bernard, in *The Future of Motherhood*, notes that people who see children only at rare intervals or for short periods show little concern about the stress toll on women who must be in the demanding company of small children for long periods of time. What's more, Bernard claims, if the physiological stresses (including noise) to which the mother-child relationship exposes women were measured, monitored, and recorded in a laboratory, they would register as "enormous."

Sources of help are available to parents in stress. Some agencies operate twenty-four-hour-a-day telephone "hot-lines" and can put you in touch with such "helping" services as child care and home visits. Parents Anonymous, one of the oldest, was started by two mothers who had abused their own children. The toll-free number of Parents Anonymous is 800-421-0353 in all states except California, where it is 800-352-0386. Check with your local Department of Social Services or your local library to see if there are branches of organizations like this in your town. Even if *you* don't need help, a friend or a relative might some day.

Waitresses can complain to other waitresses about difficult customers. Teachers bathe their wounds in faculty lounges; office workers do it over lunch. Mothers need and must find other mothers to help them through nervestretching times, to laugh with, to exchange advice with, and to hear their frustrations and anxieties.

EGO SHOCK

"The days are a mixture of many emotions. In one day I can go from a feeling that I'll never get out of the house again to a really high feeling of self-worth. As I look back I can't believe how fast the time has gone, but as I live through these years it goes very slowly."

Mother of two / New Haven, Conn.

While our children are young we invest time, energy, and often wage-earning ability in the launching of new lives. It's a "hobby" that may last longer than we do—one that provides a compelling reason to stay plugged in to the real world and to enjoy people in age groups other than our own. It is exhilarating work. But hard on the ego.

In her article "The Baby as Dictator" in the magazine *New Society*, writer Iris Andrewski pointed out that as a child becomes increasingly skillful in preventing his mother from attending to anything other than himself, her talents in other areas tend to deteriorate, adding to her feeling of inadequacy: "Since it seems to them that they can satisfy the needs of neither their children nor their households, some mothers may become seriously depressed."

British sociologist Ann Oakley, in her book *Women's Work*, says that one dangerous aspect of the normal mother-child situation is that the child can demand—and get—the total attention of the mother. "Annoying behavior produced repeatedly by the child affects the mother alone. Items such as continuous questioning accompanied by total uninterest in answers, continuous leaping on a sitting or lying parent, aggressive and monotonous singing, demands for food which is then not eaten, are present in the behavior of all 'normal' children." The effect on the captive mother, says Oakley, can be disastrous. She concludes that a more common reaction than the urge to batter is "an erosion of self-confidence and a growing feeling of worthlessness."

On top of all this, often we no longer have our old job and the instant identity (and money!) that went with it and are confronted by condescending "just a housewife" reactions from people at parties. Many women who are experiencing the enormous amount of work—and talent—it takes to be "just" a housewife as well as a new mother are frustrated and sometimes enraged by this state of affairs.

What's a new mother to do?

Not much, at first.

It is tough for a mother to find time (and perhaps money) for ego-nurturing projects during the first year or two of her child's life. And she may feel guilty when she does. But if she persists, the rewards may be great.

Dr. Hans Selye, one of the world's foremost authorities on stress, says that each one of us has only a certain amount of what he calls "adaptation energy." If we squander this energy on feelings of guilt and frustration because we are unable to achieve impossible ideals, we wind up miserable and sick. We must, he says, consider our own interests first.

During the first year, especially with a demanding baby, a mother may do well just to keep herself looking good. If she feels and looks ragged, she may come to resent the new baby. In one western state mothers undergoing counseling for child abuse were successfully treated in part by having their hair done.

One very attractive mother of three recalls that when she had her first child twelve years ago there was a long period when she never thought about how she looked. Today, despite her toddler's demands, she says, "I *make* time to exercise and to care for my own clothes. I still wear jeans, but now they're clean and they fit well. I feel better than I did ten years ago." Her friends think she looks better too.

Simply not gaining weight may be a source of justified pride. Being stuck in the house on a rainy day with a crying baby tempts some women to nibble on leftovers and anything else in sight. A friend told us about a technique that worked for her after her first child was born. She kept a surgeon's mask on the sill above the kitchen sink and put it on when preparing food for the baby or the family. All the while, she says, she sang to herself, "Brenda is a skinny lady . . . "

After a year or two at home, we all need to take stock. The most satisfying ego soother of all may be refining a talent or skill in cooking, gardening, painting, music, whatever. Volunteer work does the trick for some women; others need to be working at a paid job, even part-time.

A mother of two girls—one nearly 4, the other almost 2—wrote in the margin of her questionnaire: "It's so important to keep a portion of yourself growing that has nothing to do with your role as wife and mother. Keep a diary. Get involved in a civic or political activity. Belly dance. Anything."

It's also helpful to spend some time daydreaming creatively, thinking about the kind of life you want to be living in ten or twenty years. Analyze the life of an older woman you admire, and consider the steps it might take for you to get there.

Jeanne maintains a file of clippings and personal observations labeled "Women Doing It"—living lives that include (apparently happy) husbands and children as well as skills, paid or not, that give them individual identities. "I use the file as a goad, as a sort of prayer book," she says.

One of the four finalists for California "Teacher of the Year" in 1977 began teaching at 39. She told a reporter: "Women too often fail to realize they will live beyond the time when their children reach 18."

One mother devoted twelve years to rearing two children with, as she puts it, "great style, very seriously." Along the way she took courses, saved money, and recently opened a bookstore. "This is not a dilettante thing," she says. "It's what I want to do the rest of my life."

Historian, researcher, and teacher Fawn Brodie said in a recent *Los Angeles Times* interview, "We have three children, all grown now, and looking back I'd say that in comparison (to teaching) motherhood is easy. Housework is a breeze. Cooking is a pleasant diversion. Putting up a retaining wall is a lark. But teaching is like climbing a mountain. I struggle with teaching and I struggle with writing. . . . Why do I do it? Because I'm unhappy when I'm not doing it. Show me a character whose life arouses my curiosity and my flesh begins crawling with suspense. I simply cannot stop until I piece together all the baffling bits of evidence and solve the puzzle. Then, and only then, the clouds part and I'm surrounded by sunshine."

"First you have to develop yourself and your marriage—find out where your own values are. Then you love your kids and give them room to grow. Give few but *definite* rules. Be sure they are consistent with your own value system. My concept of mothering would never work for a woman who had different values than mine. Our kids are almost grown and we think they are terrific! We never expected them not to be." *Mother of three / Billings, Mont.*

Some of us know what is important to us; other may not have a clear idea. What is important may change from year to year. What matters is that there is something other than children, husband, house to live for. Wonderful though they are, we still need something that is ours alone.

A famous writer once observed that no one is worth living with who is not determined to find life worth living on his or her own.

Not a whit should we apologize, if we do not have to work, for taking courses. Nor should we put up with jibes about dilettantism. Somewhere along the way some women catch fire. They find an interest or skill and practice it. And they are still vibrant women at 60 or 70 or 80.

"I worked full-time for two months, but I hated being away from Karen, so I quit. I just didn't want to miss her pre-school years. I'm working part-time at home. I use the phone a lot. When I go in to pick up or deliver work I take Karen. Sometimes I even take her to meetings (I'm a programmer). But I bet other jobs could be done at home. I wanted the extra money and was determined not to leave Karen with a sitter, even two or three days a week, so I started answering ads in the paper. I picked ads for small companies. Most of them said they didn't want anyone working at home, but after four weeks of trying I got my job, and it's only three miles away." *Mother of one / Washington, D.C.*

Almost any skill or talent can be used to earn money. For many women, the ability to support themselves is crucial to self-esteem. For other women, a second income is a necessity. Apart from economic considerations, however, the mothers we interviewed reported that the forces of ego shock and isolation were minimized when they worked outside the home at something they enjoyed, even if it was just a few hours a week as a volunteer.

You don't have to be a professional woman to find ego satisfaction in work. Dr. Myra Marx Ferree did a study of wives in a working-class community near Boston and found that the employed wives were, on the whole, happier than the housewives. Although the employed women's outside jobs were not glamorous (they were supermarket and department-store clerks, waitresses, factory workers), Ferree found that they felt they were receiving "clear payoffs" in terms of money, social life, and sense of accomplishment. In contrast, the housewives felt their work brought neither monetary rewards nor social stimulation.

"I woke up every morning either very depressed or very angry," one mother told us. "Every day was the same." She had a 3-year-old son and an 11-month-old daughter. Her solution was to go back to work part-time. A former teacher with a master's degree in psychology, she now puts in five mornings a week at a weight- and smoking-control clinic. While she is working, her son goes to nursery school and her daughter stays at a grandmother's. "It doesn't pay much," she says, "but I love it. It is so good to be out part of the day."

In his book *New Wives' Tales*, Dr. Lendon H. Smith talks about his wife's intense involvement in volunteer activities: "It took me years to figure out how much healthier an influence this was on the children and the collective domestic sanity. The children look on her now as a person with rights and feelings, not as a faucet to be turned on. She has kept abreast of the community and has vital, compelling interests that will permit her to feel needed long after our children are no longer dependent. Our children also feel less guilty as they leave home." He adds: "I have the feeling that she will not miss me so much—my mother was left with little but emptiness and self-pity for twenty years after Dad died."

"HOUSEITIS"

Most of us were reared to be domestic; we have gone through what novelist Doris Lessing calls "years of conditioning for itemized responsibility." We take pride in our

homes and enjoy working in them. Before we had children—
particularly if we were married for a long time before they
arrived—we may have become accustomed to living in an
orderly, clean place, one in which things stayed where we
put them.

As this is written we have just survived a week during
which a father on his way to work searched the house for
his glasses for fifteen minutes, only to find them in a wastebasket; a ripe olive was found in an upstairs bedroom; a
hand-operated drill was found behind a living-room curtain.
We are not slobs, but neither are we obsessively neat. We
have learned to tolerate the inevitable disorder that goes
along with a houseful of active people. The secret is to draw
a line between reasonable order and the kind of perfection
that makes you cringe when people use an ashtray or leave
their shoes under the table.

"Do not be afraid to love your kids. Instead of looking at
the cookie all over their faces and on the floor, look at the
love and beauty in their eyes."
Mother of three / Boone, N.C.

You may say that the house and its work is last on your
list of priorities, but watch yourself. When you have thirty
minutes of the baby's naptime left do you read a book or
wash the windows? Call a friend or pay the bills?

Here are the words of one young mother who has, we
think, the right idea: "I find that the best days for me and
my family are when I take out an hour of time *just* for myself—to sit in a tub, stare out the window, or sew. This might
mean letting the laundry sit, leaving the dishes, or having a
lawn knee-deep in leaves. But I finally listened to my husband, who had been telling me for years, 'It will all be waiting when you get around to it.' So I let 'it,' whatever it may
be, wait for me while I enjoy the children and my life."

Mike McGrady, a New York reporter, switched roles
with his wife and stayed home with the children for a year
while she went to work. He wrote a book—*The Kitchen
Sink Papers*—about the experience, after which an enter-
prising reporter interviewed *Mrs.* McGrady on what the year

had been like for her. "I expected to come home to a well-ordered house," Corrine McGrady reported. "But it was in utter chaos most of the time." She found herself sneaking in some cleaning when her husband had his basketball night off. Consequently she began to feel that he wasn't keeping up his part of the contract. "And then," she said, "suddenly I realized . . . he had never been conditioned to think that a spotless home was necessarily a good thing."

Besides conflicting with our needs to enjoy our children and to find time for ourselves, housework can conflict with our—and our children's—need for companionship. The neater we keep our house, the less willing we may be to have other children in to play. On the other hand, the messier our house, the less willing we may be to invite other mothers—particularly new acquaintances—in to see the clutter.

One mother reported, "I just stopped going to Janet's. She made the kids put away every toy before they picked up another. I could barely listen to Janet because I was trying so hard to make sure my son conformed to the rules of that household."

Another mother we know gave a formal party for her daughter's third birthday. While the children were gathered around the dining-room table, the mother, instead of enjoying the fun, spent the time making sure the towels that had been placed over the seats of the fabric-covered chairs stayed put as the children wriggled around.

When asked what she does just for fun with her children, a mother of four said, "Walk in the rain; eat meals outside, picnic style; take hikes, telling long stories along the way." This mother lives in a home that she has decorated beautifully. But the "fun" things she remembers all took place *outside.*

"If I had it to do over again, I would try to enjoy my children even more. I think women like me were much too socially sensitive about not being perfect mothers and housewives. If you're not enjoying the children, something is wrong. With me, children and fun came first, and the house ran a poor third. But I always felt guilty about the house, and haunted by my failure to wax the floors on time. If I had it to do over, I would thumb my nose at the image of the 'perfect house' and encourage my proclivity to relax and have fun. It's the fun the children remember and not how the house looked." *Mother of five / Salt Lake City, Utah*

PHYSICAL DEMANDS

We define as a mother "pro" any woman who has several children and genuinely enjoys them. Such a one is a Denver mother who gave birth to twin girls when her first child, a boy, was 13 months old. All are now teenagers. "As I look back," she relates, "it seems that I knew a lot more about raising small children than I thought I did at the time. What horrifies me at this point are the sheer physical demands."

The lifting, dressing, changing, chasing, bathing, feeding, and cleaning up after a twenty-pound bundle of energy day after day can be exhausting. Whipping playpens in and out of car trunks, hefting a baby-filled backpack around a shopping center, trudging up and down stairs with the baby, the laundry, the baby, the groceries, the baby, the trash—these things take strength. Add in short rations on sleep and you're apt to end up with circles under the eyes and the nagging irritability that can make a person less than pleasant to live with.

We do not all have equal beauty or wit. Neither do we have equal physical stamina. Somehow we survive. But mere survival is not what most of us want. We want to enjoy our children. One key is knowing our own strength. Another is taking care of our own basic health needs. Enough sleep, good food, exercise, fun, and affection are essential for mothers as well as for babies.

When the baby naps, if you are tired, *nap*. Easy to say. Tough to do.

Fatigue is not always caused by lack of sleep. Many experienced parents knowingly give themselves and their children some extra rope during "arsenic hour" before dinner. "A large orange juice every day at five o'clock for me and my children keeps us civil at our house," says an old friend.

Paradoxically, exercise can make you less tired. A daily walk, a mother-child exercise class, a run around the football field at a local high school track, a bike ride with the baby—these are the ways some mothers handle the need for exercise. One mother of two rambunctious boy toddlers has arranged for a neighborhood girl to come over after school every day so she can go out and jog two miles with a friend.

Two children under 3 are a handful. Psychiatrist Helen DeRosis reports that young mothers she has interviewed estimate that a second child increases the workload many times. The combination is more than the sum of its parts. One more person added to a family of three creates not one but three more sets of relationships—father and new child, mother and new child, sibling and new child—plus a set of adjustments to be made on how much time everyone has for each other. Also, if you want more than one child an important factor to consider in spacing the children is your physical strength—particularly if you are over 30 when you start your family.

When your first baby is tiny, you may lean toward the "get it over with" school and be tempted to have another one fast. But remember that much more is involved than getting through the diaper-and-bottle stage. Consider these words from other mothers:

"As my children grow older, it's fun having them two years apart," says the mother of two boys, 7 and 5. "But when they were babies it was a drag. I would have help three or four times a week if I were starting again. That first year with two babies was too much. The thing I did best was to live through it until they were 3."

Another mother, who has a boy 20 months old and a girl 6 weeks old, relates, "Between the two children I don't have time to organize, schedule, cook, clean, or even shower at a regular time. I would never recommend having children that close together."

A woman whose two sons are long past babyhood says, "I did the best I could with them. The only thing I might do differently is not have them twelve months and two weeks apart. In the early years they had more fun than not, but now that they are well into school the competition and frequent fights are hard to take. I hope as they grow up the fun will come back."

It is, of course, not always that way, in this most personal of decisions.

A mother of girls 4 and 2 says, "Having children fairly

close in age has worked fine, although the first year was rough. Now we can do a lot more as a family than we could if we had a 4-year-old and a new baby. My daughters are very close and play together quite well."

Another view comes from a mother whose son is now 3. She and her husband had very much wanted to start a second child when their first was a year old. "I'm glad it didn't work then," she says. "Now I know what fun it was to concentrate on my son, to research nursery schools, to read to him many times a day and still have the time to do some things for myself. I don't think we'd have held up nearly as well if we'd had that second child right away." She adds, "I think I could do a lot more justice to a new baby and enjoy it more now."

One New York mother had it both ways—two close together, then one much later. "As I look back, those days seemed endless when I had two small babies eleven months apart," she recalls. "Getting them dressed in the winter was an ordeal. Six years later, having one baby was like playing house. It really was fun."

There is support for spacing children at least three years apart from more than a few pediatricians, psychiatrists, and psychologists. Among them is Harvard child psychologist Burton White, who feels strongly that a child's first three years are the important ones. He claims that spacing births less than three years apart means trouble for the older child because the mother must devote much of her attention to the new baby—and it's the mother who contributes most to a child's early development.

One well-known pediatrician believes that the more fun parents have with a baby, the more eager they are to relive those early "honeymoon" months. He notes that his patients most frequently ask him about spacing of children when their first is a year old.

If you wait a while, however, you are playing with more cards in the deck. The mother of a 3-year-old is plainly better equipped to decide if she truly wants another child than one who is still in the honeymoon stage.

"The worst mistake I made was trying to do everything myself when the second child came along. I ended up yelling at and spanking the older child because I didn't have the time to sit down and 'talk it out' with her. I thought I couldn't afford someone to help with the housework, but I realize now that anyone can afford a young girl of about 10 to come in and just play with the kids in order to get something done without interruptions. I should have done this, but I wanted to be a perfect mother who was with her children all the time."   *Mother of two / St. Louis, Mo.*

Pediatrician and writer T. Berry Brazelton claims that planning a second child to keep the first one company is a mistake. There is no guarantee that they will be great pals, and the more energy you spend trying to smooth out the relationship, the more energy the children spend in open competition, he says. Dr. Brazelton reports that mothers often tell him that they feel guilty about what they're *not* doing for one child or the other. Moreover, mothers sometimes feel angry when they're distracted from the demands of a new baby by those of the rest of the family. If the first child is at least 3 when the new one comes, she is already a little bit independent—which automatically, the doctor says, makes the parent's job easier.

Dr. Brazelton's advice: plan a second child for *yourself*, with consideration for your own tolerance and energy.

People don't always go along with the advice of experts. Most of us cope with what happens as best we can. Jeanne's mother had five children—four within five years and the last baby when she was 42 and all the older ones were in school. "Raising the first four together was easier than raising the last one alone," her mother says today. "The first four enjoyed each other so much."

Jeanne notes, "My mother has always had a phenomenal amount of energy. I still don't know how she did it. What she says is true, however. The rivalry the experts mention was not visible to us then or now."

Today, increasing numbers of parents are deciding to stop at one child. One mother of a 2-year-old told us, "We invest much time and energy in our son, and we don't feel we can emotionally afford a second child." She adds, "We treasure our parenthood and our relationship with John. We hope to encourage self-sufficiency and independence in him, and we feel he'll benefit from our example of pursuing individual interests."

All in all, if you and your spouse have plenty of physical and emotional strength (big "ifs" to ponder) and your first child is at least 2, we'd go along with the doctor who advised his patients: "The best time to start a baby is when you can't stand *not* to."

THE GUILT TRAP

Every day is full of opportunities to fall into the guilt trap. Forget to brush their teeth on a night when they've had ice cream. Leave them with a mediocre sitter. Overreact to a minor offense. Momentarily wish that you were anywhere but at home with your own flesh and blood. Experience the urge to strangle the well-meaning middle-aged person who says, "Enjoy it, dear, those years go so fast." Watch another parent do something with her child that you cannot do because you lack the talent, time, or money. Invoke a foolish threat. Let them watch TV for two hours straight. Demand that your son behave at the table like a 6-year-old when he is only 3.

We have been there.

"With my first child I felt trapped and confined, but I didn't know those feelings were normal. I didn't admit them to anyone! As soon as the first few months were over, I made friends with other mothers and discovered that everyone goes through some of that in the early weeks. I now have a 2-month-old; my sitter for today canceled, and I feel stuck. But I can say that without feeling guilty. I *am* stuck indoors in subzero weather with a new baby who eats every four hours. But I know how quickly these months will pass, and that my feelings are normal. Mothering has taught me a patience with myself and my children—if I don't get out today, I will get out tomorrow. If I can't manage dinner for ten this weekend, I can manage having one or two couples in for dessert or pizza after a movie. Getting frantic doesn't help."
Mother of three / Fargo, N.D.

Because having children makes us want to be better than we are, those early years offer the ideal setting for wallowing in debilitating amounts of guilt. We feel we are not hacking it at our dream job.

In his book *Working*, Studs Terkel defines the problem this way: "Most of us look, not for work, but for a 'calling.'" Mothering is a calling, mundane as some of the day-to-day tasks may be. And a calling cries for greatness.

But who can be great all the time? All of us sometimes become confused, mix up our priorities. If we're lucky, somewhere along the way we learn to perceive the difference between "good" guilt and "bad" guilt.

Selma Fraiberg, professor of child psychoanalysis at the University of Michigan Medical School, is the author of *The Magic Years*, a book more than a few mothers say helped them to look at the world through their children's eyes. Fraiberg sees guilt as a very important force in the development of a good conscience. And she is not amused by the realization that parents often feel guilt when their *children* feel guilty about patently wrong behavior.

Probably the most severe guilt we are likely to experience has to do with time—the quality and quantity of the time we spend with our children. Allied to that concern is the quality of the care we arrange for our children to have when we aren't there. We should listen to our hearts and come to terms with any uneasiness we feel in this area.

Just as guilt may be the most effective punishment a child can experience for doing something truly wrong (for example, throwing a rock at another child), it can be a positive force in helping a mother right a wrong she may have done. That is, guilt can prompt her to spend an hour having fun with a child she has been "too busy" to play with, or it can motivate her to spend a needed hour alone when she feels resentful at being pulled in too many directions, at giving too much of herself. Guilt can goad us into finding a better pediatrician, sitter, school.

The other kind of guilt—the unproductive kind—gets us into trouble all the time.

The world gives us conflicting messages: (1) mothers' work is not important and (2) if anything goes wrong it is *our* fault. Children should be happy. If they are not, we are to blame.

Someone nearby is reading a book on child development while you haven't found time to open a newspaper in a week. You feel vaguely guilty. Another mother starts her child in a recreation department exercise program. You feel vaguely guilty. Your child sucks his thumb in spite of the fact that you are nursing him and serving him pacifiers with abandon. You feel vaguely guilty. All of this is unproductive, and a waste of good guilt energy. You must learn to stop feeling guilty and embarrassed about your child's occasional lapses, particularly in public. People who do not have children of their own can't be expected to know that a child is not a miniature adult. What's more, accepting our children's faults and mistakes is an important part of allowing them freedom to breathe and grow.

Resist the temptation to feel guilt if everything your child does fails to thrill you. "One day, what seemed like a crashing insight came to me," says an old friend. "I realized that a mother may not enjoy all the ages of her child equally well." A mother of four children who are now adults confided that the years between 5 and 12 had been her favorites because of the sprouting evidence of talents and skills then. She was a star at helping her four find their long suits and go with them, producing a happy mother of three, an engineer, a cardiologist, and an interior decorator.

We may feel guilt about real trouble that cannot be avoided: sickness, divorce, money problems. This guilt is especially unproductive. When researchers at the Institute of Human Development of the University of California looked at the early years of four hundred famous Americans, they found that 70 percent had abnormal or unhappy childhoods marked by such family tragedies as divorce, alcoholism, mental illness, or abuse. Thomas Edison was beaten so often that his hearing was damaged. Eleanor Roosevelt's father was an alcoholic.

Psychologist Arlene Skolnick, who participated in the study, says, "It may be that having to cope with unhappiness makes for a more resilient and productive adult than having a comfortable, sheltered life. I'm not advocating calamities, but neither should parents feel their children will go to pieces if everything's not perfect."

The best way to minimize guilt over the mistakes we are

bound to make every day is to share what we enjoy about life and ourselves with our children as early and as often as possible.

"I struggled with guilt when, as a new mother, I worked twenty hours a week until my first child was 18 months old. Seven years later, I feel differently. It made a nice transition from career girl to motherhood. A sitter came highly recommended by my sister. I thought then, and I still think, that it is very important for a mother/wife to tend to her own needs during periods of great demands on her from others. Therefore, I can justify the time my children spent with sitters. I can also justify it because when I was with them I did a lot of listening and playing and caring.

"But I would advise young women that motherhood is their job, voluntarily chosen, and jobs are not always fun. Tending to their own needs may occupy a disproportionate amount of time; they may see their own desires as more important and the children as a nuisance. So, while I stress self-care, I also place great importance on balance."

Mother of two / San Jose, Calif.

MOTHER TO MOTHER

If we refuse to harbor unproductive guilt, if we stay in good physical shape and space our children wisely, if we put the housework in its place, if we make time for our own pursuits, if we recognize that society doesn't always place a high value on a mother's work but in our hearts know its true value, and if we get out and build a mother network, we are probably taking good care of ourselves. Paradoxically, the self-caretaking results in more, not less, energy to spend on those we love.

There is a moving description of a new mother's fight with a hospital official in a novel called *The Millstone* by British writer Margaret Drabble. Rosamund Stacey, the mother, knows that her baby is probably now regaining consciousness after a serious operation. A hospital administrator refuses to let Rosamund into the child's room. An intellectual with a lifelong habit of self-effacement, Rosamund finds herself, when calmer methods fail, pushing, screaming, and taking control of the situation in a way she had never done before in her life. She sees the baby. The child, who has been crying, stops and beams at her mother. The reader wants to pat this woman on the back.

It's a new role for many of us, that of being a determined mother. We take it on without fully realizing that we're doing so, because a child's needs are so great and because only we can fill those needs, at least for the first few years.

No one can do everything well. But the beauty of a mother's job is that our children can and will use *whatever* we have to offer. They need it and they will demand it. In response we will somehow find patience and talent we didn't suspect we had. For that we will be grateful to our own children as we grow with them and because of them.

"I try to take the long view of what I want to do in my role as a mother," one woman said. "Even though at times I feel drowned in minutiae, I know that nothing is more important to the world than what I am doing."

MOTHERS' SOURCEBOOK

Growth and Development Charts

These charts consist of lists of children's developmental "landmarks," along with the age ranges within which they can be expected to occur. While they represent the consensus of child-development specialists and mothers, these lists should be used only as a guide—a general indication of what to expect.

Although children generally develop in similar patterns, each child is an individual and will follow his own developmental plan. Although most babies roll over at 2-5 months, some perfectly normal babies roll over after that age. Although most babies begin to say "Dada" and "Mama" at 8-12 months, some begin much later. Although most babies crawl before they walk, some skip crawling altogether.

If your baby is an early developer, you will not worry. But if he is later than the norm, you will probably have some concerns. Share these concerns with your doctor, and if he tells you that everything is fine, try to relax. This advice is easy to give but not so easy to follow. One friend said, "My son was very slow in his physical development. And even though I knew better, I worried. When he was 18 months old and still not walking, I took him to the doctor. While I was expressing my worry, James entertained himself by reading the letters of the alphabet off the doctor's wall chart. 'Quit worrying!' said the doctor. 'He's just one of those kids who would rather read than walk.' Eventually, James did walk. Now he's eight, and still just one of those kids who would rather read than walk."

PHYSICAL DEVELOPMENT

New Activity	Usually Begins
Lifts chin briefly when lying on stomach	Birth - 1 month
Holds up head when lying on stomach	1 - 3 months
Holds head steady when carried or held	2 - 4 months
Rolls over	3 - 6 months
Holds up chest	4 - 6 months
Sits with support	4 - 6 months
Sits in high chair	5 - 7 months
Sits briefly without support	5 - 8 months
Attempts to crawl (stomach and legs dragging, pulling with arms)	5 - 9 months
First tooth	5 - 12 months
Crawls (trunk free, arms and legs alternating)	6 - 11 months
Can be pulled to feet, but can't support self.	6 - 9 months
Gets to sitting position/sits unsupported	6 - 9 months
Pulls self up on furniture	7 - 14 months
Climbs up onto low chairs and may climb down	7 - 14 months
Crawls up stairs	7 - 14 months
Cruises (walks around holding on to furniture)	10 - 15 months
Stands alone	10 - 15 months
Walks alone	11 - 18 months
Runs with large gait	1½ - 2½ years
Walks up and down stairs alone, usually leading with same foot	2 - 2½ years
Jumps from height of 12 inches	2 - 2½ years
Jumps into air with both feet	2½ - 3 years
Rides tricycle without pedals	2 - 3 years
Pedals tricycle	2½ - 3½ years
Walks up and down stairs, alternating feet	3 - 3½ years

HAND AND EYE COORDINATION

New Activity	Usually Begins
Glances briefly at human face or nearby objects	Birth - 1 month
Follows object with eyes from one side of head to other	2 - 4 months
Plays with hands and may hold and observe a toy	3 - 5 months
Reaches for objects	3 - 5 months
Follows distant object with eyes	3 - 6 months
Explores with hands, eyes, and mouth	4 - 6 months
Grasps small objects	5 - 8 months
Transfers toys from one hand to the other	5 - 8 months
Looks briefly at books and pictures	6 - 9 months
Deliberately drops toys, spoons, etc., from crib or high chair	7 - 14 months
Puts one block on top of another	8 - 11 months
Scribbles with crayon	12 - 15 months
Enjoys books, especially turning pages	13 - 15 months
Easily grasps small objects, using finger and thumb	14 - 17 months
Builds tower of three or more blocks	2 - 2½ years
Turns pages of book one at a time	2 - 2½ years
Moves fingers individually and draws circle	2½ - 3½ years

LANGUAGE AND SPEECH

New Activity	Usually Begins
Reacts to human voice and human heartbeat	Birth
Cries when hungry, tired, over-stimulated or uncomfortable	Birth
Develops distinct cries for hunger, pain, etc.	1 - 2 months
Coos, squeals and bleats, using vowel sounds	3 - 5 months
Babbles (strings together consonants and vowels such as "ba-ba-ba" or "da-da-da").	3 - 5 months
Accidentally imitates sounds	5 - 8 months
Consciously imitates sound	8 - 12 months
Calls some people by name ("Dada," "Mama").	8 - 12 months
Understands and responds to simple directions ("Show me your eyes," "Where is Mama?")	10 - 12 months
Calls objects by name ("cookie," "potty")	10 - 14 months
Uses words to convey messages ("dat," "no").	11 - 15 months
Talks in jargon (strings of gibberish that sound like sentences in a foreign language)	12 - 14 months
Has vocabulary of three to fifty words. Speaks for the fun of it, with no frustration if not understood.	1 - 2 years
Enjoys listening to simple stories, nursery rhymes, and repetitive songs. May sing along with songs like "Jingle Bells."	1 - 2 years
Talks in short sentences.	2 - 2½ years
Has vocabulary of more than 300 words. Talks in sentences of three or four words.	2½ - 3½ years
Understands most things said by others, and is frustrated when not understood.	2½ - 3½ years

SOCIALIZATION

New Activity	Usually Begins
Cries and gets attention of others	Birth
Recognizes mother	1 - 2 months
Smiles in response to faces or voices of others, especially mother	1 - 4 months
Recognizes father, brothers, and sisters	3 - 4 months
Laughs out loud and smiles	3 - 5 months
Interested in and may recognize self in mirror	4 - 6 months
Plays with rattle and toys and may resist if they are taken away	4 - 6 months
Shows fear, anger, and pleasure	4 - 6 months
Plays peek-a-boo	5 - 6 months
Enjoys watching children and knows they are different from adults	5 - 7 months
May begin to fear strangers and cry briefly when mother leaves.	7 - 11 months
Imitates play (pat-a-cake, so big, bye-bye)	7 - 11 months
Knows meaning of "no"; sometimes obeys simple commands	9 - 11 months
May enjoy "parallel play" (doing the same thing as another child) but does not play *with* others. Cannot yet share toys or possessions	11 - 14 months
Understands the meaning of "no" but often resists directions and must be physically removed	14 - 16 months
May become extremely afraid of strangers and cry for a long time when separated from mother	11 - 14 months

(continued)

Socialization (continued)

New Activity	Usually Begins
Knows how to keep and dominate attention of mother and other adults. Uses mother as a resource to help him out of difficult situations, give comfort and approval	1½ - 2 years
May enter strong negative stage, saying "no" to everything	1½ - 2½ years
May have temper tantrums	1½ - 3 years
Fear of strangers diminishes	2 - 3 years
Shows strong pride in his accomplishments, especially physical feats	2 - 3 years
Plays with friends, with supervision	2½ - 3 years
Expresses both affection and anger to friends (hugging one moment, hitting the next)	2½ - 3 years
Manipulates adults to get what he wants	2½ - 3 years
Competes with friends and siblings	2½ - 3 years
Occasionally shows respect for other people and their possessions	2½ - 4 years
Becomes greatly interested in outside world	2½ - 4 years
Shares toys	3 - 4 years

DEVELOPMENT OF CIVILIZED BEHAVIOR:
WHAT MOTHERS TOLD US

Fifty mothers of 4 and 5-year-olds responded to our questionnaire asking specific questions about the development of civilized behavior in their children. Here are their answers:

	Youngest Reported Age	Most Frequently Reported Age	Oldest Reported Age
Self Reliance			
Gave up pacifier	3 weeks	1 year	3 years
Gave up security blanket or toy	1 year	*	*
Was toilet-trained	11 months	2½ years	4 years
Washed face and hands	16 months	3 years	3½ years
Made attempts to dress	18 months	2½ years	2½ years
Dressed, getting help with buttons, zippers, etc.	2 years	3 years	4 years
Dressed without help	3 years	4½ years	*
Put on own shoes	18 months	3 years	4 years
Buckled shoes	3 years	3½ years	*
Tied shoes	3½ years	5 years	*
Put away toys	1½ years	4 years	*
Helped with simple household chores—putting away cans, raking leaves, etc.	1½ years	2 years	*
Cleaned own room with help	3 years	4 years	*

* 4- and 5-year-old children have not yet accomplished this task

Social Interaction

Mother could entertain friends without constant interruptions	Birth	3½ years	*
Mother could sit and read, sew, etc. without constant interruptions	Birth	*	*
Mother could take child to church or other "quiet" place	Birth	3½ years	*
Child enjoyed going to movie or "story hour" at library	2½ years	3 years	*
Enjoyed parallel play with children the same age	5 months	1 year	3 years
Played well with children the same age	2 years	3½ years	4 years
Willingly shared toys	3 years	*	*

Eating

Adjusted to a three or four-hour schedule	Birth	1 month	6 months
Weaned from breast	1 month	6 months	15 months
Weaned from bottle	8 months	2 years	4 years
Ate finger food	4 months	8 months	1 year
Ate three meals a day	6 months	6 months	1 year
Parents felt relaxed eating out with child	Birth	3 years	*

Sleeping

Slept through the night	1½ weeks	2 months	14 months
Gave up morning nap	4 months	9 months	15 months
Gave up afternoon nap	18 months	*	*

* 4- and 5-year-old children have not yet accomplished this task

GROWTH AND DEVELOPMENT NOTES

Mothers' Resource List

Note: Whenever we know that a book is available in paperback we have put "PB" after the publication date; if the paperback publisher is different from the hardcover publisher, we have so indicated. Books and catalogs marked with an asterisk are those we consider worth adding to your permanent library.

BEFOREHAND

Adventures of Birth by Elizabeth Bing (Ace, 1975, PB). An extremely useful guide with step-by-step details for prepared childbirth. The author is a nationally known Lamaze instructor.

Birth Without Violence by Frederick Leboyer (Knopf, 1975). A book that explains methods of making birth pleasant and peaceful for the newborn. If you want your baby delivered using Leboyer techniques and your obstetrician and/or hospital do not provide for this, use this book as a basis for insisting that you get what you think best.

Caring for Your Unborn Child by Ronald E. Gots, M.D., and Barbara A. Gots, M.D. (Stein & Day, 1977). The authors, a husband-wife team of doctors, have two children. Ronald Gots has a degree in pharmacology as well as medicine. If you read this clearly written book early in pregnancy, it will help you to give your baby a healthy start. Possible hazards to a fetus in your workplace, in your home, and in your diet are discussed in great detail.

The Caesarean Birth Experience by Bonnie Donovan (Beacon Hill, 1977). A comprehensive, practical, reassuring guide for parents and professionals.

* *A Child Is Born* by Lennart Nilsson et al. (Delacorte, rev. ed. 1977). A classic book of magnificent photographs of fetal development. You will treasure this during your pregnancy and share it with your children in the years to come when they ask where babies come from.

Childbirth by John Seldon Miller, M.D. (Atheneum, rev. ed. 1974). This book covers all bases and is written in a warm, informative style. "Miller's book made me wish the author could be my obstetrician," said one mother.

Choices in Childbirth by Silvia Feldman, M.D. (Grosset & Dunlap, 1978). The title aptly characterizes this book. It is an excellent guide for the mother having trouble making up her mind what she will do about methods of childbirth.

Commonsense Childbirth by Lester D. Hazell (Putnam, 1969). The best overall book on childbirth preparation. The author, who has children of her own, was an early critic of doctors and hospitals who put women in a passive childbirth role. She predicted the trend toward family-centered birth. Good section on breast feeding.

Essential Exercises for the Childbearing Year: A Guide to Health and Comfort Before and After Your Baby Is Born by Elizabeth Noble (Houghton Mifflin, 1976). Inspiration and helpful ideas for preventing problems before they start. Contains a chapter on exercises for Caesarean mothers and a thorough explanation of all muscles used in birth.

* *Every Child's Birthright: In Defense of Mothering* by Selma Fraiberg (Basic Books, 1977; Bantam, PB). Should you stop working when the baby is born? Here is a book that should be read by any prospective mother or father who is mulling over this question. Dr. Fraiberg, a professor of child psychoanalysis, fiercely stresses the crucial importance of early mothering and of finding good substitute mothers for those who can't do it all themselves.

Expectant Fathers by Sam Bittman and Sue Rosenberg Zalk (Hawthorne, 1979). This book investigates and advises the prospective father. The authors interviewed men about "their pregnancies" and share the results in this book.

First Names First by Leslie Alan Dunkling (Universe, 1977). Published in Britain and written by one of the world's experts on names, this book deals extensively with almost every Christian name in the English-speaking world, and charts the course of individual names' popularity over centuries. Dunkling advocates giving a child three names: a common one for early years when other children make fun of odd names; a more unusual one, perhaps from your own family; and a third that is more fanciful still in case your child goes into politics or the theater and needs a distinctive name.

The First Nine Months of Life by Geraldine Lux Flanagan (Simon and Schuster, 1962, PB). Story of conception and week-by-week progress of baby in the uterus. Detailed, clear, and exciting, with many photographs.

Immaculate Deception: A New Look at Women and Childbirth in America by Suzanne Arms (Houghton Mifflin, 1975). A book that looks critically at many routine birth procedures. It shows prospective parents the choices that should be, but often are not, open to them.

Making Love During Pregnancy by Elizabeth Bing and Libby Colman (Bantam, 1977, PB). The authors sent questionnaires to 300 parents who had taken natural-childbirth classes. They use the replies, along with their own research, to offer help and support to couples having physical or psychological difficulties with sex during pregnancy.

Methods of Childbirth: A Complete Guide to Childbirth Classes and Maternity Care by Constance A. Bean (Doubleday, 1972, PB). Good information on choosing a childbirth class, a hospital, a doctor. It could be of help to the mother-to-be who is having trouble deciding which method of birth she will choose.

Nourishing Your Unborn Child: Nutrition and Natural Foods in Pregnancy by Phyllis Williams (Nash, 1974). An excellent resource on prenatal nutrition written by a nurse.

Nursing Your Baby by Karen Pryor (Harper & Row, 1973; Pocket Books, rev. ed. 1977, PB). A practical guide, one of many good ones available, which can help a lot more than a busy hospital staff is likely to be able to.

* *Our Bodies, Ourselves* by the Boston Women's Health Collective (Simon and Schuster, rev. ed. 1976, PB). There's an excellent chapter on pregnancy and a photo- and drawing-filled section on childbirth in this book. See the "You" section for more information.

* *Pregnancy & Childbirth* by Tracy Hotchner (Avon, 1979, PB). A comprehensive guide that covers virtually everything an expectant mother would want or need to know about pregnancy and childbirth. The book includes discussions on some areas not always covered in other books. For example: making a decision to have a baby, difficulties in conceiving, sex techniques during pregnancy, and explicit directions for emergency delivery of a baby. Hotchner is a journalist, not a mother or a childbirth expert. The disadvantage of this is that she has gathered all of her information from secondhand sources, although the book had a medical advisor, Karen Blanchard, M.D., OB/GYN. The advantage of the book is that the pros and cons of each controversial issue are objectively presented since the author does not have any preconceived opinions.

Pregnancy, Birth, and Family Planning by Alan F. Guttmacher, M.D. (Viking, rev. ed. 1973; New American Library, PB). A classic written by a head of International Planned Parenthood who practiced obstetrics and gynecology for many years in New York. It is a Dr. Spock for pregnancy, covering virtually every physical aspect of pregnancy and birth.

Prenatal Yoga and Natural Birth by Jeannine O'Brien Medvin (Freestone Publishing—P.O. Box 357, Albion, Calif. 95410—1974, PB). Photographed yoga positions and attractive line drawings are easy to understand. The text is well written, if a bit mystical.

Preparation for Childbirth by Donna and Roger Ewy (Pruett, 1970; New American Library, PB). An easy-to-read, well-illustrated explanation of the Lamaze method for parents. One couple we know who lived in a town where there were no childbirth-education classes made it through a natural birth with the help of a cooperative doctor and a careful reading of this slim book.

The Tenth Month by Laura Z. Hobson (Simon and Schuster, 1970; Dell, PB). A companionable novel about the pregnancy of a woman who had thought she would never be able to have a child. A good novel for a time when you might especially enjoy getting into some other pregnant person's shoes.

Thank You, Dr. Lamaze by Marjorie Karmel (Lippincott, 1959; Doubleday, PB). This is the book that helped start the Lamaze movement in the United States. It's a lively personal account of two experiences with prepared childbirth, one a delivery by Dr. Lamaze in France, the other a delivery in America. Good reading, even if a little outdated.

Who Made the Lamb by Charlotte Painter (McGraw-Hill, 1965). A sparsely written, beautiful book based on the journal of her first pregnancy by a former editor for a New York publisher. If you find yourself thinking larger thoughts than you ever did before, Painter will keep you company and add to their richness. The book is out of print now, but you may be able to find it in the library.

A Woman Doctor's Diet for Women by Barbara Edelstein, M.D. (Prentice-Hall, 1978). An excellent book for any woman with a weight problem. The author tailors her diets to a woman's needs, with a special diet for the overweight pregnant woman.

Women's Work, Women's Health: Myths and Realities by Jeanne Mager Stellman (Pantheon, 1977). The author has a Ph.D. in physical chemistry. A chapter on possible hazards to reproduction found in many places of work may be helpful to those in any doubt about their own jobs.

Your Baby, Your Body: Fitness During Pregnancy by Carol Stahmann
Dilfer (Crown, 1977). A mother of two, the author has taught exercise classes for pregnant women. Each exercise is illustrated with
photographs of five different women in the last trimester of pregnancy. Despite their girth, they appear to be blooming. A book in-
spiring enough to make even a tired pregnant lady want to get up
and go.

Magazines

All of the following magazines are excellent. They contain much helpful information on pregnancy and the care of infants and toddlers that
is up to date and unlikely to be found in books.

American Baby
575 Lexington Avenue
New York, N.Y. 10022

Baby Talk
66 East 34th Street
New York, N.Y. 10016

Mothers' Manual
P.O. Box 243
Franklin Lakes, N.J. 07417

Other Sources of Help

American National Red Cross
National Headquarters
Washington, D.C. 20006

Offers classes in preparation for parenthood, first aid, and health
in the home, as well as other educational and health courses. Contact your local Red Cross chapter for further information.

American Society for Psychoprophylaxis in Obstetrics (Lamaze)
1411 K Street NW
Washington, D.C. 20005

This group purposely chose a tongue-twister name with a medical
ring to it in order to attract the medical community, in the early
1960s, to the idea of natural childbirth. ASPO pioneered in teaching the Lamaze technique and worked toward opening delivery
rooms to fathers. Today it is a recognized certifying body for Lamaze instructors. If there is a local chapter in your area, it would
be a good source for information on Lamaze classes; doctors who
encourage natural childbirth and/or other birth innovations; hospitals that welcome fathers into labor and delivery rooms, perhaps
even for Caesarean births; hospitals that offer rooming-in, a Leboyer

birth atmosphere, nurse-midwives delivering babies, procedures for immediate infant-parent bonding, and other variations in birth methods. If there is no local chapter, write to the national office.

Association for Childbirth at Home
P.O. Box 1219
Cerritos, Calif. 90701

This nationwide organization gives classes to parents who want to have their children born at home. It also sponsors a certification program for ACAH leaders to teach the parent classes and gives additional training to those who want to be midwives. The group publishes a newsletter, "BirthNotes," and has a referral service of professional and lay resources for home birth.

C/SEC (Caesareans/Support, Education, and Concern)
15 Maynard Road
Dedham, Mass. 02026

Information, education, and support for parents who anticipate a Caesarean delivery or who have experienced one. Among its publications is "Frankly Speaking: A Phamphlet for Caesarean Couples." Write for information on groups in your area that support Caesarean parents.

Caesarean Way
128 Jefferson Street
Riverside, N.J. 08075

An organization interested in finding ways to help parents prepare for and deal with Caesarean births.

County Health Departments

Services vary. In California, services are free and include well-baby and immunization clinics, pregnancy testing and prenatal care, family planning, and many others. Check with your local health department to find out what it offers.

Home Oriented Maternity Experience
P.O. Box 20852
Milwaukee, Wisc. 53220

The group's publication, "Home Oriented Maternity Experience: A Comprehensive Guide to Home Birth," is a good resource for those seriously considering home birth.

International Childbirth Education Association
P.O. Box 20852
Milwaukee, Wisc. 53220

A national group formed in 1960 and composed of 270 member

groups, all of which are strongly committed to family-centered maternity care. Sponsors conferences and conventions on recent findings in maternity care, breast feeding, and parenting. Write for information about local chapters and activities.

International Childbirth Education Association Supplies Center
P.O. Box 70258
Seattle, Wash. 98107

Offers a comprehensive source of books and publications on childbirth, infant nutrition and feeding, and general parenting. "Bookmarks" is a free twice-yearly publication listing books offered by the Supplies Center and containing helpful reviews of new books. "ICEA News" is the official publication of the ICEA, and contains the latest information on innovations in childbirth and family-centered maternity care. Subscription is $4.00 a year for this quarterly newsletter.

La Leche League
9616 Minneapolis Avenue
Franklin Park, Ill. 60131

Founded in 1956, this group is dedicated to helping women breast feed their children by having small, informal groups of mothers meet to learn about breast feeding and parenting. The League publishes "The Womanly Art of Breast Feeding" manual, the bimonthly "La Leche News," and other publications of interest to new parents. Write for information about League branches in your area or for breast-feeding hot lines.

National Foundation—March of Dimes
Public Health Division
1275 Mamaroneck Avenue
White Plains, N.Y. 10605

Aims to prevent birth defects and any life-threatening condition in babies. Health-education materials available on request, including "Genetic Counseling," a booklet describing amniocentesis, which is available free.

National Organization of Mothers of Twins Club
5402 Amberwood Lane
Rockville, Md. 20853

By the fifth or sixth month of pregnancy, many mothers and fathers have already been told to expect twins. This group offers information and support; it's good to know what to expect ahead of time. Write for information and for names of chapters in your area.

CARE, DEVELOPMENT, AND GENERAL PARENTING

Baby and Child Care by Benjamin Spock, M.D. (Hawthorne, 1968;
Pocket Books, rev. ed. 1977, PB). Dr. Spock's book has had 179
printings and is the best-selling new title issued in the United States
since 1895. His success is richly deserved. His book has held up over
the years and is still the best of many around on baby and child
care. "Sometimes I think my baby wouldn't have survived the first
year without Spock," said one mother. "And I *know* that *I* wouldn't
have survived."

Better Homes & Gardens Baby Book (Bantam, rev. ed. 1977, PB). A
general baby-care book; the bulk of the material deals with the first
year of life.

Black Child Care: How to Bring Up a Healthy Black Child in America
by James P. Comer, M.D., and Alvin F. Poussaint, M.D. (Simon and
Schuster, 1976, PB). This is an excellent guide for any parent, since
it deals with the basics of physical and emotional care of children,
but it is a must for black parents, or for anyone working with black
children.

Child Sense: A Guide to Loving, Level-Headed Parenthood by William
E. Homan, M.D. (Basic Books, rev. ed. 1977). Homan has written
a warm and witty book about the serious issues of parenting. "I
first read Homan's book when my son was 2," said one mother.
"His commonsense approach to issues like toilet training, thumb
sucking, and tantrums was an enormous help for me. I last referred
to Homan a week ago when my son, who is now 8, started telling
lies. Homan's advice helped me to cope."

A Child's World: Infancy Through Adolescence by Diane E. Papalia
and Sally Wendkos Olds (McGraw-Hill, 1975). A college textbook
that is thoroughly researched and comprehensive, yet easy to read.
It is a reference work on development of a child, from conception
through adolescence, with useful illustrations and charts.

Doctor and Child by T. Berry Brazelton, M.D. (Delacorte, 1976). A
collection of articles that Brazelton originally wrote for *Redbook*
magazine. There is especially good advice on colic, crying, and the
issue of under- versus overstimulation.

The First Three Years of Life by Burton L. White (Prentice-Hall, 1975;
Avon, PB). A professor at Harvard, after twenty years of investigating how babies learn, shares the results of his research with us in
this book. White uses a stage-by-stage, developmental approach to
help parents with the emotional and intellectual stimulation of a
baby. He emphasizes the importance of close contact between

mother and baby during the first three years of life. Don't read it through just once. As with Gesell, read the section on each stage (birth to 6 weeks; 6 weeks to 3½ months; 3½ months to 5½ months; 5½ to 8 months; 8 to 14 months; 14 to 24 months; 24 to 36 months) as your child enters it. Attacked this way, the somewhat scholarly language becomes riveting. Through White's observations you can usually recognize your own child's yearning to learn. Often his suggestions for capitalizing on this yearning are helpful.

The First Twelve Months of Life edited by Frank Caplan (Grosset & Dunlap, 1973; Bantam, PB). A month-by-month guide to a baby's growth and development, with charts and charming photographs. This book goes into great detail about what babies do, and thus can help parents decide what *they* should do.

* *Child Behavior* by Frances Ilg, M.D., and Louise Bates Ames (Harper & Row, 1955; rev. ed. 1978, PB). The Gesell Institute has published a series of books on all stages of childhood development. This one is a must for every parent. Each parent asks the question: "Is my child normal?" Gesell helps to give the answer. One mother said, "Although it took me a while to learn how to read Gesell, during my son's first few years it was my guide and gospel. But then I began anticipating—and expecting every negative stage mentioned in the book—and I finally realized that every child is different. Now I use Gesell as a *resource.* When one of my kids is acting weird, or is generally obnoxious for a long period of time, I pull out Gesell, and sure enough, it usually reassures me to discover that the behavior is normal for the age."

How to Bring Up a Child Without Spending a Fortune by Lee Edwards Benning (McKay, 1975; Doubleday, PB). Here are lots of ideas for getting the most out of the many thousands of dollars you'll spend on your child by the time she is 18.

How to Parent by Fitzhugh Dodson (Nash, 1970; New American Library, 1973, PB). A helpful book with extensive bibliographies on toys, books, and records for parents and children.

Infants and Mothers: Differences in Development by T. Berry Brazelton, M.D. (Delacorte, 1969; Dell, PB). A nurse and childbirth educator whom we know gives this book to all of her pregnant friends. They are fortunate, since with this book they'll learn that there's a wide range of normal behavior and that there are inborn differences in temperament in babies from birth. In anecdote form, Brazelton shows the daily, weekly, and monthly life of an active baby, a moderately active baby, and a quiet baby. He shows how mothers handle these babies, sometimes well and sometimes not so well, and helps a mother to relax and realize that her baby affects her at least as much as she affects him.

The Magic Years by Selma H. Fraiberg (Scribner, 1959, PB). This is a classic, the best book we know for helping a jaded adult understand what's going on in the mind of a child.

The Mother's Almanac by Marguerite Kelly and Elia Parsons (Doubleday, 1975, PB). A cheerful book by two mothers with children now in their teens. It is filled with the joy of parenting and offers marvelous hints for child-mother activities.

Nonsexist Childraising by Carrie Carmichael (Beacon Press, 1977). Offers positive advice and suggestions for parents who wish to raise nonsexist human beings instead of stereotyped "boys" and "girls." There are lots of quotes and experiences of men and women who are attempting to live nonsexist lives.

The Myth of the Happy Child by Carole Klein (Harper & Row, 1975). The author talks with children from 3 to 13 years old, and lets them reveal their thoughts and feelings of fear, guilt, anger, and loneliness.

The U.S. Government Book of Infant Care, U.S. Department of Health, Education, and Welfare (U.S. Government Printing Office, Washington, D.C.). This seventy-two-page booklet contains the first-year basics. Read it cover to cover, keeping Spock for more detailed backup information. Cost is $1.00. Also excellent is *Your Child from One to Six* for $1.75.

What Now? A Handbook for New Parents by Mary Lou Rozdilsky and Barbara Banet (Scribner, 1975, PB). A compassionate book, one of the few that covers parents' adjustment to birth. Particularly helpful chapters: "Coping with a Crying Baby," "Re-establishing Closeness as a Couple," "Feeling Comfortable as a Parent."

The Womanly Art of Breastfeeding by La Leche League International (La Leche League International, 1963). A classic written and published by the mother-founders of the organization that blazed the way for a resurgence of breast feeding in the U.S. Although some might find the view of motherhood and child care a bit romantic, there is solid information and support here for the mother who wants to breast feed. There is also information and advice on nutrition, basic baby care, and family life in general. One mother who is a former librarian and an inveterate reader says this book helped her more than any other in the early months of her two children's lives.

You Can Breastfeed Your Baby . . . Even in Special Situations by Dorothy Brewster (Rodale Press, 1979, PB). This is a book for a mother of twins, of a hospitalized infant, or any other mother with a nursing problem. Many case histories.

You and Your Will by Paul P. Ashley (McGraw-Hill, rev. ed. 1977).
A very important and often overlooked reason for having a will is
to name a guardian of minor children should both parents die. The
best guardians are usually found in a "similarly situated friendly
family" with children about the same age as yours, lawyer Ashley
contends. He also suggests that you'll need to reconsider this decision every few years. A helpful book to read *before* you go to
the lawyer.

Magazines

American Baby, Baby Talk, and Mothers' Manual

See Beforehand section for information on the above magazines.

Growing Child
22 North Second Street
Lafayette, Ind. 47902

With a subscription to *Growing Child*, you get a newsletter each
month of the baby's first year. It tells skills the baby is developing
that month, suggests toys and activities suited to his level, and gives
practical child care tips.

Parents Magazine
80 Newbridge Road
Bergenfield, N.J. 07621

An excellent magazine for parents offering up-to-date information
about child rearing from birth through the teens.

DAY CARE

The Challenge of Day Care by Sally Provence, Audrey Naylor, and June
Patterson (Yale University Press, 1977). This, the best book for helping parents understand what good day care is, describes a facility set
up at the Yale Child Study Center. There are good suggestions for
easing separation pains and for judging quality of care as well as
many anecdotes that can prepare you for the ups and downs involved
in even the best of day-care arrangements.

*Every Child's Birthright: In Defense of Mothering by Selma Fraiberg.
See Beforehand section.

*Family Day Care: A Practical Guide for Parents, Caregivers, and Pro-
fessionals* by Alice H. Collins and Eunice L. Watson (Beacon, 1977,
PB). A survey of what's available for children of working parents.
The authors report on such programs as co-op child-care exchanges,
play groups, and day-care neighbor services, as well as providing information on licensing and training. A helpful section contains taped
interviews with young mothers and babysitters.

The Day Care Book by Vicki Breitbart (Knopf, 1974). Expertly describes why U.S. child-care facilities should be expanded and improved. Also gives helpful advice on how to find the best day care for your child and tells how to start, finance, and maintain a non-profit day-care program.

Who Cares for the Baby? Choices in Child Care by Beatrice Marden Glickman and Nesha Bass Springer (Schocken, 1978, PB). A practical yet thoughtful look at finding care for children under 4. The authors, mothers themselves, recognize the day-to-day problems "experts" so often overlook. Their discussion of quality vs. quantity of time spent with babies and young children is the best we've seen anywhere. Two conclusions they reach: no single solution will work for everybody; when possible financially, part-time work for a mother is best for both parents and child.

DISCIPLINE

Between Parent and Child by Haim G. Ginott (Macmillan, 1965; Avon, PB). Ginott's book is a classic. He was the first to present workable techniques to enable parents and children to communicate constructively. Some of his ideas seem simple and basic at first glance, just plain good manners. But when we stop and think, we often realize that we don't always use good manners when we deal with our children. "I'm sure that reading Ginott has helped me avoid some catastrophic mistakes in handling my children," one mother said. Although the book deals primarily with older children, parents of young children can profitably read it. "I glance through Ginott once a year," said another mother, "just to remind myself of one of the better ways to parent."

Children: The Challenge by Rudolf Dreikurs (Hawthorne, rev. ed. 1976, PB). A useful guide to discipline that shows a parent how to help a child assume the consequences of his own behavior. For example, Dreikurs suggests the following solution to a common problem. You are driving in the car and your child is whining, crying, fighting, or screaming. Pull over to the curb and sit quietly until your child realizes that you've stopped because of him and stops his behavior on his own accord.

Child Sense by William Homan, M.D. (Basic Books, rev. ed. 1977). This book, also listed in the General Parenting section, is an excellent guide to discipline for parents of babies and young children.

Dare to Discipline by James Dobson (Regal, 1972, PB). For the parent with an authoritarian bent, this book gives practical solutions to typical behavior problems.

How to Discipline with Love by Fitzhugh Dodson (Rawson, 1977).
This book outlines nineteen discipline strategies, but emphasizes
that rewarding a child for good behavior is the most effective
method—most of the time.

Improving Your Child's Behavior by Madeline Hunter and Paul Carolson
(Bowmar, 1971, PB). The author, who has done extensive work at
UCLA's experimental elementary school, uses behavior-modification
techniques to influence children's behavior. Her book is a step-by-
step guide for parents who wish to learn behavior modification techniques as methods of discipline in the home.

The New Assertive Woman by Lynn Z. Bloom, Karen Coburn, and
Joan Pearlman (Dell, 1976, PB). If you have problems asserting
yourself, you may have problems with discipline, and this helpful
guide may be for you. It gives practical methods to help women
learn how to demand their own rights. "After I read this book, I
realized that many of the problems I thought my kids had were
actually *my* problems, in letting them walk over me, in playing the
martyr, 'poor me' role," said one mother.

Your Child's Self-Esteem: The Key to Life by Dorothy Corkille Briggs
(Doubleday, 1970, PB). A sensitively written book that helps a
mother bolster her own self-esteem and at the same time learn
techniques of discipline that will nurture her child's self-esteem.
Briggs' book is in the same tradition as Ginott's, and also discusses
problems with older children. However, like Ginott, it is well worth
reading when your child is young.

EQUIPMENT

Children's Spaces by Molly and Norman McGrath (Morrow, 1978). A
great picture book to explore in order to get yourself thinking of
ways to set up part of a house or apartment for children. Most of
the fifty architects and designers represented in the book did the
work pictured for their own children.

*The Complete Baby Book: A Total Guide to Buying Products, Toys,
and Medical Services* by editors of *Consumer Guide* (Simon & Schus-
ter/Fireside, 1979, PB). A good description of the gear and services
available to make life with a baby easier.

Good Things for Babies by Sandy Jones (Houghton Mifflin, 1976, PB).
Consumer guide to more than 250 products used during a baby's
first two years. Products are included on the basis of maximum
safety, convenience, and helpfulness. Useful drawings, especially
for the neophyte who doesn't know a stroller from a carriage.

Catalogs of Toys, Books, and Records

* Dick Blick
    P.O. Box 1267
    Galesburg, Ill. 61401
    Free "Special Education and Early Learning" catalog of music, art,
    and outdoor play materials. Among other things, the catalog offers
    a reasonably priced three-speed record player and solid oak kinder-
    garten chairs. There is a toll-free order number, and major credit
    cards are accepted.

Caedmon Spoken Word Recordings
    505 Eighth Avenue
    New York, N.Y. 10018
    The Babar, Madeline, Peter Rabbit, and other characters come alive
    in the records of this company, which usually gets superb actors to
    do the reading. A free catalog lists over 1000 cassettes and records.

* Childcraft Centers
    20 Kilmer Road
    Edison, N.J. 08817
    Free catalog "Toys That Teach"; also much more complete "Grow-
    ing Years" catalog for $1.50. It has great puzzles, furniture, learning
    aids that will bring back memories of your own kindergarten days.
    It's more fun than a Neiman-Marcus catalog for the parent of a pre-
    school-age child. Toll-free order number; credit cards accepted.

* Children's Book and Music Center
    2500 Santa Monica Boulevard
    Santa Monica, Calif. 90404
    Free 178-page catalog lists more than 5000 books and records.

Community Playthings
    Rifton, N.Y. 12471
    A free seventy-page catalog offers very sturdy climbing equipment,
    seesaws, toys, and furniture made by a Christian community, the
    Hutterian Society of Brothers.

Constructive Playthings
    1040 East 85th Street
    Kansas City, Mo. 64131
    A large supplier of educational toys, furniture, and equipment that
    may be handier for western and midwestern families than for east-
    erners since there are warehouses and showrooms in Garden Grove,
    Calif., and Dallas, Tex., as well as Kansas City. A 168-page catalog
    costs $1.00.

Creative Playthings
Princeton, N.J. 08540
"Guide to Good Toys" catalog available for 25 cents.

Edmund Scientific Company
800 Edscorp Building
Barrington, N.J. 08007
Wonderful free catalog for scientists of any age, including toy parachutes, gigantic balloons, prisms, and magnetic tape that can turn a refrigerator door into a bulletin board.

Federal Smallwares Corp.
85 Fifth Avenue
New York, N.Y. 10003
Free sixty-page catalog of dollhouse furniture and tiny dolls.

Golden Record Division
250 West 57th Street
New York, N.Y. 10019
Free catalog of long-playing and 45 rpm book and record sets.

* Scholastic Book Services
50 West 44th Street
New York, N.Y. 10036
"Starline Books" catalog of paperback book titles. Also available are more than forty book-record sets.

F.A.O. Schwarz
150 Lackawanna Avenue
Parsippany, N.J. 07054
Schwarz puts out two free catalogs each year offering wonderful toys that are fun to dream about if not to own.

Miscellaneous Equipment

For information on car restraints and catalogs of safety devices, see Safety section.

Baby-food grinder. Don't buy the first hand-operated baby-food grinder you come across. They vary widely in quality. One excellent version, the "Happy Baby Food Grinder," is made by Bowland-Jacobs Manufacturing Co., 9 Oakdale Road, Spring Valley, Ill. 61362. Smallest size (3½ oz.) is fine unless you have twins. If you can't find it in a store, write to the manufacturer.

Children's closet rod. Lee-Rowan manufactures an adjustable closet rod called the "space-doubler" that hangs from the regular rod. It can be adjusted as a child grows, so that it is always easy for him to hang up his own clothes. For names of stores that sell it, write to Lee-Rowan, 6301 Etzel Avenue, St. Louis, Mo. 63133.

Lock for the TV set. A couple who felt their own son watched too much television are now marketing a simple, inexpensive plug-locking device that can be used on any electric appliance, not just the TV. All you do is unplug the TV set, for example, then insert the plug into a small plastic locking device that can't be removed without a key. For information, write to Plug-Lok, Kenny Co., P.O. Box 9132, St. Louis, Mo. 63117.

"Lullaby from the Womb" (Capitol Records ST-11421). This is the sound of a mother's body and heartbeat. If your newborn cries steadily despite the pediatrician's assurance that he is all right, try this. After a few weeks, when the baby becomes accustomed to the sounds of his new environment, this record may not be as comforting to him as it was at first.

Picture plates. Texas Ware makes a kit that allows children to design their own dinner plates. A kit with fifty sheets of the special paper needed and a set of marking pens is available from Texas Ware, 2700 South Westmoreland, Dallas, Tex. 75224. After the picture is drawn, you send it to the company, which embeds it in a white plastic plate and returns it to you in about three weeks.

Popsicle molds. A catalog that contains toys and, more important, the best inexpensive plastic molds for making popsicles is available from local Tupperware dealers (check the yellow pages of your telephone book), or write to Tupperware, Customer Relations, P.O. Box 2353, Orlando, Fla. 32802.

FATHERS

Father Feelings by Eliot A. Daley (Morrow, 1977, PB). A beautiful book of essays about one active family. It shows that fathering can be as humbling to the ego, and as humanizing, as mothering. Daley, the father of three and a writer for children's television, writes graphically and well of the day-to-day ups and downs in store after the birth-to-3 years. How much moving around the country should children of ambitious parents be subjected to? Where is it best for a family to live—in the city or in the country? What's a good vacation for everyone? Ear piercing, cherishing the individuality of each child, TV addiction, neatness, pets or no pets: Daley covers them all. This book gives needed perspective, helping fathers (and mothers) understand both how difficult and how rewarding fatherhood can be.

Fathering by Maureen Green (McGraw-Hill, 1976). Despite the fact that this book is written by a woman, it is thought-provoking for both fathers and mothers. Green feels that until recently the father's role was much too limited; it was assumed that he would be away at work all day and when he was home he would be a sort of "mother's helper." She acknowledges that modern-day fathers are more willing to give a hand with feeding and caring for children, but asks this question: "If father feeds the infant and changes diapers, does he give his children the benefit of an auxiliary male mother? Isn't there something he should be doing that mother can't?" Green doesn't fully answer this question, but at least she raises it, and it's worth considering by mothers as well as fathers.

Father Power by Henry Biller and Dennis Meredith (McKay, 1974). If a man wants to read only one guide to fathering, this is the best. It is a thorough primer on the techniques of fathering, covering such topics as child development, discipline, and child-care basics. It also offers advice on what the authors feel is a father's role, which is to bring a child into the world and then demonstrate that civilized behavior is desirable.

The Hazards of Being Male by Herb Goldberg (Nash, 1976). It is very difficult to put oneself in another's place, particularly if the other person is of the opposite sex. This book will help a woman understand the stresses a man is under in our society, and therefore may help a new mother understand a new father's reaction to the combination of career demands and fatherhood. Psychotherapist Goldberg warns that fathering before he's ready is one of the more self-destructive ways the average man aborts his own growth and development. He sees only one "right" reason for a man to father children: "that the *process* of being a father excites him and is seen as enriching, fulfilling, and joyful, and the realities of his life allow him to participate fully."

How to Father by Fitzhugh Dodson (Nash, 1974). After writing *How to Parent*, Dodson realized that virtually all books, including his, were written for mothers. This book, therefore, is directed to fathers. It is mainly a rewrite of *How to Parent*, although Dodson has expanded the age range—from birth to the teen years—and updated his excellent lists of books, toys, and equipment.

Who Will Raise the Children? New Options for Fathers (and Mothers) by James A. Levine (Lippincott, 1977). In this trail-blazing book, Levine talks with more than 120 men who have deliberately chosen to care for children and are successful at it. Reading it, one realizes how society and the traditional working world have set things up for motherhood and have short-changed fatherhood.

FOODS AND NUTRITION

Crunchy Bananas by Barbara Wilms (Sagamore-Peregrine-Smith, 1975, PB). A cookbook with a good variety of nutritious recipes to use with your child.

A Diet for Living by Jean Mayer (McKay, 1975). The well-known nutritionist makes a good case for wise eating habits.

Eater's Digest: The Consumer's Fact Book of Food Additives by Michael F. Jacobson (Doubleday, 1972, PB). The most helpful book we know of on the subject of additives.

Kids Are Natural Cooks by Parents Nursery School (Houghton Mifflin, 1974). This is a book of child-tested recipes using natural foods. It was compiled by parents in a cooperative preschool in Cambridge, Massachusetts. We found it in the children's section of our library and have checked it out several times. The illustrations and ideas for having fun with children and food make it a delight to read. One of these days we hope to try their three-day process for making cheese.

Kindergarten Cooks by Nellie Edge (Pen-Print, 1975, PB). A spiral-bound book printed in large type with useful illustrations. A parent can use this book with a preschool child or an older child can use it alone. Except that it relies a little too much on sugar and sweets, it is an excellent cookbook. "My boys love this book," said a mother whose sons were 3 and 6. "They use it at least once a week to make dinner for the family, cooking everything from soup to dessert."

The Natural Snack Cookbook by Jill Pinkwater (Four Winds Press, 1975). Here's another good book of recipes that can be found in the children's section of the library. There is an excellent introduction to "natural" foods and healthy eating, and lots of recipes, from pizza to scones, that are fun to try.

Nutrition Scoreboard by Michael F. Jacobson (Avon, 1975, PB). Rates foods from cereals to hot dogs for nutritional value. Also available in poster form for $1.75 from the Center for Science in the Public Interest, 1757 "S" Street NW, Washington, D.C. 20009.

The New York Times Natural Foods Cookbook by Jean Hewitt (Quadrangle, 1971). Recipes for everything from appetizers to desserts.

The Rodale Cookbook by Nancy Albright (Rodale Press, 1973). Beautiful photographs and simple, clear text entice readers into learning about foods they might never have eaten before. The single best inspiration we know for planning healthy meals.

The Superbaby Cookbook by Donna Lawson and Jean Conlon (Macmillan, 1974). The best book on making your own baby food and why it is a good idea.

Too Good for the Dog: A Cookbook of Leftovers by Jane Ribbel and Barbara Geisler (Woodruff Press, 40 Woodruff Road, San Anselmo, Calif. 94960—1976). Store excess parsley in a plastic bag in the freezer and then use for cooking. Use leftover mashed potatoes as the top crust of a meat pie. Leftover beer is a good substitute for wine in a stew. Egg yolks can be frozen in ice cube tray spaces surrounded by water; whites too can be frozen, one to a section. These and dozens of other handy tips and tasty recipes can be found in this ingenious cookbook. Available for $5.50, including tax and postage, from the publisher.

For free copy of booklet on breaking dating codes of eighty-four manufacturers, write to State Consumer Protection Board, 99 Washington Avenue, Albany, N.Y. 12210.

HEALTH AND MEDICAL CARE

Baby and Child Care by Benjamin Spock, M.D. (Hawthorne, 1968; Pocket Books, rev. ed. 1977, PB). Dr. Spock still gives the best advice on medical care. See Care section for more information.

Childhood Illness: A Common Sense Approach by Jack G. Shiller, M.D. (Stein & Day, 1972, PB). Shiller is a pediatrician who has a real-life practice and also teaches at Columbia University. Used along with Spock (who perhaps tends to overworry), this book gives you enough confidence during day-to-day illnesses to wade through on your own and save money that may be necessary for more than "reassurance" visits.

Directory of Medical Specialists (Marquis). This work is updated approximately every two years and is available in large libraries. It will help you locate all the pediatricians or other specialists who practice in your area, and also gives their qualifications. A helpful reference book to know about for all family emergencies.

Good Housekeeping Family Health and Medical Guide (Hearst Corp., 1980). Expensive but good general reference for the whole family. Written by 37 specialists, it has a good index, many illustrations and charts, plus large enough type to scan fast in emergencies.

How to Raise Children at Home in Your Spare Time by Marvin J. Gersh, M.D. (Stein & Day, 1966). Helpful medical section, particularly for a mother who suspects she may be overly concerned about illness.

The Mother's and Father's Medical Encyclopedia by Virginia E. Pomeranz, M.D. (Little, Brown, rev. ed. 1977). This costs a lot so you may not want to buy it, but if your library has a copy, it's a good reference book. The same author, with Dodi Schultz, wrote the handy short *Mothers' Medical Encyclopedia* (New American Library, 1972, PB).

New Wives' Tales: Conversations with Parents About Today's Pediatrics by Lendon H. Smith, M.D. (Prentice-Hall, 1974). Amusingly written in question-and-answer form, this book gives parents a way to learn which among many medical "old wives" tales are true and which are not. Based on author's experience as a pediatrician and father of five.

* *A Sigh of Relief: The First-Aid Handbook for Childhood Emergencies* by Martin I. Green (Bantam, 1977, PB). An oversize paperback, this book has large print and many drawings. The index is listed on the back cover, and the different sections are tabbed to help a parent turn quickly to a needed section: eye injuries, poisoning, heart failure, etc.

LEARNING AND ENRICHMENT

Unless it is indicated in the title, an age range is given after the publication data about each book. Also see the Foods and Nutrition section for cooking activities with children.

An Activities Handbook for Teachers of Young Children by Doreen J. Croft and Robert D. Hess (Houghton Mifflin, 1972, PB; 2½ - 6). This detailed guide is an all-time favorite for nursery-school teachers. It gives explicit directions for hundreds of crafts, reading-readiness, and math and science activities. Although written for teachers, it would also be helpful for parents who enjoy working at home with their children.

The Baby Exercise Book by Janine Levy, M.D. (Pantheon, 1975; birth - 12 months). A free-spirited book to aid you in a program of physical development for your baby.

Baby Learning Through Baby Play: A Parent's Guide for the First Two Years by Ira J. Gordon (St. Martin's, 1970, PB). A clearly written and well-illustrated month-by-month guide with games and activities.

Children and Books by May Hill Arbuthnot (Scott, Foresman, rev. ed. 1972; 2 up). A comprehensive guide to children's literature, written for teachers but equally useful for parents.

Exploring Nature with Your Child by Dorothy Shuttlesworth (Abrams, 1972; 2 up). "Many parents are discovering in our rapidly changing world that their children have become leaders rather than followers in nature appreciation," says Dorothy Shuttlesworth. This marvelous book will help your child become a leader.

Fireside Book of Fun and Game Songs edited by Marie Winn (Simon and Schuster, 1974; from birth). An excellent collection of favorite songs, old and new.

Give Your Child a Superior Mind by Siegfried and Therese Englemann (Simon and Schuster, 1966; 2 - 4). One of the best books for parents who want a nicely spelled-out program to stimulate their child's early intellectual growth, including a clearly written section on helping a young child with mathematics. "My 9-year-old daughter is a mathematical genius," said one mother. "I'm a complete dunce when it comes to math, but I used this book with her when she was 3, to get her started in the right direction."

The Golden Song Book: 56 Favorite Songs and Singing Games by Katharine Wessells (Golden Press, 1945; from birth). A good selection of songs to sing and play with your children.

A Guide to Nonsexist Children's Books by Judith Adell and Hilary Klein (Academy Press; 2 up). This is a guide to good nonsexist books for children. The authors intend to update it to periodically include appropriate new books.

How to Play with Your Children (And When Not To) by Brian and Shirley Sutton-Smith (Hawthorne, 1974, PB; birth - 12). An especially good book for the parent with little experience with young children who might need specific guidelines for getting in touch with a baby and rediscovering the joy of child's play. Many of the ideas seem obvious, but the book serves to jog one's memory.

Learning Through Play by Jean Marzollo and Janice Lloyd (Harper & Row, 1974, PB; 2½ - 5). This useful guide, written by mothers, is filled with practical suggestions for having fun while you help develop your child's language, art, science, and reading-readiness skills. Delightful illustrations.

A Montessori Handbook by R. C. Orem (Putnam, 1975, PB; 2½ - 5). Gives an overview of the Montessori philosophy and methods and presents techniques for working on intellectual skills at home.

A Parent's Guide to Children's Reading by Nancy Larrick (Bantam, 1975, PB; 1 - teens). A book to buy and use for years. Contains specific titles and information on helping children to read at all ages.

The Play Group Book by Marie Winn and Mary Ann Porcher (Macmillan, 1967; 2 - 4). An indispensable guide if you plan to set up a play group in your own home. Good suggestions for handling discipline with a group of children.

Singing Fun by Lucille F. Wood and Louise Scott (McGraw-Hill, 1954, PB; 2 - 7). If you love music and can pick out a tune on any instrument, this book may be for you and your child. It's just what the title implies—for both children and parents.

Summerhill by A. S. Neill (Hart, 1960). A book by the founder of Summerhill, an open-structured "free school" in England, describing Neill's philosophy: children will quickly learn to read, write, and do arithmetic when they are ready, and therefore they should not be pushed academically in school.

Total Baby Development by Jaroslav Koch, M.D. (Wyden, 1976; birth - 2). Lots of good ideas, with special emphasis on encouraging physical development in infants.

Thinking Is Child's Play by Evelyn Sharp (Dutton, 1969; 2½ up). A helpful book that gives very clear directions for playing a variety of games to stimulate a child's thoughts.

Understanding Piaget by Mary Ann Pulaski (Harper & Row, 1971). Although the Swiss psychologist Jean Piaget spent years studying and developing a system for explaining the way children learn, he himself has been seriously misunderstood. This book will help an interested parent or educator understand Piaget's theories.

What to Do When There's Nothing to Do by the Boston Children's Medical Center (Dell, 1968, PB; 2 up). A great resource book, especially useful for one of those hair-tearing rainy days when you desperately need some ideas for entertaining your child.

Whole Child Whole Parent by Polly Berrien Berends (Harper's Magazine Press, 1975, PB). This book contains the best description of books for the preschool child we have found anywhere. Berends researched more than 4000 books before coming up with a recommended list of 500, along with sufficient information to enable you to decide whether a given book is suitable for your child.

Workjobs by Mary Varatta Lortin (Addison-Wesley, 1972, PB; 3 - 8). Although this book is geared toward helping a teacher equip a classroom, it is also appropriate for parents who enjoy making toys and games. It gives clear directions for making hundreds of learning toys and games that could turn a child's toy shelf into a school at home.

NURSERY SCHOOLS

Early to Learn by Joy M. Crandall (Dodd Mead, 1974). A book of lovely photographs and commonsense advice by a nursery-school pro who is also the mother of three. A useful pictorial view of what should be going on in a good nursery school when you visit.

Early Childhood Education Directory by E. Robert LaCrosse Jr. (Bowker, 1971). Description of 2000 preschools throughout the United States. Includes information on budgets, education of staff, fees, philosophies. Although not all-inclusive, it will help you establish guidelines for choosing a good school.

Montessori in Perspective edited by the Publications Committee, National Association for Education of Young Children. In separate essays, seven child-development experts put the Montessori method into historical perspective, both praising and criticizing it. You may want to read this booklet before enrolling your child in a Montessori school. It is available for $2.00, plus 20 cents for handling, from NAEYC—1834 Connecticut Avenue NW, Washington, D.C. 20009.

A Parent's Guide to Nursery Schools by Jean Curtis (Random House, 1971). Very useful advice on judging, choosing, and even starting your own nursery school from a mother who wished she had known when her first child was ready for nursery school what she did by the time her second was ready.

SAFETY

"The Gentle Art of Babyproofing" by Solomon Katz, M.D. The director of the Center for Research in Child Growth and Development at Philadelphia Children's Hospital has written a very useful pamphlet that is available free from Box 4263, Chester, Pa. 19016.

A New Vaccine for Child Safety: How to Protect Your Child from Accidents by Murl Harmon; introduction by Robert G. Scherz, M.D. (Safety Now, 1976, PB). A factual, concise guide to accident prevention from birth to adulthood. Helpful section on emergency aid.

Lists of Approved Car Restraints for Children

Action for Child Transportation Safety (ACTS)
P.O. Box 266
Bothell, Wash. 98011
Enclose 40 cents and a stamped, office size, self-addressed envelope for a phamphlet called "This Is the Way the Baby Rides." It gives detailed information, including brand names, of *infant* car restraints. This organization also has available kits, posters, articles, and films

on all areas of child transportation safety, including a guide for running a community restraint-loan program and a booklet called "Car Pool Survival." Write for the catalog.

* Physicians for Automotive Safety
P.O. Box 208
Rye, N.Y. 10580
Enclose 35 cents and a stamped, office size, self-addressed envelope for a phamphlet called "Don't Risk Your Child's Life." Revised frequently, it lists brand names and model number of car restraints that have been approved both by the government and by consumer organizations. Also, small nonprofit organizations may be able to borrow at little or no cost a twelve-minute color film, "Car Safety: Don't Risk Your Child's Life." Write for information to the address above.

Information on Hazardous Toys

Toy Safety Review Committee
Bureau of Product Safety
U.S. Food and Drug Administration
5401 West Bard Avenue
Bethesda, Md. 20016

Free Catalogs of Safety Devices

The Chris-Brooks Company
7115 SW 82nd Avenue
Portland, Ore. 97223

Safety Now Company, Inc.
Box 567
202 York Road
Jenkintown, Pa. 19046

Toll-Free Hotline to Report Dangerous Toys and Equipment

Consumer Product Safety Commission
800-638-8326
800-492-2937 (Maryland residents only)
Open twenty-four hours a day, toll-free.

Making Older Equipment Conform to New Safety Standards

"Infant Safety Kit"
U.S. Consumer Product Safety Commission
Washington, D.C. 20207

SPECIAL NEEDS

The Bereaved Parent by Harriet Schiff (Crown, 1977; Penguin, PB). Almost ten years after her son died of a congenital heart disease, this mother talked to professionals and other parents whose children had died and then wrote this small, compassionate book of advice that includes a guide to bereaved parents' organizations.

The Care of Twin Children: A Common-Sense Guide for Parents by Rosemary Theroux and Josephine Tingley (Center for Study of Multiple Gestation, 1979). Written by two Boston nurses who between them have seven children, including sets of twins, this book deals with practical matters from feeding to handling extra costs and getting help. It stresses the importance of helping each child develop his own identity. The book is based on the authors' experience and that of many other mothers of twins and triplets. (The book is available from the Center for Study of Multiple Gestation, Suite 463-5, 333 East Superior Street, Chicato, Ill. 60611.)

Cooking and Caring for the Allergic Child by Linda Thomas (Drake, 1974). Recipes and helpful advice.

Coping with Tragedy: Successfully Facing the Problem of a Seriously Ill Child by Jerome L. Schulman, M.D. (Follett, 1976). Dr. Schulman is head of the Division of Child Psychiatry at Children's Memorial Hospital in Chicago and a professor of pediatrics and psychiatry at Northwestern University. He is also the father of Billy, who died at 5 of meningitis. Thus he knows his subject from personal experience and from his work. The book was compiled from tape recorded conversations with children, parents, and doctors. It would be a help both to parents of sick children and friends or relatives of those parents.

Creative Divorce by Mel Krantzler (Signet, 1972; New American Library, PB). Offers help for both fathers and mothers in exploring ways of handling divorce without destroying their children.

Coping with Food Allergy by Claude A. Frazier. M.D. (Quadrangle, 1975). Helpful advice, with special attention to coping with the real problem of getting through holidays and birthday parties with an allergic child who requires special foods.

The Genetic Connection: How to Protect Your Family Against Hereditary Disease by David Hendin and Joan Marks (Morrow, 1978). Discusses, in clear language, various kinds of birth defects, their causes, and the tests available to help detect them. Also gives a state-by-state list of hospitals and clinics where tests and counseling are available.

Is My Baby All Right? A Guide to Birth Defects by Virginia Apgar, M.D., and Joan Beck (Trident, 1973; Pocket Books, PB). Gives causes, prevention of, and treatment for birth defects.

Momma: The Sourcebook for Single Mothers edited by Karol Hope and Nancy Young (New American Library, 1976, PB). Full of quotes from women raising children alone, giving understanding guidance for others in similar situations.

New Hope for the Childless Couple: The Causes and Treatment of Infertility by Sherwin A. Kaufman, M.D. (Simon and Schuster, 1970). A chapter called "One-Child Sterility" may help couples who, although they may have conceived easily the first time, have difficulty having future children. Dr. Kaufman says it takes the average couple four to six months to conceive. In general, he advises seeking help if a woman has not conceived after a year. If the woman is in her 30's, she should seek help after six months, he says.

The Single-Parent Experience by Carole Klein (Avon, 1973, PB). Contains suggestions for a single parent of either sex.

The Special Child Handbook by Joan and Bernard McNamara (Hawthorne, 1978). According to the authors, more than 20 percent of all children in the United States are handicapped in some way. They provide essential information for parents of "the special child."

Stepparenting by Jean B. Rosenbaum (Chandler and Sharp, 1977). The author, an experienced therapist who is also a stepparent, deals realistically with the many problems affecting natural parents, stepparents, and children: how to handle discipline; how to build a good second marriage; how children, from 2-year-olds to adolescents, feel about stepparents. This book gives excellent information and practical solutions for these and other problems. A must for any stepparent.

We Take This Child by Claire Berman (Doubleday, 1974). This book candidly covers all aspects of adoption. It begins with a modern-day fairy tale about a couple who request a newborn child and get her in a few months. Parents themselves fill the rest of the pages with realistic accounts of the adoptions of older, racially mixed, and handicapped children.

What to Tell Your Child About Birth, Death, Illness, Divorce, and Other Family Crises by Helene Arnstein (Bobbs-Merrill, 1962). This comprehensive book on helping children face change and pain will also help adults understand children's feelings and their possible reactions to unusual stress from toddlerhood through high school. Unfortunately, it's out of print, but it can be found in many libraries.

Your Overactive Child: Normal or Not? by Sidney Jackson Adler, M.D.
(Medcom Press, 1972). Gives methods of determining hyperactivity
and is written in an easy-to-understand style.

SPECIAL-NEEDS CHILDREN'S BOOKS

Preschool children can often be helped to understand problems and
change by reading books like those listed below.

Adoption

Somebody Else's Child by Roberta Silman (Frederick Warne, 1977).

Death

About Dying by Sara Bonnett Stein (Walker, 1974).
Nana Upstairs and Nana Downstairs by Tomie de Paola (Putnam, 1973).
Old Arthur by Liesel Moak Skorpen (Harper & Row, 1972).
The Tenth Good Thing About Barney by Judith Viorst (Atheneum,
1971).

Divorce

Divorce Is a Grown-up Problem by Janet Sinberg (Avon, 1978, PB).

Fears

Benjy's Blanket by Myra B. Brown (Watts, 1962).
My Doctor by Harlow Rockwell (Macmillan, 1973).
There's a Nightmare in My Closet by Mercer Mayer (Dial, 1968).
What's in the Dark? by Carl Memling (Parents', 1971).

Fighting

Alexander and the Horrible No Good Very Bad Day by Judith Viorst
(Atheneum, 1972).
The Little Brute Family by Lillian and Russell Hoban (Macmillan, 1966).
The Quarreling Book by Charlotte Zolotow (Harper & Row, 1963).

Friendship

Alexander and the Wind-up Mouse by Leo Lionni (Pantheon, 1969).
George and Martha: Five Stories About Two Great Friends by James
Marshall (Houghton Mifflin, 1972).
It's Mine!—A Greedy Book by Crosby Bonsall (Harper & Row, 1964).

Grandparents

Grandfather and I by Helen E. Buckley (Lathrop, 1959).
Little Bear's Visit by Else Minarik (Harper & Row, 1961).

Hospitals

Betsy and the Doctor by Gunilla Wolde (Random House, 1978).
Curious George Goes to the Hospital by H. A. Rey (Houghton Mifflin, 1966).
I Want Mama by Marjorie Weinman Sharmot (Harper & Row, 1974).

Siblings

Big Sister and Little Sister by Charlotte Zolotow (Harper & Row, 1966).
Go and Hush the Baby by Betsy Byars (Viking, 1971).
I'll Fix Anthony by Judith Viorst (Harper & Row, 1969).
Middle Matilda by Winifred Bromhall (Knopf, 1962).
One Morning in Maine by Robert McCloskey (Viking, 1952).
Peter's Chair by Ezra Jack Keats (Harper & Row, 1967).
Peggy's New Brother by Eleanor Schick (Macmillan, 1970).

Sex

A Baby Is Born by Milton Ira Levine (Simon and Schuster, 1949).
The Wonderful Story of How You Were Born by Sidonie Gruenberg (Doubleday, 1970).

Sexism, Countering It

My Dòctor by Harlow Rockwell (Macmillan, 1973).
Nice Little Girls by Elizabeth Levy (Delacorte, 1974).
The Summer Night by Charlotte Zolotow (Harper & Row, 1974).
William's Doll by Charlotte Zolotow (Harper & Row, 1972).

Miscellaneous

About Handicaps by Sara Bonnet Stein (Walker, 1974)
Moving Day by Helen Train Hilles (Lippincott, 1954).
Mr. Rogers Talks About: New Baby; Moving; Fighting; Going to the Doctor; Going to School; Haircuts by Fred Rogers (Random House, 1974).
The Terrible Thing That Happened at Our House by Marge Blaine (Parents', 1975). Mother goes to work.

The Bookfinder: A Guide to Children's Literature About the Needs and Problems of Youth Age 2 - 15 by Sharon Spreedemann Dreyer (American Guidance Service, 1977). If you need a book for your child dealing with the preceding or any other problem, ask your librarian for a copy of this excellent reference book.

Sources of Special-Needs Help

American Fertility Society
1608 13th Avenue South
Birmingham, Ala. 35205
Infertility is best and most quickly treated by a doctor who spe-

cializes in the field, one who will spend the time it takes to solve the problem. To find such an expert, try a medical center, a teaching hospital, or a Planned Parenthood facility with an infertility clinic. Or write, enclosing a stamped, self-addressed envelope, for a geographic list of the 6500 members of this group.

Association for Children with Learning Disabilities
    4156 Library Road
    Pittsburgh, Pa. 15234
    Can direct you to state and local affiliates set up to share information and assist in obtaining help.

Child Abuse Hotline
    800-421-0353
    800-352-0386 (California residents only)
    National headquarters of the organization: 22330 Hawthorne Boulevard, Suite 208, Torrance, Calif. 90505.
    This is the toll-free telephone number of Parents Anonymous, open twenty-four hours a day, to give help.

Children in Hospitals
    31 Wilshire Park
    Needham, Mass. 02192
    A group concerned with promoting contact between parents and children when either is hospitalized. Encourages hospitals to provide live-in accommodations for parents. This group publishes a newsletter and information sheets.

The Exceptional Parent Magazine
    Statler Office Building, Room 708
    20 Providence Street
    Boston, Mass. 02116
    An informative, emotionally supportive magazine for parents of children with disabilities of all kinds.

MOMMA
    P.O. Box 5759
    Santa Monica, Calif. 90405
    Organization for single mothers with chapters around the country. This group also publishes a newsletter; write to P.O. Box 567, Venice, Calif. 90291.

The Premature and High-Risk Infant Association
    Box A-3083
    Peoria, Ill. 61614
    Offers emotional and educational support to parents, sponsors a twenty-four-hour Help Line—309-688-0274, and publishes several booklets.

National Organization of Mothers of Twins Club
See Beforehand section of Resource List.

Warm Lines
Check with your local hospital or your pediatrician about the availability of telephone services for problems associated with child care. Several major cities have such "warm lines," staffed by volunteers or, sometimes, by professional psychologists.

TOILET TRAINING

Toilet Learning: Picture Book Technique for Children and Parents by Alison Mack (Little, Brown, 1977). A helpful book for both parent and child to use before, during, and after toilet training. Part of this book is a children's book with great pictures that describe the whole thing.

Toilet Training in Less Than a Day by Nathan Azrin and Richard Foxx (Simon and Schuster, 1974; Pocket Books, PB). Some parents swear by this book—"It worked!" said one. Others disagree. In any case, it's a book to read if toilet training becomes a problem for you and your child.

YOU

Advice to a Young Wife from an Old Mistress by Michael Drury (Doubleday, 1966). Despite the repellent title, this short book contains words of wisdom on the care and maintenance of any friendship, not the least of them that of one's spouse. Writes Drury: "The only people worth loving are those who are determined to find life good whether you love them or not."

The Book of Hope: How Women Can Overcome Depression by Helen DeRosis, M.D., and Victoria Pellegrino (Macmillan, 1976; Bantam, PB). Graphic, practical advice on dealing with loneliness, anxiety, shyness, inertia, frustration, and suppressed anger.

Boy or Girl? The Sex Selection Technique That Makes All Others Obsolete by Elizabeth Whelan (Bobbs-Merrill, 1977). The author has a master's degree in public health and is affiliated with the Harvard University School of Public Health. She is also the author of *A Baby? Maybe* and is a mother. We think this book is even more helpful than the Rorvik and Shettles book described next, although anyone who is intensely interested in the subject should read them both. The section on the history of sex selection, however, makes Whelan's book interesting to anyone.

Choose Your Baby's Sex by David M. Rorvik, M.D., and Landrum B. Shettles (Dodd Mead, 1977). A followup to the authors' 1970 book, which covered alkaline and acid-body states as one of several determining factors. We know several couples, all with one-girl one-boy families, who sing the praises of this book. We know others who say that the methods did not work.

Family Matters by Lawrence Fuchs (Random House, 1972; Warner, PB). Fuchs sees three forces undermining the strength of the American family: an overzealous striving for independence of emotion and behavior in all individuals; an emphasis on female equality with little regard for psychological differences and feelings produced by hormones; and the inherent role of motherhood today, with major responsibility put on the mother's shoulders. The book ends with a plea for reinstatement of male importance in the family.

The Future of Motherhood by Jessie Bernard (Dial, 1974; Penguin, PB). A book full of insight and compassion by a well-known sociologist who, widowed young, raised three children. She explains how outside forces are changing motherhood and how women are changing because of them. She notes that the young mother is the "most burdened" worker in our society, while the nonemployed woman in middle and late motherhood is the least burdened. Bernard ends the book with a paean to shared parenthood: "Both children and the social order will profit by opening up motherhood for men to share."

Gift from the Sea by Anne Morrow Lindbergh (Pantheon, 1955; Random House, PB). A book to read if and when you start asking yourself "Is this all there is?"

The Growth and Development of Mothers by Angela Barron McBride (Harper & Row, 1973; Barnes & Noble, PB). The author, who did graduate work in psychiatric nursing, had two children under 5 at the time she wrote this book. Written from the front lines and from the heart, it raises questions about motherhood that need to be asked. Her guiding principles: some things are done out of love and it's wrong to attach a monetary value to them; women should have some economic independence; housekeeping is too boring and child-rearing too important for one person to do alone.

A Guide for Working Mothers by Jean Curtis (Touchstone, 1977). Curtis interviewed wives and husbands for practical solutions to typical problems. She offers suggestions for housework, recreation time, and how to share being the "psychological parent"—the one who is always mindful of, who always feels a personal responsibility for, the whereabouts and the feelings of each child.

1,2,3,4,5,6: How to Understand and Enjoy the Years That Count by Patricia Coffin; photographs by James Hansen (Macmillan, 1972). A writer and mother who obviously managed, while working outside the home, to savor her last child's early years, comments briefly about happy, trying, worrisome times. The superb black-and-white photographs make you want to get out of the house and plop *your* child in a field of daisies, too.

The Joy of the Only Child by Ellen Peck (Delacorte, 1977). Deciding whether or not to have a second child can be as hard as deciding whether to have one at all. If a parent is in doubt, this book may help. Bear in mind, however, that the author is the founder of the National Organization of Non-Parents and writer of *The Baby Trap*. Peck suggests that the only child turns out as well as or even better than those from larger families. She includes a diary of a day in the life of a mother of a 4-year-old along with that of a mother whose children who are 4 and 1; a list of famous only children (Eleanor and Franklin Roosevelt, Frank Sinatra, Loren Eiseley, Lauren Bacall); and a checklist that covers the conscious or unconscious motives that may affect our thinking.

The Kitchen Sink Papers: My Life as a Househusband by Mike McGrady (Doubleday, 1975; New American Library, PB). A rueful saga of changed ideas about housewifery by a man who switched roles with his wife for a year.

Kramer versus Kramer by Avery Corman (Random House, 1977). Ted Kramer's wife, bored, leaves their young son and him and goes away to "find" herself. A warm novel that is, in part, about the growth and joy a man can experience as the primary caretaker of a child.

The Millstone by Margaret Drabble (Morrow, 1966). This novel by a British writer and mother of four describes a young scholar's pregnancy and early months as a mother. The attachment that gradually develops between mother and baby is built on blocks of sickness weathered, messes cleaned up, inconveniences overcome. This young woman had not known about the plus side of motherhood beforehand, and her earned pleasure in the baby's love engages the reader: "I certainly had not anticipated such wreathing, dazzling gaiety of affection from her whenever I happened to catch her eye." To read Drabble (she has published nearly a book a year since 1964) in chronological order is to take a course in the development of mothers. Like the author, the leading characters are invariably intelligent and involved in careers or other intense interests—and they are mothers.

Mother and Child compiled by Mary Lawrence (Crowell, 1975). Check the oversized-books section of your library for this lovely book, which contains a hundred reproductions of famous mother-child artworks from all over the world. A mesmerizing and relaxing book to look at alone or with one's child.

The Mother Knot by Jane Lazarre (McGraw-Hill, 1976; Dell, PB).
Read it. If it's not you, it may be your neighbor. An incredibly
honest book, this is a New York artist's account of her first four
years as a mother. Lazarre's two-year fight to get her husband involved in the baby's care is riveting. The second half gets to the
heart of many a new mother's conflicts: in her heart she feels a
need to be the major caretaker of her child, but at the same time
she resents the consequent stalling of her own life as her husband
goes on with his. A superb book for any couple having trouble
understanding what's hit them after the baby's born.

* *Our Bodies, Ourselves* by the Boston Women's Health Collective
(Simon and Schuster, rev. ed. 1976, PB). The new edition, like
the earlier version of this oversized paperback, is the single best
source we know on all physical aspects of being a woman. The
authors have not only researched the facts but have talked to
many different women. There are photographs, drawings, and an
extensive bibliography. Chapters on sexuality, childbearing, and
health care are particularly helpful.

Mother's Day by Robert Miner (Richard Marek, 1978). The graphic
sexual passages may offend some, but this look at mothering (of
a 2-year-old boy and a baby girl) through the eyes of a man whose
wife has left is just one thing that's worthwhile about a sometimes
shocking book. Sample observations: "Having babies is a continuous
series of crises. Nothing else will produce the necessary changes, so
intense are the adjustments you must make at each stage." Then,
"Since I've been a mother talking to women I don't think I've
had a frivolous conversation. Substance is all, spiked with intimacy."
This novel, based on the author's life, leaves a reader saddened at
what some children must go through when a single parent is under
too much stress; the father's struggle to find day care alone is
enough to flatten the strong. Here is a book that ought to be required reading for anyone who thinks it might be "fun" to have a
child without considering giving that child another parent who will
love it as well.

Parent Power—Child Power by Helen DeRosis, M.D. (Bobbs-Merrill,
1974; McGraw-Hill, PB). DeRosis is a mother and an attending
psychiatrist at Roosevelt Hospital in New York. Her book is full
of good cheer and good sense, particularly for the mother who
feels her sense of self slipping away. The chapter called "Super-
mom" is super. On how much teaching we should do: "In later
life, most people are spontaneous in direct porportion to their
parents' ability to be spontaneous. Often in trying to 'enrich' or
'teach' everything imaginable to the child, paradise is lost."

Passages: Predictable Crises of Adult Life by Gail Sheehy (Dutton, 1976; Bantam, PB). A good book for anticipating potential trouble spots in your own life, in your marriage, and in the lives of your adult friends. If you see trouble coming, maybe you can head it off.

The Summer Before the Dark by Doris Lessing (Knopf, 1973). This is *Passages* in the form of a novel. Kate Brown's four children are nearly grown, her looks are fading, and her husband is engrossed in work. What is life about now? A good scary read that manages not to be depressing.

Starting: Early, Anew, Over, and Late by Helen Yglesias (Rawson, Wade, 1978). This is a plain wonderful book, a collection of interviews and essays describing the "starting" or true blooming of many women and several men. Among them is the author herself, who wrote her first novel at 54. There are such early starters as the author's son, who had to run away from home to write his first book, and Barbara, a beautiful Maine girl who bloomed after she quit a waitressing job to do construction work outdoors, which made her happy and paid her well. There are people of 30, 40, and 50 who are starting again in careers or relationships or both, some of them pushed into it by spouses, divorce, or widowhood. This book, composed as it is of graphic vignettes of real lives, gives one the courage to try. All of us could use the inspiration it offers at some point in our lives.

What Color Is Your Parachute? A Practical Manual for Job Hunters and Career Changers by Richard Bolles (Ten Speed Press, rev. ed., 1976, PB). A helpful book for you and your spouse.

The Woman's Guide to Starting a Business by Claudia Jessup and Genie Chipps (Holt, Rinehart & Winston, 1977). The second part gives fascinating profiles of women who acted on their dreams, starting businesses in a variety of fields. The first gives facts on all the basic concerns of the fledgling entrepreneur: insurance, law, rentals, hiring and firing, taxes, and public relations.

Woman's Work: The Housewife, Past and Present by Ann Oakley (Pantheon, 1974: Random House, PB). This thoughtful book, originally published in Great Britain, describes details of the daily lives of British women of all social classes. The accent may be British but the problems are the same as ours.

Women, Work, and Volunteering by Herta Loeser (Beacon, 1974, PB). For many mothers, volunteer work is the cure for isolation and an answer to the need to maintain or develop job-related skills. This is a practical guide to volunteer opportunities and to volunteering as a training ground for a career.

Women's Legal Rights by Shana Alexander (Wollstonecraft, 1975, PB).
A state-by-state guide covering laws relating to marriage, divorce,
children, work, abortion, and widowhood. Although this book is
out of print, it may be available at your library.

Miscellaneous

Catalyst
14 East 60th Street
New York, N.Y. 10022
An organization that provides a list of companies on "flextime,"
which allows parents some choice in their employment hours.

Child Abuse Hotline
800-421-0353
800-352-0386 (California residents only)

Homemakers Rights
The Homemakers Committee of the National Commission on the
Observance of International Women's Year is now at work on fifty
versions of "The Legal Status of Homemakers," one for each state.
The booklets describe the legal rights of women during marriage,
widowhood, and divorce. Six are already completed—Colorado, Iowa,
Louisiana, Missouri, Montana, and Nevada. Order from the Super-
intendent of Document, U.S. Government Printing Office, Washington, D.C. 20402.

"Making Time: A Housewife's Log," *Ms.* Magazine, March 1976. By
keeping a daily log, the author found that, first she didn't have
time for herself, and, second, that she spent most of her time re-
sponding to family members' demands rather than actually providing the "stimulating creative environment for intellectual growth"
she had hoped to achieve by staying home when the children were
young. She effects changes, including part-time work, that appear
to work well for everyone in the family.

Martha Movement
1011 Arlington Boulevard
Arlington, Va. 22209
"Martha Matters" is the monthly publication of this nonprofit
organization devoted to mutual support and upgrading the image
of full-time homemakers, as well as to supporting legislation that
helps housewives. Local chapters are being organized in many cities.
Membership, including the newsletter, is $5.00 a year.

Naming Your Baby

Naming your baby can be a hit or miss affair, or it can be a carefully thought out decision—to give your child a head start towards success in life. Names are important! This section covers all the guidelines you'll need to consider in naming your baby. By following them, you'll not only come up with a good name, but you will also avoid inadvertently picking an awkward name or initials which can give your child unnecessary teasing from peers over the years.

Take your time in selecting a name for your baby. Don't let hospital officials interested in efficiency push you into a decision about naming your baby before you're ready to make it. Lots of us vacillate all the way to the hospital and back again. Lyndon Johnson's parents went three months without naming him. In California, a parent may take up to a full year to put a name on a birth certificate, and the law in other states allows from ten days to seven years before given names must be recorded. If you haven't made up your mind by the time you deliver, instruct hospital employees to leave the space for the child's name blank and ask them to tell you exactly how long your state allows for making up your mind. Otherwise, if you want the name changed legally, you may end up in court. In general, minors may have their names changed only by a court petition co-signed by both parents.

The guidelines that follow cover all the important considerations in choosing the first and middle given names. Keep in mind that you may decide on a *last name* other than

508

that of the father. Most states permit parents—if they both agree—to write any last name they choose on the birth-certificate form. Check your state law with municipal health department officials. Some possibilities for last names: (1) The maiden name of the mother; in medieval France it was common to give female children the mother's maiden name and male children the father's name. (2) A combination of the parents' last names, as is the custom in many Spanish-speaking countries; a child whose mother was a Smith and father a Jones could then be Peter Smith-Jones. (3) A last name that has nothing to do with either parent. Jane Fonda and Tom Hayden, for example, named their son Troy O'Donovan Garity. It's a good idea to let the doctor know your plans beforehand to avoid a hassle. The only limit on any of these options is that no fraud is intended.

Names are important as illustrated by the list of famous persons presented at the end of this section—all of whom changed given names. They apparently decided that the names their parents had given them were not suitable for the life they had in mind. Looking over the list of name changes and also looking over the lists of fifty most popular names in the U.S. over the course of this century (see the Chart on Pages 512 and 513) may suggest some suitable names for your baby.

One hint: the easiest and least expensive way of finding many thousands of names to consider for your child is to look in the back of a good dictionary. Various spellings are given along with the meaning, pronounciation, and history of the names.

One caution: When you've settled on a name do not allow others to corrupt it if *you* don't wish it to be corrupted. Grandparents or nursery-school teachers who turn Bruce into Brucie or Sue into Susie should be corrected. If you don't do it for your child, no one else will.

Guidelines in Choosing First and Middle Names

Popularity/Voguishness
Is the name you like extremely popular right now? Often you won't know this unless you do a little research. Parents naming a first child rarely know the big names on the playground. There's no way to be certain your child will not find three

others in her kindergarten class with the same name, but one way to try to avoid this is telephone the medical-records departments of several local hospitals toward the end of your pregnancy and ask them to tell you the most popular names at that time for both sexes. In the recent past, for example, parents who thought they'd come up with somewhat original names have found that Jennifer, Joshua, Heather, and Jason have hit the top-ten list in practically every area of the country. Some of the suddenly popular names appear to come out of nowhere while others can be traced to a popular TV show or hit song.

In weighing this type of popularity as well as the classic variety described in the next section, also consider your last name. A more unusual first name may help a child with a common last name such as Jones or Smith to avoid mixups in life. More important, in weighing voguishness, consider whether the name is a "new" one that will label your off-spring for life with a name that was popular in a certain decade. Sarah, for example, is an old name newly in vogue, but one that will probably always be around and will probably not be identified with a specific decade. Stacy or Tanya, on the other hand, may be. Examples of other names once in vogue but now rare are Ida, Frances, and Shirley.

Popularity/Long Term
There are some names that have stayed among the top fifty since the turn of the century, even if they are rarely in the top five. Examples: John, James, Thomas, Mary, Susan, Catherine. Among the advantages of classic names: children feel secure with a relatively common name and some psychologists say children with names like these seem to have better odds of success in life and that they are perceived as brighter by teachers; custom has usually established a standard spelling and pronunciation for the name and one or two nicknames; usually these names suit a person of 60 as well as a child of 5. Possible disadvantages: one may know many others with the same name throughout one's life; these names may not appeal to the parent who enjoys being "contemporary"; and even classic names can turn "old-fashioned" or become "dated" over the years—Mary, according to some name watchers, is destined for this fate. Check the Top-Fifty

Chart on the next two pages to see if your favorite classic name is dropping in popularity.

Etymology

The meaning or origin of a name is interesting to know but of little relevance in the life of either a child or an adult. To be aware that Anthony comes from the Latin and means "priceless" is probably something a parent who has settled on that name will want to share with the child, but it should not weigh heavily in a final decision. One should, however, be aware of a related factor, the *verbal associations* a word may have. That "john" is a slang word for toilet is something your child will probably be teased about if you decide on that name. The British are frequently surprised at hearing the first name Randy. As an adjective, "randy" means ill-mannered, coarse, and quite lusty or lewd. Check to see if there is a dictionary listing as a word for a name before making a final choice.

Stereotypes

Few parents would name a child Adolph, Judas, or even Benedict. That's what stereotypes are all about. Most of us unwittingly conjure up ideas about people just from seeing a name on paper or hearing it spoken. Test the names you are considering for a baby by asking yourself such questions as: How would I react to hearing I was going on a blind date with that person? What would my reaction be to that name on a job application if I were doing the hiring? Christopher Andersen, in *The Name Game,* offers a list of 894 stereotypes of common names based on what he calls a "wide variety of studies and sources." He claims that the stereotype idea of a Nicole is "average on all counts"; of Elizabeth, "seductive"; of Jason, "hugely popular"; and of Robin, "sissified." Interestingly enough, he uses the adjective "winner" for only three girls' names—Gina, Janet, and Patty—but twenty-four boys' names get that accolade. The "winner" boys start with Al and Bobby, go on to James and Jeff, and on down alphabetically to Stephen and Ward. Despite the difficulty in judging stereotypes, this sort of consideration should be far more important in choosing names than the etymology of the name. At the very least, parents themselves should not have poor stereotypes in their own minds for a name they choose.

The Top-Fifty First Names for Boys

Based on American university students, mainly middle-class whites, born in the years shown. The 1975 names are drawn from newspaper birth announcements. Variant spelling forms are grouped under the main spelling.

1900	1925	1950	1975
1. John	1. Robert	1. John	1. Michael
2. William	2. John	2. Robert	2. Jason
3. Charles	3. William	3. James	3. Matthew
4. Robert	4. James	4. Michael	4. Brian
5. Joseph	5. Charles	5. David	5. Christopher
6. James	6. Richard	6. Steven	6. David
7. George	7. George	7. William	7. John
8. Samuel	8. Donald	8. Richard	8. James
9. Thomas	9. Joseph	9. Thomas	9. Jeffrey
10. Arthur	10. Edward	10. Mark	10. Daniel
11. Harry	11. Thomas	11. Charles	11. Steven
12. Edward	12. David	12. Gary	Eric
13. Henry	13. Frank	13. Paul	13. Robert
14. Walter	14. Harold	14. Jeffrey	14. Scott
15. Louis	15. Arthur	15. Joseph	15. Andrew
16. Paul	16. Jack	16. Donald	16. Mark
17. Ralph	17. Paul	17. Ronald	17. Aaron
18. Carl	18. Kenneth	18. Daniel	18. Benjamin
19. Frank	19. Walter	19. Kenneth	Kevin
20. Raymond	20. Raymond	20. George	20. Sean
21. Francis	21. Carl	21. Alan	21. Jonathan
22. Frederick	22. Albert	22. Dennis	22. Timothy
23. Albert	23. Henry	23. Douglas	23. Ryan
Benjamin	24. Harry	24. Gregory	24. Joseph
25. David	25. Francis	25. Edward	25. Adam
26. Harold	26. Ralph	26. Timothy	Richard
27. Howard	27. Eugene	27. Peter	27. Paul
28. Fred	28. Howard	28. Larry	28. Jeremy
Richard	29. Lawrence	29. Lawrence	Thomas
30. Clarence	30. Louis	30. Philip	30. Charles
Herbert	31. Alan	31. Frank	31. Joshua
32. Jacob	32. Norman	32. Craig	32. William
33. Ernest	33. Gerald	33. Scott	33. Peter
Jack	34. Herbert	34. Brian	Nathan
35. Herman	35. Fred	35. Roger	Todd
Philip	36. Earl	36. Christopher	36. Douglas
Stanley	Philip	37. Patrick	Gregory
38. Donald	Stanley	38. Carl	38. Patrick
Earl	39. Daniel	39. Gerald	Shane
Elmer	40. Leonard	Terry	40. Kenneth
41. Leon	Marvin	41. Kevin	41. Edward
Nathan	42. Frederick	42. Randall	Nicholas
43. Eugene	43. Anthony	43. Raymond	43. Chad
Floyd	Samuel	44. Anthony	44. Anthony
Ray	45. Bernard	45. Andrew	45. Justin
Roy	Edwin	46. Frederick	Keith
Sydney	47. Alfred	47. Arthur	47. Bradley
48. Abraham	48. Russell	48. Eric	48. Donald
Edwin	Warren	Howard	George
Lawrence	50. Ernest	Walter	50. Dennis
Leonard			
Norman			
Russell			

Credit: *First Names First*, by Leslie Alan Dunkling, Universe Books. New York, 1977. Used with permission.

The Top-Fifty First Names for Girls

Based on American university students, mainly middle-class whites, born in the years shown. The 1975 names are drawn from newspaper birth announcements. Variant spelling forms are shown as one name.

1900	*1925*	*1950*	*1975*
1. Mary	1. Mary	1. Mary	1. Jennifer
2. Ruth	2. Barbara	2. Susan	2. Amy
3. Helen	3. Dorothy	3. Deborah	3. Sarah
4. Margaret	4. Betty	4. Linda	4. Michelle
5. Elizabeth	5. Ruth	5. Patricia	5. Kimberly
6. Dorothy	6. Margaret	6. Barbara	6. Heather
7. Catherine	7. Helen	7. Nancy	7. Rebecca
8. Mildred	Elizabeth	8. Catherine	8. Catherine
9. Francis	9. Jean	9. Karen	9. Kelly
10. Alice	10. Ann(e)	10. Carol(e)	10. Elizabeth
Marion	11. Patricia	11. Ann(e)	Julie
12. Anna	12. Shirley	12. Kathleen	Lisa
13. Sarah	13. Virginia	13. Elizabeth	Melissa
14. Gladys	14. Nancy	14. Janet	14. Angela
15. Grace	15. Joan	15. Margaret	Kristen
Lillian	16. Martha	16. Cynthia	16. Carrie
17. Florence	17. Marion	17. Pamela	Stephanie
Virginia	18. Doris	18. Dian(n)e	18. Jessica
19. Edith	19. Frances	19. Sandra	19. Christine
Lucy	Marjorie	20. Jane	Erin
21. Clara	21. Marilyn	21. Judith	Laura
Doris	22. Alice	22. Gail	Nicole
23. Marjorie	23. Eleanor	23. Christine	23. Stacy
24. Annie	Catherine	24. Sharon	Tracy
25. Louise	25. Lois	25. Donna	25. Andrea
Martha	26. Jane	26. Janice	Ann(e)
27. Ann(e)	27. Phyllis	27. Kathy	27. Rachel
Blanche	28. Florence	Lynn(e)	Karen
Eleanor	Mildred	Rebecca	Wendy
Emma	30. Carol(e)	30. Marcia	30. Christina
Hazel	31. Carolyn	31. Joan	31. Amanda
32. Esther	Marie	32. Martha	Mary
Ethel	Norma	33. Ellen	33. Christy
Laura	34. Anna	Marilyn	34. Danielle
Marie	Louise	35. Laura	35. Jodi
36. Julia	36. Beverley	36. Cheryl	36. Shannon
37. Beatrice	Janet	37. Joanna	Tanya
Gertrude	38. Sarah	38. Sarah	38. Alison
39. Alma	39. Evelyn	39. Carolyn	Lori
Mabel	40. Edith	Theresa	Robin
Minnie	Jacqueline	41. Jean	Theresa
Pauline	Lorraine	42. Michelle	42. Emily
Rose	43. Grace	Paula	Susan
44. Fanny	44. Ethel	Robin	Tara
45. Agnes	Gloria	45. Virginia	45. Heidi
Carrie	Laura	46. Vicki(e)	Jill
Edna	47. Audrey	47. Beverly	Tonya
Evelyn	Esther	48. Suzanne	48. Tammy
Harriet	Joanne	49. Helen	49. Kathleen
Ida	Sally	50. Brenda	Erica
Irene		Denise	Kara
Miriam		Ruth	Melanie

Uniqueness

For themselves and their friends, children like names that are common and easy to spell. Children who have uncommon names often say they feel uneasy with them. Indeed, studies have shown that boys and girls with "desirable" names like David, Michael, Barbara, and Carol scored higher on IQ and achievement tests than those with "undesirable" names like Bertha, Phoebe, Albert, and Maurice. Nevertheless, many adults who disliked their more unusual names as children say the tables turn in later life, when they became grateful for more distinctive names. Winston Churchill, Lyndon Johnson, and Hubert Humphrey all liked their names.

Actually, there is no way a parent can know whether an unusual name will help or hinder a child in his or her professional life. Few of us will have the luck of a Mrs. Midler or Mrs. Hoffman, who named Bette and Dustin after stars Bette Davis and Dustin Farnum. In any case, stay away from the jokes, the cute, and the faddish, and keep the child's whole life in mind when you're considering even a slightly unusual name. There is a long way between naming a child after a favorite city, as James and Pamela Mason did with their daughter Portland, and naming your twin sons Bing and Bang as did the Pistel's of Baltimore.

In the end, you don't have to worry to much about uniqueness. The number of names is proliferating, and no single name accounts for more than a small fraction of the total. In 1978 in Vermont, for example, the most popular name was Christopher among the 3,569 boys born that year. Even so, there were only 136—less than 4 percent. Among girls that year, the top name was Sarah, at 181, about 5 percent of the total.

"It is, of course, the naming of a child in a really *odd* way that I object to, not the bestowal of an *unusual* name. A rarely used name can individualize the person who bears it while causing no adverse comment. An odd name, I seriously believe, can disfigure a child for life, doing a great deal of psychological damage. Most parents are well aware of the risks, and they play safe with the well-tried names. In my view they are quite right to do so."

—Leslie Alan Dunkling, *First Names First*

Family Names/Juniors/Namesakes
Use of a surname—the mother's for example—as a middle
name or even as a first name appears to be increasing. It is
one way of making an otherwise ordinary name distinctive.
In fact, the number of corporation executives, college presidents, and foundation heads who use a family name as either
a first name or as a middle name preceded by just a first initial is remarkable. A middle name like this may allow your
child some flexibility when he decides what he wants to do
with his life. Harry S. Lewis, for example, dropped his first
name and spelled out his middle name, becoming Sinclair
Lewis, when he began publishing his novels. William Somerset
Maugham did the same. Thomas Woodrow Wilson dropped
the Thomas. Businessmen who opt for or are given the First
Initial-Family Name-Surname "uniform" (such as J. Pierpont
Morgan or C. Calvert Knudsen) are, according to Christopher
Anderson in *The Name Game*, set for success. "There is a
certain attractive arrogance attached to such names," he
notes. "In effect, the name itself is a declaration of where
the individual intends to go."

Juniors and III's and IV's, on the other hand, are decreas-
ing—and probably for good reason. As children grow up, confusion about mail and telephone calls gets wearing, to say
nothing of the psychological effect on a child of living "down"
or "up to" the reputation of a parent with the same name.
Even when, as is frequently done, parents vary the middle
name of a junior and call him by the new name, there can
still be confusion. John Joseph Hartigan's son may be named
John Scott Hartigan, but there may still be mixups over mail
for J. Hartigan.

It is a wonderful compliment to name your child after
someone, but if you give your child the first name of a relative or friend, make sure the name is one you like anyway.
Also make sure that the name is not dated; one way you can
do this is to check the Top-Fifty names chart. Rose or Myrtle
or Cornelius may be fine for a 70-year-old, but your 13-year-
old may resent it.

Sexual Ambiguity
Unisex names like Robin, Chris, and Terry and names where
just the spelling is different for boys and girls like Carroll/

Carol, Lesley/Leslie can be good or bad, depending on your point of view. Some parents think such names help children feel fewer sex-role pressures. Others think it is unfair to make a child explain which sex he or she is, a surprisingly frequent occurrence given today's attire for young children. Years afterward, John Wayne remembered vividly how he felt about being seated with the girls when school started; his name in those days was Marion Michael Morrison. Psychologists claim that boys feel more threatened when they are presumed to be girls than vice versa.

Initials

Although in the past it was sometimes considered good luck to have initials that spelled a word, it can get tiresome to listen to jokes all your life about P.U. or D.O.G. Sir Authur Sullivan of Gilbert and Sullivan had the middle name Seymour and the distinction of bearing the initials A.S.S. If your child's initials will make up a word, make sure it's a pleasant one. Also, when thinking of initials, a case can be made for avoiding duplication of another family member's initials so that there won't be mixups in luggage, messages, and the like. On the other hand, a case can be made *for* repeating initials so that monogrammed heirlooms can be passed on with the correct lettering.

Don't stop with initials alone. What happens when you put the first letter of the first name together with the last name? There really has been a D. E. Cline on the earth. At Yale University the story is still told of a meticulous professor who insisted that all his graduate students have name signs posted outside their study cubicles—just the first initial and last name, please, and no exceptions. Not even for Paul Enis.

Sound and Rhythm

Rhyming names like Heather Feather of Paul Tall set up a child for the kind of attention he does not deserve. These and any other joke names are ones that no considerate parent will put on a birth certificate. Alliteration, however—as in Sally Sloper or Tom Travis—is fine. Also when you're mulling over the sound of the whole name you have chosen, consider the ease or difficulty of pronouncing the combination of names. Pat Six is harder to say than Robert Six, for example.

A good general rule is that unequal numbers of syllables make for pleasing rythms. Elizabeth Clark sounds less harsh than Ann Clark. Alexander Graham Bell sounds better than Mark Paul Bell. When first and last names do have the same number of syllables, a middle name with a different number may create a pleasant rhythm, as in Frederick Paul Harrington. Single-syllable names can sound particularly strong together, however, if each name has a somewhat long sound, as in Charles Graves or Mark Twain.

Spelling
Ordinary spellings can save a lot of time and irritation for a child. Especially if your last name requires frequent spelling out for strangers, you may want to stick with the usual spelling of an easily spelled first name. Imagine having to spell out both first and last names to everyone from the dry cleaner to the telephone operator for the rest of your life. Even in early childhood, unusual spellings can cause discomfort. One Aimee we know had her name misspelled on gift cards from ten of the twelve guests at her seventh birthday party. What's more, there may be people in your child's world later who think it silly and in poor taste to use nontraditional spelling; they're prejudiced against every Kaytee, Thom, and Judi they meet. Check the back of any good dictionary for the "Common English Given Names" section, which gives the preferred spelling for many names.

Pronunciation
Is the pronunciation of the name you are considering in any way ambiguous? If you spell a name in an unusual way or choose a name that is little known in this country, you will surely set up your child for constant mispronunciations of his name or, worse yet, a life where people avoid addressing him by his given name. A records clerk at a Southern California hospital told a newspaper reporter recently that she had noticed an increase in new names. "In fact, a lot of them are so unusual that they're difficult for us to spell and I wouldn't even think of trying to pronounce some of them."

Religion
Religious tradition may be a factor in choosing a name for your baby. Jews traditionally choose names taken from the

Bible or use the name of a deceased relative. Orthodox Jews do not usually name a child after a living relative. Many Roman Catholics have chosen the names of saints for their children, while some Protestants choose both Old and New Testament names and most Muslims choose Islamic names.

Nationality/Ethnicity

In an era of heightened interest in "roots," parents are looking at names from different countries or those popular with other races. It may be best not to combine names with different roots, as in Rosemary Cohen or Tosca Tatarczuk, but a case can be made for the opposite view if the combination reflects reality. To find names that are popular in other countries, check with the tourist information office or embassy of the country you're interested in, or ask a reference librarian to help you out with reference books.

Nicknames

An old Chinese proverb says, "If a man has no nickname he never grows rich." You may want to encourage a lighthearted approach to naming your children, or at least to coming up with a name to be used at home. One warm Baltimore family we know with the last name of Reno lets names evolve inside the house. Mary Hall became "Halsey"; Ron Jr. became "Rusty"; William turned into Will; and when we last heard from them the youngest, Lisa, was still waiting for her nickname. Conky Johnston, president of a company that makes yogurt in Southern California, says that in Texas, where she was born, it was customary to give children a formal name and a "soft" name. Her formal name is Merly, but the soft name works fine for her life today. She has a sister named Chick, a brother Rib, and a cousin Sox, and all are listed that way in their respective telephone directories.

Certainly there is a plus side to nicknames. If you like the idea of nicknames but can't imagine yourself dreaming up original ones, consider what one name expert calls the "silver-dollar names"—ones that contain several varied nicknames suitable for different stages of life. Abigail, for example, can be Abigail on her resumé, Gail to her friends, and Abby at home. Remember Eugene Field's "Father calls me William, Sister calls me Will, Mother calls me Willie, but the fellers call me Bill"?

The basic consideration, however, is that you like the nickname, if any, that is standard for the name you have chosen. Your child's friends may end up calling him that whether you do or not. Also, be wary of giving your child a nickname as a legal name. Bobby and Jamie and Trisha will have to spend too much of their lives explaining that their real names are not Robert or James or Patricia. Finally, remember that what is a cute nickname for a baby may not sound so cute for an adult. Rickie steals dignity from Richard, and Freddie is not fair to Fred nor Bertie to Bert.

Number of Names
No law requires a person to have three names. Some name experts advocate giving a child four names: a common one for the early years; a more unusual one, such as a family name; and a name that is even more fanciful in case the child goes into politics or the theater. However, most forms provide spaces for only three names and this could cause the bearer of three-plus names—to say nothing of computers—problems from time to time.

FAMOUS NAME CHANGES

Below is a list of persons famous in politics, sports, the arts, and entertainment who changed their given names in some way. Many were able to work with the name given them by parents to fashion a name that suited them in professional life.

Fred Allen (John Florence Sullivan)
Woody Allen (Allen Stewart Konigsberg)
Julie Andrews (Julia Wells)
Ann-Margret (Ann-Margret Olsson)
Eddie Arcaro (George Edward Arcaro)
Elizabeth Arden (Florence Nightingale Graham)
Beatrice Arthur (Bernice Frankel)
Fred Astaire (Frederick Austerlitz)
Lauren Bacall (Betty Joan Perske)
Anne Bancroft (Annemarie Italiano)
John Barrymore (John Blythe)
Orson Bean (Dallas Frederick Burrows)
Warren Beatty (Warren Beaty)

David Ben-Gurion (David Green)
Tony Bennett (Anthony Dominick Benedetto)
Jack Benny (Benjamin Kubelsky)
Polly Bergen (Nellie Paulina Burgin)
Milton Berle (Milton Berlinger)
Yogi Berra (Lawrence Peter Berra)
Joey Bishop (Joseph Abraham Gottlieb)
Georges Bizet (Alexandre César Léopold Bizet)
Amanda Blake (Beverly Louise Neill)
Sonny Bono (Salvatore Bono)
Pat Boone (Charles Eugene Boone)
Willy Brandt (Herbert Ernst Karl Frahm)
Yul Brynner (Taidje Kahn, Jr.)
George Burns (Nathan Birnbaum)
Ellen Burstyn (Edna Rae Gillooly)
Richard Burton (Richard Jenkins)
Michael Caine (Maurice Joseph Micklewhite)
Taylor Caldwell (Janet Taylor Caldwell)
Maria Callas (Maria Anna Sofia Cecilia Kalogeropoulos)
Scott Carpenter (Malcolm Scott Carpenter)
Lewis Carroll (Charles Lutwidge Dodgson)
Marc Chagall (Marc Segal)
Cyd Charisse (Tula Ellice Finklea)
Ray Charles (Ray Charles Robinson)
Paddy Chayefsky (Sidney Chayefsky)
Cher (Cherilyn La Piere)
Chubby Checker (Ernest Evans)
Grover Cleveland (Stephen Grover Cleveland)
Van Cliburn (Harvey Lavan Cliburn, Jr.)
Buffalo Bill Cody (William Frederick Köthe)
Colette (Sidonie Gabrielle Claudine Colette)
Joseph Conrad (Teodor Józef Konrad Korzeniowski)
Bert Convy (Bernard Whalen Patrick Convy)
Alice Cooper (Vincent Damon Furnier)
Gary Cooper (Frank James Cooper)
Bing Crosby (Harry Lillis Crosby)
Tony Curtis (Bernard Schwartz)
Rodney Dangerfield (John Cohen)
Doris Day (Doris von Kappelhoff)
Dizzy Dean (Jay Hanna Dean)
John Denver (Henry John Deutschendorf, Jr.)

Isak Dinesen (Karen Dinesen Blixen)
Kirk Douglas (Issur Danielovitch)
Mike Douglas (Michael Delaney Dowd, Jr.)
Patty Duke (Anna Marie Duke)
Bob Dylan (Robert Allen Zimmerman)
Samantha Eggar (Victoria Louise Eggar)
George Eliot (Mary Ann Evans)
Duke Ellington (Edward Kennedy Ellington)
Mama Cass Elliot (Ellen Naomi Cohen)
Werner Erhard (Jack Rosenberg)
Dale Evans (Frances Octavia Smith Rogers)
Chad Everett (Raymond Lee Cramton)
W.C. Fields (William Claude Dukenfield)
Dame Margot Fonteyn (Margaret Hookham)
Anatole France (Jacques Anatole Francois Thibault)
Carlton Fredericks (Harold Casper Frederick Caplan)
Clark Gable (William Clark Gable)
Greta Garbo (Greta Luisa Gustafson)
Judy Garland (Frances Gumm)
James Garner (James Baumgardner)
Samuel Goldwyn (Samuel Goldfisch)
Maxim Gorky (Aleksei Maksimovich Peshkov)
Billy Graham (William Franklin Graham)
Cary Grant (Archibald Leach)
Lee Grant (Lyova Haskell Rosenthal)
Ulysses S. Grant (Hiram Ulysses Grant)
El Greco (Domenico Teotocopulo)
Haile Selassie (Ras Tafari Makonnen)
Halston (Roy Halston Frowick)
Bret Harte (Francis Brett Harte)
Laurence Harvey (Larushka Skikne)
Rita Hayworth (Margarita Carmen Cansino)
Heinrich Heine (Harry Heine)
O. Henry (William Sydney Porter)
Rock Hudson (Roy Scherer, Jr.)
Englebert Humperdinck (Arnold Dorsey)
Rev. Ike (Frederick Joseph Eikerenkoetter II)
Kareem Abdul-Jabbar (Ferdinand Lewis Alcindor, Jr.)
Tom Jones (Thomas Jones Woodward)
Garson Kanin (Gershon Labe)
Danny Kaye (David Daniel Kominsky)

Ann Landers (Esther Pauline Friedman Lederer)
Mario Lanza (Alfredo Arnold Cocozza)
Ring Lardner (Ringgold Wilmer Lardner)
Piper Laurie (Rosetta Jacobs)
Steve Lawrence (Sidney Leibowitz)
Leadbelly (Huddie Ledbetter)
John Le Carré (David John Moore Carnwell)
Gypsy Rose Lee (Rose Louise Hovick)
Nikolai Lenin (Vladimir Ilich Ulyanov)
Liberace (Wladziu Valentino Liberace)
Sophia Loren (Sophia Scicolone)
Clare Boothe Luce (Anne Clare Booth Luce)
Connie Mack (Cornelius Alexander McGillicuddy)
Gisele MacKenzie (Marie Marguerite Louise Gisele La Fleche)
Shirley MacLaine (Shirley MacLaine Beaty)
Dean Martin (Dino Crocetti)
Paul McCartney (James Paul McCartney)
Marshall McLuhan (Herbert Marshall McLuhan)
Butterfly McQueen (Thelma McQueen)
Steve McQueen (Terence Stephen McQueen)
Robert Merrill (Moishe Miller)
Ray Milland (Reginald Truscott-Jones)
Joni Mitchell (Roberta Joan Anderson Mitchell)
Marilyn Monroe (Norma Jean Mortenson)
Bill Moyers (Billy Don Moyers)
Mike Nichols (Michael Igor Peschowsky)
Peter O'Toole (Seamus O'Toole)
Drew Pearson (Andrew Russell Pearson)
Gregory Peck (Eldred Gregory Peck)
Jan Peerce (Jacob Pincus Perelmuth)
Pelé (Edson Arantes do Nascimento)
S.J. Perelman (Sidney Joseph Perelman)
Mary Pickford (Gladys Marie Smith)
J.B. Priestley (John Boynton Priestley)
Pee Wee Reese (Harold Henry Reese)
Lee Remick (Ann Remick)
Debbie Reynolds (Mary Frances Reynolds)
Harold Robbins (Francis Kane)
Jerome Robbins (Jerome Rabinowitz)
Roy Rogers (Leonary Slye)
Buffy Sainte-Marie (Beverly Sainte-Marie)

Yves Saint Laurent (Henri Donat Mathieu)
Soupy Sales (Milton Hines)
J. D. Salinger (Jerome David Salinger)
Dr. Seuss (Theodore Seuss Geisel)
Bishop Fulton J. Sheen (Peter Sheen)
Dinah Shore (Frances Rose Shore)
Jean Sibelius (Johann Julius Christian Sibelius)
Beverly Sills (Belle Silverman)
O.J. Simpson (Orenthal James Simpson)
Bubba Smith (Charles Aaron Smith)
Phoebe Snow (Phoebe Loeb)
Sissy Spacek (Mary Elizabeth Spacek)
Mickey Spillane (Frank Morrison)
Ringo Starr (Richard Starkey)
Stendhal (Marie Henri Beyle)
Casey Stengel (Charles Dillon Stengel)
Stepin' Fetchit (Lincoln Theodore Perry)
Irving Stone (Irving Tennenbaum)
Lana Turner (Julia Jean Turner)
Mark Twain (Samuel Langhorne Clemens)
Twiggy (Lesley Hornby)
Abigail Van Buren (Pauline Esther Friedman Phillips)
Gore Vidal (Eugene Vidal)
Voltaire (Francois Marie Arouet)
Mike Wallace (Myron Wallace)
Bruno Walter (Bruno Walter Schlesinger)
Muddy Waters (McKinley Morganfield)
John Wayne (Marion Michael Morrison)
Clifton Webb (Webb Parmelee Hollenbeck)
Tuesday Weld (Susan Kerr Weld)
Nathanael West (Nathan Wallenstein Weinstein)
Rebecca West (Cicily Isabel Fairfield)
E. B. White (Elwyn Brooks White)
Tennessee Williams (Thomas Lanier Williams)
Flip Wilson (Clerow Wilson)
Woodrow Wilson (Thomas Woodrow Wilson)
Stevie Wonder (Steveland Morris Hardaway)
Natalie Wood (Natasha Gurdin)
Cy Young (Denton True Young)

Acknowledgments

To the parents who shared their time, their knowledge, and
their children with us, our deepest thanks:

Linda Adler	Devra, Cindi
Barbara Albies	Casey
Lillie Faye Anderson	Ronald, Melinda
Barbara Andrews	Eric, Scott, John
Doris Arterburn	Eric, Matthew
Laura Ballard	John, Julie
Susan Ballard	Michael, Amy
Linda Barrett	Christal Lynn, Daniel Clarke
Mary Beck	Erin
Maris Berg	Danny, Michael
Martha Bill	Christopher, John, Robert
Carolyn J. Bishop	Carolyn Jenner
Sharon Blischke	Carrie, Todd
Sandy Boarts	Kori, Brian
Claire Boiko	Sue, Patty, Melinda, Robert, Elizabeth
Gertrude Bonham	Barbara, Kit
Joan Booty	Andrew
Chris Brown	Jason, Tammy
Sharon Brown	Kimberly
Clarinda E. Campbell	Karen, Christopher, Brian, Kathy, Scott, Kelly
Valerie Carricato	Drew

Dorothy Cattivera	Laura, Joe, Brian, Rob
Hassana Chahine	Hadi, Nader
Marsha Chauncey	Brett, Kai
Georgina Chrisman	Rainy, Brandy
Michele Christensen	Diane, Doug
Jennifer Coe	Amy
Susan Conger	Amy, James, Michael
Marge Cook	Cheri, Debbra
Kimberly Corson	Matthew, Gordon
Pam Cour	Cale
Patricia Crane	Laura, Bradley
Elaine Cronin	Alicia, Maureen, Michael
Paula Daniels	Kyle
Melanie Demont	Jack
Carol Detrick	Amy, Andrew
Margaret Dickie	Ananda, Ian
Mary Ann Dietz	Debora
Carol Dinn	Jennifer, Sean, Melissa
Janel Douda	Kristin
Carolyn B. Downey	Sharon, Michael
Barbara Dunsmoor	Becca, Sara, Katherine
Mary Duru	Jeremi, Kenrik
Marsha Dyer	Taryn, Allyn, Ashlyn
Melanie Ebert	Sarah, Ashlee
Laura Edge	Robert
Nikki Eick	Heidi, Carey
Marla Engel	Peter
Mary Lou Enockson	Erik, Gretchen
Kathleen Erickson	John
Mary Ernst	Samantha Mary
Shirle Farber	Jeffrey Robert, Jerold Vernon
Diana Fedrick	Chad, Shannon
Conni Ferkula	Robert
Gail Fetherston	Chelsea
Leslie Floberg	Jeremy, Brandi
Joan Floyd	Kevin
Nancy French	Sally, Ken, Bob
Eileen Frey	Jim, Steve

Mary Ann Gardner	Clinton
Barbara Geisler	Melissa, Elizabeth
Linda Goldstein	Nicole
Betty Goodin	Michael, Mark, Rodney, Gary, Heidi
Barbara Graham	Tim, Danny
Mary Kay Green	Bridgit, Cameron
Ellie Griffin	Megan
Jan Griffin	Gayle Ann
Stella Guido	Richard, Ronald, Jeffrey, Christine, Susan
Marilyn Guidotti	Crystal, Carl, Michael
Marsha Halford	Tonya, Bruce
Maria Hargett	Jan, Michael
Mary Hart	Robin, Daniel, Joey
Eiko Hashibe	Wendy, Eric
Rachel Heintz	Teressa, Lisa
Jackie Heite	Cindy, Doug
Judi Hillger	Brian, Wendy
Thomasina C. Hinman	Sarah Jane, David
Georgia Hodgkinson	Meta, Neva
Mary E. Horgan	Daniel, Elizabeth, Margaret
Barbara Hudson	Eric, Brad
Nancy Jensen	Jay
Stephanie Joe	Allison
Wanda Johnson	Michael
Gail Kaplan	David, Joshua
Jody Lynn Keech	Jeff
Ginny Kelly	Tom, Joe, Regina, John, Matt, Liz, Bill
Paulette Kelly	David, Kim, Kevin, Sheri, Mindi, Jennifer
Janie Kissel	Kara, Cameron
Susan D. Klein	Melissa, Henry, David, Peter
Linda C. Kline	Megan, Adam
Deborah A. Knauss	Jeffry, Alissa
Joyce Koelling	Joe, Jenny
Patricia Krauska	Joel Michael

Karen E. Kueck	Brian
Iyoko Kunitake	Éric, Bryan
Judith Austin Kunkel	Greg, Kristine
Leona Lacroix	Laura
Patricia A. Lang	Dennis, Sherri, Timothy, Kevin
Ann Lanton	Cherrie
Grace Lasky	Rosalind, Mannix
Susan Lattin	Trevor, Trent
Carolyn Lawson	Erika, Nikole, Mandy
Sandy Lawton	Erin, Blythe
Nina Leckliter	Ryan, Erin
Ria Ledesma	Holly, Brian, Linda
Claire Leney	Tanya
Claudia Lindwall	Kelly, Jody
Joan Livesey	Timothy
David Lobree	Lisa, Bret
Delores A. Long	Danny, Bobby, Holly
Lynda Losson	Ashley, Gregory, Bradley
Kathy Lubbs	Jeff, Dave
Jane Ludwig	Stephen, Stacy, Scott
Jan Lyman	Jessica, Eric
Candace Maccarrone	Heather, Gelane, Marisa
Linda Mack	Laura Anne
Nancy Magera	Kathleen, John Chris, Coleen, Kabrina
Cathleen S. Maloney	Christopher, Elizabeth, Ann, Catherine
Karen Mansergh	Daniel, Sarah
Florence Martin	Jack, Mary Florence
Jill Martin	Lisa
Kathy Marzalek	Sarah
Jane Singer Masser	Jessica
Becky Maynard	Ricky, Jeffrey, Scott, Johathan
Sarah McCann	Amy Kathleen, Stephen Douglas
Mary McCoy	John Paul, Brian, Kelly
Doris McDonough	Thomas Waterson, Vicki, Lisa, Eric
Mary Gaye McGahan	Lisa

Dana McGrath	Suzanne, Betsy
Lynn McIver	Kevin
Kathleen H. McKenna	Brendan, Kerry
Peggy McKibben	Bill, Tom
Susan McNutt	Joshua, Sara
Terrie Mileski	Kristi, Michael
Elsa Millen	Jennifer, Danielle
Joanne Miller	Korey Brad, Steven Jon
Gloria Milstein	Rachel Ann
Nancy Miorin	Erik, Jaime
Kris Moon	Kelsey
Kristin Mumm	Pieter, Katie
Marianne Nahay	Margot
Dale Nelson	Amy, Ingrid
Fay Nevins	Trevor
Daveen Nichols	Travis
Ruth M. O'Connor	John, Matthew, Luke
Linda Orcutt	Kristin, Jenny
Pam Paradissis	Chris, Josh
Delvia and Craig Patton	Jennifer, Craig
Eva Peli	Jeannie, Esther
Noreen Peschke	Eric, Kevin
Gayle Ann Peterson	Marni Ann
Joyce Place	Pamela, Amy, Jon Matthew
Gulli Reeves	Kris, Theresa
Chris Rezai	Theo
Eleanor Ringwald	Marian, Rosemary
Mickie Robbins	Karin, Kristin, Brian
Linda Rogers	Adam, Zach, Hank, Tori
Nancy Rollings	Sarah
Anita and Pete Rosenbaum	Todd, Michelle, Babette, Matthew
Donna Schultz	Aaron Michael
Sue C. Seagroatt	Beth Anne, Heather Lynne, Shawn Edward
Mary Ann Shaw	Stephen, Matthew
Paula Shipe	Robert, Philip
Annette Sills	Carol, Joanne, Edward
Alice B. Simmons	Blair, Sara

Frances Singer	Jane, James
Maxine Singiser	Barry, Steve
Denise Smith	Nicole Suzanne, Joshua James
Jane and Bruce Smith	Jennifer
Judy Soman	Tim, Bridgette
Carol Stark	Cara, Krista
Pamela Steele	Shannon, Craig
Mona Stepczyk	Charles, Marianne, Frankie
Nancy Stoffer	Gary, Joanna
Irene Sturiale	Christopher, Matthew
Myung Y. Sung	Kay
Joan H. Tatarczuk	Billy, Jeffrey, David, Jennifer
Linda M. Taylor	Katherine, Rebecca, Jennifer
Vivian A. Taylor	Claire, Frederick, Gordon
Mercedes Temprano	Pablo, Maria Elena
Catherine Thibault	Kathleen, Larry
Barbara Thompson	Greg, Dennis, Mark, Jim
Kay Trimm	Chris, Denise
Kim Trisdale	Dong Soon, Kenny
Gordon True	Lynn
Valerie Tudor	Sarah, Rachel
Stella Varey	Kim, Don, Rick
Kathie Vickers	Therese, Kirk, Amy
Karen Vinje	Jens
Mary Vogt	Julie, Diana, Tom
Mary Ann Vorban	Alex
Carol Walker	Christy, Cindy, Caren
Elizabeth A. Wallace	Stephen, Lee, Scott
Grace Walters	Jeanine, Tara
Connie Wambolt	Marcia, Frank
Pat Weiss	Jen, Maurine
Carole Westberg	Melissa, Brent, Gavin
Kathleen Whitehead	Stephanie, Joanne
Ann Wickler	Cristine, Bridget
Sharon Wilcox	Kimberlie
Susan Wilcox	Kimberlee
Miriam Wilhelm	Julie, Rebecca
Carol Williams	Luke

Ginger Wilson	Travis, Russ
Melinda Wolfe	Mia, Piper
Eileen Wood	Kristin, Jamie
Jeanne Wood	Timothy, Alison, Brittany
Roberta Jean Wright	Geral Shawn, Elizabeth Jean
Wanda Yetter	Lisa, Scott, Shawna
Lynn C. Zeman	Steve, Kristina

Many persons helped us during the four years this book was in the making. Our deepest gratitude to: Jeanne Henry's sisters, Joan Tatarczuk, Eileen Frey, and Kathleen McKenna, for ideas and moral support, and for cajoling friends and neighbors into answering questionnaires in New York, Vermont, and New Jersey; to Jeanne's mother for sending to California a steady stream of East Coast newspaper clippings on child care subjects; to Anne Heffernan, Jeanne's youngest sister, for help in devising the questionnaire and for trenchant criticism of draft after draft of several chapters; to Barbara Sills' sister Peggy Wilcox, her mother, and her aunt, Ruth Sawyer, for giving questionnaires to mothers in Washington, D.C. and Boston; to her sister Betty for spending a week of her two-week California vacation helping with last-minute details of this book; to our friend Leslie M. Davis, then of the *St. Louis Globe Democrat* and now of *Newsday*, for encouraging Midwestern mothers to contribute to the book; to Kathleen Whitehead, coordinator, and Bob Fish, former principal of the South Bay Adult School, for their support and guidance; to Adult School teachers Linda Adler, Martha Bill, Beth Carman, Betty Goodin, Diane Harrington, Phyllis Miller, Joanne Schepis, and Mary Vogt for handing out questionnaires in their classes; to Shirley M. Kiepper, codirector of the Emma Willard Children's School in Troy, New York, for distributing questionnaires to many mothers of her preschool students; to our friend Nancy Jensen for distributing questionnaires in Pacific Palisades, California.

We also thank: Linda Cassidy Kline, librarian, Edgewood Private Schools, Tustin, California, for help in separating the fine from the not so fine in children's books; to Ruth Robinson, former senior librarian of the Children's Room, Los

Angeles Public Library, for similar aid; to Sharon Blischke, women's health care specialist, for assistance with the chapter on pregnancy; to Dr. Robert Perens, pediatrician and learning disorders specialist, and Dr. Ken Nakamoto, emergency room physician, for criticism of the medical care chapter; to Dr. Laurence C. Reichel, children's dentist, for advice on helping children grow good teeth; to Annemarie Shelness, executive director, Physicians for Automotive Safety, for her criticism of the section on car restraints; to Barbara J. Thompson, R.D., for criticism of the nutrition chapter; to Ray C. Frodey, vice president, Gerber Products Company, for helpful information about manufacture and use of baby foods.

We are particularly grateful to: the students in Barbara's classes, children, mothers, fathers and grandparents who shared their experience and taught that there are many ways of good parenting; to Pam Paradissis and Nancy French, Barbara's teacher aides, for putting in many extra hours both in and out of the classroom; to Barbara Dunsmoor and Jane Singer Masser for reading and criticizing many chapters; to Mary Lou Enockson, Ginger Wilson, Helen Moran, Pam Steele, Gail Kaplan, Jan Lyman and Leslie Floberg for their help with other chapters; to Candy Maccarrone and Marsha and Ashlyn Dyer, who gave hours of their time posing for the photograph on the book jacket; to Sarah Christy for editorial assistance; to Carole Westberg, who savors both mothering and books as much as we do, for a painstaking reading of the book at the end and for the addition of useful information, including the best babysitter information chart we've seen anywhere; to Margaret Oldham, Lorna Clark, Heidi Thompson and Elizabeth Lutton of the St. Cross Preschool in Hermosa Beach, California, for providing examples of nursery school teaching of the finest kind in their work with Anne Henry; to Leslie Floberg and "Nana" Mulliner, who, using their gifts in the care of children with Anne, allowed Jeanne to work longer than fifteen minutes at a time on the book; to Kay Trimm, Sarah Ford, Marjorie Swabeck, Nancy Whitehead, Lesley Hamil, and Barbara Graham, who have given the best in teaching David and Jonas; to Barbara's friends Valerie Tudor, Barbara Thompson, Patricia Dorr, and Gulli Reeves, who filled in as substitute mothers at a moment's notice.

For the special inspiration they offered as mothers and/or friends, we thank: Gertrude Bonham, Georgie Chrisman, Susan Conger, Marge Cook, Kathy DeVoto, Margaret Duggan, Josephine Heffernan, Wanda Johnson, Ginny Kelly, Ann Lake, Peggy McKibben, Cathleen Maloney, Barbara Mann, Margaret Insull O'Shea, Mickie Robbins, Frances Singer, Carol Stark, Linda Taylor, Rosalind Urista, Grace Walters, Peggy Wilkinson, and Wanda Yetter.

Without the enthusiasm of one person this book would not be in the reader's hands. To Garth Bishop, our editor, goes thanks for his faith in the project and for the spurts of inspiration he fostered. To Ann Williams, copy editor and mother of four, goes our appreciation for keeping the wheat and throwing away the chaff. Copy editor Georgia Griggs started work to help polish the "finished" book and then held our hands through two more years of additions and revisions. Without her air of calm and her sharp pencil, we would not have made it.

To Anne, David and Jonas, our thanks for feeding themselves, entertaining themselves, and not interrupting more than three or four times an hour during the days and evenings we worked on the book. Anne, it warmed your mother's heart the day when—questionned about the scratch pad you were ripping apart—you confided proudly: "Me and Melinda are making a book!" Nicholas Henry, who appeared as the book was finished, we thank as the tester of information in the pregnancy chapter.

Finally, thank you to Fred Henry and to Bernie Sills. Except for the day that Bernie told a friend the book would end up being called "Grandmother to Grandmother," their understanding of what this project meant to us, their specific help in criticizing many of the sections, and their willingness to do even more fathering than they usually do is what most of all has made it possible for us to research, compile, and to write this book.

JHH
BWS

Index

Mother's Baby Notebook

BIRTH DATA

Date of birth_____

Day of week/Time of day_____

Weight_____

Length_____

Name of doctor_____

Hospital_____

Special Notes:_____

_____

_____

_____

_____

_____

DAILY ROUTINES: EATING, SLEEPING, ETC.

Infant_____ .

_____

_____

_____

Crawler_____

_____

_____

_____

Toddler_____

_____

_____

_____

2-Year-Old_____

_____

_____

_____

DEVELOPMENT DATES

Followed object with eyes_____

Smiled_____

Laughed out loud_____

Rolled over_____

Grabbed object with hands_____

Sat up alone_____

Crawled_____

First tooth_____

Stood alone_____

Walked_____

Climbed stairs_____

FAVORITE GAMES / ACTIVITIES

6 months_____

_____

_____

_____

_____

12 months_____

_____

_____

_____

_____

24 months_____

_____

_____

_____

_____

LANGUAGE DEVELOPMENT

First words spoken / Date_____

12 month vocabulary_____

_____

_____

_____

_____

18 month vocabulary_____

_____

_____

_____

_____

24 month vocabulary_____

_____

_____

_____

_____

FAVORITE BOOKS

0 - 1 year_____

_____

_____

1 - 2 years_____

_____

_____

2 - 3 years_____

_____

_____

3 - 4 years_____

_____

_____

4 - 5 years_____

_____

_____

FAVORITE TOYS

0 - 1 year_____

_____

_____

1 - 2 years_____

_____

_____

2 - 3 years_____

_____

_____

3 - 4 years_____

_____

_____

4 - 5 years_____

_____

_____

MOTHER TO MOTHER / MOTHERS NETWORK

If you would like to share your child raising hints and experiences with other mothers, write the authors in care of the publisher at the address shown below.

The authors are now working on a companion volume, *The Mother to Mother Family Care Book*, dealing with the resurgence of the family. Just as mothers do their best learning from each other, families can also do their best learning from each other.

How does a family handle everyday problems in the early years such as keeping peace between squabbling family members, and helping children cope with school difficulties? How do families deal with sexuality? In the teenage years, what can families do to avoid serious problems such as drug abuse or deliquency? How does a family handle crises like illness and job difficulties? How do families build strong bonds yet also foster the uniqueness of each individual? How does the single-parent family maintain strong family ties?

These are just a few of the concerns that the authors will explore in the *Mother to Mother Family Care Book*. If you would like to tell about your own family traditions, ideas, problem solving techniques, and thoughts on family togetherness, write the authors in care of the publisher:

Jeanne Henry
Barbara Sills
Camaro Publishing Company
Worldway Station
Post Office Box 90430
Los Angeles, California 90009